Britain and Joseph Chamberlain

BRITAIN AND JOSEPH CHAMBERLAIN

MICHAEL BALFOUR

London
GEORGE ALLEN & UNWIN
Boston   Sydney

George Allen & Unwin (Publishers) Ltd,
40 Museum Street, London WC1A 1LU, UK

George Allen & Unwin (Publishers) Ltd,
Park Lane, Hemel Hempstead, Herts HP2 4TE, UK

Allen & Unwin, Inc.,
Fifty Cross Street, Winchester, Mass. 01890, USA

George Allen & Unwin Australia Pty Ltd,
8 Napier Street, North Sydney, NSW 2060, Australia

First published in 1985

British Library Cataloguing in Publication Data

Balfour, Michael, *1908–*
    Britain and Joseph Chamberlain.
1. Chamberlain, Joseph
2. Statesmen—Great Britain—Biography
I. Title
941.081′092′4   DA565.C4
ISBN 0-04-942191-3

Library of Congress Cataloging in Publication Data

Balfour, Michael Leonard Graham, 1908–
    Britain and Joseph Chamberlain.
Bibliography: p.
Includes index.
1. Great Britain—Politics and government—1837–1901.
2. Great Britain—Politics and government—1901–1910.
3. Chamberlain, Joseph, 1836–1914. I. Title.
DA550.B24 1985   941.081   85-3913
ISBN 0-04-942191-3

Set in 10 on 12 point Bembo by Computape (Pickering) Ltd
Printed and bound in Great Britain by
Biddles Ltd, Guildford and King's Lynn

'I reminded him of the French proverb –
le bonheur qui passe.'

Chamberlain to Hatzfeldt,
25 April 1898

Contents

Contents

List of Abbreviations

EcHR	*Economic History Review*
EHR	*English Historical Review*
GP	*Die grosse Politik der europäischen Kabinette*
HJ	*Historical Journal*
P and P	*Past and Present*

The place of origin is not given for books published in London.

Preface

After my book *The Kaiser and His Times* had been published in 1964, I looked for a parallel figure in British history round whom to write a study of the later nineteenth century and fixed on Joseph Chamberlain. Having interpreted the Kaiser as a man less authoritarian by nature than his surroundings, I wanted to examine what seemed to be a reverse case. For eighteen months I read steadily and reached some provisional conclusions. But thereafter

> Fate did iron wedges drive
> And always crowd itself betwixt.

Only in 1980 was I able to get back on course.

In the interval two things happened. First a number of books on the subject appeared, including the last two volumes of the Garvin–Amery biography, with their indispensable documents, Enoch Powell's idiosyncratic commentary on his lavish illustrations and Richard Jay's careful study of the political story. These made it easier for me to write the kind of book I had in mind, which would evaluate Chamberlain in perspective and devote almost as much space to background as to foreground. Secondly I became more interested than ever in the question why it was that Britain became the first industrial nation and why she lost that position. It was during Chamberlain's lifetime that she reached and passed her zenith. I thought it would be illuminating to treat the two themes in conjunction.

I did not originally intend to write without any recourse at all to unprinted documents, but that is how things have turned out. I could not possibly have gone through all the original sources for all the ground I have dealt with. To cover only part would have meant either collecting information simply in order to condense it or else trying to marry a series of monographs to a *tour d'horizon*.

Instead I have tried to read widely in secondary sources but here too, if I had attempted to include everything, I should have been dead long before the book was finished. But the titles mentioned in the notes by no means exhaust the extent of my studies.

Any historian who ranges widely has to do so at the expense of delving deeply and is bound as a result to drive up the eyebrows of those whose specialised fields he invades. But I do not see how this is to be avoided unless we give up trying to take broad views. In my case I hope it may be excused as the harmless occupation of an old gentleman.

I am deeply grateful to James Joll, Paul Kennedy and Richard Shannon for advice and encouragement.

M. L. G. B.
Burford, November 1984

1 *The Economic Background*

The First Industrial Revolution

During the last three decades of the eighteenth century the population of England was rising by 0·9 per cent or more a year, a higher rate than had ever been achieved before. The main reason was that more people were marrying and marrying earlier; as a result fertility was increasing, and families getting larger. A further but smaller contribution was made by a fall in mortality, especially among infants.[1] Both tendencies reflected a gradual increase in prosperity. Labour was in demand, especially in the industrial areas, so that extra children could find work and in due course add to the family income. Diet was improving; the percentage of the population eating wheaten bread is thought to have risen from 60 to 66, while the consumption of tea and sugar increased at more than double the rate of the rise in numbers.[2] Epidemic diseases were becoming less virulent; smallpox in particular was being checked by inoculation.[3]

Yet about 1780 real output per head, which had been growing at about 0·3 per cent around the middle of the century, started to increase by 1 per cent per year, a faster rate than, on the evidence available at present, had ever been achieved anywhere before.[4] For the first time in human history the rate of growth in national product effectively outstripped the rate of growth in population. Hitherto, both in agriculture and outside it, production had proved capable of only slow and limited expansion. Increases in the number of persons to be fed, clothed and housed had before long been checked by growing shortages of the necessary commodities. It is untraceable that real average income per head of any continuously producing community fell much below £80 per year (at 1983 prices); if it had, most of the population would have starved (as a proportion of some populations undoubtedly did). But it is equally untraceable that the average annual income of any community ever rose much above £400 per head. Today's *average* annual income, taking the world as a whole, is £1,800 per head.[5]

The breakthrough which thus occurred in England at the end of the eighteenth century, and to which the French economist Blanqui in 1837 gave the title of 'Industrial Revolution', was therefore of crucial importance for good or ill to the destiny of mankind. Its underlying causes were so multifarious as to make a complete explanation out of the question. The human itch for knowledge was combining with the human lust for wealth in such a multiplicity of ways as to defy full interpretative understanding. Many developments occurring simultaneously interacted over a period of time with one another on such a scale as to doom any attempt at a linear exposition to inadequacy. All the same, the question why the change of gear should have occurred where and when it did is so central to an understanding of nineteenth-century Britain as to demand some sort of answer.

As convenient a starting point as any for explanation is provided by John Kay of Bury in Lancashire, the son of a 'substantial yeoman', who in 1733 invented a 'flying shuttle' which enabled a handloom-weaver to double his output. This was originally intended for use with wool and suffered from teething troubles. But by 1760 these had been largely overcome and the device was being largely adopted in the cotton industry. The result was that spinning, the previous stage in the cloth-making process, became a bottle-neck.[6] For whereas three to five spinners had previously been needed to keep a single weaver supplied with yarn, many more were now required. Although the population of Lancashire was growing, there were not enough people available to allow the weavers to reach the output of which they were becoming capable. To bring in more spinners from outside the county was hard, because it was a family affair – and families do not move easily. Fortune and fame thus awaited anyone who could show how to surmount the difficulty and, sure enough, answers began to appear before long.

First James Hargreaves, a carpenter and weaver, found in 1765 with his 'spinning jenny' a way of linking together several spinning wheels of the traditional type so that one operator could work them all. Four years later Richard Arkwright, who had previously tried his hand at wig-making, innkeeping and dentistry, showed how the use of rollers rather than a wheel to draw out the thread made possible a frame which could be driven by water-power. In putting this into practice, he got financial help from Jedediah Strutt who eleven years earlier had patented a machine for improving the manufacture of ribbed woollen stockings.[7] In 1779 Samuel Crompton, a weaver and farmer, developed his 'mule' which combined elements of both the other machines, although some twenty years elapsed before a way was found of driving it by water or steam power.

These inventions however combined to bring the bottle-neck forward again. Now it was the weavers who could not cope with the quantities of yarn becoming available. The answer was to apply power to the looms but this was more easily thought of than done; Edmund Cartwright, an Oxford graduate and parson, started to make such a machine in 1787 but its imperfections caused his bankruptcy two years later. Only in the 1820s was a suitable machine developed, significantly by a man who was a machine-maker by profession. (In the interval the gap *was* filled by finding more hand-loom weavers.) The net result was that output of cotton cloth in Britain multiplied a hundredfold between 1760 and 1827, while retained imports of raw cotton rose from 3m. lb in 1770 to over 50m. after 1800.[8] The possibility was thus demonstrated of industrial growth at unprecedented rates.

But there would have been no incentive to produce so much cloth unless it could be sold. An essential accompaniment to the innovations just described was a rise in demand. What was significant about eighteenth-century England was that such a rise came simultaneously from two directions. On the one hand there was the growth in population from 6·2m. in 1750 to 9·16m. in 1800 to 18m. in 1850, a population which was becoming gradually and steadily, although by no means uniformly, better off. Improved communications were extending the area over which it paid to distribute goods; the first turnpike had been organised in 1663, the first major canal built in 1761. Catherine the Great's ambassador attributed England's prosperity to the multiplication by five within fifty years of the speed of circulation.[9] Exports were going up as well, particularly to the more or less 'captive' markets of the West Indies and North America (where there was a comparable rise in population); the export industries as a whole expanded fivefold during the eighteenth century and at least half the total output of textiles went abroad.[10] Here too better communications were important. This double swelling in demand must have done much to induce the changes in production methods. If either the home or the overseas expansion had come in isolation, or if both had come less quickly, the cotton industry might have been able to meet the extra demand without having to devise new machines. It could not take full advantage of both by merely extending its old ways. The opportunity of profit created by the coincidence spurred men on to invent and innovate.

The new machines needed more metal, as well as better metal which would stand up to wear without breaking. But the metal-smelting and machining industries had their problems. Traditionally iron ore was heated by burning it with charcoal to produce 'pigs' of relatively pure metal. But the growing demand for metal and consequently growing demand for charcoal was outrunning the supplies of suitable wood and putting up its price. The possibility of substituting coal was known but the processes at first employed left an unacceptably high degree of impurity in the iron. Throughout the century improvements were slowly made, particularly by the Shropshire firm of Darby; in 1784 these culminated in Cort's discovery of the 'puddling' process. As a result, the demand for coal increased. But coal had to be dug out of the earth, as did the other metals such as iron, lead, tin and copper. As soon as the mines reached any depth, they tended to flood with water, which had to be pumped out; in 1702 a Warwickshire colliery was using 500 horses to do this.[11] Not surprisingly a search began for machines to do it better.

In 1705 a solution was devised by Thomas Newcomen, a Devonshire blacksmith. In his engine, steam was injected into a cylinder and its expansive force used to push up a piston. The cylinder was then cooled from outside by cold water; the steam condensed and contracted while the pressure of the atmosphere on the cylinder forced the piston down again. A see-sawing cross-beam connected the top of the piston-rod to a pump for bringing water out of the mine. The thrust exerted by the piston was weak and much steam was wasted so that the engines consumed a lot of coal but, as they were chiefly used in collieries, this was not a constraint. Between 1769 and 1784 the efficiency of the engine was transformed by James Watt, who had begun his career as an instrument-maker for Glasgow University before moving to Birmingham. He provided a separate vessel for condensing the steam, closed the open end of the cylinder and devised gear for converting the jerky to-and-fro stroke of the piston into a steady rotary motion. William Murdoch, a mechanic in Watt's firm, invented a slide-valve which enabled steam to be admitted to each side of the piston alternately. The new engines were made with greater precision and were in every way more powerful and economical, although their steam pressure was still relatively low.

Watt has rightly been regarded as a key figure in the Industrial Revolution because one of the distinctive aspects of that development was the addition of a new and more potent source of energy to supplement the age-old ones of animal muscle, wind and water. What was novel was not so much the use of machines to increase the output of the individual worker; spinning wheels are in a sense machines and lathes operated by foot-treadles certainly are. The new machines after 1760 were more complex than their predecessors but the chief factor making them more efficient was that they were, or soon came to be, operated by steam power. For steam engines were not long used merely for pumping. Others were installed to drive winding-machines bringing miners to and from the coal-face. In 1776 one was installed in a Shropshire ironworks to operate a bellows and thus, by increasing the blast of air through an enlarged furnace, remove more of the impurities from the iron. 1785 saw one in a cotton mill. Others were used to turn shafts in breweries.[12] It was the application of steam-energy as much as the introduction of more complex machinery which made it essential to move the place of production from the house to the factory – defined in 1878 as 'premises where mechanical power is employed in the business of manufacture'.[13]

More engines meant a need for more coal and coal is a heavy material difficult to transport. Much was carried by canals, much was 'sea coal' brought by coastal barges. But the problem remained of getting it from the pit-head to the nearest wharf. For this, waggons running on wooden rails had been introduced on Tyneside in the seventeenth century, copying a German example. If steam engines could turn a shaft, they could turn a wheel and not much vision was needed to light on the idea of using them to haul the waggons on such 'rail-ways'. A main difficulty was to provide a rail sturdy enough to bear a wheeled engine which had to possess a considerable weight because without such weight its wheels could not grip the rails. The first true 'locomotive' was a high-pressure machine designed by the Cornish 'engineer' Richard Trevithick which started work in South Wales in 1804 but soon broke up the tramways on which it was employed. Other experiments in Yorkshire and Northumberland led to a group of colliery-owners in the latter county commissioning the man in charge of their machinery, George Stephenson, to design and build a locomotive for them.[14] The result in 1814 was the *Blücher* whose smooth flanged wheels ran on cast-iron rails. It was Stephenson's faith in his machine which in 1825 led not merely to a railway rather than a canal being built for carrying coal from West Auckland via Darlington to the Tees at Stockton but also to the decision that passengers should be carried as well. But in the early engines the problem of raising steam to a sufficient pressure had not been solved and they were apt to stall at crucial moments. It was not till 1830 that George Stephenson's son Robert found the remedy by giving his *Rocket* on the Liverpool and Manchester Railway a multi-tubed boiler. Minor improvements, rather than any fundamental change of principle, separate the *Rocket* from the record-holding *Mallard* of 1938. Meanwhile the use of high pressure steam in factory engines increased speeds and thus cut costs.

Steam engines were first put into ships by Fulton in the United States and by 1815 there were five 'steamers' on the Thames. Yet as late as 1851 Britain had only 185,000 tons of steamships as compared with 3·66m. tons of wooden vessels.

Textiles, iron-founding, coal, railways and steamships – these were the key industries on which Britain's power and world position were built. From the point of view of external trade, textiles were the most important, providing over half of Britain's direct exports as late as the 1870s. But from the point of view of effect on the economic structure of the country, railways stood out. The increased speed and volume of movement which they permitted transformed the size of the market, thus making large-scale manufacture worthwhile. They drastically reduced costs, thereby stimu-lating consumption. Their construction and operation involved the organisation of manpower on a scale hitherto achieved only by armies. Their needs for equipment stimulated a host of other industries. Their financing, without adequate regard for economy, involved the raising of sums hitherto only handled by governments during wars; by 1850 they had absorbed some £250m. whereas the cotton industry may by then have cost £55m., the iron industry £35m., turnpikes £35m. and canals under £30m.[15] They were thus primarily responsible for raising the rate of productive investment from some 8 per cent of Gross National Product in 1760 to 13 per cent a century later. The process of transforming the world to its present condition consisted essentially in applying and extending the techniques and attitudes of mind acquired almost as an act of sleep-walking in developing textiles and railways.

Rostow has called the process 'irreversible, like the loss of innocence'.[16] But unfortunately it both can and will be reversed within the foreseeable future unless man develops new sources of energy. For the need for extra energy intrinsic in the Industrial Revolution led him to start consuming his supplies of coal (and later oil) at a far faster rate than ever before. But these owed their existence to the capacity of green plants to synthesise atmospheric carbon dioxide. The store which had thus been built up over millennia is finite and cannot be replaced in decades or even centuries.

The Preconditions for 'Take-off'

Rostow prefaces his remark by saying that 'the combination of necessary and sufficient conditions for "take-off" in Britain was the result of a convergence of a number of quite independent circumstances'. The innovations described in the previous section could not have taken place unless a variety of favourable conditions had been already in existence, so that an answer to the questions 'Why then?' and 'Why there?' involves going back to identify the most important of these preconditions.

(1) The effect of improved communications in increasing the size of the home market during the eighteenth century has already been mentioned. It was not only the home market which increased in size. If English seamen from 1497 onwards had not been venturing out into the oceans with increasing assurance and on an increasing scale, there might have been no overseas demand to add to home demand. It is a commonplace that the switch of trade from the Mediterranean and Near East to the oceans advantaged an island which was on the periphery of the former but at the departure point of the latter. A variety of desires inspired our sailors, for wealth, for knowledge, for adventure, for getting the better of rivals. Cromwell's attack on the Spanish colonies, which led to the capture of Jamaica, was due to his belief that God intended him to use the power in his hands to weaken the citadel of Catholicism. Others sought freedom to shape their own lives.

(2) Another commonplace is Britain's good fortune in possessing in her 'factor endowment' nearly all the materials needed for industriali-

sation: coal, iron and the chief non-ferrous metals. It is less frequently pointed out that most of these were possessed only in quantities which, while enabling her to start, were insufficient to keep her going. That she had no cotton added to the significance of her transatlantic communications.

(3) From the earliest times men could only be spared for fighting and praying if they could be fed by those who dug. The population increase after 1770 was only possible because improvements in agriculture meant that the existing workforce (which in 1914 showed no net increase in numbers) could produce extra food for the extra mouths. Industrialisation is always accompanied by a steady fall in the proportion of the population employed on the land (in Britain from 60 per cent in 1760 to 36 per cent in 1801 to 12·6 per cent in 1881).[17] But this can occur only if there is a corresponding increase in agricultural efficiency, or in the area being cultivated, or in the size of food imports, or in a combination of all three.

Many of the improvements in agriculture were copied from abroad, especially from Holland. But their introduction was certainly eased and even perhaps made possible by a gradual change in attitudes to land ownership which had been under way in England since the fifteenth century. A concept of land as the basis for social and political organisation gave way to a view of land as something out of which individuals made money. 'Long before Adam Smith, scattered groups of Englishmen living in the countryside began to accept self-interest and economic freedom as the natural basis of human society.'[18] The most visible result of this was the shift from the mediaeval common-field system to that of contiguous holdings enclosed by hedges and mostly let to tenant farmers by big landlords who did not themselves directly engage in producing food for the market. Only this shift, which took from the sixteenth to the nineteenth centuries, made worthwhile the introduction of new crops, improved breeds and better machinery. But the incentive to such changes was the prospect of making more money by means of them. One result was the virtual extermination of the smallholder, thereby differentiating English from continental rural society. The typical figure, in place of the peasant, became the tenant farmer. The gap in living standards between the owner/employer and labourer was greater than elsewhere. The desire to stop small plots from being further subdivided did not operate to check the growth of population but the extra mouths had to move to the towns because they could not be absorbed into the rural workforce.[19]

(4) There has been much argument as to the contribution made to industrial development by improved understanding of the physical world. Such understanding was certainly growing in Britain, although no more so than on the continent. Yet many of the initial inventions did not call so much for understanding of scientific principles as for practical ingenuity

and craftsmanship, as is suggested by the occupations of the various inventors which have been mentioned. England was not unique in possessing skilled makers of scientific instruments, clocks, carriages, guns, furniture and the like but it is significant that many people trained in such work contributed to the steady process of improvement by which the earlier machines and engines were made more efficient. Scientific knowledge did sometimes play a part, as in understanding the effect of atmospheric pressure or devising ways of bleaching cloth with chemicals, which removed another bottle-neck in the expansion of textile output.

(5) The ability of men to improve their equipment depends upon them being able to spare time and set aside materials for that purpose, instead of having to concentrate all their efforts on keeping alive. To improve the future means forgoing possibilities of present consumption, saving instead of spending. The stock of equipment amassed in Britain by 1785 (including such things as roads, harbours and buildings) was the outcome of centuries of such saving; the prospects of adding to it with new equipment depended on people being sufficiently well off and thrifty enough to set aside resources (usually in the form of money). The rise in investment's share of GNP after 1760 has already been mentioned; during the next century 'national capital' multiplied nearly four times in real terms. As Sir Arthur Lewis has said, 'The really significant turning-point in the life of a society is not when it begins to respect wealth as such but when it places in the foreground productive investment and the wealth associated therewith.'[20]

But the people who are rich or abstemious enough to accumulate spare wealth are by no means always the people who discern ways of investing it to win profit and improve production. There has to be a system for transforming saving into investment. It is natural for this to go hand-in-hand with a system of financing trade both at dates in the future and at places remote from the dealer. By the seventeenth century the activities of numerous London goldsmiths were turning them more and more into private bankers, building on examples set in Florence, Antwerp, Amsterdam and other continental cities. The second half of the eighteenth century saw country merchants like Sampson Lloyd of Birmingham move from lending money to their customers into regular banking business.

Capital was not always easy to obtain in eighteenth-century Britain; Boulton and Watt, Arkwright and Strutt were all held back by lack of finance. But it was becoming available in greater quantities than ever before. Most of it had been accumulated in trade, some by what was little better than looting in the East and West Indies. A good deal of this flowed into land, either through businessmen men turning landowners as a mark of success or marrying their daughters to indigent noblemen. Their money went not only into country houses and furnishings (thereby encouraging craftsmanship) but also into agricultural improvements where they brought business methods to bear. Successful landowners became, either directly or through the banking system, an important source of capital for industry.

The amount of capital required for the average enterprise (other than railways) should not be exaggerated. 'What became the great firms of the early Industrial Revolution were not vast combines ... but minnow enterprises which seized opportunities to keep growing.'[21] In many cases their funds came out of saved profits made by the owners of the firm, their families and friends; many earlier machines were put together at home rather than bought ready-made. The raising of capital by public issues on the Stock Exchange was (except again for railways) unknown before the later nineteenth century. Joint-stock companies were virtually forbidden from 1720 to 1844. The principle that British banks, unlike continental ones, did not provide industry with long-term loans became generally established only after 1850; previously such a source of funds, although never common, was by no means unknown.[22] Some bankers lent involuntarily when the recipient of a short-term loan could not repay it and the creditor preferred leaving the money where it was to bankrupting the debtor by recalling it!

(6) According to Max Weber, Protestantism, and especially Calvinism, enabled a man to see his ordinary daily work as a 'calling' acceptable to God which should therefore be pursued as actively and profitably as possible. Success in business could be a sign of divine approval and was certainly not incompatible with salvation. The Reformation thus contributed to the rise of capitalism. Recently this thesis has come under fire and clearly cannot be maintained in its original form. But there can be no denying that most forms of Protestantism inculcated the duties of hard work, honesty of conduct and frugality of living and that these are qualities which tend to result in worldly success, especially when combined with shrewd common sense. A Quaker told his son that 'we are saved by faith in the next world and want of it in this'! Public opinion, especially among the middle classes and Protestant sects, enjoined from the seventeenth to the nineteenth centuries close adherence to a rigid code of moral conduct. Wesley's precept was 'Gain all you can, save all you can, give all you can'.[23] The prominence of Quakers in banking was not fortuitous. The Industrial Revolution might still have occurred in Britain if it had been a Catholic, perhaps even a Muslim country. But its emphatic Protestant faith was another favourable background factor.

(7) The Protestant ethic also helped to create a climate of confidence. Men are less likely to save their money or instal expensive equipment if they are afraid that dishonest associates may make off with it before they

have derived from it the benefit which they expect. The known and upright character of businessmen who were God-fearing encouraged belief that money could be entrusted to them since they would keep their word. But a prospect of war or revolution or arbitrary rulers also undermines confidence. England had been since Tudor times a settled country in which order was well maintained. She possessed a long-established legal system which was (on the whole) predictable, integrated, impartial and enforced. According to Adam Smith, 'That security which the laws of Britain give to every man that he shall enjoy the fruit of his own labour is alone sufficient to make any country flourish'.[24]

But if the economy gained from the absence of fighting at home, it gained also from the occurrence of fighting abroad. Admittedly war put up the cost of living, besides causing the National Debt to rise from £19m. in 1709 to £844m. in 1819. But it led to the acquisition of, and growth of trade with, overseas territories. By making the Bank of England necessary as a means of raising money for the government it stimulated the financial system. It trained men to be sailors, improved the efficiency of sailing ships and developed such things as cartography, instrument-making and precision in metal-working; Watt was able to reduce the leakage of steam from cylinders because Wilkinson had shown how to bore cannon accurately.

(8) Hand in hand with confidence went enterprise. England possessed a number of individuals who were willing to take risks either to make money or extend the bounds of knowledge. Whether they were more prevalent in Britain than elsewhere is hard to say. But it is surely not fanciful to think that the spirit was encouraged by the habit of venturing overseas.

(9) The stability which enabled trade to flourish and traders to multiply helps to explain why England was the first country in which the gentry and merchants grew strong enough to challenge and defeat the monarchy. Parliament in the eighteenth century may still have been a 'committee of landlords' but the country was being run by people who were not inimical to business and often keen to foster it. They wanted to have their own hands free to run local affairs as they chose and were accordingly hostile to a strong central government with a standing army or police force of its own. They allowed much of the regulative legislation inherited from previous centuries to fall into disuse, to the detriment of those whom it had protected but to the benefit of the enterprising. The nobility was not a closed caste since newcomers were given titles (provided that they had enough land) and the children of younger sons became commoners again.

A variety of causes thus combined in Britain at the end of the eighteenth century to create a total situation which resulted in the industrial 'breakthrough'. In many of them she was not unique, in some not even the leader. Although most of the individual steps were no doubt taken for conscious and rational reasons, the overall outcome was the result of happy coincidence, not deliberate planning. Our forefathers were like a man who, while at work in an old house, accidentally touches a secret spring opening an unsuspected door down a passage to a multifarious store of treasure. If we look for something which permeates the catalogue, it is geography. We owe an incalculable debt to our position as an island, with a temperate climate, near enough to the continent to benefit from Europe's civilisation but insulated from its upheavals, accessible to the oceans, endowed with the right raw materials. The temptation to look for some distinctive British genius – whether individualism or enterprise or toleration – is great. But when one starts to examine the sources of such qualities, they themselves can be seen as the products of geography, deriving from an exceptionally stable society (thanks to the Channel) and one which encouraged enterprise (thanks to the accessibility of the New World). Even our pragmatic aversion to planning ahead can be seen as an inheritance from farmers who could not tell from one day to another what the weather would allow them to do! We were exceptionally lucky rather than outstandingly clever or admirably virtuous.

The Ripples Spread Across the World's Pool

Demand from overseas (and primarily from outside Europe) provided a crucial incentive for the mechanisation of the British cotton industry. But Britain did not grow any cotton. The relationship between the first industrialised state and the world overseas was thus from the start a double one; they were each at one and the same time suppliers and customers. Without the overseas supplies there would have been fewer manufactured goods to buy but without the income which they earned from selling their materials, the overseas suppliers could not have afforded to buy so many manufactured goods. The expansion of commerce with America and Asia may have been 'import-led'[25] but to suppose that one side of the process was more vital than the other is confused thinking.

The situation was much the same as regards money. Eighteenth-century Britain owed a significant part of her wealth to East Indian 'nabobs', West Indian sugar merchants and traders in slaves, tobacco and other exotic goods. But the ships and the wharves and the warehouses needed before such trade could flow involved the laying-out of more funds than the areas concerned would have provided for themselves. Even before large-scale overseas investment began about 1850, a certain amount of money was sunk by Britain in the 'infrastructure' of her overseas

11

dependencies and a good deal of money flowed back again to her from them. Without both expenditures, each would have been smaller.

By the time that the process reached its zenith, between 1905 and 1914, Britain would be placing over half her total annual investment abroad (on an average about £160m.).[26] But she was also receiving an even larger sum (about £200m.) from abroad in dividends on earlier investments which the countries concerned would never have been able to pay in full if she had not reinvested a large part of her receipts with them. The course which she adopted could be justified by the theoretical argument that, as rates of interest abroad tended consistently to be higher than those obtainable at home, she was letting her money go where it could be used most productively. She was bringing down her costs by getting cheaper raw materials and food (and thereby keeping down her wage levels) rather than by improving the efficiency of her production methods, as the installation of more new and better machinery might have done. This however was not a deliberate choice, except in so far as it involved accepting with little question the principles that the world should be regarded as an economic unit and that the correct thing to do with money was to earn as much as possible on it consistent with the risks which investors were prepared to accept (and which in some cases involved them in losses). She was of course investing at home as much and usually more but what made her behaviour remarkable was that in other industrialising countries the proportion going abroad was far lower; in Germany it never exceeded 20 per cent and in the nine years before 1914 was a mere 5·7 per cent; in France it was perhaps 12 per cent, in the USA never over 6 per cent (see Table 10.1).[27] Nobody would seriously suggest that overseas investment was a mistake. Without it the world economy could never have developed to its present level. What is open to dispute is whether in the long run the exact 'mix' turned out the most advantageous to individual British investors, to the British economy as a whole and to the world in general.

Contrary to a long-prevalent belief, Britain's visible trade was never in balance between 1822 and 1913 (and indeed 1956).[28] The deficit was made good by invisible trade – shipping, banking, broking, insurance and the like. Often even these were insufficient to compensate as seems to have been the case in eight out of the seventeen quinquennia between 1826 and 1910. At such times the balance was made good by interest payments from abroad and, if these are taken into account, there always was a surplus. Until 1870 income from investments was of roughly the same size as that from shipping; thereafter it drew markedly ahead, although even at its height it provided only 37 per cent of total invisible income. This cyclical process was almost inescapable. The countries in which British money was laid out could not earn by their own visible and invisible exports a big enough surplus for them to meet their own import needs and pay the interest on their borrowings. For them to have tried to earn enough gold for the purpose would not only have been impossible but (as the USA showed after 1919) would have dislocated the world's monetary system. The benefit of the investment to Britain was that, besides bringing down her import costs, much of the money was spent on orders for goods from British firms or in payment to British providers of services so that it created employment and profits at home in the course of passing into the country and out again. Moreover it was Britain's invisible income as a whole which enabled her to afford extra imports and thus enjoy a standard of living which was, for a time, the highest in the world.

↦The popular view now is that Britain rose to prosperity and power by exploiting weaker peoples. Certainly at all stages individual Britons did take advantage of the power given them by their superior wealth and sophistication to enrich themselves disproportionately to their relative needs; there was less control and less moral protest at this during the early part of the process than later. But an Industrial Revolution confined to Britain (and even to Europe) is unthinkable. The British genuinely believed that they were acting as benefactors in bringing the Revolution (with all that it implied in the form of improved living standards) to relatively primitive economies which, without finance and training from outside, would have taken longer to enjoy those benefits. Those to whom the benefits were brought showed on the whole equal eagerness to receive them. If Britain had somehow been both able and anxious to conceal the details of her new methods from the rest of the world (as the Chinese succeeded for a time in concealing the art of making silk cloth) we should no doubt be condemned today for selfishness.

Undeniably the British accepted too easily the idea of an international division of labour by which many areas (chiefly outside Europe) produced raw materials and foodstuffs for a rather smaller number of areas (chiefly in Europe and North America) which used them to produce manufactures. But such a division of labour made sense economically since each area was doing what it was good at. The weak point about the division socially was that primary production, although indispensable, requires less specialised skills so that those engaged on it earn lower incomes than those in manufacturing. We did less than we might have done to develop the industries of countries under British control, like India, in the convenient belief that manufacturing was not their job – and might handicap us in performing ours. The need of poor nations for development aid from outside puts them at the mercy of those who have the wealth and the will to provide it. A 'fair' exchange is hard to judge since most parties have interests at stake which prejudice their views. In the nineteenth century men believed firmly that in such circumstances the best way of achieving fairness was to leave matters to the free operation of the price system. But the weaker were always inclined to doubt how far that system was genuinely fair and to complain that it operated to their disadvantage. 'Imperialism' has thus acquired moral connotations. Without them the process to which it refers merely consisted in spreading the area over which industrialisation operated, 'integrating new regions into the expanding economy'.[29]

Money was not the only thing needed for development. Trained manpower was also necessary, and not merely in the technical field. As the analysis of the prerequisites for industrialisation showed, a relatively stable government well-disposed to trade is of great importance. In some parts of the world this was not forthcoming and Britain had reluctantly to provide it. The government found itself forced to intervene in order to protect its traders or take over a function which they could not satisfactorily provide for themselves or to anticipate having doors closed against them when other developed countries did the same thing. The result has been condemned as a selfish way of finding 'jobs for the boys' – especially the less competent ones. But it was by no means only the failures who went abroad. The empire can be held to have absorbed too many skilled and able men of whom we were training too few, while the need to supply proconsuls distracted our educational system from realising the need to train technicians. British cemeteries in places like Calcutta are poignant reminders of the cost of expansion in terms of human life.

The impact of a sophisticated industrialised economy on a primitive pre-industrial one, especially at a forced pace, is almost bound to be disrupting. Had it been possible to extend industrialisation more gradually and with a fuller awareness of its implications, suffering and waste could have been avoided. But the pace of history's march is hard to control. Those who are fired with a new idea, or see a new prospect of gain, hurry impatiently to turn concept into reality. The disadvantages only become obvious later. Even if they had been foreseen, they would probably not have been thought grave enough to change the course of events. Nor is it incontrovertible that they should have done.

The Cost of Industrialisation

There has been much argument as to whether, if at all, the common people of Britain benefited from the Industrial Revolution, at any rate during its earlier years. The sufferings which it brought are notorious – long hours, low wages, bad conditions of work in factories, poor and insanitary housing, subjection to strict discipline. The question is how far these were outweighed by improved standards of life.

The figures which have so far been calculated for such things as real wages and consumption per head are subject to wide margins of error. But the broad answer seems to be that, while total national income rose substantially between 1750 and 1850, the relative share of labour fell. Such a fall need not rule out an increase in labour's share per head, and things may have got slightly better during the 1780s and again during the 1820s. But on the whole there was little improvement in real consumption of goods and services during the first six decades of industrialism. Towards the end of the 1820s the position began to change, largely but not exclusively because the workers improved their bargaining techniques by better organisation. Thereafter 'real wages rose in step with national income, thus remaining a constant share of a steadily rising total'.[30]

The following points add detail to this picture.

(1)   Overall living standards did not deteriorate sufficiently to bring into operation that check on the growth of population which had previously acted as a brake on progress (see p. 1).

(2)   The war with France absorbed many of the extra resources which might otherwise have gone to make living easier. At the peak in 1812–15, 18 per cent of national expenditure went on the war. Immediately after Waterloo demobilisation (which the administration lacked the skill to handle) caused further hardship and a quick boom was followed by a slump. Again, without the industrial changes, the hardship would have been greater.

(3)   The hardship was aggravated by the government's fiscal policy. Much of the cost of the war was met by borrowing, which led to inflation and rising prices. In so far as it was met by taxation, this was still principally indirect and placed upon commodities in mass demand, which again put up prices. It is true that income tax was levied, although at a low rate, between 1799 and 1806, but many of the people who paid it also received interest on their holdings of government stock, so that what they took out of one pocket they got back into the other. If Pitt's government had adopted the course followed by Peel after 1841 and shifted the main burden of taxation from indirect to direct, the poor would have benefited without growth being, so far as one can tell, held up.

(4)   Averages as usual conceal wide variations. The decades after 1760 saw an even greater amount of change than usual, so that increased opportunities were offered to those with personality, judgment, resources, guts or luck. On the other hand those who were disadvantaged by the changes suffered, notably the surplus population on the land who were driven into the towns and the hand-workers in those industries which were mechanising. The north, where most of the development occurred, was better off than the south. Even during the war such groups as the gunmakers of Birmingham and the growers of corn prospered. Inequalities in wealth became for a time more pronounced in Britain than elsewhere in the industrialising world. But since profit was the main

motive of those who initiated and organised the whole process, it is hardly surprising that the major share should have accrued to them.

(5) Over the period 1800 to 1850, industrial production was expanding at roughly twice the rate of population growth.[31] Although external trade was also expanding, its volume would not have been sufficient to sustain this growth of output unless it had been accompanied by a rising home demand. It has been calculated that the average family was buying British-made goods worth £25 in 1750 and £40 in 1810. Because the real price of industrial products was at the end of this period tending to fall whereas that of food was rising, the increased purchasing power showed itself in the purchase of manufactures. The poor, two-thirds of whose income went on food, fared worse than their wealthier brethren in other classes and than the more successful workers.[32]

The theory has been propounded that unequal living standards and lower-class impoverishment are inevitable during the 'take-off' period of industrialisation, since the savings necessary to promote the indispensable investment cannot be generated in an egalitarian society but only in one where the well-to-do are allowed to keep more money than they need for their immediate comfort, so that they are almost bound to save. There has to be a low limit on the share available to those who, if they possessed more, would only consume more. The example of the Soviet Union after 1926 has been invoked as showing that something parallel is necessary when a communist state industrialises.

But for the theory to be valid it would be necessary to show that the development of industry in Britain would have been held back if less capital had been available. Yet, although there were cases of innovation being impeded by lack of funds (see p. 8), such difficulties seem to have been the exception rather than the rule. On the other hand, the calculation has been made that, if domestic investment had stayed the same proportion of national expenditure in 1790–1800 as it had been in 1761–70, the level of consumption per head would only have been 7 per cent higher.[33]

What has been said about development overseas applies also at home. If the initial process of industrialisation had been carried through more slowly and with broader vision, its evil effects could have been mitigated. The British people as a whole might have been happier if their numbers had grown more gradually and if more of them had remained on the land until there had been time to catch up with the evils of the sprouting towns. But that is seldom how things happen. There is much to be said for the view that, if the governmental system and the prevailing climate of opinion had not been such as to leave freedom to the enterprising, the whole process might not have started. The spring leading into the passage (see p. 11) might not have been released. Over the long term there can be no doubt about the material benefits brought to the entire population.

Industrialisation made the idea of material equality look for the first time like a practical possibility instead of just a wild dream. But it is a nice question how far a decline in amenity is offset by an increase in material supplies.

Britain's Opportunity and the Problems It Brought

The developments described in this chapter enabled a country which, by comparison with its European neighbours, was only of medium size, to become a Great Power with a major say in world affairs. The advantages of wealth and technological pre-eminence which pioneer industrialisation brought were reinforced by the fact, partly intrinsic and partly tangential, that 1815 saw the effective end of French predominance while half a century and more were to elapse before Germany recovered from the handicaps encumbering her since the Middle Ages. Our great-grand-fathers made the most of the interval.

Yet if success made the British self-confident and self-satisfied, there was throughout their years of supremacy an undercurrent of anxiety about the future – an anxiety which was well founded. For four major question marks hung over Britain's prospects.

(1) Technological progress and economic growth brought with them changes in the distribution of wealth and ways of life. Could the political system of the country (along with the social system which it reflected) be adapted by agreement to satisfy the principal beneficiaries of the advance? Or was a violent upheaval on the French model inescapable? The size of the adjustments needed was clearly going to be considerable but Britain had the advantage of having already carried through in the seventeenth century what may be described as a first instalment of them.

(2) Some people in Britain sought reform because they considered that their growing relative wealth entitled them to an improvement in their political status. But for others the stimulus to demands for change was not provided by an improving economic position so much as by one which, if not actually worsening, was acutely unsatisfactory. Could the economy be adapted by agreement to assuage those demands? If not, two dangers loomed. That of violent revolution was obvious. But since the poor seldom have the education, organising ability and stamina to bring about a revolution, they need to be led by people who are better-off, more articulate and acquainted with the corridors of power. The prospects of such people being available in nineteenth-century Britain in sufficient quantities to act as leaders would depend on the answers given to the previous question. But supposing that such an alliance on militant lines did not develop, an almost equal danger would be the alienation of a section of

the working classes from the established system. For if hostility between the givers and takers of employment were to develop too far, it would impair the efficiency and progress of the productive machine.

(3) The workers were unlikely to be satisfied without being allowed a larger share of the extra wealth brought by industrialisation. But if their share was to get bigger, whose was to get smaller? If total wealth continued to grow, could their demands be met by increasing their share of the extra without reducing the absolute amounts held by the rest? The businessmen and middle classes would resist any encroachment on their incomes and property and, if they got political dominance, would be able at least to slow down such an encroachment. The real danger was that overall consumption would be maintained at the expense of investment, less imperative in the short run but more essential in the long one. This danger would be aggravated if a higher proportion of the national income had to go on defence.

(4) Hand-in-hand with these internal dangers went an external one. Britain was of only medium size. There were many other countries in the world with a larger area and a bigger population. All of these were bound to imitate her success, at greater or less speed and with greater or less effect. When they did, common sense suggested that some of them would outstrip her, since the advantages which had enabled her to get a head-start were neither permanent nor exclusive to her. She would soon exhaust the supplies of the industrial raw materials (other than coal) which she had enjoyed to start with.

She could hardly hope to maintain her lead. The most she could expect was to remain abreast of the other leaders. Her best chance of doing so lay in offsetting her relative lack of size and material resources by efficiency of production and continued technological innovation. The need to do this put a premium on ability to change and on internal (particularly industrial) harmony. But it also meant maintaining a rate of investment in education, research and productive equipment as high as her challengers (if not higher, since their installations would tend to be more up-to-date unless she replaced hers before they became worn out). If she could not achieve this, how could she hope to maintain her population at the standard to which they were becoming accustomed? For a time she could use her political prestige and strategic power to buttress her economy, but in the long run the former were dependent on the latter. Her position was all the more vulnerable in that she had come to prosperity in a deliberately-created interdependent world of free competition. To retire from it into isolation would mean cutting herself off from many of the sources of her wealth, besides posing the problem of how to obtain and pay for the vital supplies which she did not possess.

The subject of this book spent most of his life in trying to provide answers to these questions, although he may not have seen them as clearly as we with hindsight can; and as Britain has fallen progressively behind the leaders in the race for economic growth, he cannot be said to have found adequate solutions. Since he was at first sight well-equipped to do so, one is inevitably led to ask whether anyone else could have done better or whether Britain's decline has not been, if one allows for human limitations, inevitable. The one problem which was successfully solved was the first and it is to the history leading up to this solution that we now turn.

Notes to Chapter 1

1 E. A. Wrigley, 'The growth of population in eighteenth-century England – a conundrum resolved', *P and P* (February 1983); J. Habbakuk, *Population Growth and Economic Development since 1750* (Leicester, 1971), p. 26; R. Porter, *English Society in the Eighteenth Century* (1982), pp. 219–24.

2 E. F. Thomson, 'The moral economy of the English crowd in the eighteenth century', *P and P* (February 1971); P. Mathias, *The First Industrial Nation* (1978), p. 99.

3 Habbakuk, p. 34.

4 P. Deane and W. A. Cole, *British Economic Growth 1688–1939* (Cambridge, 1967), pp. 79–80; N. C. R. Crafts in R. Floud and D. McCloskey, *The Economic History of Britain since 1700* (Cambridge, 1981), Vol. 1, pp. 1–16; C. K. Harley, 'British industrialisation before 1841', *The Journal of Economic History* (June 1982); C. Feinstein in *The Cambridge Economic History of Europe* (Cambridge, 1978), Vol. 7, pt 1, p. 87.

5 *The Economist*, 22 January 1972; P. Laslett, *The World We Have Lost* (1971), pp. 121–3.

6 N. J. Smelser, *Social Change in the Industrial Revolution* (1959).

7 R. S. Fitton and A. P. Wadsworth, *The Strutts and the Arkwrights* (Manchester, 1938).

8 S. Lilley, 'Technological progress and the Industrial Revolution 1700–1914' in C. M. Cipolla (ed.), *Fontana Economic History of Europe* (1973), Vol. 3, p. 192; Deane and Cole, p. 185.

9 Quoted in F. Braudel, *Civilisation and Capitalism: the Wheels of Commerce* (trans. 1982), p. 349.

10 Mathias, p. 104.

11 Lilley, p. 203.

12 Mathias, p. 135.

13 W. H. G. Armytage, *A. J. Mundella, 1825–1897. The Liberal Background to the Labour Movement* (1951), p. 194.

14 L. T. C. Rolt, *George and Robert Stephenson* (1960), chs 3 to 9.

15 P. Mathias, *The Transformation of England* (1979), pp. 88–90; M. C. Reed, *Investment in British Railways 1820–44* (1975), pp. 37, 43; Armytage, p. 258.

16 W. W. Rostow, *The Stages of Economic Growth* (Cambridge, 1960), p. 31; letter from E. A. Bell, Director of Kew Gardens, in *The Times*, 10 September 1983.

17 A. Jones, *The Politics of Reform 1884* (Cambridge, 1972), p. 71.

18 Barrington Moore Jnr, *The Social Origins of Dictatorship and Democracy* (1967), p. 80.

19 D. C. Coleman, *The Economy of England 1450–1750* (Oxford, 1977), ch. 7; P. O. Brien and C. Keyder, *Economic Growth in Britain and France 1780–1914. Two Paths to the Twentieth Century* (1978), pp. 61–76, 128–132.

20 Quoted by Mathias, *First Industrial Nation*, p. 14.

21 Porter, p. 339.

22 Mathias, *Transformation of England*, pp. 108–9.

23 M. Richter, *The Politics of Conscience* (1964), p. 20.

24 Quoted by Porter, p. 203.

25 Coleman, p. 137.

26 M. Edelstein, *Overseas Investment in the Age of High Imperialism: The United Kingdom 1850–1914* (New York, 1982), Appendix 1; Mathias, *First Industrial Nation*, p. 249.

27 Mathias, *First Industrial Nation*, p. 321; M. Edelstein in Floud and McCloskey, Vol. 2, pp. 75–83; D. S. Landes, *The Unbound Prometheus* (Cambridge, 1969), p. 331.
28 W. Clarke (ed.), *Britain's Invisible Earnings* (1967), p. 16.
29 J. Gallagher and R. Robinson, 'The imperialism of free trade', *EcHR*, series 2, vol. 6 (1953–4).
30 S. Pollard in *Camb. Ec. Hist. Eur.*, Vol. 7, pt 1, pp. 161–5; C. Feinstein in Floud and McCloskey, Vol. 1, pp. 136, 159, 164; A. J. Taylor (ed.), *The Standard of Living in Britain in the Industrial Revolution* (1975), pp. l–liii; S. Checkland, *The Rise of Industrial Society in Britain 1815–1885* (1964), pp. 225–32.
31 Mathias, *Transformation of England*, pp. 122–9.
32 Taylor, pp. l–liii.
33 Feinstein in Floud and McCloskey, Vol. 1; O'Brien and Keyder, pp. 164–74.

2 The Radical Background

The Levellers

Some five hundred yards from where these lines are written, three men were put against a churchyard wall on a May day in 1649 and, on Cromwell's orders, shot. Too much political significance should not be read into the mutiny which led to the executions; most of the twelve hundred soldiers involved were primarily anxious to get their arrears of pay without being forced to join in subjugating Ireland, a cause for which they had no enthusiasm. But the ringleaders had demanded that a 'Council of the Army' (to include representatives of the rank and file) should be called. Had it met and adopted the constitutional programme which the agitators had in mind, much of the political controversy of the next two centuries would have been pre-empted. The capture of the mutineers by Cromwell's troops, and the firm treatment of their leaders, put paid to the chances of England's pioneer example of a 'bourgeois revolution' resulting in any profound social change. For that to have happened, they would have had to receive the backing rather than the bullets of their comrades in the New Model Army.

The clash of theory with the Levellers had found expression eighteen months before the clash of arms. Colonel Rainsborough's contention at Putney on 29 October 1647, although unknown to most of his contemporaries, has often been quoted since it was first made generally accessible in 1891:[1]

Really I think that the poorest he that is in England hath a life to live as the greatest he; and ... that every man that is to live under a government ought first by his own consent to put himself under that government; and I do think that the poorest man in England is not at all bound in a strict sense to that government that he hath not had a voice to put himself under.

But the aptly-named Mr Wildman was even more categorical, introducing as he did the notions of 'right' and 'justice':[2]

Every person in England hath as clear a right to elect his representative as the greatest person in England. I conceive that's the undeniable maxim of government: that all government is in the free consent of

21

the people. If then upon that account, there is no person that is under a
just government, or hath justly his own, unless he by his own free
consent be put under that government.

The notion that the individual has an inalienable right to a say over his (or
her) conditions of life, and particularly over the form of political government, is the ultimate basis of democratic liberalism. 'Liberty is a right
demanded by the very nature of human beings – not merely a freedom
from restraint but a conscious and deliberate share in such arrangements as
the community finds necessary'.[3] The claim derives in the long run from
the Platonic notion that the proper aim of human life is self-realisation – the
fullest possible development of each person's potentialities. For this,
liberty is essential.

During the Middle Ages, the issue had been obscured by the struggle
between emperor and pope. To assert the individual's corporeal rights
against the temporal power might well have had the practical effect of
strengthening a spiritual power which demanded unquestioning mental
submission. The Reformation reasserted the idea that men had the right to
think for themselves. But it only survived Rome's counter-attack because
it secured the support of the Protestant princes. The Divine Right of Kings
to rule was plausible as long as top priority was given to keeping out the
Catholics. In England however by the time that the doctrine was fully
formulated, 118 years of strong Tudor government had made it an anach-
ronism; the king rather than the Catholics had become the danger. The
Roundheads' need to justify resort to arms against his government called
attention back to ideas derived from Natural Law, from Protestantism and
from traditions erroneously discerned in the English constitution. Even if
most of the Parliamentary leaders were motivated by pragmatic common
sense rather than by theory, what Keynes said of economics is equally true
of politics – 'Practical men, who believe themselves to be quite exempt
from any intellectual influences, are usually the slaves of some defunct
economist'.[4] But once resistance to a government had been justified,
where was justification to be found for obedience to any government?

Charles I on the scaffold declared himself a benevolent aristocrat,
finding liberty and freedom in 'having government, that is, those laws by
which [the people's] lives and goods may be most their own'. He denied
that having a share in the government was anything pertaining to it.[5] To
Rainsborough and Wildman such a share pertained essentially to it. Ireton
however, whose role was to find words for Cromwell's instincts, took a
middle position:[6]

If you make this the rule . . . you must fly for refuge to an absolute
natural right and you must deny all civil right . . . For my part, I think

22

... that no person hath a right to an interest or share in the disposing of the affairs of the kingdom ... that hath not a permanent fixed interest in this kingdom ... I am sure if we look upon ... what was originally the constitution of this kingdom, [it] is this: that those who choose the representers for the making of laws by which this state and kingdom are to be governed, are the persons who, taken together, do comprehend the local interest of this kingdom; that is, the persons in whom all land lies and those in corporations in whom all trading lies ... If we shall go to take away this, we shall plainly go to take away all property and interest that any man hath.

Such words show well how the parliamentary leaders realised the danger that their movement would get out of hand, that insistence on individual rights would undermine order and confidence. Four years after the Putney debates Thomas Hobbes, in *Leviathan*, published the outstanding political treatise of the period. It is dominated by the fear of anarchy. 'The foresight of their own preservation and of a more contented live thereby' is, according to him, what leads men to subject themselves to sovereigns and once the covenant of submission has been made, 'there can happen no breach' of it on the sovereign's part.[7] Cromwell's series of experiments in government showed how hard it was to combine freedom of choice for the voters with executive efficiency. By 1660 desire for radical political and social reform was spent. Most men were ready to settle for whatever compromise between monarchy and Parliament was best calculated to provide a quiet life. But the experience of twenty-eight more years of Stuart rule provoked a reaction. With the Glorious Revolution, the Bill of Rights and the Toleration Act, a new practical basis of compromise, slightly more radical, was agreed on. This political resolution of the tension between order and freedom proved durable, with the result that its theoretical formulation by Locke dominated the thought of the succeeding century.

Locke

The first draft of Locke's *Two Treatises of Government*, written between 1679 and 1682, took as its starting point man's right to property. Every man has a natural right to self-preservation. But if a man is to live he must be free to remove from the common good and appropriate for the use of himself and his family such natural objects as are necessary to maintain existence. He also has a right to keep the fruits of his labour which he has mixed with the raw materials provided by nature. A man's labour is necessarily his own and so should its products be. But if something is a man's own he has a right to do what he likes with it, including giving it away or bequeathing it to his heirs (so that a man can acquire property for which he himself has done no work).[8] He can also transfer to other people the right to the produce of his labour in return for a wage.[9] Here we find not only a justification for the virtually unlimited acquisition of property but the germ of the labour theory of value.

In a state of nature man had a power to preserve his property – that is, his life, liberty and estate. But although Locke thought of men in a state of nature as rational creatures already possessed of rights and obligations – one being to respect the life, health, liberty and possessions of their fellows – he acknowledged that some men will behave anti-socially. Growing experience led him to the depressing conclusion that this in fact applied to the greater part of mankind. Hence the establishment of civil society and of a coercive government became desirable, so as to preserve the property rights of its members against such anti-social action. In entering into a society of this kind, men resigned those rights to the government, except in so far as they could claim them by due process of law, in order to give it the authority needed to fulfil its purposes.[10]

In 1679, in the light of the Civil War and Interregnum, Locke stressed the completeness of this surrender and therefore the absolute authority of the executive power. But when in 1689 he redrafted his *Treatises* in the light of the previous year's events, he shifted the emphasis so as to justify resistance to any executive which destroyed the authority of the legislature or to any legislature which acted contrary to the trust placed in it by the body of the people as a whole. He further distinguished between the creation of a society and the formation of a government. The dissolution of the latter left the former intact. In other words, he reserved supreme political authority to the civil society itself, as expressed by the majority of its members.[11]

At first sight he would seem to be the precursor of those such as Paine and the American Founding Fathers who attributed to all men an ultimate inalienable right to have a say in their own government. Such a view can find full satisfaction only in a constitution where each man has one vote and the basic freedoms are guaranteed. This claim rests, not on rational argument (as Locke was inclined to hold) but on an intuitive recognition that it is a right with which all men have been endowed by their creator or, to use more secular language, that it is an essential consequence of respect for human personality and for the sovereignty of the individual conscience.

But did Locke in fact consider that the right to judge the government should be extended to all men? According to some critics, he took it for granted that, as wage-labourers lived from hand to mouth, they would defer to the views of those who paid them instead of thinking for themselves. They did not have, could not be expected to have and were not entitled to have full membership of political society. Whether Locke actually believed poverty to be something reprehensible and avoidable is open to argument; a number of his contemporaries certainly did and he himself saw unemployment as caused by nothing else but 'the relaxation of discipline and the corruption of manners'. According to this essentially Whig view, only those with 'estate' could be full members of society, since only they have a full interest in the preservation of property and only they are capable of making that voluntary submission to the law of reason which is necessary for full membership. Others however deny that Locke consciously took such a restrictive view, holding that the rights and wrongs of the working class had not yet become a topical problem in his time, so that he should not be interpreted as having committed himself one way or another.[12] All the same, the view that the individual had a right to a say in society led on easily to the view that he had a duty to learn and labour truly to get his own living.

Locke can therefore be claimed as a forerunner by those who thought that every man has a right to a vote and also by those who like Hume replied that, as the function of government is to protect property, votes should go only to persons whose ownership of property gave them a stake in the country. Locke's difficulty was essentially that of Cromwell. He wanted to justify the distance to which revolution had been carried and at the same time to deny it the right to go further. But like many who stand in the middle, he could not prevent some of his successors from using some of his doctrines to justify revolution and others using different ones to oppose it.

Failure to Change 1763–97

For 75 years after the Glorious Revolution had brought a constitutional settlement, most people in Britain attached more importance to maintaining that settlement than to reforming it. But George III had been on the throne for only three years when the first of a series of collisions between his ministers and John Wilkes suggested that the crucial issue had ceased to be the rights of the king against Parliament and become the rights of the king in Parliament. The monarchy had built up a position in which, provided it could count (as it usually could) on the support of a number of unrepresentative MPs or their patrons, it could pursue whatever policies it chose. It came to grief because the policies which it did choose, first against Wilkes and then more seriously against the American colonists, encountered such strong opposition outside Parliament that they had to be abandoned as failures. The way thus seemed

25

open for changes which would make Parliament more representative and ministers more attentive to it.

This opportunity was however lost, except for some limited measures of 'economic' reform which reduced the patronage possessed by ministers and the inefficiency of the government system. There were several reasons for this failure. Many of the would-be reformers merely wanted changes of person within the existing system. Wilkes was chiefly concerned with personal advertisement, the Rockingham Whigs with inducing the king to take them on in place of his existing ministers, the Yorkshire Association with increasing the influence of country gentlemen like themselves (who had to own land worth £6,000 before they could stand for Parliament). There were of course a few who called for more drastic structural change. Major Cartwright, brother of the inventor (see p. 2), in 1776 published a book *Take Your Choice* which advocated, as a return to a supposed pre-Norman constitution, adult male suffrage, voting by ballot, equal constituencies, annual Parliaments and payment of members. He argued that 'Personality is the sole foundation of the right of being represented and Property has in reality nothing to do with the case'.[13] Had his proposals been accepted, much of the constitutional debate of the nineteenth century would have been rendered unnecessary (just as similar debates in the USA were obviated by the laying down of broad general principles in the Constitution). But he and his trend-setting Society for Constitutional Information, founded in 1780, were by no means strong enough to upset the government's majority in Parliament. Moreover, although the Gordon Riots showed how easy it was to 'raise a mob' which would vent its dislike on the well-to-do by burning down a few of their houses, the organisation needed to sustain agitation for a principle was not yet practicable. The ingredients were still lacking for that coalition between the middle classes and workers which was to achieve reform in the next century.

All the same, defeat in the American War might have precipitated more drastic changes if various human accidents had not intervened, such as the death of Rockingham four months after he had at last come into office, the misjudgment which Fox showed in allying with North and the inability of Shelburne to inspire confidence among his colleagues. But what counted more than anything was the royal acquisition of a competent executive politician in the shape of the younger Pitt. Although in favour of redistributing seats, he was not prepared to treat Parliament's refusal to agree as a reason for resignation, yet nobody was in a position to challenge him. To him goes the credit for most of the 'economic' reforms. What is harder to judge is the effect on politics of the unprecedented growth which set in during his period of office.

A second opportunity for change seemed to be presented by the French

Revolution, with its conception of government as the manifestation of the people's will. An immediate effect of this event was to call into action a bevy of organisations dedicated to welcoming and imitating it (as well as others which protested by contrast their loyalty to 'Church and King'). One of these was the Society for Constitutional Information, which had been in suspended animation since 1784. Another, more popular, was the London Corresponding Society. The two bodies did not differ much in their professed aims, such as manhood suffrage and annual parliaments, and both sent fraternal greetings to the French Assembly.

The tract for the times was of course Tom Paine's *The Rights of Man* which the Society for Constitutional Information promoted with such vigour that 200,000 copies were sold in twelve months. But their wisdom in so doing is questionable. For Paine's objects were not theirs. Their members, mostly drawn from shopkeepers and the professions, hoped 'to use the example of one revolution as a means of preventing the necessity for another'.[14] Britain could be saved from going the way of France if the apparent apathy of the public over constitutional reform could be overcome and enough pressure generated to force changes through Parliament. Paine by contrast was an atheist who wanted to sweep away the existing system altogether, to hold a convention which would establish a republic based on universal suffrage and to remedy what he saw as a fundamental defect of the British system by writing down the constitution in a single document like the American. Moreover in the second part of his book, published in February 1792, he provided a blueprint for a welfare state, with old-age pensions, family allowances, universal education and job-centres for the unemployed, financed by a graduated tax on all incomes over £500 a year. It is of course true that many of those who called for reform of Parliament looked on it as the indispensable preliminary to an overhaul of the entire social system. But their association with Paine made them more suspect than ever to ministers who in December 1792 had Part II of his book condemned by a special jury at the Guildhall. Three Scottish leaders of the Corresponding Society were sentenced to transportation in 1793. Although in 1794 juries refused to convict in prosecutions against members of both societies, the government suspended the Habeas Corpus Act and during the next two years took extra powers of repression. Agitation for change had been driven underground even before the Corresponding Society was suppressed by name in 1799.

A third more aristocratic organisation, the Friends of the People, was noteworthy in including among its founders Grey and Durham, two of the three principal architects of the 1832 Reform Bill. A motion for parliamentary reform which Grey moved in 1793 was rejected by 282 votes to 41. When in 1797 he and Fox called for household suffrage, more

county members and triennial parliaments, they had equally little success.
There were no further attempts for over a decade.

In justifying his tactics towards Paine, Horne Tooke of the Society for
Constitutional Information used a metaphor destined to become familiar:[15]

> Men may get into the same stage-coach with the intention of travel-
> ling to a certain distance; one man chooses to get out at one stage,
> another at another. When I get to Hounslow there I get out; no further
> will I go, by God.

But to many observers the important question was not whether a fellow-
traveller could get out in time but whether the coach itself could be
prevented from going any further. Doubt on that score made them regret
that it had ever been set in motion. As Windham said in March 1790,
'where was the man who would be mad enough to advise them to repair
their house in the hurricane season?'[16] It may be that the course of the
French Revolution was in itself such as to make inevitable the wave of
Tory repression which began in Britain in 1794 and postponed reform for
over 30 years. Revolutions can prove counter-productive outside the areas
in which they occur and slow down rather than accelerate change elsewhere. Napoleon's seizure of power in 1802–4 discomfited Republicans
outside France and made it easier for public feeling to be mobilised in
Britain in support of the war against 'Boney' and his countrymen.[17]

Liberal historians of the nineteenth century were wont to praise the
group represented in the Friends of the People for not abandoning their
faith in the need for change all through the years of repression but holding
fast to political reform and civil rights in the belief that their realisation
must some day again become possible. When that day arrived, enough
votes in favour of change could be found inside Parliament for that
institution to be a focus for pressure by reformers rather than an obstacle to
be overthrown by revolutionaries. More recently, opinion has turned to
condemning the better-off advocates of reform for deserting the workers
after 1794 and leaving the poor to suffer unrelieved the social hardships
induced by the industrial changes.[18] The argument is that if all those
favouring reform had stood together, a coalition such as got the Bill passed
in 1832 could have forced Pitt to grant a large instalment of it in the 1790s.
Britain would have been a happier as well as a more efficient country if she
had got her adaptation under way early rather than late. Obviously, if
more people had favoured reform earlier, it could have come sooner – but
that is not very valuable as an historical judgment. The question is
whether, given the existing strengths of the various groups, stronger
pressure for reform before 1800 would have had any other result than

provoke a more determined and irresistible repression. The forces at the government's disposal were by no means negligible.[19] By 1830 relative strengths had altered to the advantage of the reformers, there was no war in progress and the Duke of Wellington was a distinctly less formidable antagonist than Pitt.

The Utilitarians

Bentham's first book, the *Fragment on Government*, was part of the remarkable intellectual harvest of 1776, which also included the Declaration of Independence, *The Wealth of Nations*, Paine's *Common Sense*, Cartwright's *Take Your Choice* and the first volume of Gibbon's *Decline and Fall*. Bentham described it as 'the very first publication by which men at large were invited to break loose from the trammels of authority and ancestor worship'.[20] What it could not break free from were the trammels of its age. The eighteenth, more than most centuries, attached importance to happiness, perhaps because in the previous one worldly pleasures had been widely suspect. Bentham was thoroughly in tune with his time in making it the centre of his system. Locke had already hit on the idea that 'good and evil are nothing but pleasure and pain or that which occasions pleasure to us'.[21] But Bentham, borrowing from continental thinkers (through Priestley), went further and asserted that the rightness or wrongness ('utility') of any act could be settled by calculating its probable net effect in causing pleasure or pain, much as a scientist might calculate the outcome of forces pulling in different directions. This gave his teaching a strong humanitarian trend, although his ideas about what constituted 'happiness' were by no means universal.

Bentham also believed, like most of his contemporaries, that the best way to maximise happiness was for human society to be planned in the light of reason. He shared however the typical scepticism of rationalists about the ability of the average man to take reason as his guide. Instead he followed Hobbes in believing men to be essentially selfish. They were bound to pursue individual happiness above all else. But since each of them was bound to be prevented by his fellows from doing so at the general expense, and since a single individual could realise few of his desires without the help of others, it stood to reason that an individual's happiness could best be secured if he co-operated in maximising happiness for everyone else. Yet Bentham also accepted the view which Locke had come to hold that most men, if left to themselves, could not be trusted to know what their own best interests were or to refrain from irrational and anti-social behaviour of a kind inimical to the general happiness. He therefore looked to government, as the embodiment of reason, to reconcile a myriad conflicting selfish interests and thus move towards maximising happiness. Such a reconciliation could best be achieved by threats that those who trespassed unduly on the interests of others would be appropriately punished; the individual must be stopped from pursuing the promptings of self (as, for example, relying on charity instead of working) by making clear how painful the results would be.[22] Believing the lawgiver to be less susceptible to transient influences than politicians, Bentham put his faith in Codes rather than Cabinets. Reason should be embodied in law (which it conspicuously was not in the Britain of his day where, for example, the question whether theft was punishable by death depended on whether it had been committed in a shop).[23]

At the outset Bentham was not much concerned with asking who was entitled to take part in framing the laws and on what grounds. He did not, like Jefferson, claim that man had an 'unalienable right' to happiness and indeed did not pay much attention to abstract non-legal rights of any kind. He was indifferent to the idea of self-development as a thing desirable for its own sake. The doctrine of utility was not, in origin or essence, a philosophy of liberty.[24] Scientific government tends to be bureaucratic government. Bentham, like many of his followers, was primarily a paternalist or meritocrat rather than a democrat; the servant of Catherine the Great found his ideal ruler in a benevolent despot. He looked for improvement by entrusting administration to enlightened men. To give such men more influence, he contemplated turning the highly decentralised island of his day into a highly centralised one. The problem which he did not face squarely was how to ensure that despots were enlightened and that the most rational men got into the key positions.

It was here that he met disillusionment. He became exasperated with the reluctance of those governing Britain to take his advice, particularly as regards prison reform. He was excited by the spectacle of France. In 1808 he came to know James Mill, who had an almost unbounded faith in representative government and freedom of discussion.[25] The net result was that he changed his mind about the relative merits of individuals and governments, embracing the alternative eighteenth-century view that, fallible as individuals might be, governments were more so. He accepted Adam Smith's argument that leaving freedom to the individual provided a better chance of maximising prosperity (and with it happiness) than the alternative of leaving some external authority to calculate the answer and then impose it. Instead however of concluding that government should be reduced to a minimum, he argued that the least fallible system of governing would be one in which the executive was chosen by the entire adult population (including women) since it would then be best qualified to judge what was in the interest of the greatest possible number. As governors always acted in their own interests, the general interest was most likely to be served when power was as widely distributed as possible.[26] He thus became an advocate of 'radical' change.[27] But his support for it was based on prudence rather than principle. His practical programme of reform was much like Cartwright's but, in spite of an aversion to big landowners, his respect for property made him stop short of giving votes to non-householders.

The Utilitarians remained however in two minds about the individual and government.[28] Practical experience fostered the realisation that the individual often did not know or lacked the power to achieve the courses of action which were in his best interests, thereby justifying the intervention of a government possessed of greater knowledge and authority. Yet they retained the respect for the individual which the eighteenth century had possessed and which the Romantics augmented. Such respect led naturally to the view that government – and indeed all authority which lacked a rational basis – was an evil which, although necessary, should be kept as limited as possible. A tension between 'hard' and 'soft' liberalism became a permanent feature of progressive thought (paralleled by a similar tension in conservative thought).[29] On the one hand there were those whose prior concern was that the individual should be allowed to decide for himself how he would live. On the other there were those who denied that the natural order was fundamentally harmonious, so that the power of the law and the superior knowledge of its representatives must intervene if the common good was to be maximised. In respect to theory, it was a difference about the value to be attached to doing something because it was realised to be right as compared with being compelled to do it. In respect to practice, it was a difference about the need for counterbalancing social and economic constraints by legal and political ones. Those who were able to look after themselves wanted freedom; those who were not (and their sympathisers) wanted intervention. In the first half of the nineteenth century, radicalism meant broadly the removal of restrictions and limitations; in the second it began to mean their re-imposition.

The inability of the average man to know what was good for him was attributed not to inherent human fallibility or 'original sin' but to his never having been taught any better. The Utilitarians took to heart the emphasis laid by Montesquieu and Helvetius on the importance of geography and climate in forming the social institutions of each country. They believed that human behaviour could be improved by controlling the environment. This outlook led to a fervent belief in education, not primarily as something to which men have a right or as a means of social advancement but as a process of conditioning in the use of reason. In the background were several assumptions: that the prevalence of truth is beneficial to mankind, so that freedom of discussion is to be encouraged; that truth cannot be contradictory, so that discussion and the dissemination of knowledge are bound to foster agreement and social harmony; that society is capable of indefinite improvement by allowing free play to man's self-interest, provided only that that interest is enlightened.

The chief practical contribution of the Utilitarians to the reform movement was the idea of introducing rationality and system into British government, where it was badly needed. Their hope of matching the sciences of mathematics and chemistry by a science of man in society may have disregarded the impact of human nature on the subject matter. But they established the importance of finding out the facts and figures about a problem before prescribing remedies; to them must go the credit for the numerous Statistical Departments and Royal Commissions which did so much to bring home to the nineteenth century what kind of a world it was living in. The Utilitarians, and J. S. Mill in particular, further provided the reformers of that century with a comprehensive ideological under-pinning which enabled demands to be supported by reasoned justification. Their political theories however failed to explain why freedom might be felt as an imperative, just as their moral ones failed to explain why right action might be felt as obligatory and not merely prudential.

Radical Dissent

G. M. Young regarded as the two greatest disasters in British history, Ireland (about which there will be much to say later in this book) and the religious settlement reached – or rather, not reached – after the Restoration.[30] Charles II, before landing, promised 'a liberty to tender consciences' and there were a number of Puritan divines, led by the saintly Richard Baxter, who were prepared to accept bishops and some form of a liturgy. But in the 'Cavalier Parliament' which met in May 1662, the high churchmen had a majority and used it to pass the Act of Uniformity which excluded from their parishes all ministers who did not 'assent and consent' to the Prayer Book and abjure the Covenant of 1643 with its commitment to root out prelacy as well as popery. The Episcopalians wanted revenge for the way in which many of them had been treated under the Puritans.

Some 2,000 ministers refused to give the required assent and were excluded from their parishes. The more rigid Calvinists would have insisted on independence anyhow but the Church of England lost the services of many devout and reasonable men whose influence would have done it good. At first those excluded were reluctant to accept the division as final or organise themselves as a separate body. But in 1672 the Declaration of Indulgence faced them with the choice of obtaining specific leave to officiate outside the Established Church or ceasing to do so at all; 1,339 applied for a licence. These gradually became known as 'Presbyterians' although the name is misleading since their views on doctrine and church organisation were considerably more moderate than those of most Calvinist churches.[31]

The Cavalier intolerance had more important results than is often realised. It meant that for over two centuries there existed in England a substantial group of Christians, drawn mainly from the middle and lower middle classes, who were denied a number of what they regarded as rights (including freedom of conscience) and others as privileges. Their social and historical background inclined them to anti-establishment (although not always liberal) points of view. Relatively few of them were tenant-farmers or agricultural labourers and they thus had no need to defer to landowners.[32] Elsewhere in Western Europe the godly, whether Catholic or Protestant, tended to support the established order so that its opponents became atheists as well as socialists. England's difference in this respect was reinforced in the next century when Wesley's followers were also compelled to leave with reluctance the church. Having lost ground during the early decades of the eighteenth century, dissent recovered it again during the closing ones. The resentment caused by exclusion took time to fade, just as the forms which exclusion assumed took time to remedy. It contributed to hostility between classes and had particularly unfortunate results in education where progress was slowed down by the mutual fear of church and dissent that the other would get the young on its side. Yet when one considers how much nonconformity contributed to English life, one begins to wonder whether G. M. Young was right. Would there have been such vigour without the stimulus of exclusion?

Baxter was a man of 'the godly middle sort', moderate in everything except in his passion for writing. After his death in 1691 his followers kept to his tolerant spirit. In 1719 they decided that adherence to Scripture should be the only test required of members, whereas the more conservative sects wanted in addition assent to various 'Confessions'; as a result the two groups began to draw apart. Moreover the Baxterians, influenced by Locke and by the growing interest in science, were inclined to regard reason as the ultimate guardian of truth in religion as in all else, thereby exposing themselves to a dilemma which became more obvious as the eighteenth century progressed. A critical examination of the Scriptures revealed that they were often contradictory or ambiguous (one scholar showed that their text was susceptible of 30,000 variant readings!) and that they provided little foundation for a number of doctrines figuring prominently in the Confessions, such as Original Sin, Redemption and the Trinity. But reason itself does not always produce an answer which is beyond dispute and the Presbyterian trust in it could have disintegrating results.

Of those who put Scripture before the Confessions and reason before

Scripture, the leader during the second half of the eighteenth century was Joseph Priestley, unkindly described as 'Faction's dearest child'.[33] A polymath whose interests embraced theology, philosophy, chemistry and political science, without his being fully at home in any of them, he vigorously propounded an outlook which was individualist, rationalist and Newtonian. He insisted on the name 'Unitarian' being substituted for 'Presbyterian', thereby provoking into secession those who, accepting the Trinity, believed that Jesus was divine. He further rejected Original Sin and the Atonement. On the other hand he accepted the teachings in the Gospels as 'guaranteed by the Miracles and established by the Resurrection'. He described the highest stage of personal devotion as 'dwelling in God and God in him'. When associated with an assertion of the Father's wisdom, these views made him confident that good would ultimately prevail. He denied the need for a national church, while his emphasis on reason and suspicion of enthusiasm put his followers at odds with both the Evangelicals inside the church and the Wesleyans outside it.[34] Politically Methodism was less radical than Unitarianism, even if it was not what saved England from revolution, as Halévy thought.

In his *Essay on Government* (1768) Priestley wrote that 'the good and happiness of the members, that is to say, the majority of members of any state, is the great standard by which everything relating to the state must finally be determined'. This, although not original, was the spark which, according to Bentham, first kindled his ideas. Unitarianism has been described as 'Utilitarianism in its Sunday best'.[35] To be accurate, Christianity had for Priestley unique authority whereas most of the Utilitarians came as near to being atheists as was in those days prudent and gave no particular priority to any religion. But on matters concerning this world the views of the two groups were closely similar. Priestley described 'the whole duty of political man' as being 'to think with freedom, to speak and write with boldness, to suffer for a good cause with patience, to begin to act with caution but to proceed with vigour'.[36] His links with reform were many. He was a friend of Benjamin Franklin and sided with the colonies in the War of Independence. Before coming to Birmingham 'in 1780 as Minister' at the New Meeting House (see p. 78), he had been librarian to Lord Shelburne. Major Cartwright and Sir George Savile, the spokesman for the Yorkshire Association (see p. 26), were both Unitarians. It was an aristocracy of enlightened dissent, attractive to people who were both progressive and well-to-do, but criticised by the enthusiasts as 'North Pole Christianity'.

Most existing grammar schools in England used the Book of Common Prayer while admission to Oxford and Cambridge was restricted to members of the Established Church. The dissenters therefore set up academies of their own to train both ministers and laymen. The most notable were those at Northampton, run by Philip Doddridge, and at Warrington, where Priestley was for a time a tutor and Malthus a pupil. These institutions were soon providing the best education available in the country. Locke's works, regarded as suspect at the ancient universities, were a basic subject while the Warrington curriculum included chemistry, modern languages and 'pneumatology', by which was meant the study of the brain and of ethical and metaphysical systems. Priestley considered the right of a man to educate his child as he wanted essential to human liberty and all the dissenters regarded schemes for state-run education with aversion. In 1808 the Utilitarians set up the British and Foreign Schools Society to promote the kind of non-sectarian learning which they favoured and three years later the Church of England followed suit with the National Society for the Education of the Poor in the Principles of the Established Church. When in 1815 the British and Foreign Society was temporarily captured by the Evangelicals, to whom religious teaching was more essential than any other, the anti-clericals transferred their attention to higher education, starting University College in 1827 and the University of London ten years later.

The First Instalment of Electoral Reform

Between 1797 and 1831 only five proposals for reforming the electoral system were put forward in Parliament. The only one which was not voted down by a substantial majority was Russell's 1821 motion transferring two seats from the rotten borough of Grampound to Yorkshire (and not, as its author hoped, to Leeds).

Over and above the basic fear of going the same way as France, there were a number of special reasons for this inertia. As earlier, the cause seemed dogged by human accidents. No sooner was a major obstacle removed by the death of Pitt in 1807 than Fox's death ten months later deprived the Whigs of their most promising leader. Three years later, when a background of discontent throughout the country was rising to a point at which Parliament might have been expected to do something about it, the Whigs' will to act was inhibited by the King's madness. For they expected that, as soon as the Prince of Wales became Regent, he would call them to office and thereby make it easier for them to act with success. By the time it had become clear that he was going to be as much of an impediment as his father, the propitious moment had passed.

Secondly there was a notable absence, both inside and outside Parliament, of leaders who were not merely able but also determined (although such an absence may be as much a sign of uncongenial conditions as of unqualified men). The names best remembered today, Castlereagh and

Canning, were made in foreign affairs. Some of the opposition leaders, like Grey and Melbourne, not unreasonably preferred the pleasures of country life during the fifteen long years of Liverpool's premiership to fruitless politicking; others were noisy nonentities, like Burdett and Hume. Outside there were good organisers, like Place, and effective publicists like Cobbett but nobody who combined political flair with power of persuasion. In spite of the distress and discontent in 1817, the Luddite risings in south Derbyshire and the West Riding were instant failures, having been mounted by workers without middle-class help. The behaviour of the Cato Street conspirators was more gauche than sinister.

Thirdly a considerable amount of reform did occur in other fields. Indeed there were politicians like Canning who argued that not only were such reforms more important but that they would deflate the pressure for electoral change. Between 1782 and 1815 over a thousand sinecures were abolished, while a further inquiry in 1817 led to the removal or regulation of 300 more.[37] Effort was also devoted to such measures as the first but feeble Factory Act of 1802 (proposed, according to the practice of the time, by a private member), the Abolition of the Slave Trade in 1807, the ending of the East India Company's monopoly in 1813, the repeal of the Combination Act in 1824 and of the Test and Corporation Acts in 1828. In 1820 three Acts were passed humanising the criminal law; in 1823 about 100 felonies were exempted from the death penalty. Catholic Emancipation absorbed much attention from 1801 until its enactment in 1829, as did the cause of Queen Caroline, which accustomed the middle classes and the populace to working together.

Several writers have detected during the period a steady progress in the organisation of political agitation. What has been described as 'collective bargaining by riot' was giving place to systematic strikes, particularly after the repeal of the Combination Act; the idea of a general strike was first mooted in 1820. 'In 1806 both in Middlesex and Westminster the mob, though still a factor, was of smaller importance than the widespread and thorough electoral organisation undertaken by the "public" against the "placemen" and their allies.'[38] 'The poor, when suffering and dissatisfied, no longer made a riot but held a meeting. Instead of attacking their neighbours, they blamed the Ministry.'[39] The movements against slavery and for Catholic Emancipation were models of how successful political campaigns should be mounted.

The reform movement gained an important accretion of strength when the merchants and manufacturers began to support it. During the earlier war years, the 'middle classes' (a term said to have come into general use at this time) had stood behind the government. But first the Orders in Council replying to Napoleon's Berlin Decrees and later the Corn Laws were attacked by Ricardo and others as measures damaging to commerce inspired by ignorant landowners who were pocketing in rents the extra wealth which it was bringing to the country.[40] This business animosity to the landed interest was to be a major factor in politics for more than fifty years. Papers like the *Leeds Mercury* and the *Manchester Guardian*, now coming into existence in the provinces, were weighty mouthpieces for such views.

In the decade after 1810, fresh attempts were made to organise a movement for moderate reform. But the simultaneous movements for violent change so frightened the government that it insisted on treating the two things as one and, by measures like the Six Acts, drove both underground for over ten years. When serious agitation resumed, it took the form of political unions, intended not only to advocate reform but also to protect life and property against 'the detailed but irregular outrages of the mob, as well as for the maintenance of other great interests against the systematic violences of an oligarchy'.[41] The first of these was founded at Birmingham in 1829; a year later, it petitioned Parliament for the dismissal of placemen from the House of Commons, elections at least every three years, redistribution of seats, votes for all taxpayers, voting by ballot, the abolition of any property qualification for candidates and payment of members. The slogan of Thomas Attwood, its leader, was 'Peace, Law and Order' and great anxiety was shown to avoid provoking or alarming the well-to-do. Less staid were the London Radical Association and a series of meetings organised by Thomas Hetherington at the Ranelagh Rotunda.

Thus by the end of the 1820s the reform movement had at last accumulated enough intellectual respectability, competent organisation and popular enthusiasm for success to be merely a matter of time. It was too strong to repress, especially when the small size of the army and the lack of a police force were taken into consideration. Then at last accident told in reform's favour. Not only did several bad harvests and high corn prices fuel the 'Captain Swing' riots and point to the need for some remedial action but, in June 1830, George IV died. The tradition which bound Parliament closely with the monarch meant that a regal death required a general election. Before it could occur, a 'respectable' revolution in France demonstrated that even there such events did not necessarily end in reigns of terror or dictatorships. British politics were still too inchoate for the results of the polling to be precisely measurable – in any case, only a quarter of the constituencies were contested – but the Tories were judged to have lost about thirty seats. Wellington's claim that the state of the representation was incapable of improvement precipitated his defeat a fortnight after the new Parliament met.

The campaign for the Reform Bills which occupied the next nineteen months was largely successful because of the political and social spread of the coalition which promoted it. At the top, the Whig ministers, representative of that element in the landed aristocracy which had always been most sympathetic to business and parliamentary tradition, provided the indispensable leadership in the House of Commons; they alone could get the Bill through the House of Lords by inducing the King to create peers. The radicals, essentially middle class, provided the rank and file of the parliamentary majority. Outside the intellectuals and journalists provided the vocabulary, while the ultra-radicals, drawn from the lower middle classes and artisans and influenced largely by Cobbett,[42] provided the ground swell of support. This was threatening enough to intimidate the aristocracy without being immediate enough to frighten off trade and industry.

The Whigs believed in liberty in principle but might not have swallowed quite so much of it if they had not been afraid of the 'anarchy' which a more moderate measure might provoke. They were far-sighted enough to realise that they could not preserve their privileged position intact but hoped, by yielding a certain amount, to keep the rest – or at least delay its loss. Graham, Grey's First Lord of the Admiralty, said that 'a statesman's wisdom consists in recognising the proper moment for making concessions';[43] Grey himself advocated a 'large' settlement as affording some ground of resistance to further innovation. Those who believed that a voice in government was a right of man were disappointed by a measure which still confined voting to owners or lessors of property and they accused the Whigs of betrayal. They found however some consolation in the thought that, once a breach had been made in the walls of privilege, the task of enlarging it would become easier. Place wrote that 'The Bill itself is of little value, but as the commencement of the breaking-up of the old rotten system, it is invaluable'.[44] He started at once to work for the next instalment, little thinking that it would be delayed for thirty-five years.

If it was by reform that Britain was to be changed, the Act could only be a compromise. Both a more and a less drastic measure might have precipitated revolution, when King and Lords refused to give way to the former or the public refused to rest content with the latter. Of the 144 seats taken away from boroughs, 66 went to towns hitherto unrepresented and 65 to counties (the remaining 13 to Scotland and Ireland). Constituencies remained far from equal; 67 in England and Wales still had less than 500 voters. Rural England still had a disproportionate influence. In all 217,000 voters were added to an electorate of 435,000, as well as 60,500 to 4,500 in Scotland, making a new total equivalent to 14 per cent of the adult male population. It was claimed that 151,492 electors still controlled 331 of the 658 seats; 54 individuals (mostly peers) controlled 72 seats.[45] The property qualification required of candidates remained untouched, although it soon became a dead letter. The maximum duration of Parliament stayed at seven years, although there were to be four elections in the next ten. A provision for voting by ballot had been included in the original draft of the Bill but Grey objected to it as likely to reduce the influence of landlords, so that bribery and intimidation continued to play a big part in elections, the chief and, in the long run, decisive change being that the number of people to be bribed went up.

In the end both Whigs and Radicals proved to have read the situation correctly. Peers, landowners and their relatives continued for a long time to staff many offices of state. Every Cabinet until 1868 contained more people entitled to be addressed as 'My Lord' than not. Yet the Whig magnates knew that the position which they were defending was one which could not be held against resolute attack and, in order to avoid provoking such an attack, they had to pay increasing attention to the views of the middle class and intellectuals. The deference in Victorian politics was not all on one side. Moreover most of those who opposed each stage of reform showed themselves ready to accept it (or resigned themselves to the impossibility of reversing it) once it was enacted, while those who did not were soon removed by natural causes. Britain thus achieved the process of adjustment to industrialisation without revolution and without the debilitating presence of a group which refused to be reconciled to what had happened – the phenomenon which did so much to weaken France's republics. She was also saved from the refusal of a strong pre-industrial élite to surrender power, which did so much to complicate the history of Germany, Austria–Hungary and Russia. A historian could write in 1938 that 'if there is still less hatred in England than in most parts of the Western world, it is because the Whig aristocracy knew how to make concessions to the middle classes and the middle classes, in turn, to the others'.[46]

Two schools of thought find this verdict too complacent. One complains that the Whigs were too successful. Their tactics of giving ground gracefully meant that the new social groups only came to power gradually and consequently, as often in such circumstances, adopted instead of repudiating the values of the groups which they were superseding. In this process the 'public' schools played an important part. As a result too many of Britain's pre-industrial institutions and attitudes got carried over into industrial society, impeding the efficiency of all her industries other than tourism.[47] A second school reproaches the Whigs for not going far enough and as a result leaving a sense of resentment in the breasts of the workers which was inimical to good industrial relations and higher productivity. J. S. Mill in 1848 spoke of 'the widening and embittering feud between the class of labourers and the class of capitalists', while the Hammonds considered that the French Revolution had divided the people of France less than the Industrial Revolution had divided the people of

39

Britain.[48] The lesson which both schools would seem to draw is that revolution would have been a gain rather than a loss.

Two questions need to be asked in considering these attacks. First, what kind of a revolution is envisaged and to whose benefit? Presumably one which would have lessened class feeling and brought a more egalitarian and humane society into existence more quickly. But could a revolution in 1832 have done more than bring the middle classes to power and would the middle classes, in their then frame of mind, with all the emphasis laid on removing barriers to free enterprise, have been inclined to help the disadvantaged? Secondly might not a revolution at that particular juncture have done more harm than good? About ten years after reform, Britain entered on her most intense phase of economic growth, when at last industrialisation began to benefit the workers. Might not the animosities, which revolution would certainly have left, have jeopardised this expansion?

There is much to be said for counter-history; only by considering what else might have happened can one judge the significance of what did happen. And there are many contexts in which one feels that, given a few small alterations, history might well have taken a completely different turn – if, for example, the bomb placed in Hitler's aircraft on 13 March 1943 had exploded. But there are other contexts in which the course of history seems to have been decided by the relative strength of forces too deep-seated for them to have been turned aside by small accidents. In such cases counter-history amounts to little more than wishing that the world were other than it is.

Politics and Society in Birmingham

The problem of adapting Britain to the industrialised world was at its most acute in the cities which industry had swollen.

Nobody has yet produced a convincing explanation of why Birmingham grew. There were no important raw materials available, except good well-water, and transport facilities were poor, although it was the meeting-place of several local tracks. But grow it did. It was mentioned in Domesday Book and by 1550 its population may have reached 1,500. Camden about 1580 described it as 'swarming with inhabitants and echoing with the noise of anvils'.[49] But, because there was no adequate transport till a canal was opened in 1770, Birmingham concentrated on small articles with a high added value. Such things, known collectively as 'toys', tended to be made by small firms in small workshops: Burke called the town 'the toyshop of Europe'.[50]

Small men working on their own are apt to think for themselves and in

the seventeenth century Birmingham was strongly Roundhead; Clarendon said it was 'of as great fame for hearty, wilful, affected disloyalty to
the King as any place in England'.[51] This disposition was strengthened by
the Five Mile Act of 1665 which required clergymen and schoolmasters
who rejected the Thirty-nine Articles to keep at least five miles away from
any incorporated town, with the result that they frequented lesser places.
By 1700 there were two congregations of Presbyterians and one of
Quakers; Kidderminster, Baxter's centre, was only fifteen miles away. As
a town without a charter, it was a 'town without a shackle' and the
enterprise of its citizens was free from restriction by guilds.[52] 'The
industrious, the ingenious and the persevering all found their natural
home where each could develop his faculties unfettered.'[53] 'Every man
seemed to know and prosecute his own affairs.'[54]

Between 1700 and 1820 the population of London doubled but between
1740 and 1800 the 'boobies of Birmingham' (as Dr Johnson described
them)[55] increased fourfold (although with a population of just over
100,000 the town was only a tenth the size of the metropolis). 'To
enumerate some of the Birmingham products is to evoke the intricate
constellation of skills; shoe-buckles, cutlery, spurs, candlesticks, toys,
guns, buttons, whip-handles, coffee-pots, ink-stands, bells, carriage-
fittings, snuff-boxes, lead pipes, jewellery, lamps and kitchen imple-
ments.'[56] 'Almost every Master and Manufacturer hath a new invention of
his own and is daily improving on those of others.'[57] In 1757 John
Baskerville, who had made a fortune by japanning enamel, printed his first
book. In 1765 a leading button-manufacturer joined forces with a Quaker
iron-merchant called Lloyd to open a bank. If unkind critics spoke of
'Brummagem ware' as synonymous with cheap and nasty, that was partly
no doubt because of the local skill at counterfeiting. But an inhabitant said
in 1781 that the image of his city called up 'a superb picture which is best
explained by the other words – grand, populous, extensive, active,
commercial and humane.'[58]

In 1762 Matthew Boulton, a born promoter of other people's ideas who
was already active in many directions, set up a new factory at Soho to the
north of the city in which careful attention was paid to work-flow and
handling methods. Two years earlier Boulton had got to know Erasmus
Darwin of Lichfield, a poet who in 1761 was elected to the Royal Society.
They took to dining together with about a dozen kindred spirits and
afterwards discussing any scientific topic which anyone cared to raise. As
these discussions tended to be prolonged and as some of the members had
a long way to go home, they met on the Sunday nearest the full moon and
took the name of the 'Lunar Society'.[59] Benjamin Franklin, who paid
several visits to Birmingham, introduced a Dr Small who had taught
Jefferson when he was a professor at Williamsburg; he acted as secretary to

the Society till his death in 1775. Another member was Josiah Wedgwood. Both Boulton and Wedgwood were Unitarians; their friendship and the existence of the Society were what attracted Priestley to Birmingham in 1780.

The most famous member however was James Watt, who first visited Birmingham in 1767 and became Boulton's partner in 1775. The firm which they jointly set up did not manufacture complete machines but drawings and key parts. The first engine was installed near at hand in 1776 but half the early output went to Cornish tin mines for pumping. This business was not profitable and financial success came only after the gear had been devised to convert the to-and-fro stroke into a rotary motion (see p. 4). The Soho establishment became world famous but it was not typical of the district. It was a 'factory' in an area of small workshops. Industrialisation multiplied the number of producing units instead of increasing the scale of existing firms. Social gradients shelved more gently as a result and it was not uncommon for workmen to address their employer by his Christian name.[60] An artisan had a better chance than elsewhere of becoming a small master. As a result class antagonisms were less sharp than in the north and trade unions correspondingly weaker.

During all this time the budding city was being ruled as a village. Law and order were enforced by centrally appointed justices. A self-perpetuating manorial court leet annually elected two bailiffs, one a churchman, the other and more influential a dissenter. In 1769 a Board of fifty commissioners was set up to pave, light and enlarge the streets but, as most improvements threatened detriment to private property, not much was done. In 1797 the Board appointed twenty-six constables as a night watch; the strength of the force rose in time to eighty but until 1840 it remained the only civil body available to maintain order. The town had once been said to have no need of police because the inhabitants worked too hard to have time for mischief, but the claim was hardly borne out by the riots which occurred in 1715, 1743, 1750, 1762 and 1783.[61] In 1791 a dinner held to celebrate the second anniversary of the capture of the Bastille provoked several 'Church and King' partisans into considering 'how to punish those damned Presbyterians', whereupon a mob burnt the two meeting houses and several private homes including Priestley's, driving him from the town and undermining the Lunar Society.[62] There were further riots in 1793, 1795 and 1800 which needed the militia to put them down.

The French Wars began by disrupting Birmingham's trade with the continent but before long its small-arms industry had been so expanded that it was supplying two-thirds of the weapons used by the British forces. The result was a slump after 1815, when one-third of the population were said to have become paupers. A petition to Parliament in 1816 epitomised the purport of many such before and since. 'We implore your Honourable

House to remove the cause of misery whatever it may be. And we cannot but think that your Honourable House can remove it.'[63] One citizen, Thomas Attwood, anticipating Keynes, found the cause in the excessively strict monetary policy of the government and recommended the issue of £20m. in paper money and the abandonment of the gold standard. Although by origin a Tory and a Churchman, Attwood was driven (like Bentham) steadily leftwards by the refusal of ministers to heed him. He played a prominent part in founding a local Hampden Society for reform and in 1829 the Birmingham Political Union (see p. 37). When in May 1832 Place decided that, if the Duke of Wellington succeeded in forming a government and the standard of revolt had to be raised, Birmingham was the place to start, the reason was not that the town was exceptionally restive but because the best prospects of keeping a revolution under control were thought to exist there. For the middle classes were working in the Union hand in glove with the artisans.[64]

Attwood was one of Birmingham's first two MPs. Another Birmingham reformer and Unitarian, Joseph Parkes, was secretary of the Commission which drafted that essential postscript to the 1832 Reform Act, the Municipal Corporations Act of 1835. 'Municipal reform' he described as the 'steam-engine for the mill built by Parliamentary reform'.[65] At last the way was open for Birmingham's incorporation and until this was achieved the Political Union regarded its task as only half accomplished. But the proposal to seek a charter met with opposition. The Act only allowed the new town councils limited powers, for fear that they would prove incompetent or corrupt. Most of the tasks which would fall to them were already being performed in Birmingham by the Street Commissioners; this was the body which in 1830 set about building a town hall. But thanks to being personally nominated at the outset and thereafter self-elected, the Commission was predominantly Whig. Town councils however were elected by ratepayer suffrage so that transferring the municipal government from closed oligarchy to representative councillors involved a transfer of political allegiance; in the first elections the Radicals made a clean sweep of all the seats, only to be accused by their opponents of having 'gerrymandered' the ward boundaries. It also looked as though an American 'spoils system' was to be instituted; the first town clerk, coroner, clerk of the peace and registrar all had radical backgrounds.

The old regime took advantage of various obscurities in the legislation and in 1839 challenged the validity of the charter and of the council's proposed levy of a rate to pay for a police force. Just at this moment the Chartist National Convention was moved from London to Birmingham (see p. 46) and serious riots in the Bull Ring followed. The council was unfairly accused of having allowed its political sentiments to weaken its will to keep order and for three years control of the police was given to a

Commissioner appointed by the Home Office. Then Peel, to Tory dismay, put the obvious intentions of the 1835 Act into effect.[66] But another nine years were needed before the council could reach a compromise with the street commissioners and an Act be obtained amalgamating the two bodies. Not only did the constitutional wrangle distract attention from practical matters but the council's impotence meant that membership was left to butchers, bakers and candlestick makers, small men of small ideas. There was a lot of catching up to be done and they were ill-qualified to do it.

Reform Marks Time 1832–50

The results of the Reform Act proved as disappointing to the keen reformers as did its provisions. To many in the coalition which had secured its passage, the experience had been unnerving and was not to be lightly repeated.[67] If the radicals had ever looked like following up their success in other directions, the Whigs might well have closed ranks with the Tories to defend landed property, the church, the Lords and the monarchy. But although a quarter of the new House of Commons was reckoned to be radical, they were a collection of individuals without a recognised leader who did not know how to work together.[68] 'The fire is insufficient for all the irons thrust in.'[69] Each of the next three elections saw their numbers fall. Consequently the period was typified as much by an Irish Coercion Act, the sentences on the Tolpuddle labourers and the rejection of a Ballot Bill as by such reforms as the Abolition of Slavery, the second (and ineffective) Factory Act, the Poor Law Amendment Act, the Municipal Corporations Act, the Marriage Act, the Commutation of Tithes and the establishment of the Ecclesiastical Commissioners to overhaul the running of the Church of England.

The Municipal Corporations Act gave a vote in all borough elections in England and Wales (outside London) to all ratepayers and empowered each council to establish a police force.[70] But when in 1836 the radical MP Joseph Hume tried to get the representative principle extended to the counties, he came up against the determination of the landed interest to preserve the power which they exercised through quarter sessions. The absence of elected bodies outside the towns led during the next fifty years to a number of specialist bodies being set up to perform the various public functions such as poor relief, education and health which came to be seen as socially necessary. In the case of the Poor Law Bentham's disciple Chadwick was bent on imposing a system which, if it was to realise the benefits he expected from it, needed to be administered with more rigour than locally elected amateurs would be prepared to use. He therefore gave the task to Boards of Guardians covering thirty or more parishes who, although elected, had to work through paid officials and were up to a point controlled by a central commission. Amendments to his scheme as it went through Parliament made its rigours less rational without much reducing them, and if the Commissioners who were implementing it had not slowed down when they turned from south to north, they might well have produced a mass protest similar to the mediaeval peasant revolts. For a system intended to discipline men who would not work was ill-suited for relieving men who could not find work.

In education an even bigger opportunity was missed. Schools in England and Wales were generally agreed to be insufficient in numbers and inadequate in quantity. But the Church of England had never taken kindly to what it regarded as its monopoly of teaching being invaded by the nonconformists who, for their part, were afraid that any state system would be run for the benefit of the church. There were others who regarded education as pre-eminently a field for private enterprise and opposed suggestions that the state should have any part in it, let alone spend money on it. Accordingly any extension of state activity was bound to be fiercely resisted; even supposing that a majority could be found for the necessary legislation in the House of Commons, it would have no chance of passing the Lords. In 1833 J. A. Roebuck MP proposed a comprehensive plan 'for the universal and national education of the people' but got little help from his fellow radicals; O'Connell objected to state education as 'regimentation' while Cobbett attacked it for increasing the number of teachers, 'the new race of idlers'.[71] The government, seeing no hope for the proposal, induced the House of Commons, by 50 votes to 26, to pay the two existing religious societies £20,000 a year (0·1 per cent of the compensation given to slave-owners) for school-building. Even this innovation only got through because it came before an empty House late in the session and did not require endorsement by the Lords.

Six years later, at the prompting of Queen Victoria,[72] responsibility for education was given to a special Committee of the Privy Council, another solution designed to avoid trouble in that it did not involve creating a new department with a minister of its own – which did not prevent the House of Lords from protesting about it to the queen. As time went on, the number and purposes of its grants increased and a corps of inspectors was formed to keep an eye on the results; the church insisted on choosing those for its own schools, who had to be clergymen. Policy decisions rested with the Societies; the function of the state was to pay part of the bill, according to an agreed scale, and occasionally, by manipulating the scale, influence the policy. Meanwhile higher education was confined to the 400–500 persons admitted each year to Oxford and Cambridge, most of whom became clergymen, and to the graduates of London. (Scotland did better with four universities and a yearly intake of over 1,000.) Thus in a field of vital importance for her future Britain, already behind, was only advancing slowly.

The parliamentary stalemate explains why in 1837, when over-investment had caused output to exceed demand and thus brought on a depression, the agitation for change was taken up by articulate artisans outside Parliament. The Grand National Consolidated Trades Union, set up in 1833, had lasted only a year. But in 1836 William Lovett, a Cornish-born cabinet-maker, developed into the London Working Men's Association an organisation through which he had just succeeded in reducing the Stamp Duty on newspapers; it was widely copied. In 1837 Roebuck was asked to present in the House a petition for reform with 3,000 signatures; he suggested instead a Bill for universal suffrage. By the time that this took definite shape under Place's guidance early in 1838, it had developed into a 'People's Charter', making six demands closely resembling Cartwright's proposals of 1778; manhood suffrage, equal constituencies, the ballot, short parliaments of fixed duration, the abolition of any property qualification for candidates and (as a corollary) the payment of members.[73]

In Birmingham, Attwood's Political Union had been revived as the LWMA's counterpart and this was the body which in May 1838 organised a meeting in Glasgow to start the campaign. Delegates were to be elected to a 'General Convention of the Industrious Classes', to meet in London, receive a petition with mass signatures and present it to Parliament. The implementing of this plan took nine months; meetings were held all over the country at which the delegates were chosen and many wild things said, particularly by torchlight, but signatures unevenly collected. Arms of sorts began to be procured. But when fifty-four delegates met in Cockspur Street in February 1839 it soon became obvious that they had no precise plan of campaign beyond presenting the Charter to Parliament. Some hoped to overcome opposition in time by 'moral force'; others thought physical force would be needed but most of these claimed that a mere show of it would suffice. Even the handful (predominantly Irish) who really expected to use it had no clear idea of how to set about doing so.

First of all the districts which had been backward in collecting signatures were given time to catch up. Then the Convention was blown off course by the 'Bedchamber Crisis' which deprived them for two months of a ministry and Parliament to receive their petition. Before this was remedied the Birmingham delegation had withdrawn for fear that the advocates of physical force would have their way, while those who favoured using force also moved to Birmingham so as to be more secure if the government should use it against them. Early in June the riot in the Bull Ring brought the Convention back to London, only for it to be nonplussed by Parliament's refusal to even discuss the petition. After much argument an attempt was made in August to launch a general strike (more euphemistically called a 'National Holiday' or 'Sacred Month'). When this collapsed the Convention was dissolved. In November twenty-four Chartists were killed in an unsuccessful rising at Newport and movements in Yorkshire intended to coincide were equally short-lived. By this time the government had almost all the leaders behind bars; the inadequacy of the organisation is illustrated by the fact that, although the LWMA was supposed to act as a focus for the whole country, Lovett was its only full-time officer so that, when he was arrested, its activities stopped.[74] Between 1 January 1839 and 30 June 1840, some 500 were convicted of various offences from high treason and sedition downwards – but nobody was actually hanged.[75]

This helps to explain why the rest of 1840 and 1841 were fairly quiet. In 1842, described as 'the worst year of the century' although in fact it saw the start of the great expansion,[76] another meeting in Birmingham led to another National Convention and the presentation of another petition to Parliament, duly followed by another rejection, more riots, strikes and arrests. When it emerged that a number of signatures to the petition had been written in the same hand, the public began to laugh the agitation out of court.

By this time the more highly-organised and skilful campaigning of the Anti-Corn Law League had diverted attention from constitutional reform. Some middle-class elements, led by a Birmingham Quaker and corn-miller Joseph Sturge, had tried at the end of 1841 to draw a lesson from the Tory electoral victory earlier that year and consolidate the forces of reform in a 'Complete Suffrage Union' but this collapsed two years later when the Chartists insisted that any alliance must take their document as the basis for action. In 1843 a railway-building boom set in, culminating in the 'Railway Mania' of 1847. These years also brought a crop of measures deliberately designed by Peel and his ministers to sap the roots of Chartism; the cheapening of working-class living by substituting direct for indirect taxation; the limiting in 1844 of factory work by women and children; Chadwick's Sanitary Report of 1842 leading to the first Public Health Act of 1848. Chartism subsided for five years and even when in 1848 events on the continent excited minds made restive by a renewed recession, the agitation proved as impotent as ever. A firm front on the part of the government and a cold front on the part of the weather deterred the leaders from attempting open violence. Demonstrators clashed with police in London and with troops in the north but the situation never got out of hand. In 1850 the overall standard of living began to rise beyond all possibility of argument and was to go on doing so without a relapse until 1873; the consumption of sugar is a convenient yardstick and, helped by Peel's reduction of the duty, this rose from 19 lb per head in 1840–9 to 54 lb in 1870–9.[77] During the 1850s it would be foreign rather than home news which filled the headlines. Many frustrated radicals emigrated.

Chartism was the protest of Britain's urban workers against the conditions which the industrial miracle had involved for them. It was the nearest that the country came to revolution. Just how near that was is impossible to judge. Chance, or a leader possessing both experience and determination or a bad mistake on the part of the authorities might have produced a spark which, given the amount of inflammable material around, could soon have become a forest fire. As things were, the attempted risings lacked supporters and organisation. The agitation got little backing in Parliament. Ministers, whether Whig or Tory, kept their heads and their human sympathies, showed that they had force in reserve without displaying it too provocatively and avoided making either massacres or martyrs. Railways and the electric telegraph enabled them to move troops quickly to points of danger. At no time does there seem to have been serious doubt as to the loyalty of the army, in spite of working-class hopes to the contrary.[78] Princess Lieven called the masses cowardly and the classes courageous – but does not this reflect the relative strength of the two sides?

The Reform Act had been achieved by co-operation between the middle and working classes. But Chartism was more of a working-class attack on the middle classes. In particular the Chartists resented the priority which the middle classes gave after 1839 to repealing the Corn Laws. A speaker in the winter of 1840–1 told his hearers not to be deceived:[79]

> When we get the Charter we will repeal the Corn Laws and all the other bad laws. But if you give up your agitation for the Charter to help the Free Traders, they will not help you to get the Charter. The middle classes and the rotten Whigs have never remembered you . . . 'Cheap bread', they cry. But they mean 'Low wages'.

And indeed there was a substratum of truth in this view. The Corn Laws were the last major target of the manufacturing interest in its struggle with the landed interest. Even the removal of the remaining nonconformist disabilities was becoming of secondary importance to people whose growing prosperity meant steady absorption into the established order. Once virtually complete free trade had been secured, the way was open for that movement of the middle classes into the conservative camp which was the outstanding feature of West European politics in the later nineteenth century.

On the other hand the resentment at hardship and the impatience at timid reform which had fuelled Chartism were not extinguished when the movement fizzled out.[80] They were the roots from which a distinctive working-class consciousness was growing and sooner or later that consciousness would find expression in a constitutional bid for political power. The two developments would threaten to turn British politics into class politics and replace the antagonism between landowner and radical by one between employer and employed. If this polarisation was to be avoided (as it was to be on the whole in the United States) middle class leaders would be needed who had enough empathy, humanity and insight to adapt the radical tradition to the new circumstances and thereby win the trust of the workers. Gladstone filled this requirement in his own special way but he lacked successors of anything like the same calibre.

The gap to be bridged was as wide as it had been two centuries earlier. In 1838 a Chartist speaker added a new dimension to the idea of natural rights:[81]

> If any man asks me what I mean by universal suffrage, I mean to say that every working man in the land has a right to a good coat on his back, a good hat on his head, a good roof for the shelter of his household, a good dinner on his table, no more work than will keep him in health while at it and as much wages as will keep him in the enjoyment of plenty and all the blessings of life that reasonable men could desire.

By contrast Cobden, in 1856, spoke in the spirit of an Ireton become economist:[82]

> So far as the wages question goes, I think the only sound and honest course is to tell the people plainly that they are under no delusion as to their assumed power to regulate or permanently influence in the slightest degree *by coercion* the rate of wages. They might as well attempt to regulate the tides by force.

He may have been right in thinking that no lunch could be free. But he failed to see that politics could not be kept out of the question as to who should pay the bill.[83]

Notes to Chapter 2

1 G. E. Aylmer (ed.), *The Levellers in the English Revolution* (1975), p. 100.
2 Aylmer, p. 109.
3 G. P. Gooch, *English Democratic Ideas in the Seventeenth Century* (Cambridge, 1898), pp. 173–4.

4 J. M. Keynes, *The General Theory of Employment, Interest and Money* (1936), p. 383; see also Epilogue to M. Freeden, *The New Liberalism* (Oxford, 1978).
5 J. Buchan, *Oliver Cromwell* (1934), p. 315.
6 Aylmer, pp. 100–01.
7 T. Hobbes, *Leviathan*, chs 17 and 18.
8 J. Mabbott, *John Locke* (1973), pp. 147–50; J. Plamenatz, *The English Utilitarians* (Oxford, 1958), p. 19.
9 C. B. Macpherson, *The Political Theory of Possessive Individualism* (Oxford, 1964), pp. 220–1.
10 Mabbott, pp. 144–6.
11 Mabbott, pp. 151–6.
12 Macpherson, pp. 223–6; Mabbott, p. 165.
13 Quoted by E. Halévy, *The Growth of Philosophic Radicalism* (trans. 1928), p. 124.
14 R. R. Fennessy, *Burke, Paine and the Rights of Man* (The Hague, 1963), p. 169.
15 Fennessy, p. 227.
16 Quoted by S. Maccoby, *English Radicalism 1786–1832* (1955), p. 38.
17 E. P. Thompson, *The Making of the English Working Class* (1963), p. 454.
18 Thompson, pp. 177–8.
19 J. Stevenson, 'Social control and the prevention of riots in England 1783–1829' in A. P. Donajgrodski (ed.), *Social Control in Nineteenth-century Britain* (1977).
20 Quoted by M. Bruce, *The Coming of the Welfare State* (4th edn 1968), p. 78.
21 Quoted by Mabbott, p. 122.
22 Halévy, pp. 487–9.
23 Halévy, p. 80.
24 Halévy, p. 84.
25 O. Macdonough, *Early Victorian Government* (1977), p. 24.
26 Halévy, p. 491.
27 The word 'radical' was first used, as an adjective, by Fox and Horne Tooke in 1802 to denote the kind of reform which involves returning to roots, i.e. supposed principles of politics. Radical reformers wanted to alter the constitution in accordance with some sweeping plan. Moderate reformers were content with piecemeal alterations to particular faults ('social engineering'). The word did not appear again until 1810–11. It was not used as a substantive till about 1819. The first recorded use of 'Liberal' was in 1816 when Southey compared English advocates of reform to the *Liberales* in Spain. It came into common use in the 1830s (Halévy, p. 261; I. Bradley, *The Optimists* (1980), p. 17).
28 Macdonough, p. 24.
29 H. Eysenck, *The Psychology of Politics* (1954).
30 G. M. Young, *Victorian England: Portrait of an Age* (Oxford, 1936), p. 186.
31 C. C. Bolam, *The English Presbyterians* (1968); R. V. Holt, *The Unitarian Contribution to Social Progress in England* (1938).
32 H. Perkin, *The Origins of Modern English Society 1780–1880* (1969), p. 34.
33 A. Holt, *Joseph Priestley* (1931).
34 Articles on Unitarianism and Priestley in Hastings, *Encyclopaedia of Religion and Ethics*.
35 M. St. J. Packe, *John Stuart Mill* (1954), p. 127.
36 A. H. Lincoln, *Some Political and Social Ideas of English Dissent 1763–1800* (Cambridge, 1938), p. 63.
37 N. Gash, *Aristocracy and People 1815–65*, (1979), p. 49.
38 Maccoby, pp. 208–9.
39 Thompson, p. 424.
40 M. E. Rose, 'Social change and the industrial revolution' in R. Floud and D. McCloskey, *The Economic History of Britain since 1700* (Cambridge, 1981), Vol. 1, p. 256; Maccoby, p. 20.
41 *The Times*, October 1831.
42 Thompson, pp. 760–2.
43 Quoted by H. Kissinger, *A World Restored. Metternich, Castlereagh and the Problems of Peace* (1957), p. 195.
44 G. Wallas, *The Life of Francis Place* (1898), p. 326.

45 N. Gash, *Politics in the Age of Peel* (1953), p. 65; E. L. Woodward, *The Age of Reform* (Oxford, 1938), p. 84; S. Maccoby, *English Radicalism 1832–1852* (1935), pp. 50, 162.

46 R. V. Holt, p. 133; see also R. H. Hartwell, 'La Revolution manquée' in D. Coleman and P. Mathias (eds), *Enterprise and History* (Cambridge, 1984).

47 Barrington Moore jnr, *The Social Origins of Dictatorship and Democracy* (1967), p. 505; M. J. Wiener, *English Culture and the Decline of the Industrial Spirit* (Cambridge, 1981).

48 J. L. and B. Hammond, *The Town Labourer* (1911), p. 325.

49 Quoted by J. Langford, *A Century of Birmingham Life* (Birmingham, 1870), Vol. 1, p. xix.

50 Langford, p. xix.

51 Langford, p. xxiii.

52 Quoted by C. Gill, *The History of Birmingham* (Oxford, 1952), Vol. 1, p. 39, from W. Hutton, *A History of Birmingham* (1783).

53 Langford, Vol. 1, p. 197.

54 Gill, Vol. 1, p. 60.

55 J. Boswell, *The Life of Dr Samuel Johnson*, 23 March 1776.

56 Thompson, p. 239.

57 Quoted by R. Porter, *English Society in the Eighteenth Century* (1982), p. 214.

58 P. J. Corfield, *The Impact of English Towns 1700–1800* (Oxford, 1982), p. 125.

59 R. Schofield, *The Lunar Society of Birmingham* (Oxford, 1963).

60 A. J. Fox, 'Industrial relations in nineteenth-century Birmingham', *Oxford Economic Papers*, New Series, 7, 1955.

61 Gill, Vol. 1, p. 72, quoting Hutton.

62 A. Holt; Schofield; Maccoby, *English Radicalism 1786–1832*, p. 50.

63 C. M. Wakefield, *The Life of Thomas Attwood* (1885), p. 62.

64 Wallas, p. 300.

65 J. Buckley, *Joseph Parkes of Birmingham* (1926), p. 129.

66 Gill, Vol. 1, ch. 12.

67 W. E. S. Thomas, *The Philosophical Radicals* (Oxford, 1979), pp. 440–4.

68 Packe, p. 193; S. Maccoby, *English Radicalism 1832–1852*, pp. 133, 432.

69 D. Southgate, *The Passing of the Whigs 1832–1886* (1962), p. 71.

70 Macdonough, pp. 171, 175.

71 Maccoby, *English Radicalism 1832–1852*, p. 83.

72 G. Balfour, *The Educational Systems of Great Britain and Ireland* (Oxford, 1898), p. 5.

73 Wallas, pp. 359–75. The demand for equal constituencies was omitted from the document as presented to Parliament because of the advantage it would have given to Ireland.

74 A. Plummer, *Bronterre: A Political Biography of Bronterre O'Brien 1804–1864* (1971), p. 142.

75 Maccoby, *English Radicalism 1832–1852*, pp. 280–2.

76 R. A. Church, *The Great Victorian Boom* (1975) contains a useful discussion of its dates and continuity.

77 P. Mathias, *The First Industrial Nation* (1978), p. 435.

78 Gash, p. 7.

79 Plummer, p. 160.

80 A. Briggs, *Chartist Studies* (1959), p. 14; G. Rudé, *The Crowd in History* (1964).

81 Briggs, p. 34.

82 Quoted by F. Gillespie, *Labour and Politics in England 1850–67* (Durham, N.C., 1927), p. 108.

83 Maccoby, *English Radicalism 1832–1852*, pp. 317, 436.

3 'Young Joe': 1836–65

The Family Background

The village of Lacock in Wiltshire is nowadays celebrated for the early photographs taken there by William Fox-Talbot. But it made another indirect contribution to the Victorian scene by housing in the eighteenth century one Daniel Chamberlain, maltster, the earliest traceable ancestor of the statesman. This may have been the Daniel who was buried in the churchyard of St Lawrence Jewry, next door to the Guildhall, in 1757 and a continuing connection with the City would support the tradition that a seventeenth-century Daniel had moved down to the country to escape the plague.[1]

The younger brother of Daniel, the maltster, was certainly established in London as a confectioner, since it was to this uncle that Daniel's son William was apprenticed about 1730.[2] But he is said to have broken the sweet bottles by trying to balance a broom on his nose, an achievement which may have suggested that he was better suited to a more pedestrian occupation and he was therefore apprenticed instead to a shoemaker – or 'cordwainer' as the fashioners of Cordova leather were called. In about 1745 he set up on his own at 56 Milk Street off Cheapside and by 1769 was Master of the Cordwainers' Company. His premises were in the parish of St Lawrence Jewry and as its 'vestry' administered many local matters which were not in any strict sense religious, a say in its councils was important to the parishioners. William Chamberlain was a Unitarian but, like many nonconformists, qualified himself for office as churchwarden by communicating every now and then – even baptised members of the church would only do so seven times a year.

Of William's eldest son, also a William, little seems known, although he lived till 1830. The second was born in 1752 and named Joseph. He inherited the shoe business and married first in 1783 Elizabeth, then after her death in 1786 her sister Martha Strutt. (Marriage to a deceased wife's sister was at that time forbidden only by the church and not by the law of England.) They were daughters of Joseph Strutt, another London merchant, and nieces of the Derbyshire hosiery manufacturer Jedediah Strutt who had helped Arkwright to revolutionise cotton-spinning (see p. 2). Moreover they traced descent through their mother from Richard Sargeant of Kidderminster who in 1662 shared eviction with his friend Richard Baxter (see p. 32), as well as from one John Spicer who had earned a place in Fox's *Book of Martyrs* by being burnt at the stake in 1556. The Chamberlains thus belonged to the inner circles of Unitarian society.

The first Joseph died in 1837. His son, Joseph II, was born in 1796 and did not marry until he was 39. His bride Caroline Harben belonged to a Sussex family which, unlike the prudent Chamberlains, had been reduced to cheesemongering by taking risks which did not pay off (Disraeli was on more solid ground than he may have realised when he said that the newly-elected member for Birmingham looked and spoke like a cheese-monger).[3] The Chamberlains used their marriage as the occasion for making that break with the tradition of living over the shop which was to have such a profound effect on the political and social outlook of the commercial classes. They acquired a house, built some twenty years earlier, in Camberwell Grove[4] and it was there on 8 July 1836 that the third Joseph was born.

Psychologists say that the earliest years of life are the most decisive in shaping character; biographers have to contend with the fact that these are precisely the years about which least is known. This adds importance to the likely behaviour of parents. Joseph II had the face of a man who knew his own mind and stuck to it. He is said to have been a reserved and austere character, upright and sincere, pleasant and quiet in manner but occa-sionally narrow in outlook. He once told a child who had borrowed from its nurse to purchase sweets, 'You never buy what you can't pay for'.[5] His physique was frail and although he lived to 79, it was only by taking care of himself. His grandson Austen described him as a man of few interests, the chief being religion, but all his relations went to him for advice.[6] It was to the mother that the children owed their intellectual tastes, as well as their human sympathies and enjoyment of life. The contrast between the unbending father with high standards of conduct and the loving but submissive mother who urges the children to live up to her husband's example is said to be the classic situation for the development of an authoritarian personality. But on such a test many a Victorian house-hold would come under suspicion. Yet the end of the century did not produce the generation of high-handed autocrats which on this hypothesis should have been forthcoming (unless of course they all found outlets in ruling the empire!) Perhaps the family discipline was counterbalanced by the firmly established Liberal beliefs which pervaded society. We had better rest content with saying that from one parent Joseph III inherited determination, industry and care for detail, from the other quickness of mind, energy and *joie de vivre*.

There were five younger sons and three daughters. One son died in infancy and, to soften the mother's grief, the family moved in 1846 from south to north London and rented a house dating from 1775 at 25 Highbury Place,[7] presumably a shift up-market. On this house Joseph III must have looked with affection, since when in 1880 he built himself a home of his own outside Birmingham, he called it Highbury. On every day of the year Joseph II is likely to have journeyed down to the City, presumably in his own carriage (for the railway did not start till 1851), since the Milk Street premises were open all week, and on Sundays the Chamberlains worshipped at a Unitarian chapel in Carter Lane, between St Paul's and the river. The Carter Lane people were 'few but united', being composed 'for the most part of the higher sort of tradesmen, plain, honest and sincere'. The same adjectives seem to have applied to the building itself, although its surroundings demonstrated that squalor was no monopoly of the new industrial towns. The repeal of the Test and Corporation Acts in 1828 had removed the need for occasional conformity, although the vestries remained till 1855. But there is no evidence that Joseph II ever took part in local politics. He did however become Master of the Cordwainers' Company in 1846.

Joseph III, after going to a dame-school in Camberwell and to a school kept by an Anglican clergyman in Highbury, was sent in 1850 to the school opened in 1830 in Gower Street as an adjunct to University College (see p. 35); several of the masters were also professors. Its origins ensured that it embodied Utilitarian ideas about education, besides carrying on the tradition of the older Unitarian academies, so that it probably provided the best secondary educational available in England at the time. Latin and Greek were taught by 'a new method', while mathematics, French, German and natural science all received attention. The school was also remarkable for doing without corporal punishment and for arranging its curriculum on what is now known as 'the cafeteria system', with each pupil choosing his own courses. The headmaster, Thomas Hewitt Key, had been a Cambridge friend of Macaulay and had tried without much success to teach Edgar Allan Poe at the University of Virginia. There cannot have been many professors of Latin who have also held chairs in mathematics and comparative philology, as well as being Fellows of the Royal Society! His teaching was lively enough to make up for its somewhat cavalier treatment of facts. His political views were naturally those of the men who had founded the school but he supported Palmerston's foreign policy and in 1859 took an active part in the Volunteer movement. Chamberlain, in his two years beneath Wilkins' classical dome, acquired enough Latin to be able to bring in the occasional word even if he could not, like Gladstone, quote Lucretius at the drop of a hat;[8] he also won prizes in French, mathematics and mechanics. Neither he nor the school cared much about games.

The rules required pupils to leave at sixteen.[9] Although Oxford and Cambridge were still barred to dissenters, the door to London was open and at hand. But a university education was at that time only regarded as appropriate to those intending to enter the professions; the Taunton Commission was told in 1865 that 'universities were places where young men stayed until they were twenty-three to learn at great expense habits which made them unfit for business or anything else'. Joseph II was ready to finance any son who chose to train for the ministry but none did. So for a couple of years Joseph III learnt how to make and sell shoes – an occupation which has often bred radicalism. He also taught in the Sunday School attached to the Carter Lane chapel. Both occupations brought him into close contact with the working classes and at this stage of his life he can have been under few illusions as to how the poor lived. At home he indulged in a passion for dancing, joined in amateur theatricals, wrote dramas and led an active family life.

For the next twenty years he read widely, both to complete his education and to improve himself as a teacher.[10] One writer he is sure to have come across was Harriet Martineau, since she belonged to a Unitarian family known to the Chamberlains and destined in the next generation to be connected with them by marriage. J. S. Mill said that her *Illustrations of Political Economy* (which sold better than his own *Principles*) 'reduced the *laissez-faire* system to absurdity by merely carrying it out in all its consequences'.[11] She later translated Comte's *Positive Philosophy*. An account survives of a dinner party which the Chamberlains gave in 1859 to her brother James, the leading Unitarian thinker of his generation. No 'seeming inspiration' could in his view establish anything contrary to reason. This made him give a ready ear to the German Higher Criticism and the Unitarian creed soon came to consist of little more than trust in God as the cause of the universe and the revealer of righteousness in man, along with veneration for Jesus as an exceptionally wise but not infallible human being.[12]

But in 1854 there came a climacteric. Three years earlier there had occurred the Great Exhibition, owing some of its inspiration to an industrial exhibition in Birmingham in 1849. Two of the exhibits in Hyde Park were patent American machines for making wood-screws (i.e. iron screws for use in wood). From time immemorial these had been made, largely by hand, in a succession of processes. During the 1840s a German clockmaker had invented a series of steam-powered machines for these processes, but the cutting of the thread was still controlled by hand and the screws were unpointed so that a hole had to be drilled for each before it could be used. One of the American machines prepared blocks and cut the heads; the other cut the thread and gave the screw a point. Both were mechanically fed and could be operated by relatively unskilled or female labour.[13] It was a good example of the standardisation and mechanisation in which the United States excelled, possibly stimulated by their scarcity of population which put a premium on replacing human hands with tools and machines.[14] It had happened with pins in 1824;[15] it was to happen with guns later.

Joseph II's sister had married a fellow Unitarian, John Sutton Nettlefold, who was an ironmonger in Holborn. About 1835 he set up a small screw factory on the Thames which was moved in 1842 to the Birmingham area where the drawing of wire (the first step in screw-making) had long been established. He came to the Great Exhibition, saw the machines and saw also their possibilities (although he is unlikely to have realised that the screw-cutting lathe was to be the foundation of precision engineering).[16] But they were expensive and in addition the patent rights would have to be bought. He could not himself raise the £30,000 necessary but realised that, unless he managed it, someone else might do so and drive him out of business. An appeal to his brother-in-law led in 1854 to the founding of the company Nettlefold and Chamberlain; it was a good example of how many of Britain's big firms were originally financed. But the Milk Street business continued to run for another nine years so its proprietor needed a resident representative to keep an eye on his venture in the midlands. His solution showed that his eldest son had won his confidence. 'We will send Joe.' The emissary is said to have taken with him a school prize for mathematics called *Eldorado or Adventures in the Path of Empire*.

Arrival in Birmingham

Evidently the Nettlefolds and Chamberlains had decided, after careful pondering, that they were on to a good thing. But they are unlikely to have realised quite how good it was. Two main reasons made it so.

The first is that the years between 1850 and 1873 covered a period which has been described as 'the Great Victorian Boom' (see p. 47). Both before and since there have been times when the economy was growing faster but few or none during which the growth was so sustained. This was also the last period in which Britain was acting as the main supplier of industrial products to Western Europe which, by 1873, had gone a long way towards installing the capacity required to meet its own needs. In markets outside Europe, manufactured goods were following the lead given by textiles. There have been few junctures at which it was easier for an Englishman to make money – and it should be remembered that income tax fell from 1s 2d in 1854 to 2d in 1874.

Secondly the nature of the product dictated a relatively modern form of organisation. Many of the older businessmen in Birmingham had done relatively little manufacturing themselves but had concentrated on financing and organising, procuring raw materials, handing them out to smaller men who actually performed the various processes and then selling the product in bulk to factors or merchants who would undertake the distribution. In some cases they did not even hire their labour directly but negotiated through group leaders who would make themselves responsible for the actual recruitment. But the whole advantage of the new process of screw manufacture depended on elaborate machinery which required a factory building and, owing to its cost, had to be used as intensively and efficiently as possible. The firm therefore managed its workforce directly and was responsible for a good deal of its own distribution and selling. Its employees were however forbidden to join unions, a ban which was some embarrassment to Chamberlain after he had ceased to be a partner.

John Nettlefold senior had a son of the same name and it was he and his cousin Joseph who soon established themselves as the driving force of the business, the first concentrating on the manufacturing, the second on trading and sales promotion. They had an office in Broad Street, Birmingham as well as a factory at Smethwick. Given energy and common sense, there was not much which could go wrong. The chief problem outside the home market was that the patent rights had been acquired only for it, so that elsewhere domestic manufacturers provided competition. Chamberlain's method of overcoming this was to insist that foreign customers must be addressed in their own language (for which purpose he worked hard to improve his own already fluent French) and must have their tastes suited in such matters as measurements and packaging; elementary as these principles may seem, concentration on markets which were English-speaking or contained a number of expatriate Englishmen ready to act as agents led many English firms to disregard them. Willingness to meet customers' requirements was not allowed to interfere with long runs of production. In 1850, 70,000 gross of screws a week were made in the whole country; by 1865 the figure had risen to 130,000 in the Birmingham area alone, of which Nettlefold and Chamberlain made 90,000. By 1874 they were selling in fifteen overseas markets. The number of their employees rose to over 2,000 in 1866 and 20,000 in 1874.[17]

Several competing firms were bought up while those who stuck to the old methods were naturally driven out of business. In the 1880s, after Chamberlain had left the firm, stories went round of the ruthlessness and sharp practice by which a near monopoly had been established. Several witnesses and even one competitor came forward however to deny these while any who may have been worsted kept silence. In due course the firm acquired its own facilities for making wire and ultimately merged with Guests of Dowlais in a vertical combine which included blast-furnaces and collieries.

Besides working from nine to six at the office, Chamberlain found much to do. He took rooms in Edgbaston, 'the Belgravia of Birmingham'.[18] He attended service at the New Meeting House, with its memories of Priestley (see p. 34), and got to know most of the leading Unitarian families in the city. He taught in a Sunday School and helped to found a Working Men's Institute at Small Heath, which might be described as the Dalston of Birmingham. He joined and, in due course, became president of the Edgbaston Debating Society where he acquired 'by painful experience' the art of public speaking. For this and other purposes he continued his reading, keeping a commonplace book and writing down the occasions on which he had used each item in it, so as to avoid saying the same thing twice. He gave a hostage to fortune in the guise of caricaturists by starting to wear an eye-glass (his defective vision was confined to his right eye).[19] He went on walking tours in the Alps but the unpleasantness of going up a peak in bad weather cured him of mountain fever. Then in 1861 he married Harriet Kenrick, whose Unitarian family had come from Wrexham in 1791 to make shoe-buckles at West Bromwich; when the invention of shoe-laces and the fashion for trousers combined to take the sheen out of the buckle business, they became one of the leading hollow-ware firms in the country.[20] Two years later her brother William became engaged to Joe's sister Mary who had recently moved to Birmingham when Joseph II abandoned shoemaking for brass-manufacture. But in 1863 Harriet died two days after giving birth to a son, Austen, the future Foreign Secretary. The effect of her death on her husband may well have been underestimated by his biographers, although they have all stressed his grief and the way in which, as a distraction, he flung himself with redoubled energy into the business. She had determined to make him into a 'real gardener'[21] and as a memorial to her he took to the occupation with a zest of which a habitual orchid in his buttonhole was to be an outward and visible sign. In due course it led to him becoming vice-president of the Royal Horticultural Society and having a screw-shaped orchid named after him.[22] Her loss was the first serious misfortune which he had encountered. Later in his career he was said to particularly resent being frustrated and to nurse a grievance against those responsible. It would not be surprising if he had now conceived a grievance against life and a determination to get compensation of some kind at all costs. His religious faith was shaken; 'no God who treated him so badly, could exist, or if he existed, deserve worship'.[23]

When he began again to lift his eyes from his ledgers, it was to be drawn actively into politics. There, with the death of Palmerston in 1865, things were ripe for change.

The Great Victorian Lull 1848–65

Palmerston was no dyed-in-the-wool reactionary. He had been a follower of Pitt and Canning, Foreign Secretary to Grey and Melbourne and has been described as 'the most progressive Home Secretary of his day'. In 1853 he spoke with feeling in favour of limiting children's hours of work. In 1854 it was he who prevented the General Board of Health from being abolished. He opened the path to the front bench for radicals like Forster and Milner-Gibson.[24] When he meddled in the affairs of other nations, it was usually with a view to increasing the liberty enjoyed by their subjects. But it is true that in 1864 he was provoked by Gladstone into privately denying, in words reminiscent of King Charles I (see p. 22), that every man has a right to a vote:

> What every man and woman has a right to is to be well-governed and under just laws, and those who propose a change ought to show that the present organisation does not achieve these objects.[25]

There were other weighty reasons why a strong movement for further widening of the franchise took time to develop.

A major political breakthrough, such as the 1832 Reform Act, is usually followed by a period of confusion while the next political issue is identified and the various interests formulate their attitudes towards it. The standard development is that some of the interests which have supported the last change decide that enough is enough and join those who have opposed it in order to resist the next change. But this reinforcement of the conservatives is counteracted by natural causes which weaken the generations wanting to maintain the past and strengthen those wanting to hasten on the future. On a long view this is what happened in early-Victorian Britain. But several factors complicated the development.

(1) There was the survival into the nineteenth century of a progressive party in eighteenth-century terms – enlightened but not democratic, aristocratic and landowning rather than bourgeois and commercial. Whiggism was a hereditary attitude as much as a creed; Gladstone said that to be a Whig one had to be born a Whig (which suggests a realisation that to marry into a Whig family, as he did, was not enough). For Whigs to turn reactionary was for them to repudiate their tradition and most of them therefore preferred conducting a rearguard action from inside the progressive camp to crossing over into the conservative one. But their position was being steadily eroded by irresistible developments. One was the relative unprofitability of land as an investment by comparison with trade and industry.[26] Another was the growing realisation, in the spirit of the Utilitarians, that administration demanded skills and intellectual

competence which patronage could not guarantee.[27] Already the Whigs in the House of Commons came from Scottish, Welsh and Irish rather than English constituencies.[28] Russell's government between 1846 and 1852 is said to have demonstrated that the Whigs could no longer run the country by themselves.[29]

(2)   Any group of interests which has been compelled to admit to a share in power a significant number of interests hitherto excluded has thereafter to face the fact that, under a representative constitution, its chances of returning to power merely by reiterating its old objectives are slim. It has to present a new image calculated to appeal to those whose aspirations have been satisfied by their admission to power. Where any substantial section of the conservative camp refuses to see this, those who do have to move leftwards before they can hope to persuade satisfied ex-progressives to move right. This was the function of the Peelites, a group of liberal Conservatives which included beneficiaries from the industrial changes. But such a political group, brought into existence by events at a particular moment (whether 1846, 1886 or 1931), suffers from an inability to attract recruits among younger generations who will usually prefer to join a party defined by reference to the future rather than the past.

An interval was therefore almost inevitable after 1832 in which first the Whigs and then the Peelites adjusted themselves to the new face of British politics. During that interval they provided between them most of the staff of most of the governments (the Tories only getting into power for short intervals while their opponents were divided). Their hold on power has often been ascribed to their administrative competence[30] (regardless of the fact that it was a Peelite–Whig coalition which during the Crimean War provided a classic example of administrative incompetence). But even in combination they did not have enough followers in the Commons to provide a majority. For that they depended on two other groups.

(3)   The conservative 'Liberals' amounted to 74 in 1859.[31] These were drawn from those members of the growing middle and professional classes and 'clerisy' (as Coleridge described Britain's substitute for an intelligentsia)[32] who had 'arrived' and were accordingly disposed to conform by adopting established ways of behaviour in society, religion and education. Although they were acquiring estates as a badge of success, they still thought that the balance of law and taxation needed to be adjusted in favour of industry. They still wanted to open careers to talents. While these views divided them from Whigs, the distinction between them and the Peelites grew steadily thinner. They believed in representation for individuals rather than for classes. In their view, ideas played as big a part in politics as interests. Their ideal was a meritocracy; government should be responsible rather than exactly representative, the concern of those

with knowledge and experience which qualified them to conduct it effectively. The existing system could with advantage be made more efficient but did not need drastic change.

(4)   More obviously distinct were those who had not been tempted by worldly success into abandoning their radical traditions. Their core was provided by some fifty businessmen, mostly nonconformists, who had achieved personal advancement by fidelity to a code of conduct deriving from the Puritans. They believed in hard work, thrift and plain living. They disapproved of attempts to shelter people from the hardships of life in the belief that the overcoming of them was what formed character. They were reluctant to mortgage the future by diverting too high a proportion of income from investment to consumption. They believed that only by providing rigorous incentives to work could the innate human tendency to idleness be overcome. All these attitudes set them at odds with the landowners whose position rested on inherited wealth, while they equally resented the privileges reserved to the Established Church and its members (who only composed a bare half of the worshipping public). They wanted the state to set its subjects an example by frugality and took seriously the noun in the term 'Political Economy'. They by no means objected to helping their poorer and less fortunate neighbours but thought that this was a field for private charity. The best way for the government to assist was by reducing taxes and prices.

These Radicals ostensibly believed in the nobility of man and hence in the individual's right to a voice in how he is governed. Bright, speaking for the first time in Birmingham as one of its MPs in October 1858, to an audience including Chamberlain, said he had no objection to the widest possible suffrage that the ingenuity of man could devise.[33] But such benevolence was made easier by the knowledge that any suffrage likely to get past the existing Parliament would be pretty narrow. Bright also said that there would be no greater folly than starting up a coach by which the middle classes would not travel. As he was to say in 1865 that he had never been in favour of universal suffrage and in 1867 that 'the residuum' was a class which would be better off if they were not enfranchised, he would seem by his earlier remarks to have meant by 'possible suffrage' variations of household suffrage.[34] Cobden was even more cautious, judging that extension of the suffrage should wait until education and the acquisition of property had made the workers more responsible. He preferred to help individual workers to qualify for votes under the existing franchises, for example by becoming freeholders.

As time passed it became increasingly clear that with the existing electorate a majority was unlikely to be forthcoming for many of the causes favoured by the Radicals, such as disestablishment and universal education. The realisation bestowed allure on the idea of giving votes to the skilled workers who were by then earning twice as much as the unskilled and aspired to become 'respectable and respected'.[35] The workers for their part gradually absorbed the lesson that, no matter how many other issues separated them from the Radicals, their only chance of achieving those objectives by peaceful means lay in getting Radical help for a broadening of the suffrage. But each side had to be convinced that an alliance was necessary and the process of generating conviction took time.

Bright said in 1864 that 'nothing except foreign politics seems to occupy the attention of the people'[36] but much the same could be said of the whole period from the Don Pacifico affair in 1850 to the end of the American Civil War in 1865. Louis Napoleon's *coup d'état* in 1851 was followed by the Crimean War, the Opium Wars, the Indian Mutiny, the Risorgimento, the invasion scare of 1859, the Polish Revolt of 1863 and the war over Schleswig-Holstein in 1864. English Liberalism was in two minds about these events. The 'softer' Radicals thought that relations between states should be governed by the same high standards of morality which they applied both to private and public life. They condemned as unnecessary the use of violence in international affairs; too much money was spent on arms and war. But there was a 'harder' school of thought which followed Palmerston in believing that Britain's influence should be exerted, by force if necessary, in the cause of freedom against autocracy everywhere.[37]

Bright's opposition to the Crimean War cost him his position as MP for Manchester in 1857. His relative lack of interest in Italy and Poland was taken by some workers as a sign of indifference to oppression whereas Gladstone, by his passionate involvement in Italian liberation, helped to build up his reputation as a champion of freedom. Over America, on the other hand, it was Bright's turn to declare that the cause of the North was the cause of freedom from slavery and privilege everywhere, while Gladstone in an unguarded moment praised Jefferson Davis for making a nation.

After Bright was turned out of Manchester, he was invited to represent Birmingham and in his first speech there dealt not only with reform but also with war. A few days later the Edgbaston Debating Society failed by one vote to adopt a motion condemning both the principles and the spirit of the speech. Chamberlain, who supported the motion, said afterwards that from the first he did not agree with what he regarded as 'practically a peace-at-any-price policy'. Soon afterwards he met Bright at a dinner party and, in a David-and-Goliath act, contested the Quaker's assertion that Gibraltar should be given back to Spain.[38]

In spite (or perhaps because) of the excitement and passion, the exceptional element in the epoch escaped notice. Never before and never again was Britain to have so little need to interest herself in the affairs of other countries or so much power to make her interest effective. This resulted from a combination of politics and economics. The Great Powers of the past – France, Spain, Tsarist Russia, the Habsburg Empire and Turkey – were in decline (although, as regards France, the British found this hard to believe). The Great Powers of the future – Germany, the United States, Japan and Soviet Russia – were not yet ready to make themselves felt. In the interval Britain could rule the waves at a relatively low cost.

> The ability to build more and faster than anybody else, the virtual monopoly of the best stoking coals and the immense financial resources of the nation – it was on these very foundations that Britain's maritime mastery rested for the remainder of the century, together with the sheer experience and professionalism of the crews.[39]

What got overlooked was Britain's inability to make herself quickly felt inland.

In the 1840s and 1850s relations between the four components of the progressive camp were informal. The results which could be achieved by party discipline were as yet unrecognised and the private member had wide freedom. In such circumstances the pursuit of a cohesive legislative programme was hardly feasible. But in June 1859 a meeting at which all four groups were represented decided to support a parliamentary motion by the Duke of Devonshire's heir young Lord Hartington, in favour of replacing Lord Derby's Tory government by one under Palmerston. This has been taken as marking the date from which the Liberal Party began to operate as an integrated body. In broad terms, it represented a reassembly of the Reform tradition, the Anti-Corn Law tradition and the Chartist tradition. The immediate results were certainly unspectacular. The new ministers, in spite of squabbles between Palmerston and Gladstone over defence expenditure, did hold together but only by dint of doing nothing remarkable. After Palmerston's death a crucial interval of upheaval elapsed before the accession to power of the first government which can be described as genuinely Liberal. And even then, as will be seen, Whigs, Liberals and Radicals were to make uneasy partners. Harcourt was later to say that the Liberal Party resembled the kingdom of heaven in being a house with many mansions. But that tends to be the nature of any party in an adversarial system.[40]

The Second Reform Act

Palmerston died two days before his 81st birthday and was succeeded by Russell, 'the last Doge of Whiggism', who was only 73. Having abjured in 1848 the attitude towards reform which had in 1837 earned him the nickname of 'Finality Jack', he had made it his ambition to pass into law before quitting politics a second edition of the measure which he had done so much to get enacted in 1832. But two efforts in 1852 and 1854 proved abortive and when in 1859 the Tories tried to produce their own version, it provoked the meeting just mentioned at which the Liberals proved united enough to agree on turning them out. A timid alternative was then introduced, only to be withdrawn in face of back bench protests.

By 1865 Russell was a peer in his own right and in the Commons the leader was Gladstone who in 1864 had said casually that 'every man who is not incapacitated by some consideration of personal unfitness or of political danger is morally entitled to come within the pale of the consti-tution'.[41] Although he proved to mean by these cloudy words consider-ably less than excited radicals gave him credit for, there could be no doubt about his readiness to see the electorate slightly extended. This lost him the favour of the Whigs and of a considerable number of Liberals whose habitual aversion to any disturbance of their comfort was enhanced by the high cost of the 1865 election; any serious effort at reform was bound for one reason or another to involve a fresh election and was therefore something to be postponed as long as possible.[42] Accordingly when in 1866 Gladstone brought in a Bill which was in several ways even more limited than that of 1854, all the Liberal malcontents gathered like the Israelites of old in the Cave of Adullam and joined with the Tories to defeat it. The natural sequel would have been an anti-reform coalition made up of all who had rejected Gladstone's Bill. But the Adullamites were not prepared to serve under a Conservative and Disraeli talked Derby into refusing to serve under a Whig. Instead they took power themselves with a minority of 70 and passed the 1867 Act.

For by this time the necessity for some measure had become apparent to almost everyone from the queen downwards (although her chief concern was that ministers should have their hands free to cope with the Austro-Prussian War, one foreign affair which interested her subjects less than it should have done). There were two main possibilities; the first was to introduce household suffrage as the qualification for voting in boroughs. This would be marginally consistent with the thesis that the right to vote should depend on the possession of property, whereas the alternative of manhood suffrage would mean abandoning this principle in favour of the view that voting was a human right.[43] The latter was the demand of the workers who had organised themselves in the National Reform League, although they qualified it by saying that voters must be 'registered' and 'residential'; the spokesman of a League deputation to Disraeli in April 1867 called for manhood suffrage on the principle of a vote for a man because he was a man.[44] Bright, who spoke for the League at a series of mass meetings, seems to have favoured household suffrage in principle but to have been ready to rest content with the maximum that Parliament could be induced to enact. Most politicians wanted to move towards household suffrage but to find some defensible pretext for stopping short of it. One way of doing this was to lower the value of the property qualification without abandoning it altogether; the other was to counterbalance votes for all householders by giving second votes to people with reassuring qualifications, such as a bank balance or university degree. Whichever solution was chosen involved a 'leap in the dark' because accurate assessment of the effects of each called for an administrative competence as well as a fullness and precision of statistical information which mid-Victorian Britain still did not possess.[45]

Although the Conservative decision to introduce a Reform Bill was taken by Derby, its enactment was stagemanaged by Disraeli. Pre-eminent among his multifarious motives were the desires to remain in power, to gain credit for his party which would otherwise go to the Liberals and to score off Gladstone. Broadly speaking he preferred the option of ratepayer suffrage with 'fancy franchises' but, since he lacked a majority, he could not control the details. When it came to the crunch, he had to choose between accepting whatever amendments his opponents might persuade the Commons to pass and losing office as a result of defeat. To Gladstone's dismay the radicals exploited this situation in a House which had become only too anxious to be rid of the whole subject.

How far Disraeli knew what he was doing depends on what he was trying to do. The claim about 'educating his party' was almost certainly a justification devised after the event. The calculation that some skilled workers would vote Conservative may have been based on the belief that they would not want to vote on the same side as their Liberal employers. The main safeguard from the Conservative point of view went little noticed at the time and for long afterwards. The widening of the franchise was accompanied by relatively little rearrangement of the constituencies. In 1873 half the House of Commons was still elected by half a million electors and the other half by two million; the west and south were still favoured at the expense of the north and midlands.[46] The chief change which was made in boundaries involved bringing into boroughs 700,000 voters living in built-up areas on the outskirts who had previously belonged to the neighbouring county seats and who, if left as they were, might have tipped those seats against the Tories. Thus most of the extra votes went to people living in constituencies which already sent Liberals to Westminster . Although the Liberal majority of 70 in the 1865 Parliament rose to 110 in the 1868 one, the majority in English constituencies stayed static at 26. The extra votes came from Wales (9), Scotland (13) and Ireland (18), the last-mentioned increase not being due to the suffrage reform at all (which barely applied to Ireland) but to Gladstone's promise that he would disestablish the Irish church![47] In the event, the Conservatives were to be in power for 22 of the next 46 years and the Liberals for 24. This balance might have been different if the Liberals had proved able to hold together but if some prophet had on this ground reproached Disraeli with the risks which he was taking, that shrewd old contriver would probably have replied that cohesion was a quality of which Liberalism is incapable. What he had done was to signal beyond doubt to the middle classes that the society which his party was now concerned to conserve was an industrialised rather than an agrarian one.

As in 1832, reform only became practical politics when it had a coalition behind it but this time the role of the Whigs in that coalition had been taken by the Conservatives. An important consequential difference was the absence of a clash with the House of Lords which might never have accepted the Bill if its parentage had been Liberal. But the essential alliance was between the Radicals inside Parliament and the Reform League outside it. An unenthusiastic House of Commons was converted not merely by the argument that skilled artisans were as much entitled to vote as shopkeepers. The fear of the consequences of giving the vote to such persons was changing into a fear of refusing it. This was not simply due to the League's mass meetings, including one in Birmingham of 150,000 people. It was not simply due to the greatly increased circulation of the Liberal press since the abolition of the newspaper tax in 1855 and of the paper duty in 1861. It resulted even more from the spectacle of two Hyde Park demonstrations. The earlier, in July 1866, is the one most often mentioned because, although not ranked by connoisseurs of riots as being in the first class, it impinged itself on opinion-formers like Stafford Northcote and Matthew Arnold by personal experience rather than second-hand report. But the second one of April 1867 was arguably even more important. Admittedly it passed off peacefully but that was because the law officers had advised the government that there was no legal basis for prohibiting it and ministers shrank from using the considerable forces collected to regulate it. What was more, it occurred just as the Bill was going into Committee and may well have been in Disraeli's mind when he decided to accept the Radical amendments.[48] Britain could only avoid the risks of democracy by adopting the risks of authoritarianism.

The Act increased the electorate (which had doubled since 1832 by natural growth) from 1,430,000 to 2,470,000, or about 47 per cent of the adult male population. Skilled workers were reckoned to number some 830,000 in 1867, of whom 125,000 had the vote already.[49] On these calculations and assuming that all the remaining 705,000 were brought 'within the pale of the constitution', there remain some 335,000 new voters unclassified of whom some might conceivably have been unskilled.[50] Most of the 'fancy' franchises came to nothing but one which was to have significance gave third seats to Birmingham, Leeds, Liverpool, Manchester and Glasgow while allowing electors in those cities only two votes apiece (in the hope that minorities might thereby get more representation). Mill's motion to substitute 'person' for 'man' was lost by 196 votes to 73 although, if the matter of sex had never been raised, the granting of the vote to 'ratepayers' would have enabled female ones to get on the register.[51]

Compiling the new voting lists took time and it was not until December 1868 that Gladstone, the Liberal leader since Russell's resignation a year earlier, took office. His was the first Cabinet in British history in which peers and sons of peers were outnumbered by commoners. It also contained, in the person of Bright as President of the Board of Trade, the first Dissenter to become a Cabinet minister, while the number of Dissenters in Parliament rose to 63. The course which it would follow was fairly clear. Gladstone had promised to deprive the Church of Ireland of its privileged position. His high church background made him unlikely to accept the Dissenter demand for disestablishment in England as well but as a substitute the abolition of church rates could be expected. Those who believed the new voters to be irresponsible considered that they needed better education while those who believed the reverse considered that they were entitled to it – and this was another Dissenter demand. Fenian terrorism in Canada, Ireland and England was interpreted as indicating a need for Irish agrarian reform and Gladstone's first remark, on learning of the queen's summons, was 'My mission is to pacify Ireland'. A recent decision in the courts which prevented trade unions from recovering funds stolen by dishonest officials produced demands from the Trades Union Congress (founded in 1868) for a revision of the law. The army still needed reform and a battle loomed over the purchase of commissions and promotions which was only resolved by their abolition by royal warrant in 1871; the appointment of civil servants by examination rather than patronage had still to be made comprehensive. The Local Government Board was created in 1871 to take over central responsibility for both the Poor Law and Public Health. The Judicature Act of 1873 slightly reduced the chaos of the law courts.

Like most measures of liberalisation, the Reform Act of 1867 made it more likely that further proposals for change would be listened to, so that the end-result would be what the future Lord Salisbury described as 'revolution by inches'. But time was needed for the new voters to make their influence felt and the changes brought in the Act's immediate wake were not drastic. Nothing had angered the League's members more than the charges made by Robert Lowe and others that they were 'impulsive, unreflecting, violent people, guilty of venality, ignorance, drunkenness and intimidation'. Accordingly they set out to prove themselves worthy of their newly-acquired votes. Already one London hostess could be heard saying to a friend, 'It would be such a comfort to cease being a Radical'.[52]

Doubts about Individualism

John Stuart Mill provided the classic formulation of the Liberal doctrine that the rational individual should be free to judge for himself, unintimidated by class, wealth or prestige. The community was only justified in interfering with that freedom in order to prevent other individuals from being harmed. But although generally recognised as the last apostle of the Utilitarians, Mill in fact transformed the basis of their theory. Under the influence of the German humanist Wilhelm von Humboldt and the English Romantics, he made the self-development of the individual into the chief end of life. It was the successful pursuit of self-chosen ends, valued in themselves, which brought true happiness; only in this sense did happiness remain the goal of human endeavour.[53] He held that man should be enabled to act deliberately in the way most likely to contribute to such self-development. But this view, although superficially similar to the radical one, differs from it as being based on reason rather than intuition. He called it a 'creed' and 'a theory of life' but it was neither a duty nor a right so much as a reasonable inference from enlightened common sense.[54] Persons were to be respected as bearers of capacities for autonomous thought and action rather than as possessors of rights stemming from their humanity.

Individuality can however be developed only where freedom of choice exists, which can be achieved only when the individual is allowed to participate in decisions about the society to which he (or she) belongs. But since self-development is desirable for all, it should be encouraged in all, including the unprivileged and underprivileged (among them, women) who deserved to be helped to acquire it. Progress consisted in increasing the proportion of the population who were capable of such development. This approach reinforced the demand of Bentham and James Mill for all adults to share in the state because only if they did could the interests of the rulers approximate to the general interest. John Stuart Mill also extended the principle from politics to include co-operation in industry which led him to regard with approval limited forms of socialism, while still objecting to extensive state control or to the elimination of competition.[55]

But having gone thus far in the direction of full democracy Mill, under the influence of de Tocqueville, at once began to back away from it. He saw that the principle of individual self-development could be used to justify individuals in behaving exactly as they chose. As a preventive, he distinguished between actions done deliberately and those done on impulse. The task of man is not to follow impulse but to amend it. Instead however of defining precisely the directions which amendment should take, he proceeded to prescribe means by which the effect of actions taken on impulse could be checked. The chief of these was universal education which he held that the state should impose and make available either gratuitously or at trifling expense (although not necessarily administering itself); until the effects had had time to spread, the suffrage should only be extended slowly. Secondly he advocated a variety of devices for giving extra influence to the educated, such as proportional representation and second votes. He abandoned his belief in the ballot, considering that the danger of intimidation involved in open voting was less than the danger of voters exercising their selfish particularities if left to vote in secret. He also abandoned the demand for more frequent elections, in the belief that they would make MPs undesirably subservient to their constituents.

The earlier Utilitarians, in the climate of the eighteenth century, had concentrated their attacks on the reservation of political power to minorities – and in particular landed ones – in the belief that groups of men were bound to abuse their power in their own self-interest. J. S. Mill, in the climate of the mid–nineteenth century, was principally concerned to prevent the majority from abusing the power which was being given to them. In his view there was a limit beyond which neither government nor public opinion was entitled to interfere with the individual personality, respect for which was fundamental to liberalism. As far as possible, people should be left free to do and say what they thought right. Somewhere in society there needed to exist a source of protection for minorities and for heterodoxy. 'If the American form of democracy overtakes us, the majority will no more relax their despotism than a single despot would.'[56] It was consistent with this approach for him to have diverged from Bentham in maintaining that one pleasure could be *qualitatively* different from another.

The net result was that in the latter part of his life Mill suffered from being chronically in two minds; he managed to combine enthusiasm for democracy with deep pessimism about its probable results. On the one hand he was anxious to see the suffrage extended and even favoured such measures as the taxation of increments in land value (although not progressive taxation which he thought likely to relieve the prodigal at the expense of the prudent and to reduce the incentive to save).[57] On the other hand his fear of the excesses to which precipitate democracy might lead made him adopt attitudes not far removed from those of Charles I. The people must be supreme but must not attempt to govern. That task they must leave to a picked assembly, which in turn must leave the details to expert officials. 'It is not useful but hurtful that the constitution of the country should declare ignorance entitled to as much political power as knowledge.'[58] To take self-development as the goal of human conduct might imply that all human beings were capable of such development and must therefore be allowed the freedom and privileges which were essential preconditions for it. Yet day-to-day experience suggested that in most cases such development still had a long way to go.

Two friends of Mill enjoyed a considerable vogue but in the long run proved less influential for what they were than for what they led to. Comte like the Utilitarians sought to apply scientific method to the study of man in society, as his invention of the term 'sociology' implies. His 'positivism' assumed that the laws of causation apply throughout the universe, to human affairs as well as to the rest of nature. Comte set himself to discover what laws governed the behaviour of man in society, in the conviction that, once these had been found, the problems which had hitherto frustrated even the most talented politicians would be readily capable of a rational solution. But he spent so much time organising the other sciences into a coherent system that he died before getting to grips with his main quest. The failure of the project did not prevent many of his contemporaries from believing in its feasibility. Since he could not decide whether God existed, he recommended men to worship humanity – which at least provided benevolence with a motive. But although he paid lip-service to the common man, he exalted the uncommon one. The proletariat might be 'the great substance, bulk, body and reality of the nation' but he allowed it no more direct say than did Mill in administration. He was by instinct a meritocrat and a planner, a rationalist and a humanitarian, a precursor of Socialism rather than a Liberal.

Herbert Spencer, another thinker claiming to be a social scientist, described his ultimate purpose as that of 'finding for the principles of right and wrong in conduct at large a scientific basis'.[59] He criticised orthodox Utilitarianism because, by failing to define happiness, it provided no clue as to how that desired state could be achieved. Spencer borrowed from Lamarck and anticipated Darwin by introducing the idea of evolution. He saw history (including pre-history) as the record of steadily increasing differentiation between types and ultimately between individuals, a progressive evolution towards 'that constitution of man and society required for the complete manifestation of everyone's individuality'.[60] Attempts to interfere with this process were ill-advised, even futile, because, like Comte, he considered it to be governed by the law of cause and effect. Like Marx, he expected that as awareness of the process became explicit, and individual behaviour became as a result increasingly rational, the need for state intervention to reconcile conflicting interests would wane until ultimately, in a society held together by voluntary co-operation, it would wither away. Unlike Marx, he did not regard this condition as incompatible with the survival of private property.

Spencer no more than Comte ever quite decided whether this development was something which ought to be made to happen or something which was bound to happen. If causation operated universally, the future was determined and could not be changed (just as the Socialist Revolution was inevitable for Marx): in that case motives for action were just as much predetermined as the action itself and had no ethical significance. Spencer's main justification for optimism was his firm belief that humanity was bound to develop, but few Victorians were prepared to leave the inevitable to its own devices. Moreover he never clearly explained why the development was bound to be from bad (incomplete happiness) to good (complete happiness). Advancement was due to the working of the universal law, in virtue of which it must continue until the state called perfection was reached. God had been ousted from a mechanical universe but a scientific Providence seemed to have been brought in to operate in his place. Spencer complicated matters still further by introducing the notion that it was the fittest who survived. This begged the question of what constituted fitness. To him it was presumably harmony with the world process and ability to develop individuality. But his own ideas were losing relevance as answers to the problems of the day and it was not long before the Social Darwinists had modified the term to imply that life was a struggle for survival in which the ultimate arbiter was strength. Such a view of the world was hardly compatible with belief in the rights of man. The use of power to impose change received a justification which put in question the liberal doctrine that civilised man ought to achieve change by agreement.

Although Spencer may not have drawn this conclusion himself, he did inveigh against the view that suffering could be avoided and that society was to blame for such suffering as existed. Increasing numbers of his contemporaries were however coming to an opposite conclusion. Three influences combined to challenge the tenet that the hardships brought by industrialisation must be left to find in due course of time their own remedies. One was benevolence, inspired alike by religion and humanism; Christians of varied persuasions joined with free thinkers to question the justice as well as the mercy of the condition to which the people had been brought. When in 1865 a vociferous but ultimately unsuccessful attempt was made by Mill and other Liberals to bring to book Eyre, the Governor of Jamaica, for having used unnecessary cruelty to quell a revolt, Carlyle, Kingsley, Ruskin and Dickens retorted that time should not be wasted on such causes as long as English working men were subjected to unnecessary cruelty by the factory system. Secondly came fear, if not of revolution then of division leading to inefficiency and weakness. The cholera epidemics of 1848, 1853 and 1860 knew no class distinctions and thus drove home the parallel lesson that the health of the poor could not be a matter of indifference to the rich. Thirdly there was the desire to forestall others in winning the votes of the newly-enfranchised, who in turn did more and more to help themselves. The attempt of Benthamites like Chadwick to tackle the problems by centralised bureaucracy fell foul of the English predilection for parish pumps and individual freedom. But the forces making for action were too strong to be held up for long.

The Poor Law Reform of 1834 had been based on the belief that an effective distinction could be drawn between poverty and pauperism. It was assumed that every man could, if only he exerted himself, earn enough to support life for himself and his family on tolerable terms. Illness was admittedly something which could overtake even the most industrious but the prudent saved a provision against it as well as against old age; to supplement self-help was the function of charity. Those who failed to look after themselves were therefore 'undeserving'. 'Pauperism was a hereditary disease endemic among a substantial section of the labouring classes.'[61] The remedy was to make the terms on which public assistance could be obtained so unattractive as to spur the idle and feckless into exertion. Hence the desire to prevent relief being given outside the workhouse and the insistence that conditions inside that institution should be less attractive and 'eligible' than anywhere else.

By mid-century the false assumptions involved in this outlook were becoming clear. A series of official inquiries and the work of charitable bodies was disclosing that about a third of the population lived either in penury or on the margin of it.[62] Few earned enough to save against a rainy day. Thus to make conditions inside workhouses even harsher than those outside meant treating the inmates worse than felons. Only a small number of them were in any case able-bodied. What justification could there be for giving such treatment to the old, to the sick (in mind and body) and to children?

Nor was it necessarily a matter of a man's choice whether he worked or not. Comprehensive statistics on unemployment did not begin being collected till 1910 and different views are held today as to how much of it there was in the nineteenth century. But in the middle of that century a well-informed observer estimated that only a third of the labour force in London were regularly employed, while a third were 'casually' employed and a third not employed at all.[63] This may have been pessimistic and was certainly not typical of the country as a whole. But the probability is that, as with poverty, the scale of the problem went for long underestimated. Gradually however special emergencies, like the cotton famine in Lancashire during the American Civil War, drove home the lesson that employment could fluctuate irrespective of the worker's diligence. The nature and effects of the trade cycle began to attract attention and there was a growing realisation that the whole problem was more complicated than previous generations had supposed.

Concern showed itself in a variety of directions. This is not the place to enumerate the laws which were passed to protect the lower classes, the charities which were founded or the institutions and organisations which were brought into being. The Poor Law began to take the shape which its reformers in the 1830s had intended but which had hitherto been held up by concern for the pockets of ratepayers. Instead of all the indigent being herded together into single institutions, the children began to be sent to special schools and the sick put into special hospitals, which were in due course to provide a starting-point for a National Health Service. Experience soon showed the drawbacks of making regulations without arranging for them to be administered and enforced. The application of scientific methods to social affairs began to bring into existence officers, inspectors and commissions. And while bureaucracy, once established, can be an impediment to action, there were in its Victorian embodiments a number of alert spirits who not only saw what needed to be done but campaigned to get it done.

Two firmly-held beliefs however stood in the way and, deeply embedded as they were in the whole individualist Protestant ethic, time was needed before their limitations became generally acknowledged. One was respect for individual enterprise, self-help and thrift. The middle-class leaders of the Charity Organisation Society, set up in 1869 to regulate the boundary between public and private aid, insisted on confining themselves to the 'deserving' poor, leaving to the Poor Law those who showed little or no prospect of ever becoming able to fend for themselves. This might help to maintain economic growth but hardly reflected Christian compassion. Obstinate and high-principled opposition was offered on similar grounds to all schemes for old-age pensions which were not contributory. For long, the attitude prevented public money being spent for the welfare of such of the poor as were not paupers.

Secondly there was still a tabu on the idea of interfering with the right of a man to do what he chose with his private property. This particularly held back remedial action on housing. Time was needed to demonstrate the incapacity of private enterprise to reconcile economics with benevolence. Insufficient houses had been built to keep pace with the population growth, making overcrowding inevitable. Too many of those which did go up were at one and the same time inadequate in standard and yet excessive in rent, if one was to judge by the wages of those expected to live in them. Providing people with decent living conditions was increasingly seen to be an indispensable step towards eradicating ignorance, disease and inefficiency. Yet for it to be done, either wages had to be raised or building costs subsidised. Again the solution was first sought in private charity, such as the Peabody Trust set up in 1862. Several more decades were needed to demonstrate that enough could never be done on such a basis; as late as 1914 a Birmingham Corporation Committee, chaired by Neville Chamberlain, while recognising that it would have to step in if all else failed, was still feeling strongly that 'public money could be used to much better advantage than in building houses'.[64] Some slum landlords were themselves poor so the compulsory purchase of their premises, although an essential first step to improvement, raised heartburning about the adequacy or excess of compensation.

Suffering was not the only aspect of the Industrial Revolution against which more and more people were rebelling. Ugliness was another. Critics such as Arnold, Carlyle, Ruskin and (later) Morris attacked not merely the aesthetic results but also the underlying values and in particular the emphasis on material gain.[65] Instead of pride being taken in what had been achieved and calls being made for further progress, there was a disposition to suggest that too much of value had been lost. Those who had newly acquired money were exhorted to adapt themselves to the life-styles of those whom they had fancied they were going to supersede. The new middle classes were gentrified; Barchester, not Coketown, was seen as the true embodiment of the English spirit. Not only did this involve some sentimentalising of history. Voices are now heard suggesting that, by thus disowning the qualities which had enabled her to lead the world into the new society, Britain was jeopardising her ability to stay competitive. Such an accusation leaves out of account the question how far the cult of the craftsman and of simple country life, of leisure and understatement, was new or peculiar to Britain. It raises deep questions of value and purpose, illustrated by the arguments about the possibility and desirability of zero growth. But that the criticism affected the course of Britain's history can hardly be gainsaid.

Common to both the compassionate and the cultured reaction was the refusal to let profit and loss be the final arbiter of what was to be done. Such a departure assumed that the industrialised economic system would bring enough extra wealth into existence for both welfare and amenities to be provided over and above bare necessities (unless of course existing wealth was to be redistributed). Paradoxically the benefits to be expected from economic growth began to be taken increasingly for granted just as that growth itself began to slow down.

Notes to Chapter 3

1 J. Austen Chamberlain, *Notes on the Families of Chamberlain and Harben* (privately printed 1915).
2 Daniel Chamberlain is said to have been descended from an Abraham Chamberlain of Bread Street – which is just where a confectioner might be expected to live! It is also next to Milk Street.
3 M. Hurst, *Joseph Chamberlain and Liberal Reunion* (1967), p. 23 (no source given).

4   N. Pevsner, *The Buildings of England: London except the Cities of London and Westminster* (Harmondsworth, 1952), p. 81.

5   D. W. Laing, *Mistress of Herself* (Barre, Mass., 1965), p. 83.

6   J. Austen Chamberlain, *Notes on the Families*.

7   Pevsner, p. 239.

8   J. Morley, *The Life of Gladstone* (1903), Vol. 3, p. 19.

9   H. J. K. Usher, C. D. Black-Hawkins and G. J. Carrick, *An Angel Without Wings. The History of University College School* (1981), p. 13.

10   Chamberlain is said by N. M. Marris, *Joseph Chamberlain, the Man and the Statesman* (1900), p. 419, to have read Marx. But he is unlikely to have read more than *The Communist Manifesto* since nothing else was translated into English until 1885 and Chamberlain's German would probably not have been good enough for him to read the originals. One person however who did read them (about 1879) was the Crown Princess Victoria, who sent Sir Mountstuart Grant-Duff to see the author. Grant-Duff was a friend of Dilke and Chamberlain and may well have described the visit to them, including the conclusion that 'it will not be he, whether he wishes or not, who will turn the world upside down' (Egon, Count Corti, *The English Empress* (trans. 1957), p. 212). Chamberlain mentioned Marx in an article on 'The Labour question' in *The Nineteenth Century*, November 1892.

11   Quoted by A. J. Taylor, *Laissez-faire and State Intervention in Britain* (1972), p. 27.

12   Article on J. Martineau in Hastings, *Encyclopaedia of Religion and Ethics*.

13   J. Chamberlain, 'The manufacture of iron wood-screws' in S. Timmins, *Resources, Products and Industrial History of Birmingham and the Midland Hardware District* (1866).

14   J. Habbakuk, *American and British Technology in the Nineteenth Century* (Cambridge, 1962).

15   G. C. Allen, *The Industrial Development of Birmingham and the Black Country* (1929), p. 109.

16   P. Mathias, *The Transformation of England* (1979), p. 56.

17   J. Austen Chamberlain, *Notes on the Families*.

18   F. M. L. Thompson in *The Times Literary Supplement*, 20 February 1981, reviewing D. Cannadine, *Lords and Landlords, the Aristocracy and the Towns*.

19   Dr B. S. Benedikz, of Birmingham University Library, informs me that this has been established in discussion with the family.

20   N. Kenrick, *Chronicles of a Nonconformist Family* (Birmingham, 1932); R. A. Church, *The Kenricks in Hardware* (Newton Abbot, 1969).

21   J. Austen Chamberlain, *Politics from the Inside* (1936), p. 15.

22   A. Swinson, *Frederick Sander, the Orchid King* (1975).

23   B. Webb (Potter), *Diary* (eds N. and J. Mackenzie, 1982), 18 November 1888.

24   W. L. Burn, *The Age of Equipoise* (1964), p. 18; O. Macdonough, *Early Victorian Government* (1977), p. 71.

25   Morley, Vol. 2, p. 128.

26   F. M. L. Thompson, *English Landed Society in the Nineteenth Century* (1963), pp. 244–6.

27   Thompson, pp. 297–9.

28   H. J. Hanham, *Elections and Party Management* (1959), p. 276.

29   B. Southgate, *The Passing of the Whigs* (1959), ch. 9.

30   J. Vincent, *The Foundation of the Liberal Party* (1976), p. 20.

31   H. Browne, *Joseph Chamberlain, Radical and Imperialist* (1974), p. 11.

32   W. E. S. Thomas, in *The Philosophical Radicals* (Oxford, 1979, pp. 437–53), has suggested that the British lack of an intelligentsia was due to the fact that the British universities were not producing more educated men than the institutions of society could employ. Consequently there was never any appreciable number of persons who were learned but unoccupied and hence disaffected. 'Professional men are not intellectuals; the latter live for ideas, the former on ideas.'

33   F. Gillespie, *Labour and Politics in England 1850–67* (Durham, N.C., 1927), p. 151.

34   K. Robbins, *John Bright* (1979), pp. 80, 176.

35   Burn, citing G. D. H. Cole, *Studies in Class Structures* (1977), p. 558; A. Briggs, *Victorian People* (Harmondsworth, 1965), p. 187.

36 S. Maccoby, *English Radicalism 1853–86* (1938), p. 79.
37 H. Eysenck, *The Psychology of Politics* (1954).
38 J. L. Garvin, *The Life of Joseph Chamberlain* (1932), Vol. 1, p. 60 in J. L. Garvin and J. Amery, *The Life of Joseph Chamberlain*, 6 vols (1932–69); Vincent, p. 84.
39 P. Kennedy, *The Rise and Fall of British Naval Mastery* (1976), p. 172.
40 Harcourt to Morley, 6 January 1891, quoted by D. A. Hamer, *John Morley* (1968), p. 268.
41 Morley, Vol. 2, p. 126; Hanham, p. 350.
42 Maccoby, p. 89.
43 F. B. Smith, *The Making of the Second Reform Bill* (Cambridge, 1966), p. 2.
44 Smith, p. 188.
45 Smith, p. 152.
46 Maccoby, pp. 53–86, 97.
47 Hanham, pp. viii–xii.
48 Hanham, p. 216; Vincent, p. 50.
49 Smith, pp. 8, 67; Maccoby, pp. 84–94.
50 R. Harrison, *Before the Socialists* (1965), p. 128.
51 Smith, p. 204.
52 As reported by Lady Houghton, 21 November 1866, quoted by Smith, p. 142.
53 J. S. Mill, *On Liberty* (1859), ch. 3; J. Gray, *Mill on Liberty, a Defence* (1983), ch. 4.
54 M. Cowling, *Mill On Liberty* (Cambridge, 1963), ch. 4.
55 I. Bradley, *The Optimists* (1980), p. 172.
56 Quoted by J. H. Burns, 'J. S. Mill and democracy' in J. B. Schneewind (ed.), *Mill, a Collection of Critical Essays* (1968).
57 H. V. Emy, *Liberals, Radicals and Social Politics* (1973), p. 190.
58 *Considerations on Representative Government* (1861).
59 *Principles of Ethics* (1892), ch. 7, quoted by J. B. Burrow, *Evolution and Society* (Cambridge, 1966), p. 215.
60 *Social Statics* (1851), p. 434, quoted by Burrow, p. 225.
61 F. Duke in D. Fraser (ed.), *The New Poor Law in the Nineteenth Century* (1976), p. 67.
62 According to Gregory King (1688), the number of people who could not exist on their income exceeded those who could. See P. Laslett, *The World We Have Lost* (1971), ch. 2; P. Mathias, *The First Industrial Nation* (1978), ch. 2.
63 H. Mayhew, *London Labour and the London Poor* (1851), Vol. 3, p. 103.
64 A. Briggs, *The History of Birmingham* (Oxford, 1952), Vol. 2, p. 86.
65 See M. J. Wiener, *English Culture and the Decline of the Industrial Spirit* (Cambridge, 1981); W. J. Reader, *Professional Men* (1966), pp. 202–6.

4 'Brummagem Joe': 1865–80

Success in Birmingham

A Liberal Association was first formed in Birmingham in 1865; Chamberlain was from the start a member but not an officer. He was present at the Reform League's demonstration which Bright addressed in August 1866 (see p. 66). In 1867 the Birmingham Education Society was set up, in imitation of the Lancashire Public Schools Association of twenty years earlier: although only an ordinary member, he worked as hard as if he were secretary. In 1868 the Liberal Association was reconstituted to fight the December election; his first recorded speech was made when he took the chair at a dinner of the Edgbaston Liberal Election Committee.[1] Thanks to a highly organised campaign, the Liberal electorate was so drilled to distribute its votes that the intention of the Reform Act (see p. 67) was frustrated and all three seats captured.

Early in 1869 the Education Society was converted into the National Education League as a pressure group to make the Gladstone government bring in an Education Bill and to influence the character of its contents. The moving spirit behind the League was the chairman George Dixon. But he was also one of Birmingham's MPs and as such often away in London, so that much of the work fell on Chamberlain as vice-chairman; a third of the funds were provided by Chamberlains and Kenricks. In June the Liberal Association held a mass meeting to support the Irish Disestablishment Bill; Chamberlain was chosen to second the resolution. The meeting ended in a riot but not before he had delivered a philippic against the House of Lords for frustrating the peoples' wishes by holding up the Bill. In October the first annual general meeting of the Education League was held; at it Chamberlain successfully moved that a Bill representing the League's views should be drafted for introduction in the next Parliamentary session. A few weeks later a deputation called on him to stand for the town council. He did so and was elected. Four years later he was chosen mayor, an office which he held for three years and only vacated when in June 1876 he nudged Dixon into resigning so as to make a Birmingham constituency available for its first citizen.[2]

The group bringing him the invitation to stand for the council was headed by William Harris, who was a councillor himself and also leader-writer for the Liberal *Birmingham Daily Post*. Harris was associated with Dixon and with a quartet of dissenting ministers, George Dawson of the

Baptist Church of the Saviour, R. W. Dale of the Carr's Lane Congregationalist Chapel, H. W. Crosskey of the Unitarian Church of the Messiah (opened in 1862 to replace Priestley's New Meeting House) and Charles Vince of the Baptists. Dawson may have been the biggest personality of the four but it was Dale who most clearly expressed their dominant – if hardly unprecedented – idea that true Christianity must show itself in social action. He said of one councillor who belonged to the team that 'he is trying to get the will of God done on earth as it is done in Heaven just as much when he is fighting St Mary's Ward as when he is teaching in his Bible class on a Sunday morning'. And again, 'In a country like this where the public business of the state is the private duty of every citizen, those who decline to use their political power are guilty of treachery to God and man'.[3] Dawson said that 'a great town exists to discharge towards the people of that town the duties that a great nation exists to discharge towards the people of that nation'.[4] One of their primary objectives was to raise the calibre of the men engaging in Birmingham's public life which still left something to be desired (see p. 44). Their scouts had spotted Chamberlain's talent and the invitation was the result.

Municipal progress had been held up not merely by the dispute as to what the council could do but, even after that was settled, by the unwillingness of the councillors to do what they could. The concept of the nightwatchman state was at its most influential and to small men small expenditure seemed a council's chief virtue. Except for its town hall (and even there Manchester had been ten years ahead) Birmingham lagged behind other comparable towns. It did not for example acquire a Medical Officer of Health until required to do so by the Public Health Act of 1872; Liverpool had appointed one in 1847.[5] Manchester had started a municipal gas supply in 1823; Leeds had put the water supply under public management in 1852. In Birmingham both were in the hands of private companies; in spite of the finding of the Royal Commission on Health in Towns that four houses out of every five were without water, a proposal for the municipality to acquire the water company was defeated in 1854. Drainage was the responsibility of three distinct sets of commissioners and four boards of surveyors, all at loggerheads.[6] But the death rate rose from 14·6 per thousand to 27·2 within ten years and opinion was changing.[7] There were demands for more vigour but in 1871 a reform of the system stalled for lack of cash.

Chamberlain, on becoming mayor, said that 'in twelve months, by God's help, the town will not know itself'. He first set out to take over the two gas companies. He got the approval of the council and ratepayers, negotiated with the owners and obtained parliamentary sanction. He enunciated the doctrine, which he claimed to have learnt from Mill, that 'all monopolies which are sustained in any way by the state ought to be controlled by representatives of the people, by whom they should be administered and to whom their profits should go'.[8] In the first year of public ownership these profits had risen to £34,000 which by 1880 (in spite of two cuts in the price of gas) had gone up to £57,000. Birmingham had hitherto possessed no revenue-earning property such as docks, so that all expenditure had to be financed out of rates or loans. Now the money made on gas enabled the sewerage scheme to be revived.

For water came next. Seeing that one of the explanations for the town's rise was its possession of a good water supply, it was paradoxical that Chamberlain could ask the council what they thought of the citizens 'being compelled to drink water which is as bad as sewerage before chlorination'. But many of the wells had been polluted by inadequate drainage and the two problems needed to be tackled together. Again the negotiations with the private companies were carried through successfully and again the system, under public management, yielded a profit. But this time it was devoted to reducing the price – another policy which Chamberlain fathered on Mill. In 1877 advantage was taken of a permissive clause in the Public Health Act passed a year earlier by Disraeli's government to set up a United Sewage Board, bringing in nine local authorities whose effluents had all been discharged into the same small River Tame.

Another Conservative measure which came in handy was the Artisans Dwellings Act of 1875 which authorised municipalities to acquire, clear and rebuild slum areas, thereby relieving individual towns of the need to get private Bills passed for this purpose. Chamberlain, who had made suggestions to the Home Secretary about the Bill during its preparation, exploited it to drive a swathe through the centre of his city, replacing an irregular jumble of alleys and yards (some of them owned by members of his family) with the shops and offices of Corporation Street – rather than with dwellings for the artisans who had been living in the 635 houses demolished.[9] He argued that the cost would be under a quarter of the sum which the community was losing through the ill-health of the slum population. He also justified the project on moral grounds:[10]

We bring up a population in the dank, dark, dreary, filthy courts such as are to be found throughout the area we have selected; we surround them with noxious influences of every kind . . . And what is the result? I think Mr White said the other day that to some extent the position of the people was their own fault . . . But I am sure that he only meant that to be true in a very limited sense . . . Yes, it is legally their fault, and when they steal we send them to gaol, and when they commit murder we hang them. But if the members of the Council had been placed under similar conditions, does any of us believe that we should have run no risk from the gaol or the hangman? It is no more the fault of these people that they are vicious and intemperate than it is their fault that they are stunted, deformed, debilitated and diseased!

The scheme was not completed till 1903. Its financial success was in doubt until 1892; Chamberlain admitted that the council had had to pay more than fair compensation for the land it acquired and the resulting deficit was not wiped out till 1938.[11] This helps to explain why Birmingham's debt was the highest of comparable cities and why even a radical like Harcourt could describe it as 'the metropolis of reckless expenditure'. But Chamberlain's reaction was that 'a corporation that is afraid to borrow is too timid to do its duty'.[12] Local authorities were machines for spending rather than for saving – but for spending wisely.[13]

It is not on grounds of expense that he would be criticised today. The worst gap in the scheme was the absence of anyone in the shape of a supervising architect. Admittedly contemporaries congratulated themselves that they were not building during 'the ugly classical period in architecture'[14] and, as fashionable taste involved the choice of Scott as heir to Adam, and of Waterhouse to Nash, Birmingham stood little chance of acquiring another Charlotte Square or Regent Street. But if gas and water were to be taken out of private hands, some restriction might have been expected on individual freedom of design. Corporation Street proved to be an object lesson in material affluence and aesthetic mediocrity. Chamberlain was hardly building for posterity since he insisted on ground leases being reduced from ninety-nine to seventy-five years. It would be pleasant to suppose him to have done so in the hope that the 1950s and 1960s would be capable of remedying what he recognised as shortcomings in his own generation but any such hypothesis would be as inherently unlikely as it has been assuredly unrealised.

It would be easy to belittle Chamberlain's achievements by arguing that all he did was to seize an exceptionally favourable opportunity for putting into practice ideas borrowed from other people and places. If he had lived anywhere else, much of his work would have been done already and he might have had to rest content with putting up municipal buildings and an assize court. Although the 'Great Depression' (see pp. 102–6) is often taken to have begun in 1873, the variety of Birmingham's trades made the town relatively immune while the money diverted from investment overseas could be made available for building at home so that his years as mayor were years of prosperity. But any such verdict would disregard the drive and salesmanship which he brought to each operation and the way he combined fixity of ultimate aim with flexibility as to the means of reaching it. His quickness of mind made him an adroit negotiator while his fluency often meant that the argument was decided in his favour before his opponents had managed to frame their case. He preferred getting things done to arguing about the best way of doing them, an attitude typical of a society with plenty of resources and consequently one which has been more conspicuous in America than in England. He was not the first leader, or the last who, in the effort to fire his team with enthusiasm, exaggerated somewhat the importance and originality of his achievement.

But if in general he was little inclined to

> look before and after
> And sigh for what is not,

there was one direction in which his sighs were heartfelt. In 1868 he had married Florence Kenrick, a cousin of his first wife. They went to live at Southbourne, a medium-sized house in Edgbaston. In February 1875 she too died in childbirth, leaving him with four more children, Neville, Ethel, Hilda and Ida. The blow seems to have completed the collapse of his religious faith and in his distress he leaned more on his recently-acquired agnostic friend John Morley than on the ministers with whom he was working so closely. It was by work that he sought to sublimate his grief, which made it all the more important for the work to be rewarding.

Immediately after becoming mayor, he resigned from his firm. As the two brothers who had joined him did the same, the name Chamberlain was dropped from its title. The retiring partners are said to have received £600,000, which suggests that the firm had multiplied its capital twenty-fold in as many years. His share however would only seem to have been £120,000.[15] He later lost money in the Argentine and £50,000 in a misjudged attempt to grow sisal in the Bahamas, so that for a time about 1890 he had to commit the great Victorian sin of living on his capital. On his death, he left £125,000.[16]

Chamberlain's activities in these years were far from being confined to Birmingham but turning to deal with them involves some retracing of steps.

The Storm over Education

When Gladstone had his farewell audience with the queen after his defeat on Home Rule in 1886, their talk turned to education as a safe subject on which they could agree that it ruined the health of the higher classes uselessly and rendered the working classes unwilling to remain servants and labourers.[17] Not many people would have shared their views but the reasons given for holding different ones would have varied.

Robert Lowe, who from 1859 to 1864 held in the Privy Council

81

Committee (see p. 45) the post of vice-president which had been created to provide representation for it in the Commons, did not quite use in 1867 the phrase often put into his mouth that 'we must educate our masters'. But he did say that 'from the moment you entrust the masses with power, their education becomes an absolute necessity'.[18] The message of Matthew Arnold's book, *Culture and Anarchy*, published in 1869, was that only the former could fend off the latter. Kay-Shuttleworth, the secretary of the Committee from 1839 to 1849, said soon after his appointment that 'a good secular education' was needed 'to enable the workers to understand the true causes which determine their physical condition and regulate the distribution of wealth among the several classes of society'.[19] Not that secular education by itself would suffice; religious teaching as well was needed to inculcate morality. W. E. Forster, the Bradford ex-Quaker who was Arnold's brother-in-law and vice-president from 1868 to 1874, said that 'the standard of right and wrong is based on religion'.[20]

Secondly concern was already rising about Britain's future ability to compete in the world. The public were left in no doubt, particularly by Arnold, that English education compared badly with that in some other European states, notably Prussia, so that Sadowa and Sedan were taken as portents. Forster, in introducing his 1870 Bill, said that[21]

> upon the speedy provision of elementary schools depends our indus-
> trial prosperity . . . Civilised communities throughout the world are
> massing themselves together . . . and if we are to hold our position . . .
> we must make up for the smallness of our numbers by increasing the
> intellectual force of the individual.

Thirdly came the claim that education was something to which individuals had a right and that it was as much the duty of the state to see that
children were educated as to see that they were fed.

It was for all these reasons that the Birmingham Education Society had been founded, with the primary aim of having more accommodation provided for teaching and financial help given to children whose parents could not afford to pay. It soon announced that barely half the children in the town were going to school at all. But this should not have come as any surprise. In 1861 the Newcastle Commission, although putting the total of the relevant age-groups who were in schools at two-thirds, had added that only a tenth of these were getting an education which could be regarded as satisfactory.[22] The Privy Council's Committee had sought to improve on this standard by its maligned system of 'payment by results', i.e. making the size of its grants and as a result the size of the teacher's salary depend on the number of pupils in the school who could pass an examination in the three Rs. But although the merits of this reform are now rated higher than they were then, it did nothing to solve the problems of the children who did not stay long enough at school to take the examination or of those who did not go to school at all. Although expenditure on education was already the second largest civil vote (after the cost of administering justice) and although the number of schools had risen from about 1,750 in 1820 to 8,800 in 1871, the voluntary system had by general consent proved inadequate. How should it be replaced?

The National Education League, of which Chamberlain quickly became the leading spirit, was in no doubt. While it differed from the Liberation Society (founded to secure disestablishment) in holding that education was a matter for state action, it looked more to local than to central government for getting the job done. Councils and parishes should be authorised, even compelled, to establish free schools wherever the need was proved. These should be maintained as to a third from the rates and as to two-thirds from central taxation. They should be managed by representatives of the ratepayers but inspected by the state. All children not being educated privately should be required to attend. No religious teaching should be given in them, the various denominations being left to make their own arrangements outside school hours. The existing voluntary schools should either be taken over or deprived of their grants and left to wither. As in the United States, the new system would be universal, compulsory, unsectarian and free.

If England had previously had no system of elementary education at all, there would have been much to be said for such a scheme and, if its introduction had been practicable, later history might have run more smoothly. But a great deal of work and money had been put into building up the voluntary system. To scrap it and start again was doubtful wisdom. With extra accommodation needing to be found for some two million fresh pupils, there would have been a time-lag before compulsion was practicable. The new system could hardly expect to inherit much help or goodwill from those who had been running the old. By doing away with fees and subscriptions from private sources, it would greatly increase expenditure and so win the hostility of all who held that governments should be economical and individuals self-reliant.

But that was not all. Three-quarters of the existing schools belonged to the Church of England and were managed by people who considered religion the most important element in education. The church was well aware that the advocates of the new system were the people who wanted to disestablish it, as they had just disestablished the Church of Ireland. The forces of the establishment were therefore bound to be mobilised against the League's proposal. Bright was the only Dissenter in the Cabinet and was proving a failure; more Liberal MPs were churchmen than were dissenters. The Prime Minister was a high churchman who said that he could not join in measures of repression against voluntary schools. Even if the Cabinet had consented to introduce a Bill embodying the League's ideas, it would probably not have got through the Commons and would certainly have been thrown out by the Lords. The League however was not worried by these difficulties. Remembering 1829, 1832 and 1846, it believed that, with public opinion running in the Liberals' favour, the government had only to show courage and in a year or two a clamour in support of a Bill could be whipped up to a pitch at which the Commons could no longer resist. And Radicals were spoiling for a clash with the Lords.

Forster, who only became a member of the Cabinet in July 1870, went a considerable way to meet the League. His Elementary Education Bill proposed first of all a nationwide inquiry to ascertain the need for more schools. Where such needs were found, School Boards were to be set up in each borough or parish and their members chosen by the ratepayers; if any locality failed to do this on its own, the government could step in. The voluntary societies were given a year to fill the gaps (which resulted in about a million extra places being provided by 1876); thereafter the School Boards themselves were to build and manage schools which were to be paid for from a special rate and, up to a maximum of 50 per cent, from a Parliamentary grant. Control was to rest locally, a principle which nobody contested. School Boards were given power to make attendance compulsory and to pay the fees of children whose parents could not afford to do so, although required to exact from all other parents fees not exceeding ninepence a week.

The provision for compulsion met with ridicule and that for fee-paying with wrath (although it later transpired that the principle had already been established in 1855).[23] A considerable proportion of the children who would get their fees paid for them would be going to a church school (as the only one in the district) which meant that nonconformist ratepayers would be indirectly assisting people who had discriminated against them for so long. One grievance of the dissenters, the church rate, had at last been abolished in 1868; it now seemed to be returning by a back door. Considerably less was heard about the middle-class Church of England ratepayers who would be financing schools to which they would not dream of sending their own children.

But it was the question of religious teaching which made passions boil over. The Bill as introduced left each School Board free to arrange such religious teaching as it thought fit, although parents who objected to the result were left free to withdraw their children. The radical dissenters claimed that many Boards would be controlled by Anglicans who would see to it that Anglican forms were taught, while invocation of the 'conscience clause' would incur a social stigma. They also objected to the possibility of money from the rates being used to support schools at which the only religious teaching was Anglican. As the Bill went through Parliament, the government made a number of concessions. In particular they accepted an amendment proposed by an evangelical MP called Cowper-Temple by which the religious teaching in Board Schools was to be strictly 'non-denominational' (which meant in effect nonconformist). As a corollary 'voluntary' schools were to get no money from the rates (although they were to have their grants from the state increased instead). Schools were not to become ineligible for grants if they taught no religion at all. Admission to a grant-aided school could not be made conditional on attending a particular place of worship. The state was to have nothing to do with denominational religious teaching in future. Inspectors were not to concern themselves with it; their appointment was no longer to require church approval and few clergymen were thereafter appointed.

Such safeguards might have been thought enough to satisfy any reasonable sectarian, but the government was not prepared to stop giving money to voluntary schools and Forster was not prepared, as he put it, to 'drive the Bible out of Board Schools' – and Bright told Chamberlain that he doubted whether a majority for such expulsion could be found even in Birmingham![24] Nor was the government willing as yet to make school attendance compulsory or to give up demanding fees. Until the League's views were met on these points, it was loath to rest content; when it failed to get any satisfaction on them in Parliament and the Bill became an Act, it fastened on paragraph 25, the clause allowing School Boards to pay fees to poor children, and encouraged its supporters to refuse payment of the rate as long as such children were admitted to church schools.

The controversy was conducted with venom, Forster being a particular target of attack, although his real sympathies lay more with the dissenters than with the church. Two centuries of resentment against the discrimination practised since 1662 were finding belated outlet. Many nonconformists must have expected the Parliament elected in consequence of the 1867 Act, with its big Liberal majority, to end such discrimination and put all religions on an equal footing; their indignation was all the greater when it failed to do so. Chamberlain attracted attention by the leading part which he played in fomenting opposition. In March 1870, before the Bill's Second Reading, he spoke at No. 10 Downing Street on behalf of a League deputation of 500; it was the first time he and Gladstone met. (Another person whom he met then was a young Radical MP called Sir Charles Dilke.) A member of the deputation long remembered the finesse with which Chamberlain secured the attention of the Prime Minister while deliberately ruffling the temper of Forster.[25] Over 60 Liberals voted against the government on the Second Reading, while 255 (out of 384) abstained or opposed on one particular amendment. If the Conservatives had not come to the rescue, the government might have fallen.

Thereafter the campaign was carried up and down the country. 'We are powerless in this House', wrote Chamberlain, 'and I doubt whether anything short of a General Election will give us what we want . . . But we shall endeavour to test the feeling of the country this autumn at every by-election.'[26] Right at the outset he met with disappointment in Birmingham itself. During the debates on the Bill, an amendment had been accepted by which voters, in electing School Boards, might distribute their votes in any way they chose, including giving all to a single candidate. The church party and the Catholics were generally quicker than the Radicals to exploit this and in Birmingham won nine seats out of fifteen. Until the next election three years later, the Liberal nonconformist town council was at continual loggerheads with the Tory–Anglican School Board.

It was the high-minded Dr Dale who proposed that nonconformity should modify its relations with the Liberal Party and insist on Liberal candidates at by-elections either pledging themselves to work for the amendment of the Act or promising to resist any further inroads into religious equality. For the next three years an effort was made to put this strategy into effect. But in many constituencies the selection of candidates rested with local Liberals who were not prepared to listen to the League, leaving it to choose between throwing in its hand and bringing in a rival candidate of its own from outside whose intrusion was likely to be resented and who would have to spend money with little hope of success. Where candidates refused to meet the League's requirements, its members abstained; where they agreed to do so, church-going Liberals abstained. The government lost twenty by-elections in a row.

At first this did not worry the hotheads; Chamberlain said that he 'would rather see a Tory Ministry in power than a Liberal Government truckling to Tory prejudices'.[27] The real object of the campaign however was not to put a Tory ministry into power but to persuade a Liberal government to change its policies. When Gladstone and his colleagues showed no sign of doing so, and when the League ran into difficulties over finding men and money to fight forlorn hopes, what was in effect a bluff had been called. The topic was not calculated to win many votes. Those who felt keenly about it were more noisy than numerous. In August 1873 Chamberlain sent to John Morley what came close to being a confession of failure:[28]

I have long felt that there is not force in the Education question to make it the sole fighting issue for our friends. From the commencement it has failed to evoke any grand popular enthusiasm. Education

86

for the ignorant cannot have the meaning that belonged to Bread for the Starving ... the assistance of the working classes is not to be looked for without much extension of the argument. I do not expect, nor do I care, to have Gladstone entirely with us, and am quite satisfied if he will not let his private prejudices stand in the way of our claims.

What this overlooked was that the assistance of the working classes might have been won if education as such had been the issue; he should not have been so surprised at their failure to feel keenly about the exact arrangements for religious education. The beliefs which meant so much to the small master and shopkeeper left most workers cold; some of them anyhow resented having to send their children to school and thus losing the income which could otherwise have been earned. After all, he was himself exploiting for political purposes something in which he was ceasing to believe.

In the same month of August 1873 Bright, in the hope of helping Gladstone, rejoined the Cabinet as Chancellor of the Duchy of Lancaster. Although he had been an open critic of the Forster Act, his Radical friends did not expect much of him and were not therefore disillusioned when he proved as ineffectual in office as ever. But it gave them a pretext for suspending their campaign and, except for securing from 300 of the 425 Liberal candidates in the 1874 election a pledge to repeal paragraph 25 of the Act, the League was hardly heard of again. In the autumn of 1873 the Radicals won hands down in the second election to the Birmingham School Board; Chamberlain became chairman at virtually the same moment as he became mayor, so he had plenty of other issues to absorb his energies.

How far the League's lack of enthusiasm for the government contributed to the loss of the February 1874 election is therefore debatable, especially as there were plenty of other factors at work. As a pressure group it had been rivalled by the United Kingdom (Temperance) Alliance, which sought to withhold votes from candidates who would not promise to seek for localities the option of prohibiting the sale of drink in their area. In a modest bid to propitiate them Gladstone's Home Secretary had added to the limitations on the sale of intoxicants; this had provoked riots among the drinking classes. The Victorian workman's liking for one of the few reliefs in his drab life made him all the more angry over attempts to take it away. Hitherto the liquor trade had been relatively evenly balanced in its politics but it now began to shift into the conservative camp; the beerage joined the peerage. The trade unions were dissatisfied with the scope of an Act passed in 1871 to protect their funds and had taken offence at the Criminal Law Amendment Act of the same year which declared picketing to be illegal (since the threat of coercion involved in it was distasteful to many Liberals – though not to Chamberlain).[29] In general the Tories were offering the working classes as much as the Liberals. A private member's Act to prevent the adulteration of food was blamed on the government; one unsuccessful candidate said that 'every milkman and every grocer voted against me'.[30] The Church of England could feel secure against being disestablished under a Conservative government, whereas a Liberal one was less calculable. Gladstone's idea of an election-winning item was to promise the abolition of income tax; the implications for the defence estimates put the Services up in arms.[31] He made things harder for his campaign managers by dissolving without warning late in January. Except in Birmingham (which they did not even bother to contest, in spite of the multiple vote) the Conservatives were at least as well organised as the Liberals. With so much going for them, their clear majority of about 50 was hardly surprising. Yet had not the British electoral system been already displaying its notorious distorting effect the Liberals, who won 1,263,000 votes to the Conservatives' 1,107,000, would have come out on top.[32]

Even if the Education League was not wholly to blame for the result, it was by no means blameless. Its attacks on the government were bound to have inspired some of the Liberal abstentions which were the party's chief handicap in the polls. Nor would its leaders have disowned such responsibility. Their underlying aim was to drive out the right wing as a necessary prelude to a shift leftwards in policy. Chamberlain wrote 'if only we can break the power of the moderates – the respectable Whigs – and leave Toryism and Radicalism face to face, there will soon be an end to the reaction'.[33] His comment, when Gladstone resigned the leadership in January 1875, was that 'advanced Liberals' would receive the news with 'comparative equanimity'.[34] This attitude disregarded the lesson that the left are seldom strong enough to achieve reform by themselves but need the support of the centre. It also assumed too easily that Gladstone's disappearance from the British political stage was going to be permanent, leaving the way open for a younger generation to assume the leadership of the Radicals. Twenty months later the atrocities of the Turks in Bulgaria, and the effect which they had on Gladstone's humanitarian feelings, suggested that this assumption would prove invalid, in which case Britain's 'Young Turks' would have to decide whether to challenge his leadership or try to capture him. Already in October 1876 Chamberlain was writing to Dilke:[35]

I can't help thinking that [Gladstone] is our best card. If he were to come back for a few years (he can't continue in public life for very much longer) he would probably do much for us and pave the way for more.

Apart from the pardonable miscalculation about the date of the Grand Old Man's withdrawal, this judgment involved manipulating the 'people's William' as a tool rather than as the party's greatest moral asset. One of the processions stopped from entering Hyde Park in 1866 had carried a banner with his portrait and the caption 'Gladstone and Liberty: an honest man's the noblest work of God'.[36] A fly-sheet for the 1868 election in Whitby said that he stood as 'the archetype of all that is wise and statesmanlike in our national affairs'.[37]

The attack on the Education Act showed a failure to grasp political realities. It involved treating relative details as though they were vital principles and harmed rather than helped the cause of getting the nation better educated. A realistic radical policy would have criticised the reform for being confined to elementary education. Thirty years of squabble as to what could be smuggled through under that term were allowed to elapse before the secondary field was systematised although it was that which was arguably more vital to an industrial nation. Chamberlain, in his anxiety to find a quarrel for picking, was led by brash self-confidence into an over-estimate of what could be achieved by energy and organising. He might be excused for maiming the Party if that had been the price of getting his own way but he only succeeded in doing the damage, not in attaining the desired end. He was fond of describing his behaviour in Birmingham as 'sagacious audacity'. His behaviour over education displayed more of the noun than of the adjective.

The Caucus

In his *Recollections*, Morley said that although Chamberlain was not one of the politicians who are forced into action by ideas, he was quick to associate ideas with his actions. From this point of view Morley's friendship will have been of particular importance to him since he must have become acquainted in the course of talk with many authors and concepts which he would have been unlikely to come across in his own reading. Moreover Morley, who had succeeded G. H. Lewes in 1866 as the editor of the *Fortnightly Review*, was making it a forum for the ventilation of new ideas, in the belief that a society which did not prepare for peaceful change would sooner or later find itself changed by violence. Chamberlain, by having its columns opened to him, was brought a step forward from the local to the national stage.

The already quoted letter of August 1873 covered an article on 'The Liberal Party and Its Leaders', presumably designed to illustrate the kind of arguments thought suitable for winning the votes of the newly-enfranchised. A programme was outlined under four heads: a Free Church (disestablishment); Free Schools (abolition of fees in Board Schools); Free Land (abolition of primogeniture and entail); Free Labour (repeal of the Criminal Law Amendment Act). 'The programme may seem advanced to the large class of politicians who never recognise any reform as desirable until it has been accomplished but no one of ordinary foresight and intelligence will doubt that every item in it will be secured before twenty years have passed away.' The aim was still the removal of restrictions; there was no mention of enforcing a ten-hour day, limiting ages of employment or requisitioning property to rebuild slums. Nothing was said about republicanism, which suggests that the author's occasional sallies in that direction about this time were primarily bravado.

This broadside had no noticeable effect on the Liberal appeal at the 1874 election and perhaps for that reason Chamberlain returned to the attack with another article in the following October which he himself described as 'rabid' and in which, like many left-wing leaders after a lost contest, he set out to argue that too little radicalism rather than too much had been to blame:[38]

> Some definite programme is necessary for the reunion of the Party and it is pure hallucination to imagine that Liberalism can be made popular by a close imitation of Conservatism. On the contrary, the greater the resemblance, the less reason for another change ... To have in hand a reform of some sort is not for Liberalism a question of choice, it is the absolute condition of its separate existence as a Party. Without a 'cry' the Liberals will never regain office.

He repeated his advocacy of the 'Four Fs' and added electoral reform to them. But, as a concession to Morley's view that one issue at a time should get priority, he suggested giving pride of place to disestablishment, a goal better calculated to involve a collision with all that was established than to be the base of that reunion between the workers and the Dissenters which he described as essential.

A new policy however was only one part of his recipe for Radical success; it had to be matched with a new organisation. A model for this had just been created in Birmingham. Its authors and its enemies alike tended to exaggerate both its novelty and its potentialities. The very label 'Caucus' was stuck on to it by *The Times* in the hope that it would acquire guilt by being associated with smoke-filled rooms, wheeler-dealing and the unholy Halls of Tammany. The reality was both more prosaic and more inevitable.

Any group formed for a common purpose finds, if it grows in size, that it reaches a point at which it has to choose between changing its methods and falling into confusion. The old haphazard face-to-face collaboration between people who know one another personally has to be replaced by rules, regular meetings, formal minutes, files, premises and accounts. The independent individual is put at a disadvantage; Organisation Man takes over. In the past, progressive politics had been conducted in each locality by a handful of men with recognised social status, familiar with one another, ready as a rule to put their hands in their own pockets for the cause, meeting only when occasion demanded action – which usually meant when an election was impending. They could as a rule settle between themselves on a candidate and the backing which they conferred made the chances of any rival poor, although cases did occur where the necessary political or social consensus was lacking or where a candidate pushed in on his own. At the centre, co-ordination was achieved in a somewhat similar way through people meeting in the London houses of the leaders, in clubs or in salons.

Various developments made this informal way of doing things inadequate, chief among them being the increase in the number of electors from 435,000 (predominantly rural) in 1830 to 2,470,000 (predominantly urban) in 1868 (and although some small constituencies remained, they were counterbalanced by a number of big ones – 60,000 people voted in Birmingham in 1868). Secondly the Ballot Act of 1872, which introduced secret voting 96 years after Major Cartwright had first demanded it, made the exercise of social or financial influence harder. With the growing electorate, the traditional methods of electioneering were becoming prohibitively expensive – at any rate in the larger constituencies; in the smaller ones some voters accepted bribes from both sides. Moral qualms and considerations of economy reinforced each other. In 1868 Disraeli's government strengthened the Corrupt Practices Act of 1854 by transferring the hearing of petitions from a Committee of the House of Commons to a judge sitting in the constituency, which not only reduced political bias but made evidence easier to get, so that disregard of the rules became more risky.

With the electorate getting bigger and less easy to control by crude methods, the need to devise alternative ones became all the greater. One way of achieving this was to replace individual bribes by collective inducements in the shape of promises to introduce measures benefiting particular groups of voters. Hence the demand for 'Programmes'. The other lay in organisation, not that moves in that direction had been wholly lacking in the past. Chapters 2 and 3 contain the names of many organisations set up to work for political causes on a nationwide scale whose members were by no means confined to people with votes, although pressure groups for particular causes (like the Abolition of Slavery or the Corn Laws) could make organisation for general political objectives more rather than less complicated. Francis Place had been renowned for the skill

91

with which he devolved the task of managing voters in Middlesex, the largest constituency prior to 1832. Methodist organisation is said to have rubbed off on party practice; businessmen no doubt brought with them into politics the more elaborate procedures which they were evolving to deal with expanding markets. Bright is said to have divided Rochdale into canvassing districts after 1832;[39] something very like a caucus was operating in Leeds in 1863.[40] The existence of seven different franchises (with many people entitled to vote under more than one) gave unusual importance to the extensive and detailed work of identifying potential supporters in advance and seeing that they were on the register. Registration Associations were set up in many constituencies. A Liberal Registration Association with offices in London was started in 1860; the Conservatives followed within three years and in 1867 established the National Union of Conservative Associations, which has been described as the first central mass organisation to be formed by a British political party.[41]

In Birmingham the Political Union had as far back as 1831 divided the town into seven districts, each subdivided into two, with its own 'station house'.[42] In 1837 it was divided into sixteen in order to facilitate contact between the MPs and their constituents. As has been mentioned, a Liberal Association was formed in 1865 and remodelled in 1868, presumably to make the best of the three-seat, two-vote franchise (see pp. 66–7). The resulting organisation was said to be the work of the William Harris who invited Chamberlain to stand for the town council.[43] Chamberlain certainly played an active part in the 1868 campaign but there is no evidence that any particular feature was devised by him. The loss of the School Board election in 1870 suggests that the system still needed improvement but the victory of the Liberals in the 1873 Board election and the failure of the Conservatives to contest the 1874 parliamentary one suggest that improvement was made.

In each of the town's thirteen wards a meeting was held annually to which anyone was admitted who professed to accept the Association's objects and organisation; payment of a subscription was not required. Each such meeting elected a ward committee, as well as representatives to sit on a general committee with a membership of 400 and an executive committee of over 100. As so large a body was better suited to answering previously formulated questions than to deciding what questions should be asked, it not surprisingly elected a management sub-committee of eleven which did the bulk of the work. The ward committees chose candidates for municipal elections, the general committee those for School Board and parliamentary elections.[44] A key clause in the constitution laid down that anyone who consented to be nominated as a candidate must, in the event of his not being elected, agree to accept the decision of the relevant committee and not present himself as an independent candidate.[45]

The more active Liberal policy which Chamberlain formulated in 1873–4 was obviously more popular outside Parliament than inside and therefore his chances of getting it adopted would be improved if he could find a way of inducing constituents to put pressure on their members. The Birmingham model of association seemed likely to give rank and file voters more influence at the expense of established party managers, so that a chain of such associations offered a promising means of generating such pressure.

For the moment however his Birmingham duties kept him busy and it was only after his arrival in Westminster in the autumn of 1876 that he began to exploit the matter seriously. Early in 1877 the decision was taken to close down the dormant National Education League and substitute a National Liberal Federation. The founding meeting was held in Bingley Hall, Birmingham on 31 May. Public attention at the time was however concentrated on foreign rather than home affairs; Gladstone's campaign against Disraeli's Eastern policy had given him the attention of all ears. Chamberlain, to whom Bulgaria was essentially a far-away country of which he knew little, hit on the astute if cheeky idea of offering its advocate a Birmingham platform for his cause and thus luring him to the town at the moment when the new Federation was being launched there. Some of the prophet's charisma could hardly fail to enhance a body for which he would otherwise have yielded in enthusiasm to many. Although Granville told him he was being exploited,[46] Gladstone fell for the bait but showed himself characteristically unwilling to accept Chamberlain's ideas about the logistics of the operation. In four rotund but nebulous sentences at the outset he congratulated the town on having held up the banner of a wider and holier principle of selecting the party's representatives by the voice of the people rather than by the power of the purse and professed himself sanguine enough to predict with confidence that, 'if freely and largely' adopted, it would be a success. Otherwise he devoted himself to Eastern Europe and to the House of Commons which had just rejected his resolutions about that area. Chamberlain managed to get in a reference to three of the four Fs but the main business of founding the Federation had been done at a separate meeting earlier in the day. There he had encouraged his audience to look forward to 'a real Liberal Parliament outside the Imperial Legislature and, unlike it, elected by universal suffrage'.

Although 95 local Liberal organisations came to Birmingham, only 46 had areas coinciding with constituencies; 56 more came in over the next eighteen months. Two concessions had to be made to overcome fears that local associations would lose their freedom of action if they joined the central one. Associations were left to decide their own terms of membership and allowed to demand subscriptions as a condition of admission. And no political programme was to be submitted for formal acceptance (although this did not save the Federation's general committee from frequently finding resolutions on individual points of policy in front of it).[47] Birmingham had a predominance which might have been thought injudicious; not only did it house the central office but the president was Chamberlain, the chairman of the general committee was Harris and the part-time secretary Schnadhorst who continued to perform the same function for the Birmingham Association. Manchester was kept at arm's length for fear it would pour water into the midland wine. A surprising weakness was finance; even in the early 1880s the Federation only had an income of £1,500 a year.[48]

In describing the new body in the *Fortnightly Review* for July 1877 Chamberlain claimed that, while Conservatism worked from the top downwards, Liberalism best fulfilled its function when it worked upwards from below. He went on to say that 'the Caucus does not make opinion, it reflects it'. But this was over-ingenuous; the real movement was of course two-way. Any body organised on several levels, with the members of each electing the one above it, is subject to both upwards and downward pressures. Those at the bottom want their voices heard, those at the top want their wishes carried out. Exactly which prevails depends on such varied factors as the personalities involved, the traditions and pro-cedures established in the body, the kind of sanctions which can be brought against dissidents and the degree of interest or loyalty which the underlying ideas can arouse. Much depends on the amount of time and energy which individuals are prepared to put in; unless the rank and file attend meetings sedulously, they will find themselves without the votes needed to alter the proposals put in front of them by the top management. Chamberlain undoubtedly hoped that pressure from below would be brought to bear higher up, so as to make the Cabinet and parliamentary party change course in his desired direction. But he certainly also intended to sway the grass roots, as Gladstone had been doing, so that he could claim their support.

A major aim of the Federation was to improve Liberal chances of victory by eliminating rival candidates.[49] When in 1874 Chamberlain had stood with Mundella, a sitting member, for the two Sheffield seats, they had not been able to stop two other Liberal candidates putting up. One of these, the veteran Roebuck, won at Chamberlain's expense, thanks largely to votes from Conservatives, who did not contest the constituency. The case was by no means unique; fission tends to be the fashion in a party which stands for freedom of thought. The British political system, thanks to its origins and nature, requires for its effective working large parties, each providing an umbrella over a wide variety of views. To win under such a system, a candidate has to obtain votes throughout the spectrum, which he is more likely to get if he has been officially endorsed, since party loyalty will then win for him the votes of many who disagree with some of his views. Moreover the Liberal Party was particularly susceptible to 'faddists' and 'crotchetmongers' – people who felt keenly about a particular reform such as disestablishment or prohibition or repealing the Contagious Diseases Act, not to mention religious education. They sought to make their cause a central issue of politics by standing as candidates on its behalf. They seldom won but might draw votes from more promising candidates, with the result that the seat went to the Tories. For both these reasons, there was growing need for an organisation which would embrace as many as possible of those who claimed to be Liberals and would also endorse one particular candidate as official, so as to reduce the chances of others standing or, if they stood, of receiving votes. To Chamberlain it was important that this organisation should not be in right-wing hands.

The 'Caucus', so far from bringing underhand or illicit pressure to bear, was in fact reducing the chances of it being brought by enlarging the number of people entitled to be consulted. It was putting into practice what Chamberlain had described as 'the cardinal principle of Liberalism – that the people shall be assisted to govern themselves'.[50] Its election-winning effects were probably exaggerated. The improvement in organisation which it represented was cancelled out once the Conservatives followed suit, as they quickly did. The drilling of voters in the three-seat two-vote constituency was only effective as long as the Tories got less than 40 per cent of the votes cast; if it had still been in force in 1885, Chamberlain might well have lost his seat.[51] But at the end of the 1870s the future looked rosy for the Liberals. A number of their Birmingham leaders were obviously sincere in claiming that they sought the welfare of the community rather than that of any particular section. As a result of the 1867 Act there were plenty of newcomers to political life who were ready to throw themselves into the work of the Association. They responded to the leadership which Chamberlain gave. Morale and cohesion were both high. There had not been time for disillusion to be bred by routine and lack of quick results. They still had to learn the difference between a day at the seaside and the long march through the institutions.

Less than a month after Chamberlain had taken his seat in Parliament, education came up for debate; the opportunity was too tempting to be resisted and the new member made a maiden speech which was competent rather than arresting. His next major speech, in March 1877, introduced a motion authorising English municipalities to copy Swedish ones by buying and operating public houses; his pet remedy for the 'disease' of insobriety won him 51 votes against 103 in Parliament and the hostility of the drink trade outside it. In 1878 he began to throw his weight about, especially as regards the contagious diseases of cattle. In 1879 he joined forces with an Irish MP called Parnell who felt as keenly as he did against the army's use of flogging. But it was only after he had needled his indolent leader Hartington into action that he got anything done to reduce it. He spoke only three times on Ireland. Nobody could have guessed where his five interventions on South Africa would lead.

The Unforgiving Heart

The English acquired Ireland by conquest and regarded its possession as essential to their security; Lord Salisbury wrote in 1872 that 'Ireland must be kept, like India, at all hazards. By persuasion, if possible; if not, by force'.[52] But they did not conquer the whole island immediately and a native peasantry lingered in the bogs and mountains; their chiefs, their language and their traditions provided an enduring focus for the emotions of the disadvantaged. Since the possessions of the proud invaders rested on institutionalised violence, their representatives never succeeded in legitimising themselves in Irish eyes and, as their title to the lands which they held was never fully accepted, the right of an owner to get the best out of his property never became taken for granted. Ireland displayed

> the unforgiving heart
> Which dwells on wrongs and will not let
> Old bitterness depart.

The Irish reply would have been that there was too much to forgive.

The basic attitude of hostility, even hatred, suggested that leaving Ireland to the Irish would mean leaving her to people who could be trusted to side with England's enemy of the moment. The eagerness for French help during the rebellion of 1798 seemed to confirm this fear. England's response was to cancel the limited and corrupt freedom granted to Grattan's Irish Parliament in 1782 and tie Ireland closer to Great Britain. To get that Parliament to vote for its own demise, Pitt held out hopes of making union the occasion for Catholic Emancipation. Unfortunately this was not to be the last example of a British government promising more than it could perform or of an Irish grievance distorting the course of British politics. Even after emancipation had been achieved the Catholic church, with three-quarters of the population, got nothing like its proportionate share of social privileges and public grants.

On this unpromising stage there supervened a demographic disaster. The population of Ireland rose from 1·5m. in 1700 to 2·5m. in 1750, 5m. in 1800 and 7m. at the first census in 1841. There seem to have been two main reasons. One was the expanding market in England for wheat as well as stock, which led many Irish farmers to turn their pasture into labour-intensive tillage. The second was the introduction of the potato which doubled the number of people, pigs and poultry a plot of ground could support. The improved prospects of employment and subsistence led to earlier marriages, larger families and the subdividing of family holdings. By 1845 24 per cent of Ireland's farms were under 5 acres and in the west the figure was 64 per cent.[53]

But the potato cannot be stored and, until fungicides were introduced about 1885, was liable to blight. The famine of 1845–8 was not the first to occur, even in the nineteenth century, but it came when population was higher than ever and English prices for wheat had begun to fall. Whereas Peel's government reacted to the 1845 shortage by promptly bringing in food, doubts as to whether this was a suitable activity for a government impeded Lord John Russell from showing equal sense in face of the 1846 and 1848 crop failures. 'God sent the blight', said the Irish, 'but the Government created the famine.'[54] Malthus' predictions, which had failed to be realised in England, proved only too valid for Ireland. Nearly a million people died between 1846 and 1851 while a million more fled to England, America, Australia and Canada, followed by a further million between 1851 and 1861. Most of them were labourers and small farmers; the proportion of holdings of over 15 acres rose by 15 per cent between 1846 and 1851. The subdividing of holdings slowed, the age of marriage went up and the birth rate down.[55] By 1871 the population was back to 5m.

Even this diminished number could be rescued from penury only by sustained investment. Ireland's factor endowment may have included a fertile climate but it omitted coal and most minerals, while she also lacked many of the features (listed in Chapter 1) which had helped to make England the scene of the industrial breakthrough. English governments, busily engaged in removing tariffs in the main island with apparently satisfactory results, could hardly be expected to give infant industries tariff protection in the lesser one. Even though supplies of men, capital and food may have been available, the prospects of making money out of industry were not good enough to attract the talented brains which the country unquestionably possessed. Her main hope therefore lay in putting money into agriculture so as to increase output for the market. But for a capital-intensive agriculture the bulk of her farms were too small and her labour force was too high; without industry to absorb it, emigration was metaphorically as well as literally the way out. Thus the results of the famine were moves in the right direction.[56] The condition of east and south Ireland certainly improved between 1850 and 1876, although in the west existence remained precarious. But peasants are not easily induced to quit their land and Innisfail's sons and daughters resented being forced to fly her lovely coast. The net result was that between 1848 and 1914 Ireland had the lowest growth rate in Western Europe.[57]

Gladstone, in introducing the first Home Rule Bill, was to say that 'the English mind is estranged from the Irish people and the Irish mind is estranged from the people of England and Scotland'.[58] The Irish in England were an unprepossessing selection, mostly there because of inability to support life in their native country. They took the worst jobs (undercutting English workers), lived in the worst slums (Taine compared the Irish quarters of Liverpool to 'the last circle of Hell'), and provided recruits in plenty for mobs and conspiracies, as well as for a third of the armed forces.[59] The Irish blamed England for turning into atheists people who had left home as faithful members of the church. The English Catholics were antipathetic to the form which their religion took among a simple-minded flock, while the Liberals despised the Irish for their devotion to an obscurantist papacy. The English regarded the Irish as backward, idle, illogical, feckless, dishonest and violent, so incapable of managing their own affairs that it was a kindness to send them rulers from outside. The Irish retaliated by denying England's boasted superiority, exaggerating what they had once done to keep European culture alive and arguing that rural penury was finer than machine-fed materialism. Under these circumstances little assimilation of the subject population could occur. Indeed the chief development was the other way round, with offspring of the Ascendancy adopting the Irish viewpoint.[60]

It has been said that 'the importance of the famine may lie less in its immediate effects than in its influence on the historical imagination of the Irish people. A subjugated people will probably always blame their rulers for whatever befalls them.'[61] The merits of English administratiion in Ireland, in such matters as education and public health, were considerable, largely because the prejudices of the administered could be disregarded to an extent not possible at home.[62] But for this very reason they went unappreciated. Education was suspect because its declared aim was to anglicise. English was the language of public affairs, with only ten per cent of the population unable to understand it in 1851, which facilitated a denial of the Irish claim to be a distinct nation with the same rights as, say, the Italians and Poles. But it was over land that the chief misconceptions flourished (partly because leading English politicians seldom visited the island). A picture was popularised of a country belonging to alien, absentee and hard-hearted landlords, who evicted their tenants as soon as they could find anyone who would pay a higher rent, refusing to give any compensation for improvements. In reality many landlords lived in Ireland, some even on their estates, and evictions for reasons other than non-payment of rent were few, at any rate after the famine. Rents were mostly left below the economic value of the land while such improvements as were made without a landlord's help did not often deserve the name. The basic problem about Irish agriculture remained the fact that too many of the holdings were too small to provide a tolerable livelihood so that any rent was too high and its extraction resented. But the remedy was to increase the average size which could not be done without evictions and without landlords financing improvements for which they would expect higher rents.[63]

To this analysis needs to be added the fact that the north-east of the country, too large to be disregarded yet too small to be decisive, was in most respects exceptional. The settlers in Ulster, chiefly Scots Presbyterians, exemplified the Protestant virtues of diligence and thrift. Their relative prosperity, agricultural as well as industrial, seemed to confirm the diagnosis of what was wrong in the three other provinces. They themselves regarded it as proof of being inherently superior. Naturally those manning the front line of resistance to Irish Catholic nationalism were averse to compromise; many of them stuck to attitudes already becoming outmoded in the kingdom with which they insisted on remaining united. Curiously enough during most of the nineteenth century neither English nor Irish took Ulster determination seriously but assumed that resistance to an otherwise acceptable settlement would not be pushed to extremes or could somehow be surmounted.

But was an 'otherwise acceptable settlement' anything more than a delusion? With mutual incomprehension coming on top of divergent interests, it seems unlikely. The example of renascent nationalisms elsewhere suggests that, as England failed to assimilate the Irish before the modernisation of society stirred them *en masse* to political and therefore to national awareness, her chances of doing so afterwards were small. Besides, English policy towards Ireland showed a familiar but fatal oscillation between coercion and conciliation. Those on the right said that all the Irish understood was force and that, once resolute action had put the trouble-stirrers behind bars, things would soon quieten down. Even Liberals deprecated concessions being made to violence. But the sad truth was that violence did often produce concessions whereas, when Ireland was quiet, the government of the moment congratulated themselves on the success of their latest policy and forgot her. Proposals for conciliation, often made without full understanding of the situation, ran into right-wing opposition, got pared down in the process of enactment and were a constant example of 'too little, too late'. As that was how the Irish regarded them even before the paring down, they were accepted with little gratitude and attention was switched to the next grievance. Such failure to appreciate magnanimity is always abhorrent to Liberals since it suggests that their trust in human good-will is misplaced. Yet Liberalism had to conciliate, since for it to be indefinitely dependent on coercion in order to rule is for it to be false to its nature. The radical principle that an individual has an inalienable right to a say over his (or her) conditions of life obviously entitled men to refuse to be ruled by people with backgrounds and interests basically discrepant from their own. In the long run the English failure to integrate the Irish into their community implied the end of British rule in the Irish parts of Ireland or the conversion of Britain into an authoritarian state.

Jeder Schuld rächt sich auf Erde. Gladstone in 1845 cast Ireland in the role of minister of God bringing divine retribution 'on cruel and inveterate and but half-atoned injustice'.[64] What made G. M. Young regard Ireland, along with the Clarendon Code, as the 'greatest disaster of our history' (see p. 32) was the absorption of English intelligence and purpose caused by argument as to how the island should be treated. Gladstone said in 1891 that throughout his political life a fraction of the population, hardly amounting to an eighth, had consumed a totally disproportionate part of Parliament's time and prevented it from performing its proper function. The peace of Liverpool, Glasgow and several other cities was periodically disrupted by riots instigated or provoked by the Irish. In 1867 a clash between Irish Catholics and the Protestant party of 'Law and Order' in Birmingham lasted for two days; Chamberlain reported that 'the roofs were gone, the fronts of the houses also'.[65] Hatred of England by Irish emigrants not only complicated relations with the United States, Australia and Canada but also provided that potent obstacle to pacification, an external source of inspiration and finance. The explosion in Clerkenwell in December 1867 which killed 12 and injured 120 may have been better evidence of venom among American Fenians than of distress in Ireland itself. But it made some Englishmen believe that the rising of the previous year had to be taken more seriously than its quick collapse suggested and left behind in Ireland a secret organisation, the Republican Brotherhood, dedicated to achieving independence by whatever means came most handy.

Gladstone's first step towards 'pacifying Ireland', which he had decided to be necessary six years earlier, was to sever the connection between the churches of England and Ireland, disestablishing the latter and taking some of its emoluments 'for the relief of unavoidable calamity and suffering'. His respect for the church was so well known that he was able to pass into law within five months a measure which, if proposed by anyone else, would have been hotly contested. But to get the Bill through the House of Lords without provoking a constitutional crisis about that body's powers, he had to reduce considerably the amount of money to be sequestrated.

He then in 1870 introduced a Land Bill, drafted by himself without Irish advice and based on the hypothesis that the root cause of unrest in Ireland lay in the law governing relations between landlord and tenant. The new Act entitled tenants to (1) compensation if evicted for any reason other than non-payment of rent (e.g. incompetence); (2) compensation if evicted for non-payment of a rent judged by a court to be excessive; (3) compensation for improvements for which they had themselves been responsible. In so far as the Act worked, it did harm by discouraging the consolidation of holdings, but as evictions were far fewer than is popularly alleged, the harm it did was mitigated. It sought to protect tenants from having to pay excessive rents but, as most rents were uneconomically low, this would have acted as a bar to efficiency had not the House of Lords, by substituting for the original 'excessive' the more stringent term 'exorbitant', gone far to make the provision a dead letter. But by authorising a court to decide over the landlord's head whether a rent was justifiable, it opened the door to the process by which in due course Irish landlords were to be expropriated. It encouraged tenants to invest when few had the resources for doing so and correspondingly discouraged landlords who mostly did have. The clauses helping tenants to buy their land, the brain-child of Bright, left too much of the purchase price to be found privately and was only taken up by 870. The many observers who failed to realise that the measure rested on a faulty diagnosis professed themselves lost in admiration for its author's grasp of his subject.[66]

For the next ten years little or nothing was done specifically for Ireland beyond Gladstone's scheme for a university which had to be dropped because the English thought it too favourable to the Catholics and the Irish insufficiently so. And many of the good effects of Gladstone's other measures were undone by the refusal of his colleagues to amnesty Fenians.[67] Yet time was beginning to run short. Hitherto British governments of whatever colour had been able to rely on Irish voters sending to Westminster representatives who would, broadly speaking, support the *status quo*. Prior to 1868 over half the constituencies had been uncontested. Where there was a contest, voters were often marched to the poll under military escort, allegedly to protect them from violence by the other side, and on arrival ordered to vote as their landlords wished.[68] But the secret voting brought by the Ballot Act of 1872 spelt the end of this cosy state of affairs, while it was becoming progressively harder to justify virtually withholding from Ireland the suffrage granted in 1867 to the rest of the United Kingdom.

In 1870 a cautious Protestant lawyer called Isaac Butt propounded the idea that the best way of securing change in Ireland without completely breaking the tie with Britain would be some form of federation in which a revived Irish Parliament, with its own executive, would be responsible for the country's internal affairs while its external ones would continue to be handled from Westminster. As a result of his initiative, a 'Home Government Association' was formed with members drawn from all parties and during the next two years candidates supporting its ideas won eight by-elections. In the general election of 1874, 58 seats out of Ireland's 105 went to supporters of the movement which had just been rechristened 'Home Rule'; only ten Liberals not committed to it won seats. In 1875 its ranks were increased at a by-election by Charles Stewart Parnell, a Protestant of English descent, ten years younger than Chamberlain.

Once Home Rule had been propounded as a goal, the chances of the Irish resting content with anything less were small. Concessions over land and other grievances might induce the Irish MPs to hold their hands for a while, but for many Irishmen the real grievance lay in being ruled by the English, so that ambitious politicians would always be under a temptation to outbid their rivals by offering to get that rule ended. English ability to resist that demand depended on the government having a majority in the House of Commons without Irish votes. But the existing party strengths in the United Kingdom made it hard to exclude the possibility of a growing Home Rule Party holding the balance in a hung Parliament.

The 'Great Depression'

In 1868 the Birmingham Chamber of Commerce referred to 'the long-continued depression which is part of the normal ebb-and-flow of economic life. If we would take wisdom from the past and avoid the trying times of depression in future, we must try to prevent the previous expansion which causes them.'[69] But the expansion which began in 1869 was accentuated by the Franco-Prussian War and developed into one of the biggest booms of the century. In March 1874 Chamberlain was still writing to Morley about 'the present prosperous state of trade'.[70] Elsewhere however the tide had already turned and the succeeding depression is often supposed to have gone on till 1896, thereby earning the adjective 'great'. British growth in general certainly seems to have been lower in 1874 than in 1873 and thereafter the indices go down until 1879. There were further troughs in 1886 and 1893.

Controversy has raged as to why this slowing-down occurred[71] and as a result there has been a tendency to forget that, if the figures were compared for any period of similar length prior to 1780 in Britain (and even later elsewhere), they would have caused satisfaction rather than concern. Having changed up from third to first gear, the world was dismayed to find that its expectations of continuing for ever in such prosperity were unfounded and that it had to accustom itself to proceeding in second. The upshot of the controversy is that the explanation of the phenomena is as usual not monocausal. A number of processes were at work which, although interconnected, were not necessarily simultaneous and the gravity of the depression to some extent depended on the extent to which they did coincide.

During any upswing, imperfect information and over-rosy estimates of the proportion of the enlarged market which he can obtain inclines each manufacturer or would-be manufacturer (what a pity that the term 'undertaker' has got appropriated for a different occupation!) to overestimate the sales and profits which he will be able to make. He therefore builds up his stocks and invests in plant on a scale which before long proves excessive. There is a general drawing-in of horns. Foreign investment in particular slows down and as a result foreign demand for the investor's exports falls, thereby intensifying the depression, which lasts until stocks have been exhausted, existing plant wears out, population has grown and savings are again beginning to seek outlets.

One outlet which is particularly likely to attract savings is investment in new processes which will make something never made before or never made so cheaply. The discovery of such inventions is one of the mainsprings of increased demand, although it can be increased demand which stimulates the invention (see Chapter 1). But such discoveries are not devised at regular pace. Sometimes a number appear together; sometimes human ingenuity seems exhausted. One of the explanations of slower growth after 1873 has been found in such exhaustion. The major inventions of the first Industrial Revolution had been exploited almost to the full; those which would characterise the second had either not been made or were not yet ready for large-scale application.

A prominent aspect of the depression was the fall in prices. If 1870 is taken as the base year, the UK price index rose to 119 in 1873 after which it fell steadily till it reached 70 in 1896. This was an extension of a process which had been going on since 1818. A fall in prices is like the question whether a bottle is half-full or half-empty. To the producer it means a loss of income and can be a serious misfortune. But to the consumer (and all producers consume) it takes another and more welcome aspect, especially as Britain's money wages rose by 50 per cent between 1870 and 1900.

Such a steady fall in prices is a rare event in the history of the world and we must therefore look for some unusual factor to explain it. There can be little doubt that that factor is to be found in the unprecedented increase in productivity brought about by high investment, mechanisation and the introduction of new sources of power. In particular the transport revolution caused by railways, steamships and the telegraph meant that supplies could be drawn from areas which, although capable of producing more cheaply than anywhere else, had hitherto been inaccessible. The vastly larger market meant that economies of scale could be achieved in both production and distribution.

One of the most notable of these price-reducing developments was the starting-up of food production, and particularly cereals, on the prairies of North America and thereafter in South America, Australasia, Asia and Africa. A necessary preliminary to this was large-scale investment not only in trains and ships but in harbours, warehouses, agricultural machinery, farm buildings and the like. The savings for this were originally local; investment by the United Kingdom did not occur on any appreciable scale until the 1850s.[72] The results began to show at the end of the 1870s when foodstuffs started to come on to the European market at prices with which no local farmer could compete. In most countries landlords and/or peasants had enough political influence to secure tariff protection for themselves at the expense of the workers' cost of living. But in Britain the issue had been decided, largely on illusory calculations, at a period when the full nature of the longer term problem could not be foreseen, namely in 1846. The prophecies of doom made by the agricultural interest at the time of the Corn Law controversy at first appeared to have been unfounded; for thirty years English farmers diversified their products, increased their investment and improved their efficiency. As a result, they throve, although perhaps at the expense of landlords; the period 1850–75 has been called farming's 'Golden Age'.[73] But disaster, when it arrived, was unmistakable for those areas which concentrated on arable farming; producers of meat, vegetables and milk suffered less. Yet many landowners already derived an appreciable part of their incomes from industry and urban estates, while the Conservative Party already contained enough industrialists to ensure that for another fifty years neither party was going to be ready to modify the 1846 decision. In consequence the most striking feature of the depression in Britain was agricultural and it is significant that the social prestige (as distinct from the political power) of the landlords was still great enough for a process, which in fact benefited most of the population, to be regarded as a national misfortune. It is true that smaller tenant farmers, agricultural labourers and all those in country districts who depended for their livelihood on purchases by farms had a hard time of it. Irish growers of wheat and to a lesser extent meat also suffered from a decline in English demand and prices.

What was happening in agriculture was not without its parallel in industry, though in a less obtrusive way. It has been said that Britain, and more particularly the midlands, lost during the depression the position of world industrial leader.[74] Other countries, notably the United States and Germany, although (or to some extent because) starting later, began to take markets away. Growing competition increased the need for Britain to shift resources away from uses no longer economic into more profitable ones. This should be a continuous process but can become necessary at times on a wider scale than others. It always causes loss and discomfort to those who are going out of business. As the amount of loss and discomfort increases, so do the cries of pain. Thus the development added to the effect of depression at the moments when the various cyclical movements were reaching their troughs (see p. 102). All the same, Britain's trade was still growing – it doubled in terms of value between 1880 and 1914 – and in good times satisfaction with the expansion distracted attention from the fact that that of her rivals was growing faster.

One other development which occurred during the second half of the nineteenth century can conveniently be mentioned here, although not strictly a result of the depression. Britain's population began to pass the point at which by any conceivable means of farming and even in the best of harvests it could be adequately fed from home resources. By 1850 a quarter of Britain's bread was being imported and by the 1870s this had risen to over a half.[75] If the political balance had allowed tariffs to be imposed, thus increasing the return available to home farmers, those proportions could have been lowered. But unless the population had been prepared to live on little better than a diet of gruel, some food would still have had to be brought in from somewhere. What would have happened if at the crucial moment the supplies from outside Europe had not begun to arrive is an interesting speculation, although not perhaps a very profitable one since we cannot even be sure that, if the means of supporting the extra mouths had not existed, they would have come into being. Even if the farmers had fared better, the rest of the population would have fared worse. But a country which had to sell enough to pay for half her food and which brought that half from the other side of the oceans was giving considerable hostages to fortune. She had not only to be able to defend her supply lines to an extent that had been unnecessary in previous centuries but had also to keep her products competitive in design and price. Moreover it was not merely food which had to be imported but also all the other materials which she no longer possessed in sufficient quantities but which she needed if she was to produce competitive goods to pay for the food. And those materials in turn would need to be paid for. Yet as long as she had to produce goods capable of selling on world markets, she could not solve her problems merely by putting up tariff barriers against imports.

Was there then a 'Great Depression' or was the historian right who provocatively described it as a 'myth'?[76] Certainly a number of changes were in progress which resulted in some people becoming poorer than they had expected, at any rate for a time. With some justice it has been called a climacteric, which suggests that change was more drastic and permanent than usual. But the phenomenon was as largely psychological as economic. People had to revise their expectations. They found themselves in the grip of unexpected and uncomfortable developments and, although they could on the whole recognise the symptoms, they could not agree on the remedies because they could not establish, or differentiate between, all the various chains of causation. It is against this background that the remainder of Joseph Chamberlain's career needs to be studied and judged.

Notes to Chapter 4

1 F. H. Herrick, 'Origins of the National Liberal Federation', *The Journal of Modern History*, Vol. 17 (1945).
2 W. H. G. Armytage, *A. J. Mundella, 1825–1897* (1951), p. 167.
3 A. Briggs, *The History of Birmingham* (Oxford, 1952), Vol. 2, pp. 3, 68.
4 A. Briggs, *Victorian Cities* (1963), p. 196, quoting A. W. W. Dale, *Life of R. W. Dale* (1898).
5 E. Ll. Woodward, *The Age of Reform 1815–1870* (Oxford, 1938), p. 445.
6 Woodward, p. 445; G. Kitson Clark, *The Making of Victorian England* (1962), p. 103.
7 S. E. Finer, *The Life and Times of Sir Edwin Chadwick* (1952), p. 215.
8 Briggs, *Birmingham*, p. 75.
9 C. Green, 'Birmingham politics: the local basis of change', *Midland History*, Vol. 2 (1973).
10 N. M. Marris, *Joseph Chamberlain* (1900), p. 120.
11 Briggs, *Birmingham*, p. 81.
12 A. G. Gardiner, *The Life of Sir William Harcourt* (1923), Vol. 2, p. 608; Briggs, *Cities*, p. 219.
13 Chamberlain in House of Commons, 23 April 1877.
14 Briggs, *Cities*, p. 23.
15 J. L. Garvin, *The Life of Joseph Chamberlain* (1932), Vol. 1, p. 174.
16 Garvin (1934), Vol. 3, p. 50; W. Rubinstein, 'Wealth élites and class structure in Britain', *P and P* (August 1977).
17 *Journals of Queen Victoria* (1968), 30 July 1886.
18 House of Commons, 15 July 1867.
19 J. Kay-Shuttleworth, *Four Periods of Education* (1862), p. 231.
20 T. Weymss Reid, *The Life of W. E. Forster* (1888), Vol. 1, p. 488.
21 House of Commons, 17 February 1870.
22 G. Balfour, *The Educational Systems of Great Britain and Ireland* (Oxford, 1898), p. 16.
23 G. Sutherland, *Policy-making in Elementary Education 1870–95* (1973), p. 115.
24 K. Robbins, *John Bright* (1979), p. 215.
25 Garvin, Vol. 1, p. 113.
26 Garvin, Vol. 1, p. 117.
27 Speech at Stroud, March 1872.
28 Chamberlain to Morley, 23 March 1873, quoted by P. Fraser, *Joseph Chamberlain, Radicalism and Empire* (1966), p. 20.
29 Speech at Sheffield, 23 September 1873; C. W. Boyd, *Mr Chamberlain's Speeches* (1914), Vol. 1, p. 34.
30 J. Vincent, *The Foundation of the Liberal Party* (1976), p. 125.
31 T. Lloyd, *The General Election of 1880* (1968), p. 5.
32 Lloyd, p. 134.
33 Chamberlain to Morley, 12 August 1873, quoted by Garvin, Vol. 1, p. 161.
34 Letter in *The Examiner*, quoted by Garvin, Vol. 1, p. 222.
35 Chamberlain to Dilke, 10 October 1876, quoted by S. Gwynn and G. Tuckwell, *The Life of Sir Charles Dilke* (1917), Vol. 1, p. 210.
36 Vincent, p. 233.

37 Vincent, p. 123.
38 The *Fortnightly Review*, October 1874.
39 R. S. Watson, *The National Liberal Federation* (1907); p. 3.
40 D. Fraser, *Urban Politics in Victorian England* (Leicester, 1976), p. 139.
41 H. J. Hanham, *Elections and Party Management* (1959), p. 106.
42 C. M. Wakefield, *The Life of Thomas Attwood* (1885), p. 312.
43 Garvin, Vol. 1, pp. 254, 261.
44 Briggs, *Birmingham*, pp. 163–74; T. R. Tholfsen, 'The origins of the Birmingham Caucus', *HJ*, Vol. 2 (1959).
45 H. W. Crosskey, 'The Liberal Association and the 600 of Birmingham', *Macmillan's Magazine* (April 1877).
46 A. Ramm (ed.), *The Political Correspondence of Mr Gladstone and Lord Granville* (1952), Vol. 1, p. 38.
47 Herrick; Watson; B. McGill, 'Francis Schnadhorst and Liberal Party Organisation', *The Journal of Modern History*, Vol. 34 (1962).
48 Hanham, p. 140.
49 Until the Ballot Act, the earlier hours of polling had been used as a first round, at the end of which the candidates with the fewest votes retired.
50 Boyd, Vol. 1, p. 26.
51 Green, 'Birmingham politics'.
52 Lord Salisbury in *The Quarterly Review*, October 1872.
53 T. W. Moody and F. X. Martin, *The Course of Irish History* (Cork, 1967), p. 267.
54 J. Lee, *The Modernisation of Ireland* (Dublin, 1973), p. 163.
55 Lee, pp. 4–7.
56 Lee, p. 16; P. Solar and D. Dickson (eds), *Ireland and Scotland 1600–1850. Parallels and Contrasts in Economic and Social Development* (1984).
57 Lee, p. 35.
58 House of Commons, 8 April 1886.
59 P. Thompson, *Socialists, Liberals and Labour: the Struggle for London 1885–1914* (1967), pp. 25–7; J. L. and B. Hammond, *The Bleak Age* (1934), p. 37.
60 See examples given in R. Hyams, *Britain's Imperial Century 1815–1914* (1976), p. 88; see also Chamberlain at Belfast, 12 October 1887:

> When it is proposed to put a race which has shewn all the qualities of a dominant people, which has proved in the history of the world that it can justify the ascendancy which it has secured – when it is proposed to put that race under the other which, whatever its merits may be, has always failed in the qualities which compel success, I say that that is an attempt against nature, an attempt which all history and experience show must of necessity fail and can only lead to disaster and confusion. (Boyd, Vol. 1, p. 287.)

61 B. L. Solow, *The Land Question and the Irish Economy 1870–1903* (Harvard, 1971), p. 202.
62 O. Macdonough, *Early Victorian Government* (1977), p. 187; Lee, pp. 27–33.
63 Discussed by Lee and by Solow.
64 J. Morley, *The Life of Gladstone* (1903), Vol. 1, p. 383.
65 Garvin, Vol. 1, p. 90.
66 See Lee and Solow.
67 Lee, pp. 62, 165.
68 Hanham, pp. 180–7; M. Hurst, 'Ireland and the Ballot Act of 1872', *HJ*, Vol. 8 (1965).
69 R. Church, *The Great Victorian Boom* (1975), p. 52.
70 Garvin, Vol. 1, p. 219.
71 For a general discussion, see S. B. Saul, *The Myth of the Great Depression 1873–1896* (1969), which contains a bibliography; R. C. Floud, 'Britain 1860–1914: a survey' in R. Floud and D. McCloskey, *The Economic History of Britain since 1700* (Cambridge, 1981), Vol. 2; D. S. Landes, *The Unbound Prometheus* (Cambridge, 1969), ch. 5.
72 M. Edelstein, *Overseas Investment in the Age of High Imperialism* (New York, 1982), p. 3.
73 Church, pp. 28–30.

74 G. C. Allen, *The Industrial Development of Birmingham and the Black Country* (1929), p. 211.
75 P. Kennedy, *The Rise and Fall of British Naval Mastery* (1976), p. 200; F. M. L. Thompson, *English Landed Society in the Nineteenth Century* (1963), p. 242.
76 Saul, *The Myth of the Great Depression.*

5 'Radical Joe': 1880–85

Arrival in the Cabinet

The 1880 Election brought the Liberals a clear majority of fifty over the Conservatives and Home Rulers. They also won a comfortable lead in overall votes (1·8m. as against 1·4m. Conservatives) in a poll which rose by 35 per cent over 1874. On the other hand, a change of only 4054 votes in 72 marginal constituencies would have put them in a minority of 28 against the Conservatives and given the casting vote to the 63 Home Rulers. The decisive factor would therefore seem to have been the high turn-out.[1] Chamberlain claimed for the National Liberal Federation the credit for the victory on the ground that seats had been 'gained or retained' in 60 out of the 67 borough constituencies in which 'popular representative organisations on the Birmingham model' existed.[2]

The Federation had certainly helped to reduce the number of consti-tuencies with more than one Liberal candidate from 21 to 9, of which only one was lost. But whereas the Liberals captured some 100 seats from the Tories, in only 20 of these did the Federation have an affiliated organi-sation. Various minor issues went to help the Liberals. Thus the Irish in Britain voted for them after Disraeli described Home Rule as 'worse than pestilence and famine'. The onset of the depression must have told against the government even though few people thought it remediable by official action. But it was what a Tory described as the 'frantic ebullition of public excitement' in Midlothian[3] which had dominated the polls. No senior politician had ever before stumped the country with a series of speeches, interspersed with 'whistle-stops', as Gladstone did. Moreover he had incontestably produced a programme, although it was one stating the principles on which the nation and world should be governed rather than containing a list of concrete measures. His underlying message was that the people could and should be trusted. It was this vigour and this moral fervour rather than more thorough organisation which are likely to have spurred the party faithful into getting hesitant voters to the poll. On the other hand the distaste which the performance aroused among the well-bred, including the queen, was not negligible.[4]

The Liberal leadership however still rested formally with the men who had succeeded Gladstone in 1875, Granville in the Lords and Hartington in the Commons. Consequently the queen was acting not merely on her personal inclinations but also in accord with constitutional etiquette by sending first for them. But they had forfeited their chance of providing the next Liberal Prime Minister by refusing to oppose Disraeli's eastern policy firmly enough. Gladstone, by taking up the challenge, had cemented the alliance between himself, nonconformists and working men which had been kindled by his respect for their self-denial in the cause of freedom during the American Civil War.[5] To leave him outside the new government would have provoked a popular tempest and even if he had been willing to serve under someone else (as he was not), he could at any moment make the position of other leaders untenable by challenging their policy. The Whigs did not like to refuse him support, for fear of driving him into radical arms and ensuring that his ultimate successor would be a Radical; the Radicals preferred him to any other possible leader. Thus he could always restore discipline by threatening to resign. As his Private Secretary Edward Hamilton said, he was the sole man who could hold together the many sections of the Liberal Party. 'He impels the sluggish Whig and holds in check the impulsive Radical.'[6] But he could only do so by leaving them all in a state of chronic discontent.

The initial distribution of offices foreshadowed how the Cabinet would line up in future. Half the places in it went to Whig peers, a concession to the right which could only have been made by someone prepared to throw his own weight to the left. But at first Bright, who again became Chancellor of the Duchy of Lancaster, was the only Radical whose inclusion was contemplated. The exclusion of others was justified on a conveniently rediscovered principle, allegedly laid down (but not observed) by Peel, according to which experience in a junior office was an indispensable qualification for entry to the Cabinet.

After the early election returns were in, Chamberlain suggested to Dilke that both of them should refuse all offers unless both were given cabinet rank. As Dilke's claims were currently assumed to be stronger, this involved using a friend to give oneself a leg up. Dilke however thought it was opening mouths too wide and temporised. Chamberlain's next suggestion, made after the queen had reluctantly sent for Gladstone, was that whichever of them saw him first should say that they would both refuse to serve at all unless one was put in the Cabinet. Accordingly this was the line which Dilke took when Gladstone offered him the Under-Secretaryship at the Foreign Office and told him that Chamberlain could not expect more than the post of Financial Secretary to the Treasury.[7] The Prime Minister was thus faced with the choice between cold-shouldering both men or gratifying the ambition of one. Truculent threats by Chamberlain to Harcourt about the trouble they would stir up if left on the back benches made him reject the first course and decide Chamberlain to be the more dangerous of the two; Bright favoured him more and the queen disfavoured him a little less. He was accordingly made President of the Board of Trade. Hamilton commented that 'no doubt it was absolutely necessary to have in the Cabinet a representative of the extreme left but Chamberlain has neither from his parliamentary experience nor his party conduct deserved such a lift'.[8]

Dilke's friends thought that he had been hardly treated but the record of events disposes of any idea that Chamberlain outsmarted him. If the original proposal had been acted on, they might have done better – but they might equally have done worse. The curious may speculate on what would have happened if it had been Chamberlain who saw Gladstone first, since modesty demanded pressing the claims of one's friend rather than of oneself; as it was, he professed to have considered remaining content with the Treasury post so as to keep in line with his ally, only to have been dissuaded by Bright. But the discovery that two could play at the game of forcing themselves in where they were not wanted is unlikely to have endeared the younger player to the older.

'Mr G'

Gladstone and Lincoln, the two greatest Liberal statesmen to hold office during the Golden Age of that creed, were born in the same year 1809. But if the former had died, like the latter, at the age of 56, he would have left merely the reputation of an able Chancellor of the Exchequer who had completed the process of freeing British trade and had been a friend of Italian liberty. Even if he had retired from politics at 65, as he sought for a time to do, there would not have been much added to the popular record. But in fact he had at that stage a third of his public life ahead of him and the part moreover for which he, like Churchill and Adenauer, is chiefly remembered. Whereas most politicians, in growing older, become increasingly reconciled to things as they are, Gladstone moved steadily to the left. The man who had begun as a Tory sitting for a rotten borough, the man who had not attended the meeting at which the Liberal Party was founded (see p. 63) because he was still supporting a Tory Prime Minister, finally left office in protest against increased expenditure on armaments and against the refusal of his colleagues to reform the House of Lords.

Admittedly he was no conventional Liberal. Brought up as the evangelical son of a Tory Scot who had made a fortune out of trade in Liverpool and West Indian slave plantations, he became a high Anglican and married into the Whig landed aristocracy. 'Uncle William', said a niece in 1881, 'is in some respects the greatest Tory out' and instanced his refusal to have anything to do with the telephone, four years after Lord Salisbury had installed the instrument at Hatfield.[9] He held that 'contempt for Locke was the beginning of wisdom' and had no use for the French Revolution or its

111

spiritual forerunners. He found fault with Bentham for maintaining that the heart should be amended through the head, whereas Christianity held the opposite. He put it on record that his teachers (outside the Gospel and Homer) were Aristotle (the great systematiser), Augustine, Dante and Butler.[10] From them he learnt to judge political, financial and diplomatic issues in terms of morality and to look for the source of morality not in reason or self-interest but in self-abnegation before God. He was one of the numerous Victorians who managed to combine firm faith in freedom as an over-riding principle with an equally profound belief that human actions are continually over-ruled by a 'great governing agency'. 'Whereas many dreamed of the unity of mankind as the final triumph of the rights of man, he dreamed of it as the final triumph of the recognition of the common fatherhood of God.'[11] He sought to reconcile the spirit of freedom with that of order, to see right as relative and duty as reciprocal. He once said that the decline of reverence meant a decline of liberty and a lack of reverence was one of his charges against Chamberlain.[12]

But it is misleading to speak of him, without qualification, as 'permeated to his innermost fibre with a veneration for all ancient, established things'.[13] 'When', he asked in 1877,' did the Upper Ten thousand ever lead the attack in the cause of humanity?'[14] In 1879 he 'freely owned that compulsory expropriation was a thing which for an adequate public object was itself admirable'.[15] The Irish Land Act of 1881 has been seen as the first step in a popular attack on property[16] and in 1885 Gladstone claimed for the legislature 'an undoubted title to expropriate every landlord if it was required for the common good'. In the same year he set down among his 'most determined foes' the aristocracy, the Established Churches, the wealth and rank of the country. In 1886 he said that for 60 years 'the Classes' had fought on the wrong side but had in the end always been beaten by a power difficult to marshal yet resistless when marshalled – the spirit of the nation. In 1887 he told a Swansea audience that the trade unions had 'been productive of an enormous balance of good' and in September 1891 said that a substantial increase in labour representation was not only desirable but in the highest degree urgent.[17] For all his aversion to 'Construction' and to 'what in the days of Sir Robert Peel was universally regarded with misgiving as Socialism' (but that was in a letter reassuring the queen!),[18] he came in the end to accept the Newcastle Programme of 1892. Being far from impervious to his surroundings, the break which Home Rule brought with the *bien pensants* consummated the love affair with the workers dating from the American Civil War and his challenge to Disraeli's policy of 'brag'; as so often in love affairs, each party was under some illusion as to what the other was really like. But his new companions caused him to discover implications which had hitherto gone unperceived.

He had learnt at Oxford to distinguish with scrupulous care between propositions similar but not identical.[19] His keen and wide-ranging intellect enabled him to see interconnections between apparently distinct subjects, while his ability to grasp quickly the arguments for or against any proposal led to convoluted sentences which his enemies regarded as deliberated equivocations and his sympathisers as the outward sign of a supremely honest man wrestling with his conscience.[20] But these abilities led him, like many others, quite genuinely to believe that his starting-point had been reason rather than an emotionally-laden sense of values. 'He had a tendency to persuade himself, quite unconsciously, that the course which he desired to take was the course which public interest dictated. His acuteness soon found reasons for that course; the warmth of his emotions enforced the reasons. It was a dangerous tendency but it does not impeach his honesty of purpose.'[21]

His wife enjoined on his biographer to remember that he had two sides – one impetuous, impatient, unrestrainable, the other all self-control. Aberdeen said he was eager and impulsive, with no perspective in his views; Argyll that on any question in which he was keenly interested, he would not even entertain an opposing thought. 'Under such circumstances, his mind was essentially fanatical.' Selborne said that he could hardly be brought to interest himself at all in matters on which he was not carried away but that when he was carried away, he did not sympathise or take counsel with those whose point of view was different from his own.[22] It was not merely in his old age that he was in a hurry; he was no sooner seized with an idea than he rushed to put it into practice. His vent for aggressiveness was unsurpassed by any contemporary statesman.[23] But his deep sense of sin made him acutely aware of these weaknesses and he imposed on himself in secret a masochistic discipline to keep his strong emotions within bounds. He was given to constant introspection. He could be fascinating company; Clarendon, who did not like him but was given to bestowing nicknames, chose for him that of 'Merrypebble'.[24]

One of his constant endeavours in politics was to induce individuals, parties and even nations to rise above narrow self-interest, above a system dominated by considerations of power, prudence and tactical advantage, to a moral world based on mutual respect and trust. 'Common action', he once said, 'is fatal to selfish aims. Common action means common objects and the only objects for which you can unite all the Powers of Europe are objects connected with the common good of them all.'[25] He would have fervently endorsed the thesis that the actions of states should be decided by the same rules of morality as should govern the conduct of individuals. Disregard of this principle was, in his view, Disraeli's great sin.

He was as a result little interested in problems of organisation, in spite of being intensely methodical in his private life. He called party 'a secondary and subordinate instrument for securing the public good'.[26] He preferred to rely on moral authority as a means of securing united action and believed that, for support to have any value, it must spring from conviction rather than coercion.[27] He told Granville that the vital principle of the Liberal Party was action and prided himself on his ability to judge when a question was ripe for action.[28] He would have agreed, had he known of it, with the remark of his great antithesis Bismarck that a statesman 'must always be on the watch to see God striding through history and then clasp hold of the corner of his garment'.[29] The way to hold a party together was not to draw up a programme since the wider the range of policies proposed in it, the more remote became the prospect of agreement. The Liberal Party ought to be an instrument for the attainment of great ends and it was the process of fighting for such ends which generated unity. In setting them he saw no particular need to consult his followers beforehand, although they might have to be educated. Followers had obligations as well as leaders and he expected those obligations to be realised. Such was his stature that they often were.

Not that his judgment about the rightness of events was infallible. A case in point was his decision to fight the 1874 election on the issue of abolishing income tax (because he disliked the idea of requiring free citizens to reveal details about their sources of income).[30] After the Liberal defeat Chamberlain publicly described his leader's manifesto as 'the meanest public document that has ever proceeded from a statesman of the first rank',[31] and said that 'advanced Liberals' would receive Gladstone's decision to retire 'with comparative equanimity' (see p. 88). When Gladstone published a pamphlet condemning the course which the Vatican was following under Pius IX as 'declining to acknowledge the high place assigned to liberty in the counsels of Providence',[32] Chamberlain commented that 'an ex-Minister of the first rank who devotes his leisure to a critical examination of the querulousness of an aged priest is hardly in sympathy with the robust commonsense of English Liberalism'. This was less than perceptive. Whereas English Liberalism may have had other foundations for its creed as well as the Christian religion, Gladstone did not, so that it was a matter of profound concern for him to find the spiritual descendant of St Peter weakening rather than strengthening the moral unity of the world. Such concern however was unlikely to be understood by a lapsed Unitarian.

After his visit to Birmingham in 1877, Gladstone wrote of Chamberlain as 'a man worth watching and studying; of strong self-consciousness under most pleasing manners and I should think great tenacity of purpose, expecting to play an historical part and probably destined to it'.[33] But they had not worked as colleagues for long before a mutual antipathy grew up behind a screen of effusive courtesy. The one has been well said to have chiefly feared the abuse of power, the other the neglect of problems. Gladstone found himself repeatedly having to defend remarks and actions by the younger man which had provoked remonstrances from the queen or members of the Cabinet. Chamberlain, without showing much gratitude, resented Gladstone's failure to back him up more strongly, especially as on many subjects they stood closer to one another than they did to most other ministers (except Bright, who again proved ineffective in office). The importance which Chamberlain attached to party did not extend to the need for holding it together and he was insensitive to many of the conventions which had grown up about correct ministerial behaviour. One practice to which the Prime Minister and most of his colleagues took particular exception was the way in which Chamberlain and Dilke leaked to journalists details of what went on in the Cabinet room, with a view to mobilising public opinion on their side. While this had been done on a small scale in the past, was not done at the time as often as was suspected and was to be done on a much more extensive scale in the future, the extension was big enough to shock those who regarded the keeping of confidences as an important element in public life. The emotional elements in the characters of both men made them headstrong, so that each easily put up the back of the other without intending to do so.

This mutual antipathy of two men who should have worked together was important for the future of British politics. By 1874 traditional Liberalism was beginning to suffer from the effects of success. Most of the essential objectives had been achieved and were even being carried over by the middle classes into the opposite camp as elements in society which were to be conserved. Those which remained – manhood suffrage, free and compulsory education, disestablishment, local option and the like – were regarded as important by small groups only and, as Chamberlain said, were hardly the cries by which elections were won. The natural development would have been for a 'new Liberalism' to lose its fear of the state which it had captured and supplement liberty by equality in a programme which included such things as the Eight Hours Bill, old-age pensions, social insurance, payment of members and votes for women – causes which might appeal to the working classes on whom the party would have to depend more and more for votes. Chamberlain could have been the natural leader for such a course; Gladstone could not, because he either had little sympathy for the aims in question or was actively hostile to them.

Yet it was Gladstone who frustrated the trend by discovering and forcing into prominence two issues which were clearly in the old tradition – 'anti-Beaconsfieldism' (or the role of morality in foreign affairs) and justice for Ireland. To achieve them in the teeth of opposition, he used his moral authority to bring them to the centre of the political stage and went on dominating it for far longer than anyone could have reasonably expected. On neither did Chamberlain prove to be a Liberal in the true sense and on the second he preferred splitting the party and driving it into the wilderness for twenty years, perhaps rendering inevitable its subsequent withering, besides forfeiting his own chance of becoming Prime Minister. Laurence Housman's perception was just when he made Mrs Gladstone say in 1894 that 'no one except Mr Gladstone could have kept Mr Chamberlain from leading the Liberal Party. And now he never will.'[34] The question one is bound to ask is how far Gladstone by his choice of policy brought to light elements in Chamberlain's make-up which were always there or how far Chamberlain allowed personal animosity towards Gladstone to tempt him into adopting antagonistic political attitudes which would not otherwise have been his.

Ireland 1880–83

When the new Parliament met in May, eager to start reforming, the only Bill presented to it was one authorising tenants to shoot rabbits. This, although assuaging the Radical thirst for landlord-bashing and outraging Tory notions about freedom of contract, was not much to be going on with. But Gladstone had so little anticipated taking office that nothing else was ready. The House of Commons thereupon got bogged down in the controversy over the right of the atheist Bradlaugh to take his seat without involving the Almighty, while the government occupied itself with liquidating 'Beaconsfieldism' in the Balkans and Afghanistan. Typical ignorance of Ireland suggested that her affairs could wait and Disraeli's warning that they should not went unheeded. In fact the political situation there was deteriorating in the wake of the economic. The arrival of grain from across the seas (see p. 104) had not merely reduced the amount which the English would buy from Ireland and the price which they would pay for it but was also reducing the ability of English farmers to employ Irish migrants at harvest time. On top of this came two sodden summers followed by one in which the rain broke all records; the quantity and value of the potato crop fell to a quarter of what it had been. Few tenants could pay their full rent; many could pay no rent at all. The menace of eviction was added to the imminence of starvation. The basic unviability of Irish agriculture was reaffirmed.[35]

In the spring of 1879 the ex-Fenian Michael Davitt suggested to the despairing tenants of his native Mayo the idea of a mass refusal to pay rents. Parnell, realising that he must take control of the movement or lose control of the situation, helped to found and then assumed the presidency of the Land League. Its objects were to protect tenants from excessive rents

116

as well as from eviction and in the longer term to make them owners of their farms by expropriating landlords. Butt had died four months earlier, having already lost the allegiance of the Irish MPs by being a gentleman first and an Irishman second and as a result failing to win concessions at Westminster. Parnell, chosen unexpectedly to succeed him, had already made clear his view that 'England respects nothing but power' and that 'the Irish would never get anything from England unless they trod on her toes'.[36] The 1880 election had brought into Parliament 63 members who regarded themselves as 'Home Rulers'; they were more inclined to work as a team than was usual in those days.[37] The new leader thus possessed the means of making himself felt both outside and inside Parliament – precisely the combination which, as has been repeatedly shewn, is needed to secure results in British politics.

In so far as the new Cabinet did give attention to Ireland, its intentions were admirable. It decided to try dispensing with special coercive measures when the Tory Peace Preservation Act expired five weeks after the Liberals took office. The Cabinet laid down, at the prompting of Gladstone, Bright and Chamberlain, that conciliation must have priority over repression. But a second bite at the cherry of Irish land, if it was to have a chance of being more successful that the first, would take time to prepare and the problem of bridging the interval was made all the more awkward when one of Parnell's lieutenants brought in a Bill requiring compensation for all tenants evicted because they could not pay their rents. The government, to save face, took it over and, although the Irish MPs thereupon turned against it, it got through the House of Commons by the end of July. Whigs and Tories in the House of Lords then combined to throw it out by 282 to 51. The wise course for a government which wished to win Irish confidence would have been to have broken into the parliamentary recess (which then lasted from September to January) and re-introduce the Bill in an emergency session. But Gladstone was ill and Chamberlain found himself a lone voice in urging this course. The other ministers either shrank from a constitutional clash or did not know a powder barrel when they saw one.

Ireland replied with a crop of violence, financed from America. Parnell, afraid of things going too far, urged his countrymen to 'put into a sort of moral Coventry' anyone who took over a farm from which the previous tenant had been evicted. Boycott, the name of an early victim, was soon applied to the practice by a priest who found his flock unable to 'wrap their tongues round "ostracisation"'.[38] And although one of the attractions of the method to the Irish leaders was that, being non-violent, it did not involve breaking the law (as the failure of an ill-judged prosecution soon showed), there were those among the rank and file who had no intention of leaving violence out. Gladstone had thought that, in making Forster

Chief Secretary for Ireland, he had chosen a large-hearted and capable man whose moderation could be relied on. But Forster's officials in Dublin won him over to the false but persistent theory that the agitation was the work of a few extremists who did not have the people behind them and could therefore be halted if stamped on firmly enough. In November Chamberlain found himself once again crossing swords with his old opponent over the latter's demand for a new Coercion Act, including the suspension of *habeas corpus*. Chamberlain compared this to firing a rifle at a swarm of gnats and insisted on the need to amend the Land Act which, in the exceptional circumstances of the country, had worked unjustly.[39] By a threat of resignation and with Gladstone's support, he got a decision postponed for two months but then, as the situation grew no better, reluctantly gave in. He would have liked this suspension to have been matched by that of a landlord's power to evict but the Cabinet thought it hopeless to put such a proposal to the House of Lords. He showed no interest in Gladstone's own view that the right solution was to enforce the existing law more stringently rather than to amend it.

The net result was that a Protection of Person and Property Bill and an Arms Bill got precedence over the new Land Bill, to the detriment of the latter's impact. The government's priorities had by degrees been reversed, without a deliberate decision to that effect ever having been taken. Had an opportunity for reconciliation been missed? The answer depends on the further question as to whether the aims of the Irish inside and outside Parliament were such that the government's measure of conciliation could have satisfied them and to this the answer is almost certainly 'No'. Parnell had been primarily interested in the land problem as a means of increasing support for his political demands believing, as he said publicly in 1879, that 'if we had the farmers the owners of the soil tomorrow, we would not be long in getting an Irish Parliament'.[40] He had further said that 'Home Rule would necessarily entail the repeal of the Union'.[41] The Irish aim was freedom from English rule and they saw no reason why Gladstone should not give them what he made such a fuss about obtaining for the Bulgarians from the Turks.

Although Chamberlain admitted that the objects of the Land League were not in themselves improper, he saw clearly where the Irish wanted to go and the point at which he intended to stop them:[42]

> Mr Parnell and those who follow him have never concealed the fact that their chief object is not removal of grievances but the separation of Ireland from England . . . How can we satisfy these men? . . . Our object is not the same as theirs . . . We want to bind the Irish people to this country in . . . cordial union.

It is impossible to concede the present demands of the Irish party – national independence cannot be given to Ireland.

I say to Ireland what the Republicans said to the Southern States, 'The Union must be preserved. You cannot and you shall not destroy it. Within these limits there is nothing you may not ask and hope to obtain.'

And he was the minister prepared to go furthest in conciliation.

Not content with making trouble in Ireland, the Irish members were making trouble at Westminster. In 1875 the ex-Fenian Biggar had had the idea of exploiting for the purpose of holding up business all the procedural provisions which Parliament had devised over the centuries to ensure free speech. This abuse of liberty was now intensified and contributed not a little to the failure of the second Gladstone government to fulfill the hopes which English Liberals had set on it. By spinning out a debate on the Protection Bill for forty-one hours, they forced the House to adopt for the first time a procedure for curtailing discussion. Next day thirty-six members were suspended in succession for protesting against the Home Secretary's action in cancelling Michael Davitt's release on parole. The extremists wanted to use this as the occasion for quitting Parliament altogether and declaring a 'No Rent' campaign. The moderates wanted to remain until the Land Bill was introduced, vote for it on Second Reading and seek to strengthen it in committee. Parnell decided that, as a compromise, they should leave in a body before the vote on Second Reading and then return to propose amendments. But only ten of his followers acted on his orders.

Gladstone, in spite of being Chancellor as well as Prime Minister, found time to draft the new Land Bill and added to its complications by casting it as amendments to the old Act, so as to suggest that no new policies were involved. It dealt with all the three topics, fair rent, free sale and fixed tenure, which the Land League had identified and a Royal Commission just reaffirmed, misleadingly, as the main things wrong with Irish agriculture. But the only part of it which had much effect was that entitling tenants (and landlords) to apply to a court to fix a fair rent, which was then to remain unaltered for fifteen years (thereby, as it turned out, disadvantaging tenants since the price of land went down). Nothing was done for 150,000 leaseholders or for the 130,000 tenants who were too poor to pay off the arrears which had accumulated; three-fifths of the farmers in Connacht did not qualify for consideration. The schemes proposed by Chamberlain and Bright to enable tenants to buy their land (described by Gladstone as 'wild') were so watered down that a mere 733 took advantage of them. The House of Lords had been sobered by the reaction to their previous intransigence and contented themselves with one relatively minor amendment. The Act transferred from tenant to landlord some of the loss being made on Ireland's farms but did little to reduce it.[43]

Once the Bill was law, Parnell proposed that the adequacy of its provisions should be tested by having selected cases brought before the courts – something which he could not have prevented even if he had tried. He excused himself to the extremists by saying that the cases chosen would be ones which the courts would be bound to reject, thereby discrediting themselves. He further allowed himself to be so carried away by the heady atmosphere of Cork as to say that 'those who want to preserve even the golden link of the Crown must see to it that that shall be the only link connecting the two countries' and to argue that Irish rents needed to be cut from £17m. to £3m.[44] This was too much for Gladstone who, like many Radicals, had been riled by the Irish refusal to show any appreciation of the considerable concessions which in his view had been made to them (concessions which the Irish of course regarded as far less than they deserved). In a speech at Leeds he castigated not only Parnell for trying to sabotage the Act but also those Irish moderates who failed to back the authorities in suppressing terrorism. 'If it were to come to a clash in Ireland between law and sheer lawlessness, the resources of civilisation against its enemies are not exhausted.' Parnell's reply was that Gladstone did not have it in his power to trample on the aspirations and rights of the Irish people without moral force behind him.[45]

By this time the tenants were flocking to the courts which had been left to decide for themselves what constituted a fair rent; they proved to interpret it as involving a cut on average of 20 per cent.[46] The Land League began to lose ground and the government might have been better advised to leave well alone. Parnell's speeches look like the trailing of a coat in the hope of provoking something which could be presented as a new 'outrage'. Some have even suggested that he wanted to get himself locked up as the only way to stop himself from seeing Kitty O'Shea and preventing his infatuation for her from becoming public knowledge. But by this time all the doves in the Cabinet had become allergic to olive branches. Bright had been soured by obstruction and agrarian violence. Chamberlain, although still uneasy, was not prepared to say that 'the refusal of demands for No Rent and Separation' constituted a grievance. 'We are in a state of war and I will use every conceivable means to come out victorious.'[47] So, when Forster insisted on lodging Parnell and four comrades in Kilmainham jail for incitement to crime, none of his colleagues gainsaid him. When the prisoners called for all rents to be withheld, the Land League was declared illegal and lost even more of its influence. But, as Parnell had foretold, the secret societies flourished instead. 'Captain Moonlight' took over.[48]

Prisons however are not good places from which to conduct parliamentary campaigns – or love affairs. By the spring the member for Meath
was finding his enforced inaction irksome. In April 1882 a nephew's death
in Paris gave him an excuse for getting released on parole. He broke his
journey to the funeral in order to see not only his Kitty but also her
husband. That 'gentlemanly adventurer'[49] was induced to write to Mr
Gladstone, not for the first time, and outline conditions which might cause
outrages to decline in Ireland and obstruction at Westminster. The Prime
Minister played this delivery with a very straight bat, sending it on to
Forster, whose opinion was unfavourable. But two days later, without
waiting for an answer, O'Shea sent a copy to Chamberlain with a covering
letter which apostrophised him as 'a Minister without political pedantry'
(or in other words somebody less likely to play with a straight bat). The
President of the Board of Trade had of course no direct responsibility for
Ireland but the politician holding that post was on the look out for a way of
mending his fences with the radical wing of his party. Accordingly,
instead of consulting the Prime Minister forthwith, Chamberlain replied
in terms calculated to encourage further discussion, albeit with a hint that a
spirit of conciliation would be needed on more than one side.

Once he had created the opening, he asked Gladstone for authority to
explore it; not only did he receive this but Forster authorised him to offer
an extension of Parnell's parole. Parnell was too wary an operator to put
himself in the wrong with his associates by giving priority to his own
comfort but, before re-entering jail, he settled with O'Shea the terms to be
conveyed to Chamberlain and, in case O'Shea were to introduce any
variants of his own, wrote a letter in much the same terms to a novelist MP
Justin McCarthy. (Another Irish MP on the very same day put a third
version to Gladstone's son Herbert.)

The concessions which the Irish were demanding through this plethora
of channels were things which Chamberlain had already failed to talk the
Cabinet into accepting, namely an extension of the Land Act to leaseholders and some release of impecunious tenants from their arrears. The
chances of his prevailing would increase if he could demonstrate that a
favourable Irish reaction was not just a hope but a promise. What was not
clear was whether the *quid pro quo* offered by the Irish was merely an
assurance that such concessions would improve the atmosphere or an
undertaking that they themselves would actively help to improve it by
encouraging well-off tenants to pay up. What Forster wanted before
agreeing to release the prisoners was a public affirmation that they would
not revert to their agitation against the law and Chamberlain encouraged
O'Shea to visit an unwelcoming Parnell in prison in the hope of extracting
this. All he got back was a 'Private and Confidential' letter expressing a
belief that a settlement on arrears (on which ministers had by then decided)

would enable the Irish leaders to stop outrages, while further action over leaseholders, tenure and land would constitute 'a practical settlement of the Question and enable us to co-operate cordially for the future with the Liberal Party in forwarding Liberal principles and measures of general reform'.[50] The Cabinet, judging it to be adequate, agreed to release Parnell and his henchmen, whereupon Forster, judging otherwise, resigned.

Many people expected his successor to be Chamberlain, the advocate of the policy which the Cabinet had accepted. Instead Gladstone appointed Lord Frederick Cavendish, his nephew by marriage and Hartington's brother who, while Financial Secretary, had worked out a plan for land purchase. A few days earlier the resignation of the Viceroy Lord Cowper had been announced, along with the appointment of Lord Spencer in his place. Spencer had already been Viceroy from 1868 to 1874 and since 1880 had been Lord President of the Council; he was to keep his seat in the Cabinet. Only for one month (January–February 1886) between 1800 and 1919 were the Viceroy and Chief Secretary both members of the Cabinet and, if the experiment had been tried for longer, awkward questions must have arisen as to where responsibility for policy towards Ireland lay. Gladstone later described Forster as 'a very impracticable man in a position of great responsibility'; the impression had been gaining ground that the strain of his job had been telling on his judgment and that he was glad to have a pretext for escape.[51] The Spencer appointment may have been intended as a step towards his supersession; Lord Frederick was not given Cabinet rank.

Gladstone afterwards denied ever having been aware of Chamberlain's desire for the job and Chamberlain himself went on record as favouring William Shaw, a moderate Home Ruler who had been Parnell's rival for the leadership after Butt's death. But there is evidence that Chamberlain was not overlooked as a possibility and the inference must be that he was considered unsuitable.[52] Reasons for such a view are not hard to guess. He had already circulated to his colleagues a paper sketching what he thought should be done; in addition to the items asked for by Parnell, it included an inquiry into the condition of Irish labourers and an extensive programme of public works. He made clear to his friends that, if he went to Ireland, he must have his own way there and would set out to 'smash the system', i.e. override or remove the permanent officials in Dublin who were widely and with justice regarded as a major obstacle to conciliation.[53] If this did not bring on a conflict with Spencer, it would certainly do so with the Whig wing of the Cabinet. Gladstone had reason for fearing that with Chamberlain he would be pushed further and faster than he judged politically opportune. Hamilton said that Chamberlain's appointment would 'have struck terror among the would-be law-abiding Irish people – they would have thought the game was over and would have thrown up the sponge'.[54]

The sequel is notorious. On the afternoon of the day on which Lord
Frederick arrived in Dublin, he was murdered in Phoenix Park along with
the chief permanent official. The hatreds generated by the past intervened
to blight the hopes of the present. Again the post of Chief Secretary had to
be filled and in spite (or perhaps because) of popular demands for
retribution, Gladstone decided to fill it with a Radical – although still not
with Chamberlain. Instead it was offered without a seat in the Cabinet to
Dilke who, on those terms and against Chamberlain's advice, refused it; it
then went to George Otto Trevelyan, Macaulay's nephew (who a year
later asked to join the Cabinet and was refused).

A new Crimes Bill, even tougher than the one which the Cabinet had
been already contemplating, was brought in and, after twenty-four days
of argument, passed; only then did the Arrears Bill receive consideration.
Chamberlain tried to get the new powers limited to something which the
Irish MPs could accept but, although Gladstone was sympathetic, the
majority of ministers and the temper of all classes in England were against
him. Parnell did not help when, in giving to the House his version of the
events which had led to his release, he used a text which – perhaps without
his realising it – left out a vital sentence from the letter forming the basis of
the negotiation. Forster thrust the full text into O'Shea's hand and made
him read it then and there. The impression was strengthened that Parnell
had been hand-in-glove with the secret societies (an impression which
recent evidence shows to have had something behind it)[55] and that the
Irish were a pack of rascals who had exploited Chamberlain's naïve
benevolence. To make matters worse, it was about this time that Harcourt, as Home Secretary, told ministers about Parnell's relations with
Mrs O'Shea. He and other hawks in the Cabinet took the view that Parnell
was neither trustworthy nor influential enough to have concessions made
to him in the hope of strengthening his hand against his own hard-liners;
this impression was reinforced when details came out about the way the
Phoenix Park murders had been planned. As it turned out, Ireland and the
Irish in Parliament were, for various reasons, entering on a period of
relative quiescence; falling prices were being matched by reduced rents
and it was the turn of landlords rather than tenants to complain. The
members of the Cabinet, with much else on their minds, took the calm as a
sign that their double policy had been successful and were at a loss for ideas
about what to do next.[56]

If Chamberlain had been Chief Secretary there would have been action
of some sort, whatever the consequence. He told Trevelyan to spend
£50m., 'It does not matter on what'.[57] Again one has to ask whether an
opportunity was not missed by the refusal to let the apprentice try his hand
at sorcery. Once again the answer depends on an estimate of the readiness
of each side to modify their views. Undoubtedly Chamberlain's measures

would have improved the atmosphere in Dublin, if not in Downing Street or Belfast. But it is hard to believe that the Irish would have stayed content with anything less than what came to be known as 'Dominion status', which he had already said firmly that he would not grant. But would the actual experience of governing Ireland have modified the firmness of his opposition, as is said to have happened with Spencer? Things might have been different if he had approached the question gradually, as a result of reflection on personal experience, instead of having it presented to him by someone with whom he was temperamentally out of sympathy.

There is some evidence that his mind was not as rigidly closed at this stage as it later became. He had expressed sympathy for Butt's scheme of federation in 1874. In 1880 he had advocated an extended franchise for Ireland and an assembly in Dublin. Early in 1881 he told Hartington that he believed the time to have passed when Ireland could be ruled by force.[58]

In January 1884 Derby was to record him as admitting[59]

to almost universal hatred of England [in Ireland]; thinks it may die out, as a similar feeling in Scotland has done; he seemed to me to admit that a federal union is practically impossible and that federation is only a step towards separation. He did not say in so many words that he was ready to accept separation as a possible solution but implied it by arguing that, after all, the danger which could arise from Ireland being free was rather imaginary than real; that the Irish could do us no harm, 'a miserable little island at a few hours distance'; but he seemed to me to ignore the possibilities of a French or American alliance.

Foreign Affairs 1880–85

In foreign affairs, the second Gladstone ministry set out to fulfil the promises made by their leader in Midlothian and to put the policy of their predecessors into reverse. They were however to find that the most they could do was to alter the method of application; the ends remained the same because they were based on a principle which no British leader in the nineteenth century was prepared to challenge or reverse (and which still awaits the sceptical historian to balance burdens against profits). This principle was that at all costs Britain must maintain her position in India and therefore her ability to move men, goods and money freely to and from India. Not only was Britain's prosperity still thought to be inseparably connected with the possession of her Indian empire (as it undoubtedly had been in the past). Gladstone, who wrote in 1877 that India did not add to but took away from Britain's military strength, saw the need for her to keep up her position in the sub-continent as 'a capital demand upon her national honour'.[60] The country could not be left to anarchy until a reliable substitute for British rule had been gradually built up. Therefore although Liberals could substitute a stationary policy for a forward one, as by withdrawing from Afghanistan or coercing instead of supporting Turkey, they could not remain indifferent to the safety of the Suez Canal or Cape Town – 'perhaps the most important strategical position in the world in the age of sea power'[61] – or allow the Cape or Egypt to come under the control of any government which might be indifferent or hostile. Indeed Gladstone's own policy of weakening Turkey made Egypt more vital than ever.

Gladstone recognised that Britain's position in India had little moral justification. 'It came to us through the Company, and after proceedings which will not bear being scrutinised and which would not be tolerated nowadays.'[62] But since he could not liquidate the past, he tried to live it down by pursuing a Liberal policy over the consequences in the present and over Egypt in particular. There he adopted a sympathetic attitude towards other interested parties, such as the French and the Egyptians, seeking to agree rather than to dictate. He repeatedly expressed his desire to find and apply 'the public law of Europe'. In line with the outlook already described (see p. 113), he believed that, when the interests of Great Powers conflicted, solutions should be reached by discussion between them in a Concert of Europe, a sort of League of Nations in embryo. But if the Concert of Europe had ever been more than a situation in which no power was able to predominate over the others and no formal alliances existed, it had been brought to an end by the creation of the German empire, an over-strong power at the centre of the continent. Bismarck, to whom Europe meant 'a lot of old men in a hot room',[63] had brought the Second Reich into existence by methods which earned for it the implacable hostility of France. As a result he could not afford to give that country any opportunity of acquiring an ally. It therefore suited him for Britain to be on bad terms with both France and Russia, since all three powers would then be more inclined to seek German support and be less likely to ally against Germany. He preferred a Europe out of concert and encouraged France to be awkward in Egypt while he extracted concessions from Britain as the price of German support. Gladstone incorporated all that he disliked.

The French threw themselves with alacrity into the part assigned to them. What exactly they were trying to do in Egypt is impossible to say because the instability of Third Republic governments made it hard for them to go on doing the same thing for long. Their desire to protect the interests of the bondholders inclined them to intervention. The unwillingness to let Britain establish herself inclined them against it. Having taken a lead in imposing control over Egyptian finances, and thereby provoked a nationalist anti-European rising, they backed out when the show-down came and even managed to make British ministers suspect them of trying to do a deal with the rebels. By refusing to join in re-establishing order themselves and refusing to accept any international arrangement for doing so, they ended by leaving the British with a stark choice between acting alone and seeing Egypt dissolve into anarchy. Yet the predominant position which Britain thereby acquired in Egypt was for the next twenty years to be a grievance keeping France and Britain apart.

A further problem lay in the inadequacy of British Liberal doctrine about self-government. Profoundly satisfied with the system which they had evolved for themselves in an exceptional historical and geographical environment spread over a millennium, British political thinkers accepted too easily the idea that an institutional solution had been discovered to all the problems of organising human beings in society and that all would be well if peoples could be set free to govern themselves on a basis of national self-determination. This view had of course in its favour the undoubted fact that industrialisation of an economy leads of necessity to the modernisation of the society in which it occurs; workers cannot be ruled as if they are still serfs. But unless a pre-industrial society has evolved a relatively high degree of integration and a sense of moral responsibility, a grant to the public of a voice in their government is apt to result in dissension and corruption. It was over two thousand years since Egypt had been a model among pre-industrial societies. Turkish rule had done harm rather than good while exposure to open-market investment by European profit seekers had brought a veneer of modernisation without really changing the infrastructure:[64]

> The capital invested was not producing enough new wealth to cover its cost. European bankers who charged the Khedive high rates of interest were partly to blame; but the vices of oriental administration played their part in bringing on the eventual disaster. Immense sums were expended on unproductive works after the manner of the East or on productive works carried out in the wrong way or too soon.

Whether such a society could ever learn to rule itself democratically was questionable; what was not was that the process of inculcating the necessary attitudes would be lengthy. Yet when at last the British government lost patience and decided to plunge in on its own, it excused itself to its followers as well as to the rest of the world by promising to come out again quickly. It would stay only as long as was necessary to restore order and set the indigenous government on a sound basis. Its failure to realise how long that meant was not just a matter of political

126

convenience but also the result of misplaced idealism. Gladstone said in 1884 that[65]

> the British task in Egypt is one which we are executing not alone on our own behalf but on behalf I may say of civilised mankind. We undertook it with the approval of the Powers of Europe – the highest and most authentic organ of modern civilisation! But having under- taken it at their valuation, or with their concurrence, we must fulfil it as we received it from them.

Such a claim to be performing a duty made withdrawal all the harder. Yet it was considerations of power and not of duty which really kept Britain in Egypt. If she withdrew and anarchy resulted, another country might acquire control not only of the Nile but also of the Canal. And there was always a lurking doubt whether an independent Egyptian government would pay adequate regard to vital British interests.

If on one of the two main routes to India British Liberals were faced by the phenomenon of a pre-industrial civilisation in decay, on the other, as luck would have it, they encountered the phenomenon of a vigorous agrarian society convinced that its chances of survival depended on the exclusion of Liberal ideas.

> The Boers fought for the right to live and govern the Transvaal according to the ideas of rough farmers untrammelled by British ideas of progress or the rights of man or of philanthropy or humani- tarianism.[66]

But paradoxically they, like the British, took advantage of the Liberal belief in self-government and made it the basis for their claim to be left alone. In the British reaction, moral disapproval of the idea of ruling people against their will combined with lively appreciation of the diffi- culty of doing so. Derby, as Colonial Secretary, spoke for most of the Cabinet when he said, 'We do not want another Ireland in South Africa'.[67]

At first sight compromise might seem to have been easy. To render secure the basic route to India, Cape Town was what the British had to hold. Why need they concern themselves with what was happening in the hinterland 1,000 miles to the north? Derby's predecessor Kimberley however maintained it 'an entire delusion to imagine that we could hold Cape Town, abandoning all the rest. If we allow our supremacy in South Africa to be taken from us, we shall be ousted before long from that country altogether.'[68] But not only were the people of British origin out- numbered in the whole area by nearly two to one by non-British whites; three-fifths of the white inhabitants of Cape Province itself were Afrikaners. This did not prevent either the Beaconsfield or the Gladstone governments from seeking to escape from their difficulties – and save money – by making the colonists look after themselves, with a faint hope that those who had remained near the sea would prevail over the more recalcitrant ones who had moved inland. But their effort to set up a Union broke down on the steadfast refusal of the Cape to take on the responsibilities and cost involved. The British were presented with the choice between leaving the Boers in the Transvaal and Orange Free State to their own devices and sending troops to reduce them to subjection. The Conservatives opted for the latter and, although the Liberals put the choice into reverse, they were impeded by their other preoccupations from moving fast enough to escape humiliation at Majuba in February 1881. Gladstone refused to let the defeat divert him from conciliation and the Transvaal leaders were talked into satisfying Britain's basic requirements by promising to keep out other European powers and filch no more land from the natives. But the Boers regarded any limit on their freedom as an indignity and treaties as incitements to violation. Having made the 1881 Convention of Pretoria into a dead letter, they were allowed in 1884 to substitute the Convention of London, which soon seemed destined for the same fate. The Cabinet were advised that, if it again came to fighting, the sympathies of the Cape Afrikaners would be on the other side. Ministers therefore judged it imprudent to disturb sleeping dogs, even if this meant remaining deaf to humanitarian pleas about duties to natives.

For a further constraint on British policy-making in the later nineteenth century was the failure of leaders and public alike to appreciate how much effort they would henceforward have to make if they wanted to put their wishes into practice. Britain's apparently unchallengeable position rested on the absence of rivals and on her industrial lead (see p. 63). Both were dwindling assets. Although the real challenge did not emerge until the first German Navy Law was passed in 1898, the Battle of Hampden Roads in 1862, by demonstrating the superiority of the 'iron-clad' over the 'man-of-war', was the writing on the wall for those with the vision to read. The industrialisation of naval warfare was going to send costs rocketing; the equivalent of what could be had for £108,000 in 1850 would require £1m. by 1893.[69] Moreover ships could quickly become obsolete in an age of technical progress; Britain managed to keep ahead of her rivals in 1905 by building the novel *Dreadnought* at a cost of £1·8m. but it made her forty-seven existing battleships vulnerable to any other navy which followed her example.[70] The French navy, still regarded as the chief rival, was weakened by political intrigue and vacillating strategy. But in 1884 a scare that it possessed as many first-class battleships as the British drove a government dedicated to economy and international conciliation into raising the naval estimates by 50 per cent before the alarmists could be silenced. Moreover Lord Salisbury brought out another difficulty when he said that he could not make the British iron-clads manoeuvre in the mountains of Armenia. Military costs were going up too; Tommy Atkins was not paid much but conscripts came cheaper.

Disraeli said in 1876 that 'there is no country so prepared for war as England because there is no country whose resources are so great'.[71] But the fact that Britain was a European as well as an overseas power has made the calls on those resources abnormally great, since the requirements for performing the two functions are not the same. In the 1880s Britain was in no position to fight a continental war and gravely embarrassed if she had to fight more than one colonial war at a time. Sending Wolseley with 40,000 men to Egypt was an added reason for keeping South Africa quiet. In 1885 fear of a crisis with Russia in Central Asia contributed to the decision not to conquer the Sudan. Those members of the public who objected to the government spending money at all particularly objected to it being spent on arms, while those who were keen for force to be used were considerably less keen about paying the bill.

Unrealistic ideals, unreliable allies, irreconcilable enemies, inadequate forces – to this prescription for confusion were added agents on the spot who gave misleading information (as that no serious trouble was to be expected on the veldt when in reality the Transvaalers were to attack within four weeks) or 'prancing proconsuls' (as Harcourt called them)[72] who exceeded their instructions (Colley, Seymour and above all Gordon). With Ireland demanding attention as well, it is hardly surprising that the Cabinet should have been turned from a decision-making body into a debating society in which Gladstone once hissed at Harcourt and at times allowed weeks to pass without calling his fractious colleagues together. His personal influence alone prevented the break up of the government, although frequently foretold, from ever quite taking place, but the cost of keeping it in existence was that policy became a succession of compromises, mostly decided on too late. The forward policy in Egypt was in part the price paid to reconcile the hawks to appeasement in South Africa and Ireland.

Chamberlain usually found himself on the same side as the Prime Minister, although with little sympathy for the latter's hankering after international agreement. He was apt to want what was done ultimately to be done immediately, disregarding the risk that this, while easing matters abroad, would precipitate resignations at home. In August 1880 he was invited to speak for the government in the Commons on South Africa (Kimberley being in the Lords). It says a good deal for Cabinet dissensions, and for the way in which collective responsibility could still be interpreted, that five months later, in the debate which followed Majuba, when Gladstone put up a masterly display of stone-walling about the government's intentions, the man who had accepted this responsibility should not only have kept silent but walked out before the division, along with three other ministers! Yet his behaviour, so far from unleashing a political crisis, hardly occasioned comment. Five weeks later he, Dilke and Bright threatened resignation to prevent Kimberley from yielding to popular clamour for a bash at the Boers. Gladstone sagaciously defused the crisis by first of all delaying the decision and then, in the time thus gained, talking Kimberley into a quieter mood.

When soon afterwards the policy of conciliation came under fire Chamberlain was asked to defend it publicly. This he did, with considerable vigour but only after openly admitting his view that the government had been too slow in putting it into effect. Gladstone protested that this was an admission he himself was not prepared to make. Chamberlain earned forgiveness by emphasising in another speech that the Boers could be kept in the Empire only by Britain maintaining enough troops in South Africa to overawe not merely the Transvaal but the Orange Free State and Cape Colony as well. Later he allowed himself to be enlisted by the missionary Mackenzie as a member of a 'South Africa Committee' designed to press the interests of the natives. But when in 1882 the London Missionary Society called on the government to do its duty by them, he pointed out that the price of doing so might be 'the most costly, unsatisfactory and difficult of all the little wars we can possibly undertake'.[73] As Kimberley put it:[74]

> Either we must hold South Africa strongly by force and maintain our policy whether the colonists like it or not; or else we must acquiesce in a great many things being done in these Colonies which the majority of people in this country do not approve.

In the autumn of 1884 a new factor intruded itself. Bismarck, chiefly for reasons of internal politics which were imperfectly understood in Britain, decided to placate the German enthusiasts for colonies whom he had previously derided and not only began to increase the support he gave to German merchants overseas but laid claims to assorted areas in East Africa, West Africa, South-west Africa and the Pacific.[75] He won Britain's compliance by exploiting her need for German backing against the French in Cairo. Gladstone refused to be alarmed at the snapping-up of land which nobody had previously considered to be worth having and reminded his colleagues how salutary a French presence in Canada had been in keeping the Thirteen Colonies on the leash. But others, including British colonists in the vicinities, gave their new neighbours no welcome. Although Chamberlain had earlier (if the German account is to be trusted, which is probably only in part) told Bismarck's son Herbert how delighted he would be to see Cape Colony left to its own devices, he was somewhat less Olympian when Germany upset the Australians by acquiring a toehold in New Guinea.

What drove him into indicting a memorandum to his colleagues in October 1884 were the 'salami tactics' adopted by the Transvaal freebooters in order to acquire native lands west of the line which their government had accepted as their new frontier. His exasperation led him to propose that Her Majesty's Government should take active steps 'to maintain the trade route to the interior' as well as its own rights and those of the native tribes.[76] In fact this broadside proposed little more than Derby, as Colonial Secretary, himself recommended – and a good deal less than the War Office favoured. It emphasised that action should depend on the willingness of Cape Colony to co-operate (although irrespective of the attitude of the Transvaal government). When the colonists said smugly that they could do the job perfectly well themselves, Hartington and Chamberlain, for once seeing eye to eye, were incredulous enough to sweep their more cautious colleagues into assembling an expedition and, when 'doing the job' proved to mean giving in to the Boers, sending it up to the scene of the dispute. Its proceedings had a touch of comic opera about them but all the same led to the annexation of Southern Bechuanaland in the hope that the Cape colonists would soon take it off Britain's hands.[77] When they proved to have no such intention, so that Britain had acquired a new possession with which she was going to be burdened until the days of Seretse Khama, the best was made of a bad job by declaring the rest of the country a protectorate and, as such, not up for Boer or German grabs. But that was the doing of the Salisbury government after Gladstone's had found a welcome escape from the cares of power.

Over Egypt Chamberlain's attitude hardened in much the same way. When he took office his conviction that the bondholders were chiefly to blame would have done credit to Lenin. He and Dilke were all for pulling out with the greatest possible speed; curiously enough, their knowledge of and liking for things French did not lead them to give much consideration to Gallic susceptibilities. When Arabi's rebellion developed, Chamberlain thought that it might prove the basis of a popular government and in January 1882 argued that the British government should think twice before accepting a French proposal to back the Khedive against the rebels. He found himself however alone with Gladstone in the minority and, unlike the latter, was not won round by assurances that no commitment to action was involved. But when the Egyptian nationalists refused to be intimidated and anarchy seemed to be spreading, Chamberlain began to think that action of some kind was imperative and went along with his colleagues in accepting a French proposal for a naval demonstration. When this proved provocative rather than pacifying, and Europeans in

Alexandria began to be massacred, he concluded that Arabi was only an adventurer and sided with the hawks under Hartington who insisted that action to assert Anglo–French authority, once begun, must be carried to a point at which it was effective. When Arabi seemed to be threatening the security of the joint fleets, and the French withdrew theirs to avoid trouble, the moment of truth had arrived, especially as it coincided with the aftermath of Phoenix Park. Gladstone, to keep the Cabinet together, reluctantly allowed the British fleet on its own to bombard the Egyptian shore batteries; Chamberlain, while still emphasising that the ultimate aim must be to let the Egyptians choose their own government, was one of the four ministers keenest on action. But Arabi retaliated by declaring a holy war and urged Moslems everywhere to rise against the British. The Canal seemed threatened. In a Cabinet at loggerheads, despite Gladstone's protests, the forward party in which Chamberlain was still prominent won a majority for sending troops to Egypt to show beyond a doubt who was in control there. The only drawback about this course, accomplished in September at the battle of Tel-el-Kebir, was that, control once having been established, a safe moment for relinquishing it never seemed to arrive.

Over the next few years Chamberlain and the other left-wing ministers, including Gladstone, made repeated efforts to fix a date for withdrawal, regardless of the bondholders' interests. But as he himself said, 'We cannot leave anarchy behind us and we have to see that our interference has produced some benefit for the Egyptian people'.[78] Moves to substitute a neutralised Egypt under international guarantees got nowhere. Moreover control over Egypt proved hard to combine with indifference towards the Sudan. Chamberlain, unlike Dilke, had no hand in the choice of Gordon, whom he never met (any more than Gladstone did). He shared the suspicions that Gordon would prove insubordinate and was chiefly concerned to prevent the Egyptian experience from being repeated further south and Britain finding that, having gone in, she could not creditably get out again. As he was to say in 1896, 'That [i.e. fixing a date for withdrawal] is an experience which I do not think we are likely to repeat'.[79] When a threat of resignation by Hartington and Selborne led to a belated rescue expedition being decided on, Chamberlain urged that it be confined to a compact force moving quickly rather than a bigger one which would take more time to mount. After Gordon's death, he joined but took no prominent part in the general agreement not to stay in the Sudan.

In a much-quoted phrase, Granville described Chamberlain at the time of the decision to bombard the Alexandrian batteries as 'almost the greatest Jingo in the Cabinet'.[80] Bright also identified him as the man most responsible for action being taken at that juncture. Those historians who have not accused him of inconsistency have discerned the shape of things to come. The explanation is surely to be found in the businessman's appreciation of power, combined with the growing realisation that, as he was to tell Milner twenty years later, 'political decisions are always a choice of evils'. Without at this stage abandoning his distaste for national self-assertion overseas, he was learning that a refusal to exercise power might involve abandoning other aims which were morally desirable or strategically essential, yet that on occasion the price of putting the world to rights might be too high. In Pascal's words, force without justice might be tyrannical but justice without force was impotent. And when the balance in his mind tipped in favour of action, he wanted to make sure that the action was effective. A deep impression is likely to have been left by the experience of how limited was the ability of both Britain and a Liberal government to shape events as they wished. Meanwhile his apparent movement from one extreme to the other cannot have made Gladstone think any better of him.

Votes for Hodge

In the Cabinet's first discussion about its programme, Chamberlain had wanted to see suffrage reform given priority. But he himself said later that 'a Reform Bill has this peculiarity – it is fatal to the Parliament in which it is carried'.[81] A change in the voting system must deprive the existing House of Commons of its legitimacy and, if agreed on, must be followed by an election on the new basis; if rejected by either House, an appeal to the country becomes equally inevitable. Gladstone had therefore good grounds for arguing that the subject was more suitable for the later than the earlier years of a Parliament. Yet as he did not oppose it on principle, he made it progressively harder to postpone with each year that passed. To Chamberlain passing years suggested that in none of them was the existing Parliament likely to approve a really radical programme, so that voting reform was once again the key to social reform. By the time that the National Liberal Federation met at Leeds in October 1883, it hardly needed the encouragement which it received from its leader to tell the government that the moment for action had come. The next major Bill should deal with franchise.

Gladstone's mind had been moving in the same direction and he promptly proposed to the Cabinet a measure which would be moderate in that it would introduce no new qualifications for voting but would all the same increase the electorate by two-thirds by extending to householders in the counties the same rights as had been given in 1867 to householders in the boroughs. Although the more thorny question of redistribution was to be left till later, the Bill was to cover the whole United Kingdom; in contrast to 1867, Ireland was to receive exactly the same treatment as the other three parts. As a result the Irish electorate would be trebled since a far higher proportion of it lived in the countryside than was the case in England.

By comparison with hints which Chamberlain had been dropping about manhood suffrage, equal electoral districts and payment of members, this was milk-and-water. In the light of what had happened in the past seventeen years, doom could hardly be expected to ensue if the country was treated like the towns. Indeed Chamberlain had some fears (which over the long term were to be realised) that ingrained rural deference would make the county seats into Tory strongholds. What he failed to appreciate was that the extension to Ireland (about which he was emphatic) would increase the number of Parnell's followers and so make Home Rule a burning issue.[82] But to those ministers who thought Ireland should be treated fairly were added those who hesitated to present the Irish with an additional grievance, not to mention those who thought Ireland so difficult already that nothing could make it worse. Above all the strategy, as well as the drafting, of the Bill was dominated by Gladstone who could meet any attempts to change it by a threat of resignation. One of the few things which his colleagues had in common was a fear of the confusion which his withdrawal would precipitate, especially as that withdrawal might well not extend, either immediately or permanently, to politics as a whole! There had already been a Second Coming – might there not be a Third?

As a result, he got his measure through the Cabinet without even Hartington quite deciding to resign. In the Commons the Irish MPs supported it as a step towards the autonomy of their country, although there was some doubt as to the effect it might have on the authority of their leader; on everything but Home Rule, he was moving rightwards whereas the new voters might go to the left.[83] More influential support came when Lord Randolph Churchill and his friends of the 'Fourth Party' realised that the chief Tory opponents of the Bill were the very people opposed to 'Tory democracy'. Thereafter other Conservatives lost heart about fighting what some of their fellows were prepared to accept and compromised by abstaining. Amendments to exclude Ireland and give votes to women were easily defeated and the Bill went on almost unaltered to the Lords, where on 8 July 1884 its Second Reading was shelved until the government had produced their proposals for redrawing constituency boundaries. The Tory managers calculated that on the existing pattern the Bill would give forty-seven seats to the Liberals whereas any redistribution seemed almost bound to increase the number of suburban seats where their own influence was growing.

The government, taking to heart the lesson of 1880, decided to reintroduce the Bill in a special session in the autumn and to drop all other measures (including the Board of Trade's Merchant Shipping and Railway Rates Bills) so as to concentrate on getting it passed. Chamberlain thought that the long-awaited moment had come to make Radicals stand up and be counted by precipitating a major constitutional clash between the two Houses. Previous Reform Bills had needed pressure from the streets to get them through, so that the generation of excitement could not but be salutary now. A year earlier he had allowed a provocative speech made by Lord Salisbury on the sacrosanct soil of Birmingham to lure him into denouncing a 'class who toil not neither do they spin' (a specification which fitted his own colleagues Hartington and Granville equally well).[84] A little later he had said that, if Salisbury tried to force a dissolution rather than pass the Bill, 'then the issue will be between the peers and the people'. This had produced (not for the first time) what Gladstone delicately described as 'disturbance at headquarters'[85] but, although the culprit denied any intention of attacking the queen, he refused to retract his opinions about the legislative programme of the Lords. The Prime Minister, whose veneration for that body and for the aristocracy in general was wearing thin, and whose own stock at 'headquarters' was far from high, admitted to 'a considerable degree of concurrence'. Now Chamberlain returned to the attack with a series of speeches between July and October 1884 in the spirit of Morley's phrase, 'Mend them or end them'.[86]

Fuel was added to the queen's indignation by an unfortunate affair at Aston on 13 October. At the instigation of Lord Randolph Churchill (who had agreed to become a Conservative candidate in Birmingham if his own constituency of Woodstock was reformed out of existence and who in fact was to run Bright very close in the election of 1885), a great demonstration against the government had been planned to offset the spontaneous outbursts against the Lords which had been organised throughout the midlands. Chamberlain had written to Morley, 'The Tories will not be allowed to hold their meeting here. That is certain and there will be a blazing row.'[87] But, as on other occasions, he would seem not to have known more than he wanted to know and thus was able to plead ignorance about the forging of tickets and the fortuitous appearance of a builder's cart containing ladders outside the walls of Aston Park just as the harried Tories were retreating within them. In the ensuing mêlée there was considerable 'redistribution of seats';[88] Sir Stafford Northcote, who was to have been chief speaker, had to be hustled away by his bodyguards to avoid capture while his portrait in fireworks which was to have formed the climax of the occasion fulfilled the forecast of a blazing row by being set off in broad daylight upside down. Lord Randolph retaliated with an amendment to the Address censuring Birmingham's leader for speeches which interfered with freedom of discussion and incited to riot; the Birmingham system was depicted as a 'Tsarist despotism' (which no doubt reminded some of his audience that the member under attack had recently contrasted the coronation of Alexander III unfavourably with John Bright's jubilee). Gladstone's expectation that the two firebrands would 'tomahawk' one another[89] was disappointed, since a plethora of affidavits produced to show that it had been Tory stewards who had started the rough stuff led to the amendment being defeated by thirty-six votes. It then transpired that the affidavits had been forged too.

But four days before the riot the (Conservative class) London daily, the *Standard*, had printed the complete text of a redistribution plan on which Dilke, as President of the Local Government Board since the previous December, had been working with Cabinet sanction throughout the recess. He was nominally subject to a committee of ministers including Chamberlain, but the other members drove him 'wild with piffling points, so I got rid of the committee after one meeting and went on by myself'.[90] The authenticity of the leaked document was given the tepid denial habitual in such cases but Morley told Chamberlain that 'those who asked who had been responsible plumped for Dilke'.[91] The leak was soon seen to have done no harm and would appear in fact to have been calculated. For while Parliament had been on holiday, zealous intermediaries from the queen downwards had been trying to coax the party leaders into a compromise by which the government would get its proposals for redistribution formulated before the time came for the Lords to make up their minds about the Franchise Bill, so that if agreement could be reached on the former, opposition could be abandoned to the latter. And although Gladstone told Chamberlain on 6 October that 'the word compromise has never passed my lips', compromise was exactly what he agreed to seven weeks later.[92] The great battle was off and all the mud appeared to have been slung in vain.

The scheme in the *Standard* pointed the way to a compromise but still had to be agreed in detail. The process required to be carried out at a speed which could not possibly be achieved by open debate in the Commons. Accordingly the deal was clinched by three meetings in November between Gladstone, Salisbury, Dilke, Hartington and Northcote, of whom the last two proved mere passengers (whereas Salisbury's performance settled in his favour the question of who should lead the next Conservative government). The results were presented to the parties as a *fait accompli* and the Bill went through the Commons without a division. In the meetings Dilke (although occasionally outwitted by Salisbury)[93] played a key role. Not only was detailed knowledge required to calculate the effect of any particular proposal but the whole scheme was so intricate that a change at one point usually called for compensating changes elsewhere. Unless the proposer of a change knew where to look for such compensations or was helped to find them, his proposals were likely to be shot down as impracticable. Thus, while it had been Gladstone's adoption of the main principles which had been decisive at the outset, once they were settled the man who had mastered the small print was apt to carry the day. Moreover Dilke won much credit by his skilful piloting of the two Bills through the Commons. 'His information is inexhaustible,' commented Hamilton, 'and always ready at hand; his temper is perfect.'[94] Chamberlain by contrast had little say in the operation. His chief contribution had been his threatening speeches, which may or may not have made the Conservatives more ready for compromise but which had certainly increased the dislike with which he was regarded and damaged his chances of highest office. When next year the Radicals of Cabinet rank took to meeting twice a week, it was Dilke who by agreement presided and, if his own testimony is true, was spoken of by Gladstone as the destined heir.[95] On the other hand, he must bear the main responsibility for the failure of the Act to work in the way most Liberals expected.

Whereas in 1867 it had been the franchise innovations which were epoch-making and only in 47 constituencies were the boundaries changed, in 1884–5 things were, partly for that reason, the other way round. A new pattern was created which still to some extent persists. 99 boroughs with populations of less than 15,000 were deprived of their members and merged in adjoining county constituencies; 35 boroughs and 2 counties with populations between 15,000 and 50,000 were deprived of one of their members. The seats thus liberated were reallocated to redress the over-representation of agricultural areas and given to London and to the main industrial areas. Only the City of London, the universities and 23 boroughs with populations between 50,000 and 165,000 retained two members; all the rest of the country was divided into single-member constituencies of roughly equal size. This last was Salisbury's chief contribution to the scheme.

The part of the agreement about which Chamberlain had most doubts was the emphasis on single members (although he had often enough attacked minority voting). This reduced the size of constituencies and, by enabling residential areas to be detached from industrial ones, increased the chances of Conservatives benefiting from 'Villa Torydom'.[96] It also put an end to the Liberal practice of running a Whig and a Radical in joint harness and made it hard for a Whig to be chosen as the candidate where the local organisation was under radical control. It thus hastened the disappearance of the Whigs – or rather, their absorption into the Tories. The end of the three-member, two-vote constituency deprived the Caucus of some of its purpose but, by dividing Birmingham into a number of constituencies, enabled Chamberlain to keep the seat which he might otherwise have lost (see p. 95); the offer to give the town a seventh constituency, played by Dilke at the crucial moment, did much to bring him round to the Bill.[97]

In the end he thought well enough of the measure to predict that after it 'the Tories may periodically return to office but they will have place, not power'.[98] Yet in fact it did not have the effect which he expected. The reform which was to have ushered in a radical era was followed by twenty years during six-sevenths of which the Conservatives held power. For that, of course, there were special reasons but even they to some extent resulted from the measure. Parnell had said in 1882 that his party needed to win 80 to 90 seats (as compared with their existing 63) in order to secure the grant of national self-government to Ireland. In the first post-reform election they won precisely 85 (plus one in Liverpool) and, although there are grounds for thinking that even on the old suffrage they would have improved their position, the new one was certainly not a hindrance to them. Even 86 seats would not of course have put them in a commanding position if the Parliament had not been hung. But the ability of the Conservatives to win more seats than the Liberals had bargained for may have owed something to the shape of the reform and not everything to events between its enactment and the first election.

It was just possible under the new suffrage to claim that men still only got a vote if they had a stake in the country but that stake might amount to no more than a single rented room. Those electors whose stake was substantial were becoming the minority. Colonel Rainsborough's dream was close to realisation. Only a small step would be needed to give the poorest he in England (shes were a different matter!) a voice about the government under which he was to be put. The voting power of groups no longer corresponded to the 'permanent fixed interest' of their members in the country but rather to their existence as adult male human beings. But this approximation to the ideal was bound to bring the society achieving it face to face with certain realities.

How was a party to attract the votes of the new electorate? Clearly it must give evidence of concern for their interests. But must this mean giving those interests priority? A party which failed to do so would always be liable to be outvoted by one which did. Hitherto British politics had not been organised on a strictly class basis; the ranks of the progressives had always contained a number of the well-to-do. Was this now going to cease? The shift of the middle classes into Conservatism would make such an outcome more likely.

But if a left-wing party organised on a class (even if not an openly Marxist) basis set out to redistribute the resources of the kingdom, might there be a danger of its leaders failing to recognise the extent to which the economic position of Britain (as of any industrialised country) had been built up by a high rate of saving/investing and required a similar rate to be maintained if it was to remain competitive? Might they, in their anxiety to redistribute resources from conspicuous consumers to needy consumers, redistribute resources from people or institutions which would save them to people who would spend them (including the state expenditure on consumption)? Might there also be a danger that parties competing against one another on a class basis would between them claim shares of the national resources which, when put together, came to more than the total of those resources? The temptation for societies and individuals to spend more than they can afford has been as prominent in history as their passion for amassing wealth. But if inflation were to become the normal state of things, how could Britain hope to maintain her competitive position and pay her way in the world? Would other countries, as they industrialised, follow her example and, by similarly reducing investment, enable her to keep her position stable? Or would an improvement in standards of life and culture (particularly among the workers) make possible a rate of growth in productivity which would enable her to eat her cake without gnawing off the bit on which she was sitting? But would not a high rate of investment be essential for such a growth?

The Unauthorised Programme

The Board of Trade provided Chamberlain with persistent trivialities rather than big opportunities. Even when a fresh depression set in around 1884, conventional wisdom still ruled out the thought of government action to remedy it. In 1880 he secured the passage of an Employers Liability Act, increasing the rights of workmen in certain industries to claim compensation for accidents caused by negligence on the part of their employers. He also steered into law a Grain Cargoes Act and a Seamen's Wages Act, improving the safety and status of seamen. In 1882 came the Electric Lighting Act which encouraged municipalities to take responsibility for the new form of energy as far as lighting was concerned but inadvertently discouraged them from using it for power. In 1883 the Bankruptcy Act not merely established a Bankruptcy Department in the Board but also official receivers throughout the country, systematising a field in which confusion had hitherto abetted evasion. The Patents Act of the same year, besides setting up the Patents Office, did a little to encourage British inventiveness.[99]

On the other hand the Railway Rates Bill of 1884, which sought to relieve farmers at the expense of shareholders, and the Merchant Shipping Bill of the same year ran into storms. Chamberlain had incurred the hostility of the shipowners nine years previously when he had initiated a series of town meetings in support of Samuel Plimsoll, who was asking inconvenient questions about 'coffin ships'; when he was appointed to the Board of Trade, they had vowed they would never go 'cap-in-hand to a fellow like that'.[100] They disputed the need for the reforms which Chamberlain proposed although one in sixty of British sailors were losing their lives every year. He accused the owners of deliberately incurring wrecks; they accused him of wrecking an industry already near the rocks. He suggested to Gladstone that he should deliberately invite defeat on the Second Reading and then resign, presumably to drum up public opinion in his support (as he was to do nineteen years later). But the Prime Minister preferred his favourite remedy of 'taking a little time'. Chamberlain therefore marshalled all his energies into a four-hour speech but got little backing. The Reform crisis then intervened and the Bill, along with Railway Rates, was sacrificed so as to clear the decks for a fight with the Lords (see p. 135). A Royal Commission was agreed to as a consolation prize; the evidence which it produced provided the answer to the problem of raising public support and a Conservative government did what had proved beyond the reach of the Liberals.

The general legislative record of the second Gladstone government was not quite as bad as has sometimes been suggested:

1880	Ground Game Act (see p. 116)
	Employers Liability Act, Grain Cargoes Act, Seamen's Wages Act
	Education Act (making schooling compulsory)
	Burials Act (allowing nonconformist services in churchyards)
	Local Government Act (abolishing property qualification for town councillors)
1881	Abolition of flogging in the army (a subject on which Chamberlain, like Parnell, felt hotly)
1882	Corrupt Practices Act (limiting expenditure, etc., at elections)
	Settled Land Act (allowing such land to be let or sold)
	Married Women's Property Act (limiting freedom of husbands to dispose of their wives' property)
	Electric Light Act
	Artisans' Dwellings Act
1883	Bankruptcy and Patents Acts
	Tenants Improvements Act (giving to English tenants what Irish ones already had)
	Agricultural Holdings Act
	Factories and Workshops Act (protecting men handling white lead)
	Act prohibiting the payment of wages in pubs
	Act rationalising parochial charities in the City of London

Two linked measures which had been promised, for establishing popular government in London and in the counties, had to be shelved when they provoked as much intra-party as inter-party dissension. In the view of some, piecemeal social engineering of the kind enumerated is a more beneficial way of carrying on the business of the country than drastic constitutional and social changes. It is in any case doubtful whether there were many other substantial measures on which the Liberal Party as then constituted could have agreed. There was still no clear majority for such things as disestablishment, prohibition, free education, the excusing of atheist MPs from having to swear by God, even the repeal of the Contagious Diseases Act. There was not much more to be done to set the people free constitutionally at home (Ireland and the colonies were a different matter). What was now emerging as the main problem was inequality and exploitation, rather than discrimination, and this could only be cured by positive state action, by placing limitations on wealth and power rather than by taking them off poverty and weakness. But many Liberals who were rich and influential lacked enthusiasm for such a development.

Chamberlain believed with conviction that what the Liberal Party needed to attract the enlarged electorate was a 'constructive' policy of reform and that the sphere of the state, or at any rate of state intervention, could be usefully extended without impinging harmfully on individual initiative and responsibility.[101] But Gladstone repeatedly portrayed himself as a man nearing the end of his political career who only refrained from retiring, a step which he frequently threatened and always professed to desire, because he had certain work to finish, notably Ireland. As long as he remained leader, the formulation and adoption of a programme seemed unlikely to become a major feature in party activity. While therefore such a step could be represented as a wise preparation for the period *after* Gladstone had retired, its adoption could also be used as a weapon for hastening on that retirement. There is no doubt that Chamberlain saw it in that light and Gladstone's political antennae were sensitive enough to make it possible that he also appreciated – and resented – what was afoot.

As a preliminary step, a series of seven articles appeared in the *Fortnightly Review* between July 1883 and January 1884, followed by three more in May 1884 and July 1885. The main work of producing this series fell on T. H. Sweet-Escott, a radical journalist who was then editor of the *Review*. Chamberlain only contributed one article, on 'Labourers' and Artisans' Dwellings', a subject made topical by the study of the slums by a Congregational minister, *The Bitter Cry of Outcast London* which was serialised by W. T. Stead in the *Pall Mall Gazette* and led Dilke to appoint a Royal Commission on Housing the Working Classes in 1884. The remaining articles were written by friends such as Morley and Collings. In

July 1885 the series was republished as a 'little red book'.[102] To this Chamberlain contributed a short preface, commending the articles in general without pledging himself to support all the proposals. His own article was omitted, since by then a majority of the Commission (which included Salisbury, the Prince of Wales and Cardinal Manning) had recommended that local authorities should be given compulsory powers to buy land and that government money should be made available to pay for the workers' housing. Escott produced a new Introduction which was itself published in the *Review* in July 1885, the original one of 1883 having become out of date. The proposals were said to 'sound the death-knell of the *laissez-faire* system':

> The goal towards which the advance will probably be made is . . . the intervention of the state on behalf of the weak against the strong, in the interests of labour against capital, of want and suffering against luxury and ease.

The principal concrete proposals of the book were:

Electoral System   Manhood suffrage, equal electoral districts, payment of members by their constituents. The question whether large towns should be represented by several members or divided into single-member constituencies was in 1883 left open, with a slight preference expressed in favour of the second alternative; by 1885 the issue had of course been settled.

Institutions   The Crown was described as being 'likely to remain undisturbed for a period which a practical politician need not take account of', although 'an imperial and especially a military policy undertaken at the royal instance and wish' was deprecated. [If Gladstone and those round him had not been so discreet about royal attempts to interfere with the policy of his government, the monarchy might have been in serious danger.] The House of Lords was warned that it had to choose between submitting to the Commons and being reformed out of existence. Nothing was said about an alternative second chamber.

Urban Housing   Local authorities were to be empowered to acquire land or buildings compulsorily, paying out of the rates, at a price settled by an arbitrator on the basis of existing use. Owners of insanitary property who did not reconstruct it were to be subject to a special tax. Rateable values and rents of property were to be brought into line.

Agriculture   The Artisans' Dwellings Acts were to be extended to rural areas and local authorities given power to acquire land compulsorily. Settlements and entails were to be abolished, with a view to breaking up big estates and encouraging sales of land. The thrust of the proposals was to reverse the trend of recent centuries by recreating a body of peasant proprietors and halting the effect of industrialisation in shifting labour from the countryside to the towns. 'The object of all land reform must be the multiplication of landowners.' [The proposals smacked rather too much of being town-dwellers' ideas of how to run the countryside, besides assuming too easily that what had been true in the past would hold in the future.]

Religious Equality   A detailed scheme was outlined for disestablishing and disendowing the Church of England. [Chamberlain had it in mind to use some of the endowments to meet the cost of making education free. Today it is clear that one of the chief effects of the change would have been to shift on to the public purse the considerable cost of maintaining historic church buildings.]

Free Schools   The inequity and inefficiency of charging fees for attendance at Board Schools, while making attendance compulsory, were dwelt on at length.

Taxation   A shift was recommended from indirect to direct taxation, along with the institution of a progressive income tax [a sharp reversal of Gladstone's policy]. Moreover, while lip-service was paid to the need for economy in administration, the objections to state interference were said to be 'of diminished force when the Government is by the whole people'.

> There are many operations which have to be conducted on an extensive scale which a Government, by reason of its resources and comprehensive powers, can undertake much more economically than individuals and private associations. It would be better for the State, through Parliament or municipal authorities, to assume these functions more often than it does, rather than to encourage the creation of huge private interests and monopolies ... Take for instance railway companies [which Gladstone had contemplated nationalising in 1844 and in the 1860s].
>   Taxation, on equitable principles, for objects which the nation approves, cannot be on too liberal a scale.

Local Government   County councils, elected by all the ratepayers, were to be established [as the government had already decided, without managing to implement the decision]. In London, separate councils were favoured for the various parliamentary divisions, with a central authority doing only what was essentially metropolitan.[103] On these local councils were to

143

be concentrated the powers and duties already performed by the Boards of Guardians and School Boards and rating authorities [as was to be done for education in 1902 but for the Poor Law only in 1929].

Elective county councils were also to be set up in Ireland but that country was to have its own national council as well which would take over from Westminster all necessary control of local administration, all Private Bill legislation and various existing special Irish Boards. Wales, if it so desired, was to have a similar body and the devolution which had already begun for Scotland with the establishment of a separate Secretary of State was to be extended. Much was said about the need for relieving the burden of the imperial Parliament but there was no hint that a similar council would be set up for England. [Before these proposals were published in book form, the Gladstone government had left office and much had happened.]

On this basis Chamberlain built in speeches. These had begun as early as February 1883 but, after an interval in which he concerned himself with loss of life at sea and parliamentary reform, he laid out his views in a series of sixteen speeches between January and October 1885. In the latter month, after the Liberals had left office, a collection of them was published, whereupon Goschen, the right-wing Liberal back-bencher, described them as an 'unauthorised programme' in distinction to the official one promulgated in accordance with established practice by the party leader in his address to his constituents in Midlothian. Chamberlain accepted the label, while putting together two comments on his proposals for smallholders to make them a promise of 'three acres and a cow'.

There were discrepancies between the volume and the speeches while the emphasis in the latter changed as circumstances developed. The remarks which ranged most widely and caused most offence were contained in three speeches in January 1885. As a result of them he received a courtly reminder from Gladstone about the damage which might result to Cabinet unity if individual members began expressing their views about questions of general principle which were not immediately pressing; the Prime Minister did not add that he himself had received a similar reminder from Palmerston in March 1865 and had as a result reined in his tongue about Irish disestablishment.[104] Chamberlain argued back, claiming that the extension of the electorate had created a need for issues to be ventilated by ministers before decisions were taken on them. This view answered the accusations often made about Chamberlain's violations of confidence; he refused to accept that, as Hamilton put it, not only does *noblesse oblige* but also the holding of office. What the mouth-opener overlooked was the awkward position of a minister who nails his colours to a mast on which his colleagues later refuse to hoist sail. On this occasion the *enfant terrible* decided on a pause in naughtiness; perhaps he judged it an inopportune moment for resignation, perhaps he had just been trying to see how much he could get away with, perhaps the news of Gordon's death left him with little alternative but to stand by his colleagues.

By June 1885 however the government had become fatally divided on the subject of Ireland and took (some say, created) the opportunity of defeat on a minor issue to resign. As the new electoral register made necessary by the Redistribution Bill (which had itself still to become law) could not be ready till the end of the year, a Tory government of 'Caretakers' came into office and the parties began manoeuvring for an election (see Chapter 6). In September Chamberlain, after making two speeches at Hull in August, undertook a tour in northern England and Scotland, followed by other speeches till mid–October. These concentrated increasingly on practical points about the work to be done by the next Liberal government. A protest by Hartington was returned by a slap in the face, but this was exactly how Chamberlain regarded Gladstone's manifesto to his constituents in September.[105] A direct request to be shown the passage on land had been met but no time was then given for comment before the text was published. In October Chamberlain paid his one and only visit to Hawarden but with singularly little result. Gradually however the warnings against parading party splits and scaring moderates from voting began to sink in.

Although at the beginning of the year Chamberlain had expressed himself in favour of a further extension of the suffrage and payment of members, the impossibility of bringing in yet another Reform Bill was too obvious for such a proposal to figure in the election campaign. Equally, nothing was said about the House of Lords. Disestablishment did not get a mention beyond two admissions that, while the speaker personally favoured it, the party as a whole was not committed to it (which did not prevent a widespread fear of it from having some effect).[106] The spring speeches had included a proposal for an income tax which would not only be graduated but distinguish between earned and unearned income; as things were 'taxation pressed hardly on the poor but hardly at all on the rich'.[107] This was watered down to a graduated death tax or house tax and in the end gave way to acceptance of an opaque statement in Gladstone's manifesto that 'the balance of taxation as between property and labour must be adjusted with a scrupulousness which unfortunately has often been absent when property had exclusive control of Parliamentary action'.[108] Local government reform (by which was meant in effect the creation of county councils) was a regular item but hardly a controversial one, as it was acceptable in principle to both parties. The proposal for national councils also appeared regularly and was once so phrased as to admit the possibility of one being set up for England.

The core of the programme came down in the end to three points. One was local government. Another was the familiar demand for 'free education'. But even here reservations began to appear, since it no longer seemed to rouse much feeling among parents (who could after all get their fees paid by the Guardians if need was proved) whereas it created alarm in the Church of England as well as among nonconformists. For were fees to be remitted in all schools or only in Board ones? If the former, the taxpayer would be supporting education under denominational auspices, a red rag to dissenters; if the latter, church schools would be handicapped and in danger of extinction.[109]

The third point was the call, openly admitted as such, to bring a peasantry back into existence by authorising local authorities to acquire land and lease it as allotments or smallholdings, so as to increase the home production of butter, eggs, poultry, cheese, fruit and vegetables. Linked with this went a demand, expressed in various forms at various times, for the ownership of land to be brought under closer control and for limits to be set to the profits which landlords could make when the value of their land increased through no action of their own. (This applied more in towns than in the countryside and was the result of farmland being turned into suburbs by growing population and better transport.) The 'landed interest' had long been a target of middle-class radicalism and interest in the subject had just been stimulated by the 'Single Tax' proposal of Henry George.[110] But the attack was losing point because, as Lady Bracknell was soon to say, 'what between the duties expected of one during one's life and the duties exacted from one after one's death, land has ceased to be either a profit or a pleasure'.

In a speech at the 'Old Vic' on 24 September Chamberlain said that if free education and the compulsory purchase of land by local authorities were 'excluded from' (rather than 'included in') the programme of the next Liberal government, he would not be able to accept office in it. Instead he would 'stand aside and lend a loyal support to those who are carrying out reforms with which I agree although they are unable to go with me a little further'. On both points Gladstone's manifesto had hedged, expressing sympathy while hinting at difficulties. In subsequent discussion, the demand for free education was reduced to a demand that ministers might be left free to speak and vote in its favour.

Thus, by the time that the electors went to the polls at the end of November 1885, the Radical Programme (as distinct from the general Liberal one) might seem for practical purposes to have been reduced to the acres and the cow. One can hardly believe that this would have proved a pitfall over which a major party could stumble or (in the light of our greater experience of British agricultural problems) a step which would have transformed society. Chamberlain himself said that they would not excite the passionate fervour which he desired to see by inscribing on their banners 'Local Government' and 'Cheapen the Transfer of Land'. But, when the chips were down, he seemed to be acquiescing, for the time being at any rate, in little more being proposed. Yet in the course of the next eight months a crisis was to arrive which brought lasting changes to Liberalism and affected the whole future course of British politics. How could this be?

The first explanation is to be found in those statements of wider principle which, as has been seen, lost prominence in the speeches made during the actual election campaign. They could not be unmade and to many, such as the young Ramsay MacDonald,[111] it was for them rather than for his precise proposals that Chamberlain stood. The most famous passage of all came in the Birmingham speech of 5 January 1885:

> If you will go back to the early history of our social system, you will find that, when our social arrangements first began to shape themselves, every man was born into the world with natural rights, with a right to a share in the great inheritance of the community, with a right to a part of the land of his birth. But all these rights have passed away. The common rights of ownership have disappeared. ... Private ownership has taken the place of these communal rights and this system has become so interwoven with our habit and usages, it has been so sanctioned by law and custom, that it might be very difficult and perhaps impossible to reverse. But then I ask, what ransom [he later regretted not having used instead the word 'insurance'] will property pay for the security which it enjoys?[112] What substitute will it find for the natural rights which it has ceased to recognise? Society is banded together in order to protect itself against the instincts of those of its members who would make very short work of ownership if they were left alone. That is all very well but I maintain that society owes to these men something more than toleration in return for the restrictions which it places upon their liberty of action.

For this unusual excursion into political philosophy he was taken to task not merely by *The Times* but also by Morley who read him a lecture to the effect that[113]

> no right is worth a straw except for the good it brings and all claims to rights must depend – not upon nature – but upon the good that the said rights are calculated to bring to the greatest number. General utility, public expediency, the greatest happiness of the greatest number, these are the tests and standards of a right, not the dictates of nature.

Chamberlain's history was of course wild and he was confusing between a natural right to a say over one's conditions of life and a right to ownership. Yet he was for all that cutting through to the ultimate basis of democratic radicalism (see p. 21). Six years before the Putney debates of 1647 were rediscovered, he was speaking in the spirit of Rainsborough and Wildman.

At Ipswich a few days later he disclaimed ever having thought it possible 'to bring everything down to one dead level [or] equalise the capacities and conditions of men'. But at Hull on 5 August he proclaimed his belief that

> the great evil with which we have to deal is the excessive inequality in the distribution of riches. . . . If we can do anything to raise the condition of the poor in this country . . . we should do more for the prosperity, nay for the morality of this country than anything we can do by laws, however stringent, for the prevention of excess or the prevention of crime. I want you to make this the first object in the Liberal programme for the reformed Parliament.

At Warrington on 8 September he produced a variation of the same theme:

> Now that we have a Government of the people by the people, we will go on and make it the Government for the people, in which all shall co-operate in order to secure to every man his natural rights, his right to existence and to enjoyment of it. I shall be told to-morrow that this is Socialism. I have learnt not to be afraid of words that are flung in my face instead of argument. Of course it is Socialism. The Poor Law is Socialism; the Education Act is Socialism; the greater part of municipal work is Socialism; and every kindly act of legislation by which the community has sought to discharge its responsibilities and its obligations to the poor is Socialism; but it is none the worse for that. Our object is the elevation of the poor – of the masses of the people – a levelling-up of them by which we shall do something to remove the excessive inequality in social life which is now one of the greatest dangers as well as a great injury to the State.[114]

Comparison of these wide-ranging aspirations with the detailed proposals for reform inevitably pose the question as to which it was that mattered. The short answer is that by the end of 1885 the immediate task was to win the election and to win it without putting excessive strains on the unity of the Liberal Party. In that context Chamberlain may reasonably be assumed to have picked out one or two issues which would give him a justification for refusing to join another Cabinet dominated by Whigs without going so far as to constitute a logical bar against his doing so. But in the longer term he was making a bid for the leadership of the party after Gladstone had retired, and possibly also seeking to hasten on that retirement by creating a demand for steps which he considered that Gladstone, and knew that the Whigs would not support.

Such an answer only prompts a further question. Were the positive proposals in the book and the speeches all that a ministry led by Chamberlain would have put into operation? If so, would they have been enough to satisfy the gradually crystallising desires of the newly enfranchised? If not, how much further would the Radicals have been prepared to go? The question is important both in relation to British history and generally. Was Chamberlain, with his monocle, orchids, cigars and his sons at Rugby just an example of successful middle class individualism or, if he had had power in the later 1880s and 1890s, could he have led the transition to a new-style interventionist regime, which would begin the redistribution of wealth and the governmental regulation of the economy in the interests of the community as a whole? There are those who maintain that he had no real sympathy for the working-man and would not have been prepared to contemplate any serious limitations on individual initiative and responsibility. Such a charge implies a judgment that his earlier relevant speeches were insincere.

He certainly criticised landowners more frequently than manufacturers, but he made himself highly unpopular among shipowners and railway directors by his outspoken attacks on them for disregarding the interests of others. In this connection it is primarily his remarks prior to 1886 which must provide the evidence, since thereafter altered circumstances may have produced altered attitudes. But even in his later years he was to press on allergic Conservatives such ideas as old-age pensions on a contributory basis, voluntary insurance against sickness, full compensation for accidents, Labour Exchanges and Courts of Arbitration to diminish strikes. In 1892 he wrote an article supporting (in line with trade union policy) an 8-hour day for (initially) miners and railwaymen, further Factory Acts and loans to help workers to buy houses.[115] He certainly did not contemplate the nationalisation of basic industries but he was continually advocating the ownership of public utilities, and even of public houses, by municipal authorities, while the Radical Programme suggested that it would have been better if the railways had belonged to the state from the start. There are ample grounds for thinking that, for more than the likely span of Chamberlain's life, a Liberal programme could have been found which would amply have satisfied working-class desires.

What in any case does Liberalism mean? There are those who equate it with the views of the urban middle classes, as expressed in the nineteenth century, and who consequently hold that, as the desires of those classes were satisfied and their predominance declined, Liberalism was bound to yield ground to Socialism and Liberals to turn into Conservatives. But on an alternative view Liberalism is not to be identified with any particular economic creed or the interests of any one particular class but instead with the creation of social conditions in which individuals have the greatest possible chance of self-realisation. On this interpretation Liberalism is a permanent rather than a transient creed, which changes its detailed aims from period to period in accordance with changes in the general environment. It is perfectly compatible with state or communal interference in many walks of life, provided that such interference is on balance judged likely to enhance the freedom of individuals overall – the danger of course being that it will increase the freedom of the ruling group alone or merely put more money into their pockets. From this point of view there is no reason why a fresh left-wing party should have had to be formed in Britain to take over the function which the Liberals had hitherto played in the two party system.

That however was not to happen because social policy did not have the stage to itself. There was also Ireland where a complex situation was made even more complex by the personal relationships of the three main actors, Gladstone, Chamberlain and Parnell. Ireland's revenge was still far from complete.

Notes to Chapter 5

1 T. Lloyd, *The General Election of 1880* (1968), pp. 134–6, 144–5; H. J. Hanham, *Elections and Party Management* (1959), pp. 222–32; B. McGill, 'Francis Schnadhorst', *The Journal of Modern History*, Vol. 34 (1962); F. S. L. Lyons, *Charles Stewart Parnell* (1977), p. 123.
2 Letter in *The Times*, 10 April 1880.
3 Lord Overstone, quoted by R. Shannon, *Gladstone and the Bulgarian Agitation* (1963), p. 130.
4 Shannon, pp. 213–15; J. L. Hammond, *Gladstone and the Irish Nation* (1964), ch. 27.
5 Shannon, p. 163.
6 D. Hamer, *Liberal Politics in the Age of Gladstone and Rosebery* (1968), p. 77; E. Hamilton, *The Diary of Sir Edward Hamilton 1880–1885*, ed. D. W. R. Bahlman (1972), 27 October 1882.
7 J. Enoch Powell, *Joseph Chamberlain* (1977), p. 45 has suggested that Chamberlain took a similar line when he had a preliminary conversation with Gladstone on the afternoon of Monday 26 April. That there had been some contact between the two before Tuesday 27 April is certainly suggested by Gladstone's letter of that date, offering a seat in the Cabinet, which began 'I have made some progress since yesterday afternoon and I may add that there is a small addition to my liberty of choice beyond what I expected'. Yet, if there had been a meeting, it is curious that Chamberlain made no mention of it in the letter to Collings written apparently on the morning of the Tuesday (J. L. Garvin, *The Life of Joseph Chamberlain* (1932), Vol. 1, p. 298) nor in his *Political Memoir* written eleven years later. Gladstone may well have been referring to the indirect communication through Harcourt which certainly occurred on the Monday.
8 S. Gwynn and G. Tuckwell, *The Life of Sir Charles Dilke* (1917), Vol. 1, pp. 304–9; R. Jenkins, *Sir Charles Dilke, a Victorian Tragedy* (2nd edn 1965), pp. 128–33; Hamilton, 29 April 1880.

9 Lady F. Cavendish, *Diary* (ed. J. Bailey, 1927), November 1881; Lady G. Cecil, *The Life of Lord Salisbury* (1931), Vol. 3, p. 7.
10 J. Morley, *The Life of Gladstone* (1903), Vol. 1, pp. 82, 207; Vol. 3, p. 476.
11 R. Shannon, *Gladstone* (1983), Vol. 1, p. 178; Hammond, p. 536.
12 Lady D. Stanley, Diary, 15 January 1886.
13 G. M. Young, *Victorian England* (Oxford, 1936), p. 141; A. Ramm (ed.), *The Political Correspondence of Mr Gladstone and Lord Granville* (1952), Vol. 2, p. 228; Hamer, p. 160.
14 M. Barker, *Mr Gladstone and Radicalism 1885–1894* (1975), p. 43.
15 Address to the Electors of Midlothian, 11 March 1880.
16 W. Lecky, *Democracy and Liberalism* (1896), Vol. 1, p. 182.
17 I. Bradley, *The Optimists* (1980), p. 177; Barker, p. 134.
18 Mr Gladstone to Queen Victoria, 8 May 1885, in *Letters of Queen Victoria*, ed. G. E. Buckle (2nd series 1928), Vol. 3, pp. 700–03; Morley, Vol. 3, p. 173.
19 G. W. E. Russell, chapter on Gladstone in *Prime Ministers and Some Others* (1918).
20 Lloyd, p. 154.
21 J. Bryce, *Studies in Contemporary Biography* (1903), p. 448.
22 Morley, Vol. 1, p. 189; Shannon, *Gladstone*, Vol. 1, pp. 239, 315; R. R. James, *The English Revolution* (1976), Vol. 1, p. 19.
23 R. Shannon in *The Times Literary Supplement*, 6 January 1984.
24 G. Lyttelton, appendix to Vol. 1 of the *Lyttelton–Hart-Davis Letters* (1978).
25 Speech in Midlothian, 25 November 1879.
26 Article in *The Nineteenth Century*, November 1877.
27 Hamer, p. 60.
28 Ramm, Vol. 1, 19 May 1877.
29 A. O. Meyer, *Bismarck's Glaube* (Munich, 1933), p. 39.
30 S. Checkland, *The Rise of Industrial Society* (1964), p. 359.
31 Garvin, Vol. 1, p. 220.
32 In *The Examiner*, 23 January 1875, quoted by Garvin, Vol. 1, p. 222.
33 Ramm, Vol. 1, p. 43; Hammond, p. 77.
34 L. Housman, *Angels and Ministers* (1921), p. 72.
35 Lyons, p. 83.
36 Lyons, pp. 101, 63.
37 Lyons, p. 123; J. Lee, *The Modernisation of Ireland* (Dublin, 1973), p. 106; A. O'Day, *The English Face of Irish Nationalism* (Dublin, 1977), pp. 27, 35, 45, 176.
38 Lee, p. 91.
39 Hammond, p. 196.
40 Lyons, p. 92.
41 Lyons, p. 54.
42 Speech at Birmingham, 7 May 1881, Garvin, Vol. 1, p. 337; Letter from Chamberlain to Morley, 18 October 1881, Garvin, Vol. 1, p. 343; Speech at Liverpool, 25 October 1881, Garvin, Vol. 1, p. 345.
43 Lee, p. 87; B. L. Solow, *The Land Question and the Irish Economy 1870–1903* (Harvard, 1971), p. 198; Hamilton, 19 December 1880.
44 Lyons, p. 166.
45 Morley, Vol. 3, p. 61; Lyons, p. 168.
46 T. M. Moody and F. X. Marvin, *The Course of Irish History* (Cork, 1967), p. 288.
47 Garvin, Vol. 1, pp. 339, 345.
48 Lyons, p. 168.
49 A. Robbins, *Parnell, the Last Five Years* (1926), p. 66.
50 Lyons, p. 201.
51 Morley, Vol. 3, p. 49; Garvin, Vol. 1, p. 358.
52 Garvin, Vol. 1, p. 359; Hammond, p. 355; Hamilton, 4 May 1882.
53 Mrs Campbell Praed, *Our Book of Memories* (1913), p. 97.
54 Hamilton, 4 May 1882.
55 J. A. Cole, *Prince of Spies* (1984), p. 100–14.
56 Lee, p. 87.
57 O'Day, p. 171.

58 Speech in House of Commons on 31 May 1886 by Dwyer Gray and reply by Chamberlain on 1 June 1886; P. Fraser, *Joseph Chamberlain, Radicalism and Empire* (1966), p. 34, quoting letter of 25 January 1880 from Chamberlain to Morley: Gwynn and Tuckwell, Vol. 1, p. 361.
59 Derby's Diary, 4 January 1884, quoted by J. Vincent, *Gladstone and Ireland* (1981), p. 25.
60 *The Nineteenth Century*, June 1877.
61 Lady Victoria Hicks-Beach, *The Life of Sir Michael Hicks-Beach* (1932), Vol. 2, p. 113.
62 Hamilton, 26 April 1884.
63 I cannot find a source for this remark and suspect it has been attributed to Bismarck because it is the kind of thing he might have said. He did write on a despatch in 1876, '*Qui parle Europe a tort – notion géographique*' (*GP*, Vol. 2, p. 255) and 'a *Daily News* correspondent' said to Dilke in 1879, 'What is Europe? A number of wicked old gentlemen with decorations assembled in a room.' (Gwynn and Tuckwell, Vol. 1, p. 279).
64 W. L. Langer, *European Alliances and Alignments 1870–1890* (2nd edn, New York, 1964), p. 252.
65 House of Commons, 12 January 1884.
66 G. Bower, quoted by D. M. Schreuder, *Gladstone and Kruger 1880–1885* (1969), p. 93.
67 House of Lords, 13 March 1883.
68 Kimberley to Selborne, 12 October 1881, quoted by Schreuder, p. 15.
69 P. Kennedy, *The Rise and Fall of British Naval Mastery* (1976), pp. 178–9.
70 Kennedy, p. 193.
71 Speech at the Guildhall, 9 November 1876.
72 House of Commons, 11 April 1879.
73 Garvin, Vol. 1, p. 490.
74 House of Lords, 13 March 1883.
75 H-U. Wehler, *Bismarck und der Imperialismus* (Cologne/Berlin, 1969), criticised by P. Kennedy, 'German colonial expansion', *P and P* (February 1972).
76 J. Chamberlain, *Political Memoir 1880–1892*, ed. C. H. D. Howard (1953), p. 107.
77 Schreuder, p. 456.
78 Garvin, Vol. 1, p. 501.
79 House of Commons, 20 March 1896.
80 Lord E. Fitzmaurice, *The Life of Lord Granville* (1905), Vol. 2, p. 265; A. G. Gardiner, *The Life of Sir William Harcourt* (1923), Vol. 1, p. 514.
81 House of Commons, 27 March 1884.
82 Garvin, Vol. 1, p. 405.
83 Lyons, p. 266; C. C. O'Brien, *Parnell and His Party* (1961), p. 88.
84 Garvin, Vol. 1, p. 392; F. M. L. Thompson, *English Landed Society in the Nineteenth Century* (1963), p. 51.
85 Ramm, Vol. 2, pp. 121–5.
86 Garvin, Vol. 1, pp. 404, 465.
87 Garvin, Vol. 1, p. 472.
88 A. Jones, *The Politics of Reform 1884* (Cambridge, 1972), p. 169.
89 Ramm, Vol. 2, p. 281.
90 Jones, p. 181; Gwynn and Tuckwell, Vol. 2, p. 66.
91 Jones, p. 180.
92 Garvin, Vol. 1, p. 484.
93 Jones, p. 210.
94 Hamilton, 14 May 1885.
95 Jenkins, p. 225, quoting letter from Dilke to Mrs Pattison.
96 Phrase coined by Salisbury in a letter of 25 June 1882 to Northcote, quoted by J. Cornford, 'The transformation of conservatism in nineteenth-century England', *Victorian Studies* (September 1963).
97 Jenkins, *194*.
98 R. Taylor, *Salisbury* (1975), p. 89.
99 But see H. V. Richardson in D. Aldcroft (ed.), *The Development of British Industry and Foreign Competition* (1968), pp. 299–300.

100 Jones, p. 165.
101 Garvin, Vol. 1, p. 385.
102 Reprinted in 1971 as *The Radical Programme*, ed. D. A. Hamer.
103 Gardiner, Vol. 1, p. 472.
104 Shannon, *Gladstone*, Vol. 1, p. 535.
105 Garvin, Vol. 2, p. 96.
106 Hammond, p. 397; J. Amery, *The Life of Joseph Chamberlain* (1951), Vol. 4, p. 511, in J. L. Garvin and J. Amery, *The Life of Joseph Chamberlain*, 6 vols (1932–69).
107 Speech at Ipswich, 14 February 1885, Garvin, Vol. 1, p. 553.
108 *The Times*, 17 September 1885.
109 C. H. D. Howard, 'Joseph Chamberlain and the "Unauthorised Programme"' *EHR*, Vol. 65 (1950).
110 J. A. Hobson, 'The influence of Henry George in England' in *The Fortnightly Review* (December 1897).
111 R. MacDonald, 'Mr Chamberlain as a social reformer' in A. Milner, J. A. Spender, H. Lucy and R. MacDonald, *The Life of Joseph Chamberlain* (1912), p. 164.
112 'Imparting good education to the poorest classes is equivalent to an insurance on our property . . . No money seems to return so good an interest as that which is laid out in securing the morals of the labouring classes', E. C. Tufnell, Poor Law Inspector 1847, quoted by F. Duke in D. Fraser (ed.), *The New Poor Law in the Nineteenth Century* (1976), p. 164.
113 D. Hamer, *John Morley* (1968), p. 153.
114 H. W. Lucy (ed.), *Speeches of the Rt. Hon Joseph Chamberlain MP.* (1885), p. 188. The extract printed in C. W. Boyd, *Mr Chamberlain's Speeches* (1914), begins after this passage. Compare Gladstone's views, as quoted by M. Arnold, *Equality* (1879):

> There is no broad political idea which has entered less into the formation of the political system of this country than the love of equality. It is not the love of equality which has carried into every corner of the country the distinct undeniable popular preference, when other things are equal, for a man who is a lord over a man who is not. The love of freedom itself is hardly stronger in England than the love of aristocracy. Call this love of inequality by whatever name you please – the complement of the love of freedom or its negative pole, or the shadow which the love of freedom casts, or the reverberation of its voice in the halls of the constitution – it is an active, living and life-giving power, which forms an inseparable essential element in our political habits of mind and asserts itself at every step in the processes of our system.

115 J. Chamberlain, 'The Labour Question' in the *Fortnightly Review* (November 1892).

6 'Judas Joe': 1884–6

Ireland 1884–5

The events centering round Ireland between November 1884 and June 1886 were decisive for the history of that country and for the career of Joseph Chamberlain. But their course was complex and they cannot be judged without being studied in detail.

Ireland had become relatively quiescent during the two years after the Arrears Act of 1882 (see p. 123). The Irish MPs were allowed a say in how official patronage was dispensed and had nothing particular to shout for, since there was clearly no chance of the existing Parliament listening to demands for Home Rule.[1] Early in 1883 the Cabinet decided against a proposal of Gladstone's to create an elected council for each of the four provinces. One of his reasons for suggesting such institutions had been the belief that no extension could be made to schemes for land purchase by tenants until it was an Irish rather than an English authority which would suffer if the purchasers repudiated their liabilities. When therefore in June 1883 a Conservative MP proposed 'immediate revision' of the existing arrangements, Gladstone got the adjective altered to 'early' and in effect killed the proposal. His further argument that attention could only be given to Irish affairs at the expense of more pressing English ones reflected a widespread attitude which had already crowded out proposals made by Parnell and supported to some extent by Spencer for amending the Land Act, as well as a Bill for Irish county councils proposed by Healy. In 1884 a renewed proposal by Spencer for amending the 1881 Act found Gladstone so unwell and preoccupied that he never gave the letter an answer. Soon afterwards Parnell suggested that the Committees which the House of Commons had set up to deal with commercial and legal business should be matched by one for Irish Bills but this too was cold-shouldered. The only crumbs of comfort which Ireland received in these years of coercion under Spencer were a Housing of Labourers Act, a Fisheries Act and a Tramways Act. Parnell for his part concentrated on mending his fences with his countrymen, consolidating his followers and concealing his private life.

There was therefore an element of relaunching in the series of conversations which Chamberlain had in October and November 1884 with Captain O'Shea who professed to be, and up to an undisclosed point was, the mouthpiece of Parnell. Where the initiative came from is not clear but three impending events made negotiations of some sort irresistible. For one thing, the Crimes Act was due to expire in September 1885 and there was every sign that Spencer would want it renewed in whole or part. Secondly the Franchise Act with its trebling of Irish voters seemed bound to strengthen Parnell's position in Parliament. Thirdly there was the further imminent prospect of county councils for England and Ireland, announced as a government intention in 1881, coming into being. A deal suggested itself. Irish opponents of a renewed Crimes Act might be appeased if it were limited in scope or time and combined with a considerable dose of local government. Significantly the channel chosen for overtures was not the Viceroy or Chief Secretary, or even the Chief Whip whom Gladstone had named to Mrs O'Shea in 1883 as a suitable person to approach (although, as a right-wing Whig, he was unlikely to be very receptive), but once again a minister who had no official concern with the subject or authority from his colleagues to handle it. The choice was obviously motivated by the expectation that he would be sympathetic, as he was. It gave him a chance of moving back towards the centre of the political stage from which he had recently been displaced by Dilke. His prospects in the election made inevitable by the Reform Act would clearly be improved if he could add an Irish settlement largely of his own making to the rest of the programme which he was going to launch. Moreover it might prevent his being left out, as seemed possible, from the Cabinet which Hartington was expected to form if, as seemed probable, Gladstone's health should finally collapse or the patience of his colleagues be exhausted.

On 27 November, the very day on which the Liberal and Conservative leaders finally agreed about the Redistribution Bill (see p. 136), O'Shea brought Chamberlain a 'short note' giving, or purporting to give, Parnell's views as to the basis on which agreement might be reached. He would also seem to have brought a copy of the Crimes Act with various clauses struck through by an anonymous pen, claimed by O'Shea to be Parnell's, as though indicating that amendment should take the form of their deletion.[2] Chamberlain promptly reported O'Shea's approach to the Prime Minister, who approved its reception, thought it promising and asked that the fish be kept on the line. (Parnell's proposals were only a slight advance on Gladstone's own provincial councils of 1882.) He also said that he had himself received a similar communication from Mrs O'Shea but did not add that, under pressure of work and illness, he had sent it unopened to Spencer.[3]

At this juncture a Hibernophile solicitor in Walsall called Duignan happened to send Chamberlain an account of the impressions which he had gathered while tricycling round the Emerald Isle. He thereby provided a convenient peg on which the recipient could hang a sketch of what was desirable and what impossible. Chamberlain wrote back that he considered Ireland to have a right not merely to county councils but also to a Central Board which would settle for itself, independent of English control, questions of education, land and communications. It would have power to raise taxes for these purposes. On the other hand he stuck to the view which he had propounded two-and-a-quarter years earlier. He could never consent to regard Ireland as a separate people with the inherent rights of an absolutely independent community. 'If Nationalism means separation, I for one am prepared to resist it. I see in it the probability, almost the certainty, of dangerous complications and an antagonism which could be injurious to the interests of the larger country and fatal to the prosperity of the smaller. Sooner than yield on this point, I would govern Ireland by force to the end of the chapter.'[4] He was forgetting that most books have more than one chapter.

This letter was shown, with Chamberlain's consent, to several Irish politicians and came to the ears of others, including Parnell. It elicited a further visit from O'Shea on 17 January, with a plan for local government in Ireland which only differed from Chamberlain's thinking by being more modest. The Central Board was to be administrative rather than legislative, more influence was to be allowed to landlords and no bid was made for the control of the police. What O'Shea failed to make clear, although instructed to do so twice over by Parnell, was that 'we do *not* propose this Local Self-government plank as a substitute for the restitution of our Irish Parliament but solely as an improvement of the present system. ... The claim for the restitution of Parliament would still remain'.[5] The reason for the plan's moderation was precisely that it had to be prevented from weakening the demand for full legislative independence.

Chamberlain might have been put on his guard by the fact that the document was in O'Shea's writing and there was no guarantee, other than the go-between's word, that it fully represented the views of Parnell. O'Shea also copied to Chamberlain a letter in which he told Parnell of his interview with the minister and this so misrepresented what had passed as to suggest that the intermediary's accounts were not to be relied on. It did however contain the sentence 'as long as you are practical for the time being, Chamberlain does not appear to mind the determination which you are expressing in your speeches of recovering Grattan's Parliament'.[6] Chamberlain should not therefore have been altogether surprised when on 21 January Parnell said openly that, so far from accepting local self-government as a substitute for the restitution of Home Rule, he was not even prepared to say that Home Rule itself would provide a final settlement. In the words now carved on his Dublin monument, 'no man has the right to fix the boundary of the march of a nation'.[7] Even if this was read as a negotiating bid deliberately pitched high, Chamberlain was taking a risk by allowing it to pass unchallenged. He later claimed to have remained ignorant of the material qualification in Parnell's offer while Parnell himself claimed to have remained unaware of this ignorance. But both positions seem to have been hardened up in retrospect.

Chamberlain had in any case been thinking of his Central Board, not as a measure for the 1885 session but as one to be laid before the reformed Parliament after the election. In venting on O'Shea on 21 January for the misleading letter part of the irritation which an abscessed mouth was causing him, he said he must make it clear that the time had not arrived for any negotiation or agreement. During the next two months he is said to have sought the sympathy of all his colleagues for his ideas but in fact little seems to have happened. Ministers' minds were elsewhere, notably in the Sudan (Khartoum fell on 26 January). What set things moving again was a Cabinet memorandum from Spencer on 28 March insisting on the need to continue coercion but proposing to combine it with a scheme for local government and an extension of the land purchase arrangements. This produced on 11 April a paper from Chamberlain on the lines of the Duignan letter, while limiting the extension of coercion to twelve months. When soon afterwards it emerged that the Irish bishops would support an agreement on such a basis he sent round a further memorandum expanding on the role envisaged for the Central Board. Exactly what scope this was to assume remained somewhat nebulous, but the term 'local government' was taken to include 'not merely local and municipal affairs but also questions which may be described as national, although they do not concern Imperial interests ... The establishment of such a Board would involve the practical disappearance of what is known as "Castle" Administration'. These were the papers before the Cabinet when on 28 April it turned to Irish affairs and set up a Committee to consider them.[8]

Spencer, who had been wavering over the Central Board project, had by now become convinced by his officials that to have an Irish administrative body working under English policy control would be an infallible recipe for friction. Certainly the maximum which the English would have been likely to grant would have been unlikely to attain the minimum with which the Irish would have rested content. Gladstone, although strongly in favour, took the puritanical view that he should not try to influence a decision which could only take effect after he had left the political stage (as he was then expected to do at any moment).[9] Although O'Shea sought to strengthen Chamberlain's hand by producing another equivocatingly encouraging document ostensibly emanating from Parnell, the remaining ministers were so divided on the question of a Central Board that its adoption was decided on 9 May to be impossible.[10] Gladstone forecast that within six years the opponents would be repenting in sackcloth and ashes.

Chamberlain considered it impossible to fly in the face of Spencer. Yet, unless he could get the decision reversed, he could no longer hope, by staying in office, to get the credit for negotiating an Irish settlement (and a desire to prevent him from doing just that may have been at the back of Gladstone's passivity). He would do better to get out of office and thereby recover his full freedom of speech (see p. 144). But if he was to resign (a step which nine of his colleagues had for one reason or another threatened to take at intervals during the previous month),[11] he must do so over something which the electors could be persuaded to think worth resigning about. Manoeuvring to this end influenced the events of the next few weeks.

If a Central Board was ruled out, how far was coercion to be given up in exchange and what was to provide the sugar coating for the pill of such coercion as was not given up? A Land Purchase Bill, acceptable to Spencer, was put forward. But sensible as this would have been, Chamberlain and Dilke not only wanted revenge on Spencer for frustrating them over the Central Board but were afraid that a Land Purchase Bill on its own might weaken the case for saying that some sort of local government measure was essential. Gladstone pre-empted the decision of his colleagues by telling Parliament that the Crimes Act was to be extended for two years without any mention of palliatives and then, to calm the resulting excitement, announcing with equally little consultation that there was to be a Land Purchase Bill. His claim to have understood Chamberlain to have acquiesced has been seen by some (perhaps including Chamberlain at the time) as a subterfuge, his real aim having been to rule out a revival of the Central Board idea (although it is not clear why he should have wanted to subvert a project which he favoured). Dilke resigned without more ado but Chamberlain, although feeling obliged to follow suit, thought the squabble too minor to be a good breaking-point and got both resignations put on ice. Two days later a reasonably accurate account of the row appeared in the *Birmingham Daily Post*. Many including Gladstone pointed an accusing finger at Birmingham's chief citizen. But he not only denied having had any 'direct' communication with the paper but pointed out that much of what it said had already appeared in the *Pall Mall Gazette*, with which his relations were anything but cordial. In any case Gladstone, who had recently institutionalised non-attributable ministerial leaks by devising the 'Lobby' system, was in a weak position to complain.[12]

Ministers were still at sixes and sevens over the scope and duration of the Crimes Bill when on 8 June the government was unexpectedly defeated for putting up the duty on beer without doing the same for wine. Not only did Parnell and thirty-six of his followers vote with the opposition but seventy-six Liberals (of whom only fourteen were paired) failed to vote at all. Rumour had it that Chamberlain had organised their inaction so as to get out of office without having to find a reason for doing so.[13] Certainly he and Dilke had played a leading role in persuading the government to display such injudicious class prejudice about beverages. Chamberlain was also in fairly close touch with the mercurial Lord Randolph Churchill at this time and who can say what that pair may not have concocted? But if it was at his prompting that the abstainers were behaving, he must have found arguments to talk round a number of members whose ear he did not normally possess.

Next day the Cabinet decided to resign.[14] After a fortnight in which the Conservatives discovered that the circumstances attending their accession to office made it considerably less attractive than a more distant view had suggested, Lord Salisbury formed his 'Caretaker' government (see p. 145), thereby providing an end to the current chapter of Anglo-Irish history. But before the next one can be embarked on, there is a more personal matter to be disposed of.

Chamberlain and Dilke

On Friday 17 July 1885 Donald Crawford, Political Secretary to the Lord Advocate for Scotland and a distant cousin of Dilke, received an anonymous letter (the fourth of a series) which led him to accuse his young wife (sister of Dilke's brother's widow) of adultery.[15] She confessed and named Dilke as the man with whom she had had an affair since February 1882. Crawford brought an action against Dilke which was heard on 12 February 1886. Dilke, on the advice of his lawyers, with whom Chamberlain is said reluctantly to have concurred (primarily because a key witness could not be produced), did not go into the witness-box, on the ground that no evidence of any legal force had been brought against him. The case against him was dismissed and costs awarded in his favour; but, with questionable logic, Crawford was also given his divorce. The apparent contradiction in the verdict stirred up talk. In particular W. T. Stead, who had succeeded Morley as the editor of the *Pall Mall Gazette*, made a series of attacks on Dilke, with whom he began to associate Chamberlain, blaming the latter for keeping Dilke out of the box. Chamberlain as a result urged Dilke to induce the queen's proctor to intervene. This led to a hearing before a special jury on 16–17 July, which took the form of a case between the proctor, Crawford and Mrs Crawford. Although Dilke gave evidence and was cross-examined, he was not directly a party and his counsel could not speak in court. The verdict upheld the February decision but lurid facts which had emerged seriously discredited Dilke's reputation, while also establishing that Mrs Crawford was by no means a witness of truth.

·In the belief that he had been framed, Dilke and his friends set about collecting additional evidence. Much of this discredited Mrs Crawford still further. But hard evidence also emerged that on Wednesday 15 July (two days before the last anonymous letter) Mrs Crawford had called at Chamberlain's London house and had spent some time there while he was present. It would also seem that the letter had been posted at a pillar-box in the same street. Chamberlain, when questioned about the visit, did not deny it but never gave, in public at any rate, any explanation of it beyond saying that she found nobody at home and did not go in (which was at variance with the evidence of the detective employed by Crawford to watch his wife).

It can be argued that for Dilke to have his political career brought to a virtual halt at this juncture, when it had been tacitly agreed that, on Gladstone's withdrawal from politics, the Liberal leadership should pass to him, was greatly to Chamberlain's advantage. But it can equally be argued that for Chamberlain to lose his chief ally at this moment was greatly to his disadvantage (although for him to see this, his judgment would have had to be sounder than it sometimes was). The two men professed to be intimate friends but there had been several differences of opinion between them: when Gladstone's Cabinet was forming (see p. 110), over the question of Dilke becoming Chief Secretary in 1882 (p. 123), over Dilke's entry into the Cabinet in December 1882, over the Redistribution Bill (p. 136) – this had particularly annoyed Chamberlain – and over their resignations in May 1885 (see p. 158). J. E. C. Bodley, the historian and writer who was Dilke's secretary, believed Chamberlain to have been the man behind the conspiracy. But Dilke himself, although he considered Chamberlain's explanations inadequate and unsatisfactory, thought that Mrs Crawford's visit on 15 July had been a mere chance and refused to believe that it had a sinister significance. 'What Bodley will not see', he said, 'but what I and [my wife] can is that, although a "Red Indian", Chamberlain is loyal to his friends and incapable of such treachery.'

The conspiracy could also have been engineered by some woman or women who had hoped to marry Dilke and were angry at the announcement in the autumn of 1884 of his engagement to the widow of the Oxford don, Mark Pattison (said to have been the original of Dr Casaubon in *Middlemarch*). The two most likely persons were Mrs Eustace Smith (Mrs Crawford's mother), who had certainly been his mistress earlier, and a Mrs Rogerson; unflattering evidence about both emerged in the course of the trials.

Yet if Mrs Crawford's visit to Chamberlain admitted of an innocent and respectable explanation, why did he (a) keep silent about it until it came to light through other channels later and he was questioned about it; (b) say she had not entered the house when he must have known or been told that there was evidence to the contrary; (c) fail, so far as is known, to say what the purpose of the visit was? It is generally agreed that, when Mrs Crawford presented herself at his door, he was not at home, only arriving a few minutes later. Yet she was admitted, as she hardly would have been unless the servant knew her or had orders to let her in. Whether the two had ever met before and, if so, in what relationship, has never been ascertained; there is an undocumented verbal tradition that she was Chamberlain's mistress as well as Dilke's!

The existing evidence is inconclusive and by this time seems unlikely to be supplemented. The verdict must lie somewhere between 'not guilty' and 'not proven'. But the episode is of considerable importance to anyone assessing Chamberlain's character. Immediately the blow fell, he took Dilke to his Birmingham home and saw him almost daily through the summer. Dilke on leaving said, 'I owe to you that I was able to live at all through this awful time ... I shall never be able to repay – but I can't forget'.[16] In October Chamberlain was best man at Dilke's wedding. He wrote to several people that his friend was innocent and that the charges were impossible. For him to have engineered the conspiracy would have involved a high level of perfidy. But for him to have done so and then to have behaved as he did would put him on a par with Iago. If he were capable of it, nothing which he ever did or said in the course of his life could be accepted at face value. The question has a clear bearing on that of the genuineness of his political convictions (see p. 149). What makes the matter more difficult is that this is not the only time when a similar question arose.

Chamberlain and Parnell

Immediately after the Liberal government fell, Chamberlain asked Parnell, through O'Shea, whether the Irish leader still held to what the Liberal leader still mistakenly believed to be his own proposals for settlement (but which were in fact merely Chamberlain's own proposals to which Parnell did not object, although not considering them to go far enough). If he did, Chamberlain and Dilke would promise not to take office in any government which would not make them part of its programme. This inquiry was met by a sinister and significant silence. O'Shea merely proffered reasons why he could not obtain an answer.

Nearly four months earlier, on 27 February, Parnell had had an interview with the Conservative Chief Whip who had promised him that, in the event of the Tories coming to office, the numbers of Irish members at Westminster would not, as a result of the Redistribution Bill, be reduced nor any decisions already made about new constituency boundaries be revised. Contemporaneously the Tories and the Irish more than once acted in obvious collusion in the Commons. Rumours spread that a deal was in preparation and seem bound to have reached Chamberlain's acute ears.[17]

The next development was a conversation between Parnell and Lord Randolph Churchill, probably on the very day (9 May) on which Chamberlain failed to carry the Cabinet with him for his Central Board scheme. Churchill promised that he would not be a party to any renewal of coercion. 'In that case', said Parnell, 'you will have the Irish vote at the Elections.'[18] A bargain on such terms offered advantages to both sides. Until the election, any Conservative government must be a minority one and, as such, could not possibly carry a renewal of the Crimes Act through the Commons against the Irish and Radical members. A promise not to attempt such a feat could therefore be made cheaply. But what were the chances of the Conservatives, after the Reform Act, ever being anything more than a minority? The general expectation was that the enlarged electorate would lead to a substantial and lasting Liberal majority. The only possibility of a different result lay in the Irish vote being given to the right. Parnell was gambling – as it proved, correctly – on the outside chance of being able to give the casting vote in a hung Parliament. If so, he could make his price Home Rule. For Home Rule to be enacted, it would have to pass through two Houses of Parliament. The prospect of getting it through the Lords would be transformed if it was proposed by the Conservatives and not by the Liberals. The flaw in this calculation may seem to have been that, if both the Conservatives and a substantial number of Liberals refused to vote for Home Rule, there would be no majority for it in the Commons, let alone in the Lords. But unless the Conservative–Liberal agreement extended to more than Home Rule, Parnell could prevent a government of either complexion from passing any legislation at all by throwing the Irish votes behind whichever party was providing the opposition. In any event, the gamble was well worth taking and Parnell must have been gratified when on 20 May, five days after Gladstone had announced the government's decision to renew the Crimes Act, Churchill declared himself against it. No doubt the Irish leader's desire to get a Tory government into office accounts for the help which his followers gave to getting the Liberal government out of office on 8 June.

Parnell had skilfully given himself a free hand. Towards the Liberals, he had committed himself to nothing in his own writing and verbally had merely allowed it to be indicated that, if a scheme for a Central Board were brought in, he would support it – as he undoubtedly would have done, although only as an interim palliative. If manipulation of the Irish vote failed to prevent an overall Liberal majority, he could resume pressure.

But for the time being the Liberals were in opposition and to give Chamberlain any further encouragement might scare away the Tories at a critical moment. Moreover there were other Irishmen like O'Brien and Healy who thought it dangerous to give a Central Board scheme any support at all in case it were used as an argument for holding up a wider measure. On 27 June *United Ireland* began to publish a series of articles criticising both the Radicals and the visit which had been planned to give Chamberlain (accompanied by Dilke) his first sight of Ireland. Although the paper was the one generally supposed to have been closest to Parnell, he does not seem to have inspired the articles; on the other hand he remained deaf to suggestions that he should repudiate them. The Catholic bishops for their part showed a sudden reluctance to provide the travellers with the introductions which had been promised; while they appreciated Chamberlain's sympathy for Ireland, they did not equally appreciate his enthusiasm for making education non-denominational. It began to be borne in on him that negotiating from the uncertainties of opposition was not the same thing as negotiating from the security of office. The visit was called off.

On 11 July he sought in a letter to O'Shea to make Parnell stand and deliver:[19]

I have often expressed my opinion that the Irish people are entitled to the largest measure of self-government consistent with the continued integrity of the Empire ... With this object in view, I ventured to sketch a scheme of County Boards and National Councils. I did not suggest this arrangement as a substitute for Home Rule, as the demand for a separate Parliament ... with full powers in regard to every subject except foreign and colonial affairs and national defence, is one which may be treated independently of the question of local government. [But he *had* been thinking of the Boards, if not as a substitute for Home Rule, at least as a means of postponing Home Rule and weakening the Irish case for it. The admission was a dangerous one, since a main argument of the opponents of the scheme was that the Irish would merely exploit it as a stepping-stone to Home Rule.]

I have not concealed my objections to such a proposal nor my opinion that it could not be accepted by the people of Great Britain but on the other hand I have never attempted to obtain any pledge for its withdrawal [which would never have been forthcoming].

A complete and effectual system of local government ... may be found sufficient to satisfy the Irish national sentiment ... but if this should not be the case, no arrangement could possibly bind the Irish people not to pursue their demands further. [He could hardly have written like this if he had believed, as he later made himself out to have done as a result of O'Shea's deception, that Parnell would accept the Board as a final solution.]

Under these circumstances I was very glad to hear from you in January that Mr Parnell . . . had authorised you to place in my hands a written scheme for Irish Local Government which, although it differs from mine in important details, was based on similar principles. You informed me that Mr Parnell had declared that acceptance of this scheme in its main features would be in his opinion a settlement of the question [a studiously ambiguous phrase] and would be the foundation for amicable and cordial relations between the two countries . . . I could see nothing in his proposals to which Liberals ought to object and I have . . . therefore since that time omitted no opportunity to . . . urge their acceptance as the basis of immediate legislation . . .

I have therefore seen with astonishment and regret the bitter attacks both on Sir Charles Dilke and myself and also on the scheme for local government . . . which have been made in [Mr Parnell's] paper *United Ireland* and by some of his leading followers.

It is impossible that these attacks . . . could have been made unless the authors of them believed that they had Mr Parnell's approval, and I think Mr Parnell is bound as a gentleman . . . to take steps to correct the impression that he is hostile either to our visit or to the scheme for local government which has been proposed on lines laid down by himself.

The letter ended by arguing that the opportunity for introducing such changes might not recur and ought not to be lightly thrown away.

The only reply was an evasive letter giving the impression that Parnell was disinclined to interfere with the editorial policy of *United Ireland*, considered the state of affairs to have materially changed in recent weeks and doubted whether it was worth 'encumbering the Irish question' with a special measure of self-government until it was clear what the Conservative policy towards Ireland was going to be. According to Chamberlain, O'Shea said openly that 'he has had a better offer'. At the end of July O'Shea was told to let Parnell know that, as far as Chamberlain was concerned, the matter was at an end.[20]

The 'Radical Programme', which gave some prominence to national councils that would be both legislative and administrative, had already appeared when this message was sent but in the autumn campaign of speeches they cropped up only twice and were described as being purely administrative. Attention was switched instead more exclusively to the English scene. Chamberlain would seem to have been moving towards the conclusion that, as he was to write to Dilke on Boxing Day, Councils were a 'feasible practical plan' but open to the fatal objection that the Nationalists would not accept them.[21] This however meant that, instead of being the author of a settlement, he was without a positive policy for Ireland. The blame for his discomfiture lay partly on O'Shea. But one gets the impression that all along he had been over-excited by the political advantage which he saw himself acquiring if he could carry through a settlement on his terms and as a result paid insufficient attention to evidence suggesting that Parnell's attitude was not what he wanted it to be. If he was to succeed, he had to take risks and he trusted in his own negotiating skills to match those of the other side. In retrospect he tended to exaggerate the extent of his misapprehension. But instead of blaming himself or O'Shea, he conceived an ominous grudge against Parnell who had never in fact misrepresented his own position and genuinely thought that Chamberlain had been put in possession of it.

The Conservatives and Ireland

As his Viceroy of Ireland, Salisbury chose Lord Carnarvon, known to his friends as 'Twitters', who had been Colonial Secretary in Derby's 1866 Cabinet, when he had been responsible for introducing federation in Canada, and in Disraeli's 1874 Cabinet, when he had stirred up a hornet's nest by trying to do the same in South Africa. While wintering in Italy, Carnarvon had come under the influence of Sir Charles Gavan Duffy who, after getting himself imprisoned in 1848 for his part in 'Young Ireland', had migrated in despair to Australia and there for six years governed Victoria. In the light of his colonial experience Duffy advocated giving Ireland the embryonic form of 'Dominion status' which Canada, the Australian colonies and New Zealand already possessed *de facto*; the need was recognised for special provisions to be made in Ireland safeguarding the interests of landlords and Protestants. Carnarvon, as Salisbury knew, was attracted by these ideas. He persuaded his colleagues to abandon coercion and to bring in a new scheme for land purchase by which the state would advance to the tenant the whole purchase price of his farm and recover the cost by instalments. In the House of Lords he expressed his conviction that the 'terrible question' of Ireland could be satisfactorily solved. He established good relations with the bishops who thought that the Tories could be trusted not to involve them in popular assemblies or 'godless' education. Through Duffy he met Justin McCarthy, Parnell's vice-chairman, and on 14 August even had a *tête-à-tête* interview with a reluctant Parnell in an empty house in Mayfair. At this the Englishman certainly showed that he was sympathetic to some form of Home Rule and the Irishman certainly emphasised that no reform could be satisfactory which did not include a central legislature for the whole island. Parnell must have felt that the tide was flowing in his favour although it is impossible to say how far he really (as he later claimed) took Carnarvon to be speaking with the authority of the Cabinet.

In fact only two members of that body knew of the interview, although one was Salisbury who had urged caution and eschewance of the written word. A fortnight earlier Parnell had raised in the Commons the way Spencer's régime had handled criminal cases and in particular a vicious murder at Maamtrasna in 1882 when it was alleged that an innocent man had been hanged. Carnarvon took the bipartisan view that nothing should be said to undermine confidence in the officials and judges administering Ireland but had not been able to prevent Churchill and Hicks Beach from attacking Spencer who found nobody to speak in his defence. (Chamberlain and Dilke abstained.) Parnell no doubt congratulated himself on having induced the Conservatives to embarrass the Liberals but, since he did not know what Carnvarvon's attitude had been behind the scenes, failed to realise that the incident exemplified the limits of the latter's influence over his colleagues. In fact the Cabinet was not prepared to make serious concessions to the Irish but equally was not prepared to say so until after the election. Salisbury's recipe for governing the island had all along been to do what seemed right to the English and not bother unduly about whether it pleased the Irish; in 1890 he was to disown any desire to satisfy their national aspirations, which seems to justify his exclusion by a recent historian from the ranks of 'nature's celtophiles'.[22] In any case his chief concern at the moment was to keep his hold over his party which had only just decided that his rival Sir Stafford Northcote was too much of a Grand Old Woman to be a suitable leader. His main pre-election speech, at Newport on 7 October, was carefully equivocal. He can hardly have chosen Carnarvon for any reason other than temporary expediency.

Meanwhile things had also been moving in the Liberal camp. On 14 July Gladstone's son Herbert spoke out at Leeds in favour of Home Rule for Ireland within some sort of federation. In his enthusiasm for this cause he was apt to run ahead with embarrassing results. His father was not in fact engaged in actual negotiations, as many including Chamberlain suspected, but was trying to find out through his Chief Whip and then (when that brought no results) by direct approach through 'that bothersome woman Mrs O'Shea' (as Hamilton once called her)[23] what Parnell's terms for settlement were. In particular he wanted to know whether the document which he had mentioned to Chamberlain in the previous November (see p. 155) and which he set about retrieving from Spencer, was still valid. The answer he got was that Parnell thought the time had come for the 'leaders of English political opinion to consider giving to Ireland independence on the colonial model, though with guarantees'. Gladstone replied by invit-

166

ing greater detail but also refusing to compete for Irish favour against the Tories, whose 'heightened bidding' he took to be the reason why the schemes of the previous winter were out of date.[24]

Parnell decided that the moment had come to stake out a claim publicly in no uncertain terms, especially as certain restless spirits among his followers such as Healy were reported to be dining with Chamberlain. In two speeches in Ireland during the holidays he repudiated the idea that Ireland could be ruled like a Crown Colony and insisted that she be allowed to govern herself, with a right to put import duties on English manufactures. This induced Chamberlain to include in his speech at Warrington (see p. 148) a clear warning that those who refused to indulge in mutual scratching of backs were likely to find themselves involved in scratching of faces:[25]

> If these and these alone are the terms on which Mr Parnell's support is to be obtained, I will not enter into competition for it. If this claim were conceded, we might as well for ever abandon all hope of maintaining an United Kingdom. We should establish within less than thirty miles of our shores a new foreign country animated from the outset with unfriendly intentions towards ourselves. A policy like that would be disastrous and ruinous to Ireland herself and . . . we are bound to take every step in our power to avert so great a calamity. . . . Mr Parnell seems to me to forget the change which has come over our constitutional system. . . . He is face-to-face with the whole population of England and Scotland, reinforced as it will be by at least one-fifth of the population of Ireland itself, and to threaten thirty-two millions of people with the vengeance of four millions is a rhetorical artifice which is altogether unworthy of Mr Parnell's power and influence. But it is said by him that justice requires that we should concede to Irishmen the absolute right of self-government. . . . I cannot admit that five millions of Irishmen have any greater inherent right to govern themselves without regard to the rest of the United Kingdom than the five million inhabitants of the metropolis.

Two days later Gladstone wrote to Rosebery, 'Chamberlain says what are four millions against thirty-two? The answer depends wholly on the case'.[26] Whereas the society of the metropolis was an integral part of English society in general, the Irish would have claimed that their society was a distinct entity. As Hartington was to tell Chamberlain in March 1887, 'In Ireland the demand on the part of a large section at all events of the people and their leaders is for national recognition'.[27] Although Chamberlain said in April 1886 that 'there are two nations in Ireland', he came to see that if he was to square his refusal of autonomy to the Irish with his general political position, he must deny them nationhood. In December 1886 he said to Harcourt[28]

> I do not think that Ireland can be recognised as a nation without conceding separation. Ireland is a province and the cardinal difference between Mr Gladstone and myself is that he has treated the question from the point of view of the separate Nationality of Ireland while I have regarded it from the point of view of a State or Province.

What constitutes a nation? The objective answer of 'differences in such things as language, religion and status' hardly helps in the case of a country whose nationalists were led by a Protestant landlord ignorant (like many of his colleagues) of Gaelic. Renan however, with an eye to Alsace-Lorraine, had in 1882 given the question a subjective answer:[29]

> A nation is a soul, a spiritual principle. . . . It is summed up in the present by a tangible fact − consent, the clearly-expressed will to continue life in common. The existence of a nation is a *plébiscite de tous les jours.*

Is then any group which claims to be a nation entitled to be allowed to decide its own fate? How far can this be carried? If Ireland is to be treated as a nation, what about Ulster? If Ulster, what about Fermanagh, or Monaghan? The only answer may be the pragmatic one of allowing self-determination to any group which has enough nuisance value to make refusal a difficult and protracted business. In the letter just quoted, Gladstone told Rosebery, 'Some of you seem to me not to have taken any just measure of the probable position of a serious dispute with the Irish nation'.[30] The difficulty which a liberal state finds in coercing was something to which Chamberlain shut his eyes. It is of course true that for most of the next 36 years Ireland was to be coerced but the treatment could only be maintained as long as the Irish MPs did not have a casting vote at Westminster. Once they regained that position, they would be able to make parliamentary government impossible by refusing to support any government which did not grant Home Rule. It is true that, if Ireland had been given self-government as a single unit prior to 1914, Britain's strategic position in 1914–18 and 1939–45 might have been weakened, although it needs to be remembered that an Ireland which had been satisfied would not necessarily have been disloyal, whereas an Ireland which had not been satisfied might have been more of a liability than an asset.

Gladstone spent August 1885 on a cruise to Norway which so reinvigorated him that on return he told his chief followers of his readiness to go on leading them, provided they wished him to do so. As usual, the thought of the squabbles which would follow his departure made them express a delight which was less than heart–felt. Thus endorsed, he set out to draft the address to his Midlothian electors which took the place of a manifesto by the party. He recorded that the Irish paragraph gave him most trouble, with the result that, if Salisbury 'danced on eggs' at Newport, what his rival provided was a plate of porridge:[31]

> To maintain the supremacy of the Crown, the unity of the Empire and all the authority of Parliament necessary for the conservation of that unity, is the first duty of every representative of the people. Subject to this governing principle, every grant to portions of the country of enlarged powers for the management of their affairs is, in my view, not a source of danger but a means of averting it and is in the nature of a new guarantee for increased cohesion, happiness and strength.

There are some who have believed, and Chamberlain was probably one of them, that Gladstone made up his mind in favour of Home Rule in the first half of 1885 and started to work towards it without telling anybody. Such a simple deception would have been quite out of character, although it is closer to the truth than the view that it was the 1885 election results which converted him. The true position was more probably as follows:

(1)   As long ago as 1855 he had said that the way to deal with dependent territories was to 'govern them upon a principle of freedom'. In 1877 he had said that 'whatever the effect on party, it is better that a nation preferring self-government should have self-government'.[32] For some time past he had been in favour of greater devolution, as much to relieve the pressure on Parliament as to satisfy local aspirations, and had put forward two proposals (Grand Committees 1880; Provincial Councils 1882) to that end. Only once, in 1871, had he spoken against Home Rule.[33] In 1881 he had written to Granville about 'the perilous crisis, which no man has as yet looked in the face; the crisis which will arise when a large *and* united majority of Irish members demand some fundamental change in the legislative relations of the two countries'.[34]

(2)   He had been in favour of a Central Board and had gone further than Chamberlain in that he had been prepared, with certain reservations, to put it in control of the police. He had described the proposal as 'the only hopeful means of saving Crown and State from an ignominious surrender in the next Parliament after a mischievous and painful struggle'.[35] He drew from the rejection of the proposal the conclusion that a demand for Home Rule had probably been made inevitable but that it would involve a major political crisis. He thought that such a measure might possibly be

carried but only 'by the full use of a great leverage. That leverage can only be found in the equitable and mature consideration of what is due to the fixed desire of a nation, clearly and constitutionally expressed'.[36]

(3) As an 'old Parliamentary hand', he realised that, if the Irish knew this to be his position, it would only encourage them to demand the maximum of freedom. He had however long hoped that they would be content with something short of complete independence (as Parnell probably would have been). He therefore took care not to publicise what he thought he would be prepared to do as a last resort, especially as such publicity would split his party shortly before an election. This made it impossible to open his heart to someone who was known to talk indiscreetly to journalists and who claimed that the arrival of popular government made it impossible to keep questions under wraps until the moment of decision had arrived.

(4) His inclination to believe Home Rule inevitable was strengthened by the apparent readiness of the Conservatives to put it up to auction. Their action convinced Spencer and the chief officials in Dublin that it was bound to come.[37] Gladstone thought it a mistake to bid against them, especially as he saw that a Conservative government would have a much better chance than a Liberal one of carrying a measure through the House of Lords, as his hero Peel had done over the Corn Laws. This consideration made him more inclined that ever to lie low about his own views.

(5) He is often said to have been influenced by a desire to distract attention from the Unauthorised Programme; Chamberlain even came to believe that he proposed Home Rule to prevent Disestablishment![38] But until Home Rule was out of the way, the Irish could join with the Tories to block any other radical legislation, so that by proposing Home Rule Gladstone would be easing the way for such legislation, unless he was calculating that, once the Irish quitted Westminster, there would be no majority in Parliament for left-wing measures.

Intelligible and statesmanlike as Gladstone's position was, it had two defects. First it prevented the Liberal leaders from engaging in any thorough discussion of the form which Home Rule should take and of the way in which it could best be reconciled with the unity of the empire. This constituted an acute problem and division of opinion over it was the ostensible reason why Gladstone's proposal was destined to fail. Secondly, he did try to clarify what it was that the Irish wanted. To do so was an essential preliminary to deciding what they should be offered but when combined with his reticence about his own position, it did great damage. For news of the feelers inevitably leaked out; their purpose was misunderstood and their importance exaggerated.

In September Gladstone presciently put to Chamberlain the problem which would arise if Parnell came back from the election with 80 to 90

followers and demanded self-government for Ireland with adequate securities for imperial unity. Chamberlain discounted the possibility of this
happening but said that, if the securities were adequate, he would strive
every nerve to help the government but thought he might be able to do so
best from outside the Cabinet. At the beginning of October he made his
one and only visit to Hawarden. It had been arranged by an intermediary
and neither side quite knew what the object was. 'He is a good man to talk
to', wrote his host, 'not only from his force and character but because he
speaks with reflection, does not misapprehend or (I think) suspect or make
unnecessary difficulties or endeavour to maintain pedantically the uniformity and consistency of his arguments throughout'. Most of the
discussions were concerned with making the Radical Programme less
alarming to moderates and Ireland occupied only a small part of them.
Gladstone got the impression that they were 'pretty well agreed' except as
to the likely extent of Parnell's demands. Chamberlain found Gladstone
'very full' of the question but did not think he had a definite plan for
dealing with it [which was not surprising since the question itself had not
yet been defined in terms of Conservative policy or election results].
Gladstone claimed (although Chamberlain later denied all memory of his
having done so) to have mentioned the contingency (which was obviously
occupying his mind) of a big Irish question arising, and arising in such a
form as to promise a possibility of a settlement. 'That would be a crisis
with a beginning and an end and perhaps one in which from age and
circumstances I might be able to supply aid and service such as could not
exactly be had without me'. A fortnight later Gladstone wrote saying that
'an instinct blindly impresses me with the likelihood that Ireland may
shoulder aside everything else'. He asked Chamberlain to co-operate in
keeping the Liberal Party together until its list of agreed subjects should be
exhausted.[39]

Gladstone in short saw what was coming; Chamberlain assumed that
the Liberals would win a clear majority in the election and that Parnell
could in those circumstances be fobbed off by renewing the national
council scheme.[40] But it was not so much the prospect of not winning the
election which disturbed Gladstone; that would merely make worse the
critical problem of how to deal with a House of Commons in which 80 to
90 per cent of the Irish MPs called for Home Rule. As Chamberlain refused
to take the danger seriously, he failed to ask what Gladstone would do if it
materialised, while Gladstone, for reasons which have been explained,
was disinclined to volunteer information. Unfortunately Chamberlain
learnt soon afterwards through the garrulous Labouchere that approaches
to the Irish had been made. Gladstone's belief that he was not suspicious
proved the reverse of truth. Chamberlain assumed that active plans for
promoting Home Rule were in hand and felt not unreasonably that the

Grand Old Man had been less than candid with him. A year earlier he had rushed into Dilke's room after an interview with Gladstone saying 'I *don't* like him, really I hate him'.[41]

In the same month of October Parnell took two steps towards getting an offer out of the Liberals. He first tried to answer the arguments that any concessions made to his party would be exploited with the object of gaining more till complete independence had been extorted, and that an independent Ireland would be hostile to England:[42]

> My advice to English statesmen . . . would be – trust the Irish people altogether or trust them not at all . . . Give our people the power to legislate upon all their domestic concerns and you may depend on one thing, that the desire for separation, the means of winning separation, at least, will not be increased. It is impossible for us to give guaran-tees, but we can point to the past, we can show that the record of English rule is a constant series of steps from bad to worse, that the condition of English power is more insecure and unstable than it has ever been.

As examples of the beneficial effects which followed from the granting of self-government he cited Hungary since 1867 and the colonies; in neither case was history to confirm that magnanimity would preserve the sover-eignty of the government which displayed it.

Secondly Parnell sent on 30 October through Mrs O'Shea the detailed 'Constitution for Ireland' which Gladstone had invited in August. It provided for a single-chamber Irish parliament, with power to legislate and appoint the executive for all domestic and internal affairs (including taxes, tariffs, the administration of justice and the police). Representation for the Protestants was to be secured by special arrangements (which could not of course efface their minority status) but nothing was said about protection for landlords. Ireland was to pay £1m. a year to the imperial Treasury towards defence but in return be free from imperial taxation. The question of keeping the Irish members at Westminster was left open but, if they remained, they would be debarred from voting on English domestic matters (as defined by the Speaker). Gladstone however was not to be drawn into expressing an opinion on the document, either privately or publicly. He said that, as he was not a minister, he had no right to assume the functions of one. Parnell's reaction was to advise his country-men in England to abstain in the coming election from voting for Liberals or Radicals, whom he loaded with abuse.

Estimates of the number of English seats which this advice cost the Liberals varied from 65 (T. P. O'Connor, who had drafted Parnell's message) to 20 (Herbert Gladstone); Chamberlain himself put it at 25.[43] In

Ireland itself Liberal representation was wiped out, 85 seats being won by Nationalists (who also won a seat in Liverpool) and 16 by Ulster Conservatives. The surprise of the election lay in the English boroughs, where the move of middle class suburbia ('Villa Torydom') into the Conservative camp became unmistakable. Voices were heard, led by *The Times*, saying that Chamberlain's radical speeches had frightened away the voters; he did not really answer this by retorting that the election had been fought on a manifesto 'which had not contained a single point to which the extreme Liberals attached importance'. Some votes may have been lost by the call to replace 'free' with 'fair' trade but equally some may have been won by the fear of tariffs putting up food prices. The Liberal situation was saved by the country constituencies where 'Three acres and a cow' had won many first-time voters. Overall the Liberals won 335 seats, the Conservatives 249; the discrepancy of 86 was exactly filled by the Home Rulers.

Chamberlain, who said that 'next time we must have an urban cow', had reason to be crestfallen. The spell of the Caucus had proved shortlived; good organisation by itself was not enough to win town seats. His confidence in an overall majority for the Liberals had been unfounded; his dream of playing the leading role in a great reforming ministry was not to be realised. Gladstone and Parnell had proved shrewder judges than he had been. There could be no doubt that 'a big Irish question' lay ahead.

The First Home Rule Bill

No sooner were the election results known than Chamberlain, Dilke and Morley took counsel together. They agreed that the Liberals could be rescued from having to make up their minds about Ireland if the Tories could be induced to stay in office. They anticipated that a few years of Conservative government would work wonders for Liberalism's electoral chances. Dilke hoped that the formation of the next Liberal government could be delayed until a successful conclusion to the Crawford case made high office again accessible to him. In his penultimate significant appearance in politics, he advocated at a private dinner the strategy of leaving the other side to bat. This came to the ears of Herbert Gladstone who interpreted it as a plot to shelve Home Rule and concentrate attention instead on domestic policy, not merely because this was thought more important but also because it would bring with it the shelving of his father. The same story came to the ears of Wemyss Reid, editor of the *Leeds Mercury*, who had never forgiven Chamberlain for his treatment of Forster (a Bradford MP). Reid urged the younger Gladstone to give some public indication of what the elder's attitude might be. As a result an enthusiastic but inexperienced MP who did not know how to leak information without being revealed as its source gave an interview to two young journalists whose desire to prove their story authentic overcame any inhibitions against disclosing its source. On 17 December the 'Hawarden Kite' hit all the headlines. Gladstone was said to be prepared to take office with a view to creating an Irish Parliament to manage all domestic legislative and administrative affairs. (Hints to this effect had already appeared in the *Liverpool Post* and *Daily News*.)[44]

To Chamberlain it must have seemed that the man who had done most over the last five years to baulk his political desires (while professing sympathy with many of them) was on the point of gratifying the political desires of the man who had just, as he thought, played him false. His instant reaction was hostility. 'Mr G's Irish scheme', he wrote to Dilke, 'is death and damnation; we must try to stop it.'[45] Small wonder if, with the half-knowledge which he had of negotiations in progress, he refused to be as incredulous as Gladstone asked about the latter's views and intentions. He believed the leak to have been a put-up job (such as he might have organised himself) and to give an accurate indication of a conclusion which the older statesman had reached long before. Gladstone at this very juncture told Hartington that he had 'more or less of opinions and ideas but no intentions or negotiations';[46] while this may have been strictly true, he was no doubt concealing from himself how small a margin of choice would be left in his mind when the moment arrived for him to make it up. The election had removed one point of uncertainty; his forebodings about Home Rule strength had been realised. But there was one other question to be clarified before he took his decision and that was the way the Conservatives were going to behave. He was not merely at one with Chamberlain in wishing to keep them in office but was in the middle of overtures with Salisbury to that end through A. J. Balfour,[47] the Prime Minister's nephew. In spite of pressure from Parnell he refused to pass judgment on the scheme which the latter had sent him or go into details as to what he himself would propose. He reminded the Irish leader that the bulk of the Liberals, after the way they had been abused, would be far from keen to gratify Irish demands.[48]

But Salisbury was ceasing to keep a door open because he saw no prospect of his party going through it and was averse to doing so himself. The opponents of concession had already on 14 December carried the Cabinet in favour of coercion. Gladstone's approach, betrayed by Churchill to Labouchere who promptly retailed it to Chamberlain, was ridiculed as a barefaced attempt to set his opponents quarrelling among themselves. But the Hawarden kite suggested that the tables might be turned on Gladstone. If he had really decided to propose a thoroughgoing scheme of Home Rule, the sooner he was put back into office the better, since there was a good prospect that Hartington and the Whigs would then quit the Liberal Party and provide the Conservatives with a majority independent of the Irish. On 26 January the government announced its decision to renew coercion, thereby inciting the Irish to turn against it. The natural sequel would have been a debate on policy towards Ireland in which the Liberals would have had to show their hand. To avoid this trap, their leaders accepted a suggestion of Chamberlain's and an amendment was moved by Collings regretting the absence from the queen's speech of any proposal to give allotments to agricultural labourers. This was carried although the opposition mustered 90 less than their full strength and 18 Liberals, including Hartington, voted against their own party, while 76 more abstained. Salisbury resigned with alacrity.

Gladstone invited his former colleagues to join a Cabinet whose first priority would be to explore the practicability of satisfying the desire, 'widely prevalent in Ireland', for a Dublin-based legislature. Had he stated any more precise intentions, he would have failed to form a government, since most of the politicians who did consent to join him were doubtful about Home Rule. Hartington stood aside, telling the Duchess of Manchester that 'now he has gone as far as he has, it is necessary that he should have a fair trial and should show his hand. If he fails, and if either the English or the Irish won't have his plan, there may be some chance of governing Ireland in some other way; but if he is prevented from having a fair chance by premature obstruction or opposition. I don't believe the country will be governable at all'.[49]

Four other peers who were ex-ministers also refused to join, thereby realising Chamberlain's long-term objective of evicting colleagues whom he had recently confessed to hating more than the Tories. But he himself could not risk incurring the blame if Gladstone's attempt to form a government broke down. Although he had told Dilke they must stop the Irish scheme, he had added 'We must not openly commit ourselves against it yet – we must let the situation shape itself before we decide'.[50] So he therefore took office on condition that he could retain 'unlimited liberty of judgment and rejection' on any scheme which might be proposed, although Gladstone extracted from him a parallel promise that he would give 'an unprejudiced consideration' to any proposals which went further than he had previously advocated.

As regards offices however Gladstone could not have been more difficult if he had been wanting to keep Chamberlain out of the Cabinet, as indeed he may have been. With Dilke and the Whigs out of the running, the Radical leader had become a key figure and common sense might seem to have recommended an effort to conciliate him by the offer of a major post like the Exchequer. But perhaps Gladstone was afraid of being served as Randolph Churchill was to serve Salisbury later in that same year or perhaps he really believed that such an appointment would be too much for the City's nerves. The Treasury was therefore offered to Harcourt, whose support through the ensuing months was thus assured, and Chamberlain was offered the Admiralty. When he expressed distaste for having to entertain in an official residence, he was asked what office he would prefer and, when he gave the Colonial Office as an unexpected answer, got (by his own account) the rejoinder 'Oh! A Secretary of State!'[51] (It is an intriguing thought that, if he had had his way, he might have become so absorbed in the department's work as to lose interest in Home Rule.) He does not seem to have been told that that berth was needed for the Prime Minister's old and valued friend Granville whom everyone, from the queen downwards, thought 'past it' for the Foreign Office (but who could perfectly well have been made Lord President).

Chamberlain then suggested – and was given – the Local Government Board, where he not only prepared a draft scheme for county councils, which would have been the second item in the government's programme if it had ever got as far, but also authorised local sanitary authorities to find work of communal value for the unemployed (this circular was not quite such a novelty as has sometimes been suggested and only 75 authorities out of 673 acted on it).[52] As Parliamentary Secretary, Chamberlain asked for his henchman Collings. Gladstone, while agreeing, gave way to his mid–Victorian passion for saving candle–ends by trying (unsuccessfully) to cut the salary from £1,500 to £1,200. Morley was offered the post of Chief Secretary to Ireland, with a seat in the Cabinet (in defiance of the 'Peel principle' (see p. 110). As he had publicly committed himself in favour of getting the Irish out of Westminster, this was a pointer to Gladstone's intentions, although one which Morley himself hesitated to trust. Chamberlain realised that an old ally was being detached from him and that he would as a result find himself the only Radical in the Cabinet (except perhaps for Trevelyan) opposed to Home Rule. He said however that Morley could not keep any self-respect if the offer were refused.

Chamberlain was in a cleft stick. How could a man who had gained the reputation of being keener than most to satisfy Ireland offer point-blank opposition to Irish wishes without suggesting an alternative? Yet how could a man who had gone on record so consistently about the dangers of Home Rule and his determination to oppose it suddenly turn round and accept it? His instincts prompted him to fight the issue on principle and, seizing the initiative from Gladstone, concentrate the energies of the Liberals on social reform rather than the satisfaction of the Irish. But how could he obtain a majority for that, especially as many of the Radicals to whom he would naturally look were so 'raving mad' about Gladstone that they would vote for any Irish scheme he put forward and find it hard to forgive anyone who stood in its way?[53] And Gladstone wanted what in

General Staff terms is known as a 'big solution' not only because it offered the best chance of enduring but also because the Home Rulers were not going to settle for anything less. Chamberlain did not lack friends to point out that, if he helped Gladstone to secure Home Rule, he would secure for himself the succession to the Liberal leadership and then be able to give priority to whatever he wanted. He is often said to have been actuated by motives of personal ambition but in fact he was acting against the interests of his career. The personal motive which did influence him was antipathy to Gladstone and here his frustration warped his judgment. Perhaps too the authoritarian in him disliked the prospect of surrendering power.

To perform the Cabinet's first task of examining what could be done for Ireland, a Committee to consider alternative courses might have been thought the obvious procedure (as was to happen in 1892). A document listing the choices with their advantages and defects would have considerably clarified subsequent discussion. But discussion was not Gladstone's way. A substitute however appeared in the February issue of the *Fortnightly Review*. After regretting that Parnell was not being left to produce his own scheme as a basis for negotiation, 'A Radical' (the pseudonym with which Chamberlain affected to cloak himself)[54] went on to list eight choices:

(1) National councils: a sound idea but the Whigs had rejected it and now the Nationalists would not have it.

(2) An independent Parliament in Dublin: this would soon acquire power to deal with all internal questions. Irish representatives would have to remain at Westminster to express their country's views on defence, foreign policy and customs. There they could make things difficult since the government, although possessing a majority in Britain, might not have a majority in the United Kingdom.[55]

(3) The Canadian model: but Canada was to all intents and purposes independent.

(4) Britain to have garrison rights in an otherwise independent Ireland: probably the safest form of separation but incompatible with Gladstone's declared aim of maintaining the integrity and security of the empire.[56]

(5) Federation: this would involve the abolition of the House of Lords and the Crown, for which public opinion was not ready.

(6) Complete separation: a hostile Ireland would raise a conscript army of 150,000 and Britain would have to follow suit.

There therefore seemed to be no scheme which would be acceptable both to Parnell and to Parliament. In this case, two further possibilities should be considered:

(7) Doing nothing: Parnell's American funds might dry up, his control over his followers might slip and English Liberals (especially among the working classes) might lose sympathy for him. There was no reason to suppose that violence would increase. If the Irish gave trouble in Parliament the Speaker should act as a dictator or Irish representation at Westminster should be temporarily suspended.[57]

(8) If no generally acceptable scheme of Home Rule could be found but something had all the same to be done, Parnell should be invited to join the government to deal with the land question 'in frank concert with the Irish population'. A scheme should be prepared enabling the Irish authorities to buy land, sell it to tenants and reimburse the Exchequer out of the proceeds.

Accordingly, when Chamberlain saw Gladstone on 30 January and again on 13 February, he suggested tackling land, education and municipal government first and waiting to see what resulted from changes in these fields before reaching a conclusion on 'more extended local government'. He affected to hope that, now the Irish knew they could get nothing out of the Tories, they might scale down their terms. But when he suggested to Parnell, through O'Shea, taking land purchase before Home Rule, he got no clear response. For hopes in the Tories, the Irish had substituted hopes in Gladstone and until they saw what came of these hopes, they would settle for nothing else. But Gladstone adhered to his habit of formulating his major legislation himself, consulting from time to time Spencer and Morley (used from late March onwards as a channel to Parnell) but no other ministers. Chamberlain was invited to submit his ideas about land purchase and did so on the lines of his article. His solution appealed to the Radicals, who were concerned lest the British taxpayer should be expected to provide the money for compensating Irish landlords. But, although his proposals were circulated to the Cabinet, they were never discussed.

Instead Gladstone on 13 March disclosed his own ideas on the subject, less ingenious and more generous. Chamberlain, whose manner was described as being 'almost brutal', insisted on being told whether the money was to be advanced to a part of the United Kingdom under full control by Parliament or to what might turn out to be a practically independent nation. Gladstone replied that his plans must be considered in succession as they were submitted but did admit to thinking that there should be an Irish authority for legislative purposes, thereby showing in effect that he had made up his mind on the main issue which the Cabinet had been formed to examine without producing any of the evidence which had brought him to this conclusion. Chamberlain and Trevelyan thereupon resigned, nominally over the form of the land purchase scheme, but were persuaded to wait until the full plans for Ireland had been revealed. News of the resignation however leaked out. Chamberlain put it about that, if his resignation was not accepted, he would stay and be master of the Cabinet (because he would only stay if his views prevailed).[58]

A fortnight later Gladstone placed before his colleagues a broad resolution for submission to the House, saying boldly that a legislative body should be established by statute in Dublin, under carefully framed provisions. (He possibly chose this form, rather than that of a draft Bill, to stop the Cabinet bickering about details.) Chamberlain immediately asked:

(a) Whether the Irish representation at Westminster was to cease?
(b) Whether the power of taxation, including customs and excise, was to be given to the Irish Parliament?
(c) Whether the appointment of judges and the magistracy was to be vested in the Irish authority?
(d) Whether the Irish Parliament was to have authority in every matter not specifically excluded by the Act constituting it (as in the USA) or merely in matters specifically delegated to it?

The answers to all these questions being in effect 'Yes', Chamberlain and Trevelyan walked out and no further attempt was made to hold them back. They had decided to choose as their breaking-point the retention of Irish members at Westminster, with all that followed from it, a solution which Chamberlain had three months earlier described as 'the worst of all plans'. Gladstone showed great satisfaction that, come what might, he was rid of Chamberlain for good.[59] Six years later Chamberlain said that he had gone into the Cabinet with no intention to resign but that Gladstone had gone in with the intention of driving him out; Morley and Rosebery confirmed that they had had the same impression.[60]

Nothing more was heard about a resolution and the full Bill was tabled. A fortnight later Chamberlain used its First Reading as an occasion for justifying his departure and started to do so on the land purchase proposals as well as the constitutional ones. Gladstone, who had not for nothing described himself as 'an old parliamentary hand', tripped him up on the procedural point that, as the former had not been announced, the queen's authority to disclose events in Cabinet did not extend to them; the validity of this argument is open to question but Chamberlain, having paid too little attention to a warning from Churchill, was caught by surprise and felt compelled to defer.[61] But instead of merely objecting to Gladstone's Home Rule scheme, he now for the first time propounded in public the idea of a federal solution. He also called for an all-party Committee of the House, to be given the task of working out a solution; Gladstone retorted that such a Committee would be incapable of such a task.

In the interval between First and Second Readings the Cabinet went back on the decision to leave the Irish free to fix their own customs and excise duties. The possibility of them using this power to put duties on imports from Britain was thought capable of killing the Bill 'in every manufacturing and commercial centre in the land'.[62] But this change led logically, on the principle of 'no taxation without representation', to the decision that Irish members must attend at Westminster for discussions on matters of common interest. Various proposals were made, and might easily have been added to the Bill at the committee stage, for enabling them to do so. These went some way towards depriving the Bill of one of its chief merits in English eyes, in that Parliament would no longer be rid of 'the dry rot in the House of Commons' (as Granville described the Irish).[63]

The modifications did not however induce Chamberlain to alter his stance, thereby invalidating the theory that it was midland business fear of Irish tariffs which lay behind his opposition. During the debate on the Second Reading he repeated that any scheme of federation involved too great a disturbance of the constitution to be practicable at the moment, only to point on the following day to the Canadian federation as affording the best guide to a satisfactory solution. Various proposals were made for bridging the gap. But Gladstone, with the backing of his colleagues, was determined not to give the appearance of capitulating and Chamberlain was going to be content with nothing less than capitulation. Gladstone told his Chief Whip that 'with men like most of my colleagues it is safe to go to an extreme of concessions. But my experience is that in Chamberlain's case such concession is treated as an acknowledgment of his superior greatness and as a fresh point of departure', while Harcourt told Gladstone that 'you will be deceived if you think that Chamberlain is to be conciliated on any terms. He has no thought but of war to the knife'.[64] Mundella, the Radical President of the Board of Trade, wrote, 'he hates Gladstone. He has no sense of gratitude or loyalty'.[65] Chamberlain had told Harcourt he did not want a compromise and Dilke that 'the retention of the Irish members is only, with me, the flag that covers other objections'. Twelve years later he declared that he had deliberately seized on this item in order to kill the Bill.[66]

Two mutually antipathetic personalities were contending for power and each believed that he could win. Gladstone thought that, with his prestige in the country, he could carry the Bill at least through the House of Commons. Chamberlain thought that he could defeat the Bill in the Commons, that defeat would make Gladstone retire from politics and that the Radical Liberals would then turn to himself as leader. It was largely as a result of these attitudes that the Bill was defeated on 8 June by 343 votes to 313 and, if considerable influence was unintentionally exercised in the closing stages by John Bright writing to say that he would vote against the

Second Reading, it was Chamberlain who got Bright to write and he too who read the letter to a meeting of hesitant MPs. (The government added to its problems by choosing this moment to quarrel with the railways over freight rates.[67] But there is nothing to show that the twenty-six Liberal railway directors who voted against Home Rule would not have done so anyway.)

Britain's tragedy – and Ireland's – was that two headstrong men frustrated one another largely for personal reasons and that, instead of Gladstone achieving Home Rule with Chamberlain's help and then retiring to leave the way free for Chamberlain's social programme, neither project was realised. Most of the social legislation had to wait for twenty years and more, while it was to be in effect thirty-five years before three-quarters of Ireland received autonomy. And reforms are like fruit; if they are left too long, their capacity for satisfying is impaired. Instead of the 1885 Reform Act ushering in the era of popular government, the progressive party in British politics was out of power for twenty years and it was during those years that an independent party representing the workers established itself. Liberalism was undermined by the defection of the middle classes to Conservatism and of the working classes to Labour. There are too many variables in the situation to say with any assurance that if the left had been bearing the responsibilities of government instead of the frustration of opposition, it would have remained united and prevented the polarisation of politics along class lines, not to mention the distortion caused to Britain's adversarial representative system by the introduction of a third party. There was no reason why a Liberal government under Chamberlain could not have produced a programme to satisfy working-class demands for a decade or two. Dr A. J. P. Taylor has said that, seeing how hard it is to establish what did happen, historians should not indulge in pipe-dreams as to what might have happened. Yet it is only by judicious testing of alternatives that we can reach a proper appreciation of the realities. Is it injudicious to speculate as to what might have happened if Ireland had been set on the road to self-government in 1886, if the reforms of the 1906 Liberal government had been enacted before 1890 and if it had fallen to a government of the left not only to tackle the Boers but to hold power for ten of the twenty years between 1919 and 1939?

The objection has been made that there was no chance of Home Rule being passed in 1886. Even if it had got through the Second Reading, it would have been so changed in committee as to become incapable of satisfying Irish demands. If it had retained its form in the Commons, it would have been thrown out in the Lords. A dissolution would not have produced a majority justifying the creation of peers to swamp the Lords, to which a partisan queen would not in any case have consented. If it had got passed into law, it would have had to be imposed by force on a

181

recalcitrant Ulster. Ireland would have been left to her own devices only after all other solutions had been tried and found wanting (which was in fact what happened). This is obviously impossible to prove one way or another, although the argument can only be maintained in full rigour if no changes at all are assumed in the existing balance of forces, since under them Home Rule must have failed, as it did fail. The question is rather whether the changes needed to imagine its success are so big as to become fantastic. If they are, it is a terrible indictment of British political skills and enhances one's respect for Gladstone's effort to achieve a big solution. It is precisely the damage which was done to Anglo-Irish relations and to British class-antagonisms which makes one interested in considering whether greater imagination or humanity could not have been shewn earlier. The people who defeated Home Rule are not entitled to any particular credit.

There is the further objection that if, after the 1885 election, when the Liberals were widely expected to win, they only had a majority with the aid of the Irish, they could not have hoped for a majority after the Irish had left Westminster and the Whigs had crossed the floor (as a thoroughgoing radical programme would lead them to do). Acton, foreseeing the difficulty, suggested that the remedy was to give votes to women – a distinctly problematic solution! But the Liberal Unionists 'remained a regiment of officers without common soldiers and with little prospect of finding a rank-and-file'.[68] And in 1886 the Conservatives won 203,000 less votes than the Liberals. It was only thanks to the 386,000 votes gained by Liberal Unionists and to the peculiarities of the British voting system that the Conservatives emerged with 125 more seats.[69] (There were a number of uncontested constituencies but as many of these were won by Liberals as by Conservatives.) It is certainly true that, as Reginald Brett told him, Chamberlain was not yet strong enough to do without the moderate Liberals, a fact which would have damped down his programme. But if the Unionist breakaway had been fifteen smaller, or if the election had been fought on issues other than Home Rule, on which Liberals were less inclined to abstain, an adequate majority for them is quite conceivable.

There are of course those who would put on Gladstone the main blame for the failure of these dreamt-of blossoms to ripen. It has been suggested that if he had quitted politics in 1885 or not come back to them after 1875, the transition from Liberalism to Radicalism would have developed gradually but naturally, while a proposal to give Ireland Home Rule would have generated less passionate opposition. Gladstone undeniably behaved high-handedly; it was not in his nature to cajole or conciliate people whom he found uncongenial. But, as Harcourt said, the author of the Unauthorised Programme was hardly entitled to complain about that.[70] Gladstone had always been inclined to concentrate on one topic to the exclusion of everything else and, as we get older, we become more like ourselves. He was too precipitate both in proposing Home Rule (but here his hand was largely forced) and in proposing one particular form without allowing time for others to be examined (but he accepted several modifications and expressed willingness to consider more). He was right in seeing Ireland as a festering sore in Britain's anatomy which was not going to be healed by being repressed or even by the economic poultices which the Conservatives were going to offer. 'Our ineffectual and spurious coercion is morally worn out.'[71] Ireland was not going to be healed without surgery (any more than it will be healed today) and refusal to nerve oneself to the pains and controversy involved in surgery makes it all the more grave when finally resorted to. It needs to be shown that Chamberlain or some other Liberal leader would have proposed and could have carried a Home Rule scheme wide enough to be a durable settlement if Gladstone had left the stage.

Chamberlain by contrast gives between December 1885 and June 1886 the impression of a man casting around for an alternative solution to justify his resistance to Gladstone, and finding none. In October 1885 he had admitted to not seeing his way at all on Ireland.[72] Having been the principal opponent of coercion from 1880 to 1885, he settled for a policy which was bound to involve it. This reversal of priorities was what earned him the shouts of 'Judas' when the voting figures for the Second Reading were announced. He was condemning himself to fight on a negative programme whereas the unauthorised one had been emphatically positive; he was turning his back on the principles of Liberalism; he was cutting himself off from his closest political friends and associating instead with Hartington who was anything but a kindred spirit; he was, as it turned out, giving up his chances of becoming Prime Minister. He was much influenced by the analogy of the American Civil War, fought to maintain the Union, but failed to remember that the ultimate issue there had been slavery, not secession.

Perhaps it is a pity that he did not develop earlier or more fully the idea of federation. For it was on a failure to think through the implications of this state-form that the move to give self-government to Ireland foundered. For federation involved two Parliaments at Westminster, one to deal solely with English affairs and one to deal with affairs common to the whole of the United Kingdom. (The English Parliament might have been sited in a provincial city like Birmingham!) Scotland, Ulster and probably Wales would then have pressed for legislatures of their own and become constituent states. Gladstone's various proposals tried to make the existing Parliament perform both jobs. Every way of arranging how to do this, and what position to give to the Irish members, had objections which rendered it unacceptable. To have no Irish members there at all meant taxation without representation. To have them there nominally only for UK affairs would still allow them to influence British affairs by using the threat of withheld votes as blackmail. To have them present for all affairs would give them an influence in Britain which Britain would not have in Ireland, as well as retaining the disadvantages of the existing system when to many the strongest argument for Home Rule was that it would get rid of the Irish. (It is true that something very like the last arrangement was put into practice for nearly fifty years as regards Northern Ireland, but then it was to the interest of the Ulster MPs to maintain the system rather than to wreck it.) Chamberlain was however right in suggesting that a federal system would require a written constitution, a Supreme Court and a revised Upper Chamber.[73] While we may think that their introduction would have been no bad thing, a good deal had to happen before public opinion became ready so much as to consider them.

Would federation (if practicable) have been a solution? Federations come into being when political units wish to be associated for some purposes but refuse to be associated for all purposes. There has to be a sense of common interests alongside a sense of divergent interests. Whether the federation survives depends on whether the centripetal forces grow and the centrifugal ones weaken or vice versa. Perhaps Mr Enoch Powell was going too far when he said that 'even in its attenuated form of a customs union or preferential trading block, a Federation is a nation – a sovereign political unit – or it is nothing'.[74] But a federation without strong common interests or loyalties is vulnerable to attempts at secession.

If the United Kingdom had been converted into a federation in the 1880s, it is doubtful whether the Irish sense of common interests would in the long term have been strong enough to enable it to endure. If Ireland had included Ulster, there would have been constant friction. If Ulster had been made a separate state, the rest of Ireland would have had a lasting incentive to disloyalty. It is questionable whether Britain had the strength to impose her will on Ireland indefinitely, even if her people had had the will to try.

There were those, such as Rosebery, Forster and the Imperial Federation League, who welcomed Home Rule primarily because they saw it as a step towards a federation which would include not only the United Kingdom but also Canada, the Australian colonies, New Zealand and possibly South Africa. When Chamberlain tested the ground for such a thing ten years later, opposition proved far stronger than support. It would be hard to demonstrate that the result could have been different in 1886. There was too much fear of being dominated by the centre, which points to an awareness that interests were not sufficiently common. Geography still had more influence than accelerated communications. The only solution was the Liberal one of 'Dominion status' and that again was something in which the British public would only take a pride when there was less left to be proud about.

Chamberlain's conclusion that the only alternatives open to Britain in regard to Ireland were separation and governing by force to the end of the chapter may have owed something to a desire to prove to the Gladstonian faithful that they were being led up a blind alley. But that need not mean he was wrong. His own willingness to prefer permanent repression in turn owed something to his pessimistic view about the sequel to separation. Even if we, wise through hindsight, judge separation to have been the lesser evil, it looks as though Home Rule could have been only a staging post and not one attractive enough to induce a lengthy stay. The ultimate ineffectiveness of the Tory policy of 'killing Home Rule by kindness' showed that, no matter how comfortable the accommodation was made, the Irish travellers could not be induced to remain in it once the weather began to clear again. When all is said and done, there would have been considerable advantage in getting the journey started in 1886 rather than 1911.

Notes to Chapter 6

1   A. O'Day, *The English Face of Irish Nationalism* (Dublin, 1977), pp. 61 ff.
2   The version of events given here has been reconstructed from the following evidence:
   (a)   Chamberlain (*Political Memoir 1880–1892*, ed. C. H. D. Howard (1953, p. 140) said that O'Shea brought him on 18 January 1885 a memorandum embodying Parnell's scheme. Garvin (*The Life of Joseph Chamberlain* (1932, Vol. 1, p. 581), printing the memorandum with its date of 14 January, put the visit on 15 January, with a further visit, at which the marked copy of the Crimes Act was handed over, a few days later. O'Shea (Garvin, Vol. 1, p. 584) put it on 17 January. Chamberlain (*Political Memoir*, p. 141) said that he saw Gladstone about it on the same day.
   (b)   Gladstone was away from London from 3 to 20 January and from midday 22 January to 5 February (A. B. Cooke and J. Vincent, *The Governing Passion* (1974), pp. 175, 180, 186). Chamberlain on the other hand was confined to his house with an abscessed jaw on 20 and 21 January (Garvin, Vol. 1, p. 537; Cooke and Vincent, pp. 180, 184). Gladstone's letter of 31 January to him (Garvin, Vol. 1, p. 558) strengthens the impression that they did not meet in mid-January. The visit about O'Shea must therefore have been made before 3 January or after 6 February.
   (c)   By February attention had switched to the external situation and Chamberlain had on 21 January choked off O'Shea (Garvin, Vol. 1, p. 586).
   (d)   Chamberlain said (*Political Memoir*, p. 143) that 'at about the same time' as the 18 January visit O'Shea brought the copy of the Crimes Act. But the paper in the Chamberlain archives relating to this copy, in Chamberlain's own hand, says it was brought in November 1884 (*Political Memoir*, p. 143n).
   The simplest way of reconciling this clash of evidence is to suppose that
   (i)   O'Shea brought both his 'short note' (Garvin, Vol. 1, p. 578) *and* the copy of the Crimes Act on 27 November; Chamberlain saw Gladstone on the matter later in the same day.
   (ii)   There was no meeting between Chamberlain and O'Shea on 15 January. The only person who suggests that there was is Garvin and he quotes no documentary evidence in support.
   (iii)   A meeting between them did take place on 17 January since O'Shea, in his letter of 18 January to Parnell (Garvin, Vol. 1, p. 584), reports on the meeting which he

had had with the minister 'yesterday'. At this meeting O'Shea presented his memorandum of 14 January.

(iv) On some date prior to 21 January O'Shea sent Chamberlain, in 'an envelope . . . open on two sides', [a copy of] his letter of 18 January to Parnell.

(v) Chamberlain, writing seven years later, misdated the meeting of 17 January as having occurred on 18 January and associated his visit to Gladstone with it instead of with the meeting on 27 November. Garvin was misled by the fact that the O'Shea memorandum was dated 14 January into supposing that it was handed over on the following day and then invented a further meeting at which the Crimes Act was handed over.

3 J. L. Hammond, *Gladstone and the Irish Nation* (1964), p. 49.

4 Garvin, Vol. 1, p. 579, 17 December 1884.

5 Garvin, Vol. 1, p. 588; 5 January 1885.

6 Garvin, Vol. 1, p. 585; 18 January 1885.

7 F. S. L. Lyons, *Charles Stewart Parnell* (1977), p. 260, 24 January 1885; Chamberlain, *Political Memoir*, pp. 144–7; Garvin, Vol. 1, p. 600.

8 Lyons, p. 272; Cooke and Vincent, p. 225.

9 Garvin, Vol. 1, p. 602.

10 Dilke has often been quoted as recording that all the ministers in the Lords except Granville were against and all in the Commons except Hartington were in favour. If accurate, this would have given an 8:8 split. But, although the attitudes of individuals would seem to have been much as Dilke indicated, the official record, quoted by Cooke and Vincent, p. 231, shows that the discussion took place after some ministers, including Dilke, had left. This recent account of the episode plays down the importance of the decision. But it was from then on clear that a Central Board, the horse on which Chamberlain had put his money, was a non-starter. Cooke and Vincent (pp. 32–5) argue that at the time he was only interested in the Irish question in so far as it could be exploited to give him future control of the Liberal Party. No doubt he did have such considerations at the back of his mind but this need not mean he was using the issue of Ireland merely as a pretext.

11 E. Hamilton, *The Diary of Sir Edward Hamilton*, ed. D. W. R. Bahlman (1972), 18 May 1885.

12 *The Times*, 18 January 1984.

13 Hammond, p. 375, quoting *The Correspondence of Lord Acton* (1917), Vol. 1, p. 265.

14 D. M. Schreuder (*Gladstone and Kruger* (1969), p. 465) says that 'Hartington and Rosebery did not even bother to attend the last Cabinet – they went to the races to watch the Derby'. But the Derby was run (as always) on a Wednesday, on 3 June, whereas the last Cabinet met on Tuesday 9 June; Cooke and Vincent (p. 244) say that it was attended by all ministers.

15 The facts in this section are drawn almost entirely from R. Jenkins, *Sir Charles Dilke, a Victorian Tragedy* (2nd edn 1965). See also B. Askwith, *Lady Charles Dilke* (1969).

16 Garvin, Vol. 2 (1933), p. 43.

17 Lyons, p. 276; Hamilton, 24, 27 and 28 February, 3 and 7 March 1885; Cooke and Vincent, pp. 68–9.

18 W. S. Churchill, *Lord Randolph Churchill* (1906), Vol. 1, pp. 390–5.

19 Chamberlain, *Political Memoir*, pp. 151–4.

20 Chamberlain, *Political Memoir*, p. 157.

21 S. Gwynn and G. Tuckwell, *The Life of Sir Charles Dilke* (1917), Vol. 2, p. 200.

22 J. Lee, *The Modernisation of Ireland* (Dublin, 1973), p. 112. In an article in *The Quarterly Review*, October 1872, Lord Salisbury wrote, 'To conduct Irish affairs on any principles is hard enough; but to govern a population which does not wish to be governed by you on the principle of implicitly attending to its wishes appears to be about as hopeless a task as ever politician undertook.' See also Salisbury to Carnarvon, 27 March 1890, quoted by Hammond, p. 730.

23 Hamilton, 5 November 1882.

24 Hammond, p. 421; Lyons, pp. 291–2.

25 C. W. Boyd (ed.), *Mr Chamberlain's Speeches* (1914), Vol. 1, p. 243. Compare Hitler on

the annexation of Austria in 1938, 'What can words like independence or sovereignty mean for a state of only six million?'

26 Gladstone to Rosebery, 10 September 1885, quoted by Hammond, p. 521.
27 Chamberlain, *Political Memoir*, p. 260.
28 Chamberlain had some difficulty in deciding how to describe Ireland:
   (a) In the House of Commons, 9 April 1886, he said 'Ireland consists of two nations, [Interjection "No, no"] that is, it is a nation which comprises two races and two religions.'
   (b) In Birmingham twelve days later he said that 'There are two nations in Ireland, two communities separated by religion, by race, by politics and by social conditions' (Boyd, Vol. 1, p. 266).
   (c) In December 1886 he wrote to Harcourt in the terms quoted in the text (M. Hurst, *Joseph Chamberlain and Liberal Reunion* (1967), p. 145). See also the letter quoted by Garvin, Vol. 2, p. 284, from *The Times*, 18 January 1887.
   (d) On 12 October 1887 he said in Belfast, 'There are two Irelands. There is the Ireland which is prosperous and loyal and contented. There is an Ireland which is miserable and dissatisfied and continuously under the control and leadership of agitators.' He then went on in the words quoted in note 60 to Chapter 4: 'When it is proposed to put a race . . . under the other race'. (Boyd, Vol. 1, p. 287). By contrast Gladstone asked in Parliament on 7 June 1886 'Have hon. gentlemen considered that they are coming into conflict with a nation?'
29 E. Renan, *Qu'est-ce qu'une Nation?* (Paris, 1882).
30 Hammond, p. 521.
31 *The Times*, 17 September 1886.
32 P. Knaplund, *Gladstone and Britain's Imperial Policy* (1927), p. 225; D. Hamer, *Liberal Politics in the Age of Gladstone and Rosebery* (1968), p. 123.
33 Hammond, p. 118.
34 A. Ramm (ed.), *The Political Correspondence of Mr Gladstone and Lord Granville* (1952), Vol. 2, pp. 10–11.
35 Ramm, Vol. 2, p. 366.
36 Letter to Rosebery, 13 November 1885, quoted in J. Morley, *The Life of Gladstone* (1903), Vol. 3, p. 240.
37 Hammond, pp. 435, 445.
38 J. Amery, *The Life of Joseph Chamberlain* (1951), Vol. 4, p. 511; (1969), Vol. 6, p. 723.
39 Morley, Vol. 3, pp. 224–6; Garvin, Vol. 2, pp. 108–110; Hammond, p. 407.
40 W. H. G. Armytage, *A. J. Mundella 1825–1897* (1951), p. 229.
41 Jenkins, p. 169.
42 Lyons, p. 246.
43 Garvin, Vol. 2, p. 189; C. H. D. Howard, 'The Parnell Manifesto and the schools question', *EHR* (January 1947).
44 Hamer, pp. 115–16.
45 Garvin, Vol. 2, p. 141.
46 Morley, Vol. 3, p. 262.
47 Although both our families almost certainly originated in the same 'Place on the Orr' in Fife, the connection dates from before 1480 and has proved impossible to trace.
48 Hammond, p. 432.
49 30 January 1886, quoted by Cooke and Vincent, p. 344.
50 Garvin, Vol. 2, p. 142.
51 Garvin, Vol. 2, p. 172. See also Hamilton, 29 and 31 January 1886.
52 H. V. Emy, *Liberals, Radicals and Social Politics 1892–1914* (1973), p. 31; M. W. Flinn, 'The Poor Employment Act of 1817', *EcHR*, Vol. 14 (1961); J. Harris, *Unemployment and Politics 1886–1914* (Oxford, 1971), pp. 75–9.
53 Powell Williams to Joseph Chamberlain, 11 May 1886, quoted by P. C. Griffiths, 'The Caucus and the Liberal Party in 1886', *History* (June 1976).
54 He admitted having been the author in *Political Memoir*, p. 184, although changing the month from February 1886 to December 1885, i.e. before he had reassumed office.
55 Gwynn and Tuckwell, Vol. 2, p. 202.

56   See A. G. Gardiner, *The Life of Sir William Harcourt* (1923), Vol. 1, p. 557.
57   Gardiner, Vol. 1, p. 4; Garvin, Vol. 2, p. 128.
58   Cooke and Vincent, p. 386.
59   Hamilton, 27 May 1887; H. A. L. Fisher, *The Life of James Bryce* (1927), p. 219; Gladstone to Morley, 28 April 1886, quoted by Hammond, p. 495.
60   J. Morley, *Recollections* (1917), Vol. 1, p. 296.
61   R. R. James, *Lord Randolph Churchill* (1959), p. 239.
62   Morley, *Gladstone*, Vol. 3, p. 307.
63   Lord E. Fitzmaurice, *The Life of Lord Granville* (1905), Vol. 2, p. 473.
64   Gladstone to J. Morley, quoted by Hammond, p. 496; Gardiner, Vol. 1, pp. 584–6.
65   Armytage, p. 252.
66   Gwynn and Tuckwell, Vol. 1, p. 222; Hammond, p. 493.
67   Armytage, p. 256; also W. H. G. Armytage, 'The railway rates question and the fall of the third Gladstone Ministry', *EHR*, Vol. 65 (1950).
68   H. Sidgwick, *Memoir* (1906), p. 463, quoted by C. Harvie, *The Lights of Liberalism* (1976), p. 225.
69   C. Cook and B. Keith, *British Historical Facts 1815–1900* (1975), p. 144.
70   Gardiner, Vol. 1, p. 585.
71   Speech on the First Reading of Home Rule Bill, 8 April 1886.
72   Garvin, Vol. 2, p. 114.
73   Letter to Dilke, quoted by Gwynn and Tuckwell, Vol. 2, p. 200.
74   J. Enoch Powell, *Joseph Chamberlain* (1977), p. 152.

7 'Pilgrim Joe': 1886–95

'You know yourself something of bitter pilgrimages'
Winston Churchill to Joseph Chamberlain, 13 August 1903

The Round Table Conference

Those who expected Gladstone to meet defeat by quitting politics little understood him. Instead, he decided that even resignation would imply lack of faith and asked for a dissolution which the queen was advised by Salisbury to grant. 'Arrived at without due deliberation, this has the strongest claims to be ranked as the most foolish and irresponsible gamble of the century.'[1] The assumption behind this remarkable judgment presumably was that Gladstone should have resigned, to allow the formation of a Hartington–Chamberlain government. But such a government could only have obtained a majority over the combined votes of the Conservatives and Irish by obtaining those of all the Liberals and it is hard to believe that some of Gladstone's more devoted followers would not have wanted to pay back in their own coin the man who had brought him down. Alternatively over 200 Conservative votes would have been needed to prevail against a Liberal–Home Rule combination and it is hard to believe that the Tories would not have preferred to take office themselves instead.

Gladstone's faith rested on confidence. The secession of the Whigs and Chamberlain had split the National Liberal Federation, which gave an overwhelming vote of confidence to the Prime Minister and moved its headquarters to London. Chamberlain managed to keep a precarious hold on the Birmingham bit of the machine, which he reorganised as the National Radical Union, while Hartington formed his own Liberal Unionist Association. With the NLF headquarters had gone the head wire-puller Schnadhorst, who encouraged Gladstone to hope that the transfer of the Irish-in-England vote back to the Liberals would cancel out the loss of the secessionists. This proved illusory; as in 1874 a number of confused and disappointed Liberals abstained and 117 seats were lost in England and Wales. The Conservatives emerged with 316 seats, the Liberal Unionists with 79 (thanks to Conservatives refraining from standing against them), the Gladstonians with 190 and the Irish Nationalists with 85.[2] Gladstone thereupon resigned but made clear his intention of remaining as leader.

Salisbury was called back from the French spa to which he had retired[3] and, as leader of the strongest party, was invited to form a government.

Before doing so, he went through the motion of offering the job to Hartington. In fact, he had astutely precluded acceptance of the offer by a speech on the previous 15 May when he had not merely appeared to equate the Irish with Hottentots and to think that twenty years in manacles would be more salutary treatment than the grant of self-government, but said that emigration to Manitoba would be a better solution to Ireland's problems than land purchase.[4] For Hartington to give office to or even take office under colleagues with such a viewpoint would shock the Liberal consciences among his followers and lead some to switch back from him to Gladstone. Moreover Salisbury was not yet prepared to sit in a Cabinet with Chamberlain nor Chamberlain with him.

The secessionists refused to accept that they had quit Liberalism for good. Chamberlain wrote to Collings[5]

> The situation is dominated by the question of Mr G's action. If he retired, all would come right pretty quickly. If he remains, it is no use issuing manifestoes or anything else. All action intensifies differences which it is our object to remove and I believe we must lie low till the inevitable disappearance of the G.O.M.

In the meantime he was in a quandary. As long as the hope of reunion remained, he must manage to look distinct from the Tories. Otherwise he and his twenty followers would lose both elected members and electing voters and, worst of all, recruits from each generation as it came of age. The obvious way to look distinct was to take a radical line on domestic policy. But on this issue he was divided from the Whigs as well as from the Tories. The only issue on which he and the Whigs were agreed was Ireland, but there their position was essentially negative and a successful political movement cannot be built on negation. He told Hartington that he agreed with his strategy and would accept his leadership. But this involved acting as if Ireland was what mattered. To carry conviction with his followers however he had to play down the need for radical reform and the unlovely results of refusing Home Rule. He had to wheedle a Tory Cabinet into looking unconservative and to pretend that denying self-government to the Irish did not mean being beastly to them. Even so, he did not prevent eight Liberal Unionist MPs from reverting to their original allegiance between 1886 and 1895.

At first however all went well. Salisbury's policy towards Ireland consisted of commissions of inquiry and a compassionate commander-in-chief. Moreover Randolph Churchill's position as Leader of the House of Commons meant that reaction would not go unchallenged in the Cabinet, although it has been well said that he was keener on making democrats Tories than Tories democrats. But the arrival of American grain, soil exhaustion and tightening credit were undermining Gladstone's partial settlement of the land question, since rents which had been reasonable five years earlier were ceasing to be so. The government refused to listen when Parnell proposed adjustments and Chamberlain, although speaking in favour, allowed his anxiety over keeping out Gladstone to make him vote with the Tories whenever they were in danger and against them only when such a vote did not matter. The Irish reply was the National League's 'Plan of Campaign' by which in October 1886 tenants whose landlords refused an abatement were advised to pay their rents into a fund which, if the refusal continued, would be used to fight and compensate for evictions. Although the initial effect of this was to alienate English opinion and thus damage the prospects of Home Rule, the government was bound sooner or later to use force in support of recalcitrant landlords and thereby turn opinion round.

If an observer of the political scene had been asked at midsummer 1885 who were the coming men, he would undoubtedly have answered 'Dilke, Chamberlain and Churchill'. Eighteen months later the transformation of the picture was completed by the news of Churchill's resignation, ostensibly over the defence estimates but in reality over the whole trend of policy. What is popularly forgotten about Goschen, who succeeded Churchill, and thereby saved Salisbury from having to climb down, is that he was a Whig, although such a pronounced one as to have refused to serve under Gladstone. Thus not only was the government moving to the right but the Liberal Unionists seemed to be aiding and abetting. The Liberals who had gone unhesitatingly into the Unionist camp over Ireland without otherwise abandoning their progressive inclinations began to reconsider their priorities. Their numbers were appreciable, not least in Birmingham.

Chamberlain was summoned to defend his course on his home ground on the evening after the news of Churchill's departure had taken him almost by surprise.[6] His reaction was to emphasise the things which united Liberals, even as regards Ireland, and to suggest that 'almost any three men sitting round a table' could find acceptable solutions to the things which divided them. The result was that twice in January 1887 and once in February he, Trevelyan, Harcourt, Morley and Herschell did sit round a table.[7] Neither Gladstone nor Hartington joined in; their claims that success would delight them were balanced by their doubts as to whether it could be had. The subjects discussed were (1) Land purchase, where Chamberlain put forward a revised version of his 1886 scheme; it had the advantage of pledging much less British credit than Gladstone's, the drawback of offering landlords shaky security. (2) Local government, where it was agreed that whatever system was set up in the rest of the kingdom should be applied to Ireland as well. (3) Home Rule (about which

191

Harcourt was always luke-warm). Here Chamberlain was induced to agree that there should be 'an Irish legislative authority (or authorities)' for the management of what Parliament should decide to be 'distinctively Irish affairs', with some sort of executive to carry out its decisions. The powers given to the provincial legislatures by the Canada Act of 1867 were to be adopted as an 'analogue' for Ireland and Chamberlain, in a speech on 29 January, said he would have no objection if the Irish chose to call the head of their executive a Prime Minister, with Ministers of Agriculture, Public Works and Education to assist him.

On the other hand the four questions which he had asked Gladstone on 26 March 1886 (see p. 179) now got negative answers. Four big issues still remained undecided. There was the old point about the Irish members at Westminster; both sides seem to have agreed that they should remain for all matters, but Morley's violent dissent pointed to trouble. Secondly Chamberlain insisted on separate treatment for Ulster, which the Nationalists would be reluctant to swallow. Thirdly there was a division of opinion as to whether the English or the Irish executive should be responsible for appointing Ireland's judges. Fourthly there was obscurity as to what exactly the Canadian 'analogue' implied. Nobody seems to have grasped the nettle by pointing out that, for it to be at all close, the imperial Parliament, like that at Ottawa, should have no responsibility for 'provincial' affairs anywhere, even in England. Chamberlain seems to have considered that the Prime Minister of Ireland should not have much more liberty of action than the mayor of Birmingham.

The ex-mayor of Birmingham's liberty of action was itself small. He had two main objects. On the one hand he had to convince his supporters that he was a reasonable man and that the blame for Liberal disunity lay with the Gladstonians. He also wanted to frighten the government into believing that Liberal reunion (which would immediately put them in a minority) was perfectly possible, so that they would be well advised to moderate their policy and thus make Liberal Unionist support for it easier. For these purposes he had to make the Round Table talks look as if they might succeed. He could not afford to have them break down too soon or the insincerity behind his approach would be evident and his ability to alarm the government dwindle. This was why he agreed to talk about Home Rule at all and to accept the Canadian 'analogue', even though it implied allowing Ireland a legislature and executive of her own. On the other hand his self-respect forbade him to go too far in this direction or he would come close to admitting that he had been wrong in the previous March and was primarily to blame for the party split; he would also complicate his relations with Hartington and the Whigs. He got by, partly because the conferences were supposed to be secret and his reports to Hartington concealed how far in reality he had gone, and partly because by a speech and an article he managed to provoke Morley into advocating that the talks be wound up while he was still posing as anxious for them to continue.[8]

. Fortunately for Chamberlain, as he doubtless realised, Gladstone's position was the mirror image of his own. For the Grand Old Man had less than no desire to resume co-operation with the politician of whom he had been so thankful to be rid. In the following May he said to Hamilton that his one great apprehension about his country's future was its men – 'personalities of the stamp of Churchill and Chamberlain'.[9] He believed that the tide was flowing in his favour, as for the next three years it would be, and did not attach much importance to the extra support which Chamberlain's twenty could bring. Hartington would have been a different matter – indeed, the hope of winning Hartington back was what gave the talks their chief attraction to the Gladstonians. In the meantime their leader had no intention of modifying his ideas about Home Rule, since that would do more to complicate his relations with Parnell than improve those with Chamberlain. A visit by the latter to Gladstone on 5 April made it clearer than ever that neither was going to be the first to budge.

Thus the Round Table Conferences were doomed to achieve nothing beyond irritating the people who took part in them, thereby making reunion more difficult instead of easier (except perhaps for Trevelyan who treated them seriously and as a result went back to his original allegiance, saying that Chamberlain was not a loyal colleague).[10] The latter's chances of becoming Liberal leader received a worse set-back than he can have reckoned with. For when Parliament reassembled on 27 January, the government announced its intention of introducing a Criminal Law Amendment (Ireland) Bill and, to ease its passage through the Commons, an extension of the Speaker's powers to curtail debate. The Crimes Bill (as it was called for short) had, unlike its predecessors, no time limit and could be brought into force for a particular district whenever a Viceroy saw fit. Where it operated, Resident Magistrates (Englishmen who did not have to be qualified as lawyers) could deal with a number of offences without a jury, could treat a public meeting as an unlawful assembly and punish anyone who attended it. Soon 3,000 men and women, including 20 MPs, found themselves behind bars, often in England. A. J. Balfour, who became Chief Secretary in March, administered the law with an unruffled determination which showed no trace of philosophic doubt as to its desirability. In August 1887 the National League was proclaimed an unlawful association; in September a clash between police and public at Mitchelstown provided a minor Peterloo. The government did however bow to accumulating evidence and go back almost completely on its attitude to rent reductions, thereby conceding that the evictions of the previous ten months had been unjustified. Pressure from the Liberal

Unionists had some share in bringing about this retreat; their objections to the rigour were over-ridden. Chamberlain with five other Radical Unionist MPs from the midlands voted with Gladstone but against Hartington and forty-six Liberal Unionists in condemning the suppression of the League, thereby inducing Salisbury to look for a way of quarantining him. Earlier however he had defended coercion and more than once taunted the Nationalist MPs with living on money sent them from America, 'the subsidised agents of a foreign conspiracy'.[11] But practical experience of the alternative to Home Rule was reinforcing the arguments for it. Liberal and working-class opinion was rallying to Gladstone, whose followers won a series of by-elections. The man identified in the public mind with defeating him inevitably found it harder to look convincing as a Liberal. Perhaps it was at this time that in a speech at Birmingham he said 'the allegation is false and the alligator knows it'.[12]

Sensational relief was however at hand. On 7 March 1887 *The Times* had begun to publish a series of articles on 'Parnellism and Crime', which described the Home Rule movement as 'essentially a foreign conspiracy' and claimed that its leaders had been 'in notorious and continuous relations with avowed murderers'. On 18 April, the day of the crucial vote on the Crimes Bill, a facsimile was printed of an 1882 letter supposedly written by Parnell's secretary and signed by him in which approval of the Phoenix Park murders was implied. The alleged author repudiated it as a forgery. Next day the Prime Minister implied that he considered it authentic.

Crime and Parnell[13]

The letter incriminating Parnell had in fact been forged by an impecunious Irish journalist called Richard Piggott who in 1885 had approached Lord Richard Grosvenor, then still the Liberal Chief Whip (see pp. 155, 166), asking for cash to finance a pamphlet about Parnell's links with lawbreakers. Grosvenor put him in touch with one Edward Caulfield Houston, a former Dublin employee of *The Times* who became secretary of the chief Unionist society in Ireland. Houston commissioned Piggott to ferret for evidence; Piggott found forgery more expeditious. In July 1886, meeting Houston in Paris, he was paid £605 for a sample of his products which he claimed to have obtained from 'two men downstairs', whom Houston, aglee with his acquisition, did not insist on seeing. Back in London, Houston appears to have hawked his wares to a variety of politicians. On 29 December 1886 Chamberlain wrote to Dilke 'There is no secret as to Parnell's letters. They prove him to have been a liar but I do not know that they have any other interest just now.'[14] It does not necessarily follow, of course, that it was the Piggott letters which were being referred to, but these were certainly shown to Hartington, who sent Houston packing. But either then or earlier the sedulous *colporteur* got in touch with his former employers on *The Times*.[15] Evidence in the paper's archives proves that its chiefs consulted the government;[16] W. H. Smith, the First Lord of the Treasury, while still a stationer, had been a close friend of Buckle, the editor. Over the next few months the paper's representatives were given privileged access to the Irish official archives in their hunt for evidence. Doubts about the authenticity of the material did arise but after five weeks were brushed aside.

Parnell at first believed O'Shea to have been the source but there is no evidence of any contact at this stage between him and Houston or Piggott, although later Chamberlain put him into touch with *The Times*.[17] The target of the attack repudiated it as based on forgeries and, in spite of the paper trailing its coat by remarks which bordered on libel, decided against suing it on the advice of Morley and others that he would neither get a fair trial in an English court nor clear his name in an Irish one. Gladstone called for the matter to be examined by a Select Committee but did not press his demand for fear that a political inquiry might bring out evidence of Parnell having behaved injudiciously though not criminally.

Over a year then elapsed during which the only development was that F. H. O'Donnell, a former colleague of Parnell who had later fallen out with him over Home Rule (although not so far as to prevent them from going together to examine *The Times'* documents), sued the paper for libel, alleged, on far-fetched grounds, to have been contained in one of the articles on 'Parnellism and Crime'. The case did not come on until July 1888. It collapsed before there had been time for Parnell to give evidence but not before the leading counsel for *The Times*, who happened (as was still admissible in those days) to be the Attorney-General, had had a chance to repeat in court, with embellishments, the allegations made in the original articles. One cannot help suspecting that some person or persons, disappointed at not having provoked Parnell into an action where he could be cross-examined, put up O'Donnell so as to create an opportunity for the allegations to be repeated in such a way as to make the continued disregard of them by Parnell unacceptably damaging to his reputation.

By now Parnell had a shrewd idea where the letters came from. A libel suit was still thought injudicious and instead he asked for a Select Committee; when the request was refused, he repeated it. W. H. Smith, in a take-it-or-leave-it fashion, offered instead a Judicial Commission to be appointed by Act of Parliament. The change of mind was publicly attributed to 'artful Mr Chamberlain', who believed that he had a score to settle and seems to have believed that some at least of the documents were genuine.[18] The terms of reference of the Commission were arbitrarily widened by the government to permit inquiry into 'the allegations and charges made against certain Members of Parliament *and other persons* by the defendants in the recent action of *O'Donnell* v. *Walter*'; it was thus authorised to spread itself over the story of British dealings with Ireland during the previous eight years. The amount of muck to be raked over thus became so great that any deficiencies in the evidence might get obscured. When the Attorney-General, who had been taken to task publicly for his dual role in the earlier case, jibbed at once again appearing for *The Times*, he was firmly told that he must go on. Salisbury said that, if he and the junior counsel were let off, 'there will be no persuading the outside world that they have not run away from the case because on scrutinising the evidence they satisfied themselves that it was bad'. The galley-slave wrote to a colleague, 'Every day I curse Chamberlain and the Unionists for their obstinacy' – presumably in insisting that the case must go forward.[19]

Before it came into court Chamberlain had occasion to do his own cursing. Speaking on the Second Reading of the Bill setting up the Commission, he said that the opinion which he had formed of Parnell's honesty, sincerity and patriotism made it hard for him to credit the charges. The only thing which shook his belief was Parnell's reluctance to face a full inquiry. Only by allowing the whole record of the Land League to be investigated could Parnell and his colleagues clear themselves convincingly from the charge of complicity in outrage.

A week later Parnell replied:[20]

I have not, Sir, had an opportunity before this of thanking the right honourable gentleman the member for West Birmingham, for his kind references to me and for the unsolicited character which he was kind enough to give me . . . He spoke of not long ago, when he said he entertained a better opinion of me than he does to-day. I care very little for the opinion of the right honourable gentleman. I have never put forward men to do dangerous things which I shrank from doing myself, nor have I betrayed the secrets of my colleagues in council. My principal recollection of the right honourable gentleman before he became a Minister is that he was always most anxious to put me and my friends forward to do work which he was afraid to do himself, and after he became a Minister my principal recollection of him is that he was always most anxious to betray to us the secrets and counsels of his colleagues in the cabinet, and to endeavour, while sitting beside those colleagues and while in consultation with them, to undermine their counsels and plans in our favour. If this enquiry is extended into these matters, and I see no reason why it should not [be], I shall be able to make good my words by documentary evidence which is not forged.

Chamberlain in reply justified himself on the grounds that both in 1882 and in 1884–5 he had acted with the full knowledge and approval of Gladstone. But he also said that Parnell himself had been the author of the Central Board scheme 'until he dropped it in the hope of getting more elsewhere'. Parnell denied this; Chamberlain claimed to have as proof letters 'in his own handwriting and not in that of his secretary'. He must have forgotten in the heat of the moment that this was just what he did not have. O'Shea wrote to *The Times* in his support. Parnell wrote to the same paper demanding that the documents in his handwriting be produced, including the amendments to the Crimes Act which had by this time been mentioned. 'It is not to be supposed for an instant that an astute politician of the Chamberlain–O'Shea type, having got hold of so important a document as "Mr Parnell's own Coercion Bill" would have been so careless as to mislay or lose it'. Intemperately Chamberlain telegraphed to *The Times* accepting the challenge.

When he sat down with O'Shea to decide what was to be said, he came face to face with three unpalatable facts. One was that he had nothing in Parnell's hand-writing and that the Crimes Act merely consisted of the original text with certain paragraphs struck out. The second was that, as he had known since late in 1886,[21] O'Shea had concealed from him Parnell's two letters emphasising that the Central Boards were not to be regarded as a substitute for Home Rule. The third was that on 19 January 1885 O'Shea had written Parnell a letter which such an astute politician would never have been so careless as to mislay or lose but which Chamberlain himself had sharply criticised as misleading. If Parnell were to produce it, Chamberlain would have to repudiate it and, in doing so, repudiate his chief witness against Parnell. If O'Shea could misrepresent the one man, was he not highly likely to have misrepresented the other? Humble pie was the only dish on the menu and in a long letter published in *The Times* on 13 August Chamberlain with a bad grace ate it. He really had only his own credulity and hastiness to thank. But the episode cannot have reduced his rancour against Parnell.

To the discomfiture of the right-minded an equal degree of incompetence had been displayed by *The Times*. To anyone acquainted with Ireland, the name of Piggott would have set alarms ringing. But the bells did not ring loudly enough in the confident recesses of Printing House Square. The well-known results were first seen on 21 February 1889 when Piggott not merely betrayed himself as a forger by mis-spelling 'hesitancy' but also betrayed himself as a liar by denying that he had known of *The Times* attack in advance when letters proving the contrary were in the defence's hands. Eight days later he blew out his brains in Madrid. Further incompetence would seem to have been displayed by the police in letting him slip out of the country. The curious circumstance of his having been seen in a café on the previous day by none other than O'Shea presents an almost irresistible temptation to connoisseurs of detective fiction but nobody has yet succeeded in proving it to be anything other than coincidental. We are not told whether Chamberlain was in the House of Commons on that same first of March when Parnell began to speak and all those on the Opposition benches, with the exception of Hartington, rose to their feet as an act of retribution. But his Liberal image must have been a good deal tarnished by his obvious association with the men who had been hounding Parnell and with the government which, when the Commission finally in February 1890 gave the Irish a virtual acquittal, signally failed to express any regret for the wrong which they had inflicted. When Randolph Churchill introduced a motion condemning that government, it was Chamberlain who spoke up on their behalf. If an election had been held before the autumn of that year, Home Rule would have been quickly accomplished. But in this singular tragedy the peripeteia was already at hand.

On Christmas Eve 1889 Captain O'Shea filed a petition for divorce against his wife, citing Parnell as co-respondent. The timing can be adequately explained by the fact that Mrs O'Shea's aunt, on whose wealth the family had been living, died in May 1889 aged 96; the need to avoid antagonising her by a public scandal was removed (a point which did not become generally known till long afterwards). But the background is more intricate. As early as February 1887 a Nationalist MP had told Dilke that O'Shea 'is going forward with his divorce case against Parnell, who has no defence possible'.[22] In November 1888 O'Shea had written to tell Chamberlain that his wife was under a written engagement not to communicate with Parnell and vice versa. 'I daresay a great many people have some notion of the state of affairs but I am most anxious for my children's sake that nothing should actually be published because a very large fortune may depend on it not coming into print.' Chamberlain in reply admitted to having felt that 'I could not say a word to you on the subject until you spoke to me'.[23] The London correspondent of the *Birmingham Daily Post* long afterwards stated that in August 1889 he had been asked by 'one on the inside of the Liberal Unionist machine' whether Parnell would be politically ruined by a divorce, as Dilke had been. The Unionist managers were said to be 'wavering'.[24] In October 1889 O'Shea sent Chamberlain an explanation of some personal matters including detail about the 'perfidy' with which his wife and Parnell had behaved towards him. Chamberlain in reply said that he never listened to scandal about his friends 'and in your case I have heard nothing and know nothing beyond what you have told me. I am not sure that the boldest course is not always the wisest'.[25] About this time O'Shea spent a night at Highbury but for what purpose is not known.[26] To a further letter from him in

January 1890 announcing the filing of the petition, Chamberlain replied that 'I have never presumed to refer to your private affairs . . . but now that you have taken the decisive step, I may be allowed to say that it seems to me to have been forced upon you'.[27] In 1890, when O'Shea was anxious to clear himself of suspicion of connivance, he is said to have got Chamberlain to write him a letter saying that in 1885 Parnell had only helped him to get nominated as a candidate in Galway out of deference to the strong wishes of Chamberlain himself and 'another person'. In February 1891[28] Chamberlain lent O'Shea £400 (one wonders if it was ever paid back) but the Captain was unusually hard up at the time.[29] The allowance paid him by his wife's aunt had stopped with her death. The terms of her will and the fact that the family contested it meant that he could not lay hands on any of the capital which he had hoped to inherit. It is tempting to speculate whether in this situation he may have accepted a financial inducement to bring his case but there is no evidence one way or another. Any large sum however would have been unlikely to come from Chamberlain whose financial difficulties (see p. 81) were then beginning.

Parnell told the *Freeman's Journal* of Dublin that O'Shea had been incited to move by Houston, on behalf of *The Times*. Having failed to assassinate his character by forged letters, his enemies were resorting to other means. The *Freeman's Journal* not only attacked O'Shea in its comments but mentioned Chamberlain specifically among his accomplices. This led to a charge that the divorce was deliberately launched by the 'Chamberlain–O'Shea combination' as a means of cancelling out the damage done by the Piggott affair.[30] Chamberlain's two letters of October 1889 and January 1890 are, on this showing, dismissed as being pretence pieces sent to safeguard the writer in the event of his involvement ever coming to light. Parnell's intimacy with Mrs O'Shea had been a 'notorious and recognised fact' for many years[31] and Chamberlain must have known about it long before, even supposing that he was not among the ministers to whom Harcourt confided it in 1882 (see p. 123). But this does not necessarily invalidate his statement that he said nothing on the matter to the husband until November 1888, three months after his controversy with Parnell had made him realise just how unreliable O'Shea was. The natural inference of the evidence is that, once the aunt's death had removed the disincentive to action by O'Shea, Chamberlain and other friends brought pressure on him to act; a Tory MP wrote later about O'Shea 'having been kept to his guns'.[32] But there is nothing to prove it was this pressure which was decisive. Nor is there anything to show that such pressure had been exerted in earlier years – but then until February 1889 Parnell's enemies could still hope to accomplish his downfall by other means. As in the Dilke case, the verdict must be an open one but here the alternative to 'not proven' is 'guilty', although not of any action which was legally a crime.

The morality of the day may seem to have concentrated unduly on one type of wrong–doing and even to have tolerated that type provided it kept out of the courts. But Parnell's position set him at odds with two groups of opinion whose support, or at least tolerance, was vital to him – the nonconformist conscience and the Roman Catholic church. The case for doing justice to Ireland by granting Home Rule had been seen in England as predominantly a moral one. The people sensitive to it were the kind of people who lived by principle, unlikely to exonerate a man in a responsible post who disregarded principle. Any inclinations which Gladstone may have had towards reticence on grounds of Christian charity after the divorce was granted in November 1890 had to be subordinated to his sense of the politically possible – although he need not have made his views public quite as quickly as he did. And the anomaly of Parnell's position in Irish politics had always been that a Protestant sprung from the Ascendancy was leading a movement with strong Catholic and Celtic associations. He could no more afford to offend the Catholic church than can a mayor of Chicago. The Irish Party, which had always united a wide variety of views beneath the national banner, split and the cause of Home Rule received a body blow from which it took a generation to recover. The misguided attempt to swim against the tide was too much for Parnell's precarious health and in October 1891 the President of the Immortals finished his sport with him just as he did with Tess in the self-same year.

Private Fulfilment and Public Frustration

If the upshot of the Round Table Conferences was that the Liberal Unionists were not going to reunite with the Gladstonians, what did the future hold for Chamberlain? Was he committed to walking with a handful of cronies for the rest of his political life? In June 1887 he wrote to his son Austen:[33]

> Gladstonianism is becoming more sectional and more irreconcilable and I do not want to reunite with such a party . . . I see the possibility of a strong Central Party which may be master of the situation after Mr G goes.

Yet, apart from the fact that a moderate course was the very thing to which he was temperamentally least inclined, such parties have been said to suffer from being all centre and no circumference. A month later Randolph Churchill started talk about a 'National Party'. But his wife has described what came of Chamberlain's effort, while on a Jubilee cruise, to enlist

Hartington's rather indispensable support for such a venture. She was sitting next to the intended recruit when Chamberlain[34]

> drew up a chair and suddenly plunged into the matter without preliminaries and with his usual directness. Lord Hartington looked uncomfortable and answered very shortly. Mr Chamberlain, full of his scheme, pressed the points home, taking no notice of the mono-syllables he got in answer. But after a time the frozen attitude of Lord Hartington began to take effect and the conversation languished . . . I imagine that Lord Hartington was a difficult person to persuade against his will and most uncompromisingly definite in his likes and dislikes. I have always thought that there existed a gulf between him and Mr Chamberlain that no political expediency could really bridge.

There was no alternative to the repulsive course of tagging along behind the Tories. By the autumn of 1887 the momentary gleam had faded and Chamberlain was brought up roundly against the implications of the course he had chosen:[35]

> Every day of coercion adds to the Gladstonian strength and I see no probability that the strong measures which are disgusting our friends in England will effectively dispose of the League in Ireland. I cannot see how Mr G. can be kept out much longer. If he comes back he will dissolve and most of the Liberal Unionists will go to the wall. I do not feel absolutely certain of a single seat, though I think I am safe myself.

Relief came from an unexpected quarter. Lord Salisbury invited him to go to the United States as chief British spokesman in an Anglo-American negotiation on Canadian fishing rights. Although pity may have played some part in the offer, the main motive was undoubtedly to be rid for a time of 'an embarrassing colleague who demonstrated almost daily the differences of emphasis . . . in the Unionist camp'.[36] That joker of American politics, the need to get treaties ratified by the Senate, almost led to Chamberlain's reputation being impaired rather than enhanced by his three months stay. The situation was saved by the neat device of an interim protocol which only the ratification of the permanent agreement could abrogate. The Christmas break was devoted to a visit to Toronto where he invested with rhetoric the idea that the federation of Canada might be not merely the clue to solving Ireland's problems but even 'the lamp lighting our path to the federation of the British Empire'.[37]

He brought back not merely success but also a bride, a girl younger than his own elder children whose father, Judge Endicott of Salem, was Secretary of War in President Cleveland's Democratic administration;

Richard Baxter was joining hands with Cotton Mather in a world which would have surprised them both. During the previous summer Beatrice Potter had finally seen that, for a woman with views of her own, domesticity with Chamberlain would be anything but bliss and her four-year fencing with him had ended. Mary Endicott was quite prepared to let him rule the roost ('I am not in the habit of making suggestions to my spouse')[38] and content herself with seeing that his household, including the thirty-three greenhouses at Highbury, ran on oiled wheels. Her desire to support him in all respects resulted before long in her knowing as much about British politics as he did; not for nothing had his first gift to her been John Morley's study of Burke. The feline Potter comment was 'a plain little thing, but sweet and good and simply-dressed'.[39] Many people, including Lord Salisbury, referred to her as 'the Puritan Maid' and her unassuming good-nature won her the favour of many, from the queen downwards and including her step-children. Reversing the usual pattern of Anglo-American marriages, it was she who smoothed down his brashness and accelerated his absorption into the establishment which might anyhow have come with his approximation to the Tories and his chagrin that the loyalty of the masses had gone to Gladstone rather than himself.

He got home in March 1888 to find the situation worse rather than better. The Gladstonians were winning by-elections and even gaining ground in the midland 'duchy' on which his entire political position by his own admission rested. No sooner had he sailed from Liverpool than Gladstone moved a multitude when the National Liberal Federation met in Birmingham; thereafter Schnadhorst captured the 'Caucus'. Chamberlain built a new one with a Liberal Unionist label but its power, as indeed the Liberal Unionist power throughout the country, depended on Conservative complaisance. Were they to run a candidate, the anti–Home Rule vote would be split and a Gladstonian capture the seat. To prevent this happening Chamberlain had more than once to throw his weight about and the thought that he might have to do so again restricted his ability to exert pressure in matters of policy. In 1892 he told A. J. Balfour that he had to expect to be refused three times out of four but hoped for a hearing the fourth time;[40] in 1895 he threatened to quit politics if he were not shown more consideration.

In compensation however the more intelligent Tories realised that, to coax a majority out of the new electorate, they must genuflect to the idea of progress. The result until 1892 was an uneasy compromise. 'Three acres and a cow' shrank to an Allotment Act which proved almost a dead letter; a Smallholdings Act was equally unsuccessful because ministers refused to give the local authorities power to acquire land compulsorily. A Housing Act allowed councils to use rate income for building houses to rent but few did. County councils (but not district or parish ones) were at last advanced from notion to reality and Chamberlain was able to prevent a proportion of places on them being reserved for magistrates. He could not however stop the elected members being allowed to nominate aldermen, which in practice came to much the same thing. The job of licensing was not handed to them and Salisbury objected that to let them replace the Poor Law Guardians would, in view of the amount of patronage involved, mean 'putting the cat in charge of the cream jug'.[41] Moreover their extension to Ireland was delayed until 1891 and then hedged about with so many limitations that it had to be abandoned. Chamberlain's admirers made much of the virtual abolition of school fees in 1891; his detractors complained that, to secure it, he had dropped his objection to voluntary schools sharing in the grant which was given in place of fees. A more pertinent criticism is that the compromise could have been reached earlier if he had put his weight behind it. Another success which misjudgment had delayed came in laws protecting seamen on lines recommended by the Royal Commission appointed after the failure of his single-handed attempt to force them through an unprepared Parliament (see p. 140). The Irish Land Purchase Act of 1891 disregarded his ideas about how compensation should be financed (see p. 178) but represented a major step in the process by which most English owners of land in Ireland were to be bought out at the expense of the British taxpayer; the Congested Districts Act of the same year embodied ideas which Chamberlain had propounded a decade earlier (see p. 122). It must have been galling to think how much more effective these measures could have been if they had emanated from an unsplit Liberal Cabinet. But in November 1891 he publicly interred the hopes which he had once cultivated of an early reunion.[42]

A month later Hartington succeeded to the dukedom of Devonshire and Chamberlain was unanimously elected by the Liberal Unionists as their leader in the Commons. But although ministers consulted him about the date of dissolution their back-benchers disregarded his desire to delay it and, although the polls showed that the Liberal tide was ebbing, it had not ebbed far enough to prevent Gladstone from winning, thanks to the Celtic fringes, a majority of 40. The Liberal Unionists dwindled to 47, 30 of whom came from the midlands. The new government's strength was not enough to carry Home Rule, although the Irish insisted on it being given first priority; it was got through the Commons by the new procedural device of 'the guillotine' but lost in the Lords by 419 to 41, an action which led Chamberlain to express approval of that body for the first time in his life. As introduced, the Bill allowed 81 Irish MPs to remain at Westminster for matters affecting the whole United Kingdom. When it was objected that they would use their votes to make mischief, the proposal was amended to let them vote on everything. Chamberlain rejected both proposals, having come firmly to the view that the only satisfactory solution would be federation, which was unobtainable. He was throughout the moving spirit in opposition to the Bill.

Ireland took up so much time that little was left for enacting the programme of internal reform which Gladstone had authorised at Newcastle in 1891 and on which Chamberlain poured scorn regardless of its considerable similarity to the programme which Gladstone had not authorised in 1885. The most important measure was a codicil to the County Councils Act by which district and parish councils were set up. Chamberlain not only voted for it but exerted himself to stop it being emasculated in the Lords, thereby depriving Gladstone of a good stick with which to beat that body. In return the government allowed an Employers Liability Bill to die rather than contest the Lords' amendments; Chamberlain, who scored a debating success over the young Home Secretary Asquith, was coming to the view that liability was the wrong way to tackle a problem where often nobody had been at fault.

Gladstone's retirement in March 1894 made painfully clear the sad state the Liberals were in. A party which would henceforward have to rely on working-class votes would have been well-advised to choose a leader with popular appeal. Instead, jealousies inside the Cabinet allowed the choice to be made by the queen and she was bent on appointing Rosebery, a peer who had married a Rothschild.[43] The rank and file in the Commons were allowed no say whatever. (To be fair, there were objections to everybody else.) Rosebery in turn insisted on making Kimberley, another peer, Foreign Secretary, so that between them they could replace the spirit of Cobden and Gladstone by that of imperialism. To Home Rule Rosebery showed an indifference which was later to become active hostility. The only memorable achievement of his sixteen months in office was a measure of which Chamberlain thought better than he did himself, namely Harcourt's Death Duties. Gladstone's successor completely lacked his ability to reconcile personal feuds and policy divergences; the government quickly became so demoralised that defeat on a minor issue was grasped as an excuse to resign. The Unionists won the ensuing election and Salisbury offered places in his Cabinet to Chamberlain and four other Liberal Unionists.

Nine years are a long time in politics and the sixth decade of a man's life is often the most valuable one. Chamberlain had, by his own volition, spent it out of office, without much positive achievement to show. He no doubt would have argued that the defeat of Home Rule had made the sacrifice worthwhile but in fact that snake was only scotched. Now he was doing what he had at first vowed not to do and entering a government which did not need to rely on Liberal Unionist votes since the Tories had a clear majority by themselves. In February 1895 Lady Bracknell was already counting the Liberal Unionists as Tories; they might not yet dine at the best houses (although in practice many of them had been doing so for some time) but they could certainly come in afterwards. Their leader might not like this trend but would he prove strong enough to prevent it? With the insight of a woman who had done the scorning, Beatrice Webb (as she had become) speculated in her *Diary* over his future:[44]

> The majority of the Liberal Unionists in the House of Commons have been anti-Chamberlainites – more hostile in their hearts to Joe than the bigoted Tories. It is a testimony to the marvellous force of his personality that he pervades this election – no one trusts him, no one likes him, no one really believes in him and yet everyone accepts him as the leader of the united Unionists. His position in the Tory Party is, in fact, very similar to his position in 1885 in the Liberal Party. Is it equally unstable? Will he play again the role of the usurper to keep his seat on the throne and does he believe sufficiently in his new party to serve it faithfully? I am inclined to think that, barring accidents from evil temper, the cause of property is sufficiently attractive to him to keep him from wilful wrecking.

Britain's Slip Begins to Show

The drop in Britain's economic activity which set in about 1884 and lasted until 1887 affected attitudes as well as behaviour. Although real wages do not seem to have suffered, the workers were disturbed by the reminder that things could not be relied on to get steadily better. From 1885 a series of meetings and marches in London caused considerable concern. In April 1886 Chamberlain, who had at that particular moment reasons for wanting to make flesh creep, forecast that, if the next two winters were bad, the people would take the bit between their teeth.[45] 1887 saw 'Bloody Sunday' in Trafalgar Square; 1888 a strike of match-girls; 1889 a strike of London dockers, so successful as to encourage others. But the most significant beneficiaries of the discontent were the trade unions, which not only grew in numbers but changed in character; the staid craft ones were pushed aside by militant industrial newcomers which proceeded to make their muscle felt by a series of strikes. In 1880 barely 4 per cent of the working population belonged to unions; by 1914 the figure was over 25 per cent.[46] The alarm felt by the well-to-do provoked two debates: how to improve the condition of the unemployed and how to provide more employment. A Royal Commission was set up to discover why trade and industry were depressed.

There was and is no doubt that in the late nineteenth century Britain failed to maintain the growth-rate which she had established a century earlier, while in the seven years after 1900 the slowing-down became even more pronounced. Although her exports, after marking time from 1885 to 1900, began to increase again thereafter, they did so less fast than those of her main rivals while her share of world trade went down.[47] Partly this was a result of having started first; other countries with bigger populations and better resources were bound, as they industrialised, to catch up. 'Half a continent is likely in the course of time to make more steel than a small island.'[48] But this was no danger as long as Britain could continue to pay her way in the world and thereby make possible a steady rise in living standards. The needs of mankind had only to be converted into effective demand for there to be plenty to keep everyone busy. But the increasing relative inefficiency implied by slower growth threatened in due course to price her out of the world market and render her unable to make ends meet except at the cost of considerable impoverishment.[49]

Many villains have been made responsible for this retardation and the blame cannot be pinned exclusively on any. (It may of course be that, as economies become older, they get, like individuals, stiffer in the joints!)[50] In general, weaknesses which had not mattered as long as Britain was dominant became serious once customers turned into competitors. The factors which had enabled her to start were by no means necessarily those which she needed to keep going.[51] Her neglect of education, and particularly technical education, told against her when craftsmanship had to be supplemented by technology. The fact that many of her pioneers had been self-made men using rule of thumb methods fostered an outlook which discounted scientific knowledge. The fact that British goods had for long sold themselves discounted salesmanship. The lack of concern for the welfare of the workers resulted in a labour-force more concerned to maintain employment than to maximise income. The tendency of firms to find their own finance meant that banks did not assume the function of channelling private savings into home industry.[52] Many family firms preferred to stay small for fear of wider ownership leading to loss of control, but smallness discouraged specialisation in management, expenditure on research and readiness to take risks. (Kenricks, the firm of Chamberlain's relatives, was an object-lesson in this.)[53] The cult of the country gentleman led to undue keenness about making money being deprecated. The population growth came to the point at which in an industrialised nation the birth-rate begins to fall.

At the time the cause of the trouble was frequently found in 'overproduction' – the UK was producing more goods than were in effective demand.[54] The Sheffield and Birmingham Chambers of Commerce told the Royal Commission that more markets must be acquired.[55] They glossed over the difficulty that unsophisticated markets might not be able to pay while sophisticated ones might prefer non-UK goods as being cheaper or better. (They would probably have met this objection by saying that it was political intervention in the shape of tariffs which was making UK goods uncompetitive in the sophisticated markets and that the UK's unsophisticated markets, whether existing or new, needed the protection of similar intervention.) The desire to find new markets for existing types of goods threatened to distract attention from the need to find new types of goods to sell in existing markets.

J. L. Hobson countered this diagnosis by finding the explanation in 'under-consumption' at home. If purchasing power were redistributed, there would be quite enough demand to absorb UK output.[56] This remedy overlooked the UK's need to sell enough in overseas markets to pay for the imports on which it had come to depend (see p. 105). To expand home demand would increase the quantity of imports which were needed and, although it might induce home manufacturers to expand their capacity, an over-buoyant home market might distract them from efforts to raise the quantity of exports to correspond. In Hobson's day the machinery of the gold standard would have operated automatically (at any rate in theory) to check the expansion of home demand as soon as it threatened to cause inflation, so that the sacrosanct monetary system might have had to be tampered with before buyers could be found for all the surplus products. Hobson's ideas involved replacing the 'present competitive price system' with one in which goods were distributed 'on a conscious basis of the satisfaction of human needs', so that, all in all, he was calling for a bigger reconstruction than he perhaps realised.[57]

With hindsight, three ways can be identified by which the UK might have sought escape from its dilemma.

(1) An attempt might have been made to isolate the economy from the outside world by official controls on the movement of goods, money and men. Something of this kind was advocated by the Fair Trade League in the 1880s and in the Minority Report of the Royal Commission on the depression. It would have meant abandoning the principle of locating production where it could be done most cheaply and thus refraining from maximising the standard of life. Britain's dependence on imports for existence would have made it hard to pursue this course very far unless the population had been reduced by emigration. Isolation would not have solved the problem of remaining competitive in third markets.

There were however two even bigger objections. The UK owed its prosperity to trade, finance and services as much as to industry and for these to flourish, the economy to which it belonged needed to be as wide and free as possible. Moreover from about 1890 the pattern of world trade began to move from a bilateral to a multilateral basis. Industrialised countries other than Britain began to buy primary products, often from the empire and particularly from India. They paid by selling manufactures to the UK, which it in turn paid for by selling other manufactures to the empire. Had Britain kept out the manufactures of other countries, the process would have been halted, growth in world trade would have slackened and competition in such markets as remained open or could be opened by political pressure would have intensified.[58] For Britain to quit the world which she had done so much to create was hardly a practicable option. (See below pp. 285–9)

(2) Britain could have concentrated on becoming an international rentier, exporting her savings to the world, accepting payment chiefly in primary products and balancing a deficit on visible trade by an invisible surplus. This is in fact largely what she did. Most of the money invested overseas went to provide orders and work for her export industries, which were as a result geared to supply underdeveloped rather than sophisticated markets. The big question mark over this solution concerned its permanence. By themselves the investments would in 1913 have sufficed to pay for only between five or six years imports;[59] it was the dividends and orders brought in by them which mattered. But would the countries involved remain ready to treat the world as an economic unit? Would the primary producers remain content with their role? Would nationalist régimes put up barriers, repudiate debts, confiscate capital? If home consumers spent more, would Britain continue to generate the necessary volume of savings? Above all, would the whole system become dislocated by war, when Britain would find it difficult to transport and pay for all the things for which she had become dependent on others? As we know, all these dangers were to a greater or less extent realised and many of Britain's present economic problems are the result.

Chamberlain and the tariff reformers were to welcome investment in the empire but deplore it in foreign countries, on the ground that the first would come back in the shape of orders for UK manufactures, whereas the second would build up industries which would take orders away.[60] But this distinction either implied that empire countries would remain producers of primary materials when foreign countries would not, or it could not be maintained as each British territory overseas began to follow Canada and Australia along the road of industrialisation. UK industry could anyhow profit in the short term by providing overseas countries with the wherewithal for industrialising. But what to do in the long run was the nub of the problem.

(3) The third course was to solve that problem by developing the production of goods and services which required high technical knowledge and skills and to keep prices down by concentrating on efficiency. This can be conveniently labelled 'keeping one jump ahead': by the time Britain's customers became able to make for themselves the things with

which she had hitherto been supplying them, she would be able to offer them more complex things which they could not hope to produce for themselves for a considerable time, if ever.

Such a course involved extending drastically her provision for research and scientific training. The Liberal Imperialists, with their emphasis on better technical education and 'national efficiency', were in due course to see this. But they failed to appreciate the even greater importance of a high rate of capital investment in producers' equipment. Yet not only was the proportion of the Gross National Product devoted to capital formation lower in Britain than in Germany, France and America (see Table 10.1). The proportion of that capital invested abroad was higher than in any other country at any time. There were a variety of reasons for this. The rate of return on overseas investment was higher, while fixed-interest bonds offered by empire or American governments, railways, mines, etc., were regarded by the private investor as better security than shares in home companies! The insufficiency of the channels by which domestic savings could reach domestic enterprises was partly a result, partly a cause. Insufficient long-term investment handicapped growth in productivity, which in turn made investment less attractive.[61]

In addition, the average British manufacturer became more reluctant to take the risks involved in developing new products and processes as long as he could find customers for his established lines. Innovation is often costly and in its early stages unrewarding. Consequently there is little evidence that it was inability to get adequate capital which held up the installation of new plant. To have kept abreast would in some cases have meant scrapping plant before its cost had been fully recovered. In cases where British industry seems to have missed opportunities, closer examination often shows that the decisions taken were sensible ones for the firms concerned in the prevailing British conditions. Individuals can hardly be blamed for failing to foresee what consequences their choices will ultimately have for the whole economy.[62] The doctrine that investment decisions should be left to the individual unit, which should take them on the basis of cash advantage, was so deeply rooted that even if the problem had been seen there would have been little which could have been done about it. Freedom to be enterprising had had much to do with Britain's original breakthrough; at a later stage failure to be enterprising helped towards her undoing. For the net result was that in 1907 70 per cent of her export earnings were still provided by the industries on which she had built her supremacy. And they were no longer the sectors where technology was advancing fastest and which were therefore those most likely to attract investment.

It would of course be as absurd to suggest that Britain failed to adopt this third course altogether, as it would be to suggest that she was totally mistaken in following the second course. The question rather is whether a different balance, giving more emphasis to development at home and less to expansion overseas, would not have left her in a stronger competitive position. Her politicians and men of business worried considerably about her ability to maintain her position in the world with which they were familiar. Perhaps they would have been wise to allow a little more for the possibility that the world would turn unfamiliar.

Empire – Burden or Salvation?

It was Major Cartwright, ahead of his time as usual, who in 1771 propagated the idea of a 'firm and brotherly League' to be called the 'Grand British League and Confederacy'.[63] But another seventy-five years were needed before Liberal ideas began to be applied to Britain's relations with her colonies.[64] Then, in 1846, the Whig Colonial Secretary, Grey (son of the Prime Minister and brother-in-law of Durham) authorised the fullest adoption of the principle of representative government in Canada and said it was of general application to all colonies with a similar form of government. The removal of import duties and the repeal of the Navigation Acts established what was intended to be a free trade area. Economy as well as liberality figured among the motives; colonies were considered not to pay so that a transfer to often unwilling colonists of responsibility for their own defence would lighten the burden on the home taxpayer. But although the burdens were off-loaded, only a few voices called for the whole enterprise to be wound up. The colonists were no longer to be kept in and were expected gradually to drop out – but they were not to be pushed out. The best way of holding the empire together was seen to lie in not trying to do so.

Hardly was the process achieved than its wisdom began to be doubted. An institute to generate interest in the colonies was founded in 1868, a colonial society in 1869. In 1869–70 the Gladstone government in general and Granville as Colonial Secretary in particular were harried into promising that no sinister intentions lay behind the withdrawal of the last British troops from Canada and New Zealand. In 1872 Disraeli at the Crystal Palace deplored the failure to extract in return for the devolution of power acceptance of some organisation for collective action. But he did not suggest that the missed opportunity could or should be recovered. The mid-Victorian enthusiasts for empire may have underestimated the strength which local patriotisms were bound to develop but most of them were realistic enough to recognise how limited colonial enthusiasm for closer reunion was. Even the action of some colonists (led by Canada in 1859) in putting duties on all imports, including those from 'home', was allowed to pass. The advocates of federation, formed in 1884 into the Imperial Federation League (whose first president W. E. Forster had in 1876 coined the term 'commonwealth'), remained persistent rather than influential. The most striking success was achieved by the Fair Trade League which in 1886 staged a colonial exhibition and inspired the Conference of Colonial Premiers at the Golden Jubilee. Salisbury however brought the Fair Trade League down to earth in 1891 by insisting that they should produce a definite plan. After much heart-searching, they produced an indefinite one which had as its chief positive proposal a scheme of preferential duties. Gladstone, who by this time had succeeded Salisbury, told them that this was totally unacceptable whereupon they decided, as nobody could think of anything better, to disband.[65]

That the future lay with 'the great empires' was a commonplace of the time.[66] Only by making a reality of her colonies could Britain keep up with the United States and Russia. The wave of pride in possession, stimulated by such writings as Seeley's *Expansion of England* (1882) was, in spite of appearances, a defensive reaction, counter-attack rather than unprovoked aggression. One element in it was the assertion, contradicting those writers who were denigrated by being called 'Little Englanders', that colonies *did* bring wealth. Whatever the truth as to this may be, the rest of the world can hardly be blamed for thinking that there must be something in it when the chief colony-owner was so obviously wealthy.

Underlying the new approach was a renewed emphasis on power, as the main subject matter of politics. Disraeli in 1863 had stressed the need for Britain to obtain and maintain possession of the strong places of the world. This was a direct challenge to Liberalism. While men like Cobden, Bright and Gladstone were not pacifists, they believed in moral rather than physical power. The use of force was to them only justified as a last resort when reason and compromise had proved unavailing. If Liberalism was about liberty, how could Liberals be justified in using force to deprive subject peoples of it? 'If', wrote Chamberlain in 1882, 'the people of Egypt prefer native administration with all its consequences to the inflexible severity and honesty of European control, it is not England's business nor right to force on them an unpopular system.'[67] To refuse individuals a say in their own destiny because they belonged to the 'lesser' races was incompatible with that basic right to such a say which was the ultimate foundation of the Liberal creed. Unless men are taught to rely on themselves, they can never be truly worthy of the name of free men.[68]

In this context Gladstone stood out as a persistent seller of passes. His part in handing back the Ionian islands to Greece may have been exaggerated but it was certainly large in the settlement of the *Alabama* dispute with the USA. It was his first government which was suspected of scuttling in Canada and New Zealand. The 'Beaconsfieldism' which was the main target of the Midlothian campaign consisted in readiness to use force in promoting national interests, as in sending the fleet to the Dardanelles, bringing Indian troops to Malta and taking over Cyprus for no very convincing reason. Back in office, Gladstone withdrew from Afghanistan and accepted defeat in South Africa after Majuba. It was largely his doing that Bismarck's colonial claims were settled with relative harmony in 1884–5. But the head and front of his offending was his refusal to avenge Gordon and his willingness to give Ireland Home Rule.[69] The overall result was that he alienated a preponderant fraction of Coleridge's 'clerisy'; Ireland, in Salisbury's words, 'woke the slumbering genius of Imperialism'.[70] All the same his policy was much better attuned to Britain's long-term capacities than was its counterpart. Her best hope of retaining influence in the world as her relative physical power decreased would have been to put her peace-keeping activities, so to speak, into commission and persuade as many as possible of the other major states to join her in arrangements designed to get international disputes settled by agreement rather than war. Although such arrangements, to have any chance of success, would have had to include provisions for peaceful change, they would inevitably have benefited the satisfied powers. To get the necessary co-operation and good-will from the rest of the world, British policy would have had to be conducted much more in the spirit of Gladstone than in that of Palmerston, Disraeli and Chamberlain.

But so deeply had liberal ideas taken root in British society that recourse to the empire, and especially to the non-white empire, as the answer to the country's looming difficulties left many people uneasy. 'Imperialism' was something disreputable engaged in by French emperors. How could a good Liberal justify engaging in it? Four answers presented themselves, for use in isolation or in a variety of logical or illogical combinations.[71]

(1) Undoubtedly the most popular idea was that of trusteeship, originally propounded by Burke with reference to India, which saw it as Britain's task to use her powers in the interest not of herself but of humanity at large. The art of ruling other peoples, as the British reminded themselves in their favourite Vergilian quotation, was to bring mercy to the subjugated and justice to the arrogant. By British help alone could backward societies be raised to a level of education and public morality at which they could be conscientiously allowed to look after themselves. Meanwhile the white man had a burden to carry and often a grave to die in. Ultimately this approach amounts to a claim that, rightly conducted, the governing of subject people is entitled to respect on moral grounds. 'The Government of India', said Gladstone, 'is the most arduous and perhaps the noblest trust ever undertaken by a nation.'[72] But the claim went uneasily with assertions that empire building paid off and it was open to charges of hypocrisy which could be rebutted only by carrying the process

through to the point at which the promised self-government was bestowed.

(2) By many however that promise was regarded as something for the distant future, if ever. The highest ranks of civil employment must continue to be held by Englishmen because they alone possessed the habits of mind and vigour of character which were essential to the task. Whether Asiatics or Africans could develop those qualities was questioned. Indeed many involved in governing the empire had serious doubts as to whether they were even possessed by the home public. Hence the curious spectacle of men who claimed to be benefiting their inferiors by inculcating British principles, criticising bitterly the state of affairs to which the pursuit of those principles was in their view leading in Britain herself. They were meritocrats conscious of their own capacities and loath to have their well-intended policies submitted to popular control. In questioning why good and benevolent despotism should not be allowed to continue indefinitely, they paid too little regard to the need of all governments to win a measure of consent and to the tendency of governments which do not win it to degenerate into tyrannies.

(3) A third school of thought were so convinced that Britain's rule brought benefits as to have no hesitation in justifying most things which could be regarded as essential to its continuance. Strategic needs were over-riding. This was the strongest argument for refusing Home Rule to Ireland. It was the main reason why British governments during the 1870s and 1880s overcame an undeniable reluctance to take on more burdens and acquired four-and-a-quarter million square miles of extra territory and sixty-six million more subjects. To criticise such moves on the ground that Britain was thereby over-extending her limited and stretched resources would not be entirely fair, since the people who justified the acquisitions were mostly very concerned as to how she was to maintain her position in the world. Taking over more lands might add to the burdens but not taking them over would add to the dangers.

(4) The people who pleaded strategic imperatives mostly justified the means by pointing to the general welfare as the end. But there were some who, with one eye on Darwin and another on Bismarck, frankly abandoned Liberalism for *Realpolitik*. Oxford's training for proconsuls included the passage where Thucydides makes the Athenian imperialists claim that 'by a necessary law of their nature, men rule wherever they can'. Chamberlain said that 'because we are a great governing race, we are predestined by our defects as well as our virtues to spread over the habitable globe'.[73] In the view of Edward Dicey, the editor of the *Observer*, the British Empire had been established for the sole benefit of Great Britain. 'To say that we have been influenced by any higher motive seems to me self-deception.' But such an outlook left unans-

wered the question how Britain was to stop her power from being eroded.

Much ink has been expended in trying to settle why the last twenty years of the nineteenth century saw a sudden rush on the part of the Great Powers to acquire colonies. The chief answer is that the ripples were reaching the edge of the world pool (see p. 11). The process of incorporating non–industrialised countries into the world economy was beginning to affect even the most backward areas, which hitherto had hardly been attractive enough to justify the cost of development. Many of the markets which were becoming increasingly important to British exporters, worried about 'over-production', were in primitive lands where native governments seemed incapable of providing the security and justice needed for European traders to operate. In addition Britain's first followers on the path of industrialisation were taking at face value her claims about the benefits of empire; investment overseas seemed to pay off. France and Germany had internal pressures which led their governments to welcome chances of external distraction. As they sought to grab such bits of the world as were still unclaimed, the British government was driven rather reluctantly by commercial and public opinion to make formal its claims where informality had previously sufficed. The limits of spheres of influence had to be pegged out and this was something which only governments could do. Most of the land concerned was in Africa since in the Americas most states claimed to be civilised and even banana republics were protected by the Monroe Doctrine. In Asia predatory eyes were turned on the Turkish empire, Iran and China. But the danger of precipitating war by trying to get in first was obvious enough to curb greed. The brink became a place where one bargained uncomfortably rather than fell in.

Concern Outmodes Self-help

As the nineteenth century advanced, talk about 'natural rights' dropped increasingly into the background. Neither the Utilitarians nor J. S. Mill (see pp. 29, 68) had attached importance to them. They are a typical mode of thinking for disadvantaged members of society who are claiming a share in the advantages; their hey-days were the English, American and French Revolutions. After 1867, and still more after 1885, the only men excluded from a share in Britain's government (women were a different matter) were those without property and largely inarticulate. It had never been easy to see what moral obligation there could be behind the call to achieve the greatest happiness of the greatest number, but the pioneers of the British Socialist movement abandoned even J. S. Mill's reinterpretation of that objective. 'I prefer to define my end', wrote Beatrice Webb, 'as the increase in the community of certain faculties and desires which I happen to like – love, truth, beauty and humour'.[74] She and her friends were more concerned with the practicalities of improving society than with deciding exactly why society should be improved. Socialists seemed short on categorical imperatives; some, like Shaw, even approved of writers such as Nietzsche and Ibsen who denigrated duty and sacrifice.

The vogue of the British idealist philosophers needs to be seen against this background. Prominent among them was T. H. Green, who taught at Oxford from 1860 to 1883; his works however were only published posthumously in 1883–7 and it was not until then that his disciples (who included Goschen, Curzon and Milner) began to move into posts of influence. Through them he caused a generation of the 'clerisy' to rethink its obligations to society and modified the attitudes of many who never read a line of his works (although a number will have read *Robert Elsmere*, the best-selling novel of 1888 by Matthew Arnold's niece, Mrs Humphrey Ward, in which he played a key role).[75]

The exponents of 'natural rights' had set the individual over against society; freedom for the individual was the outstanding demand of early-Victorian Liberals. But to Green the individual and society were unthinkable apart. This applied even in the sphere of cognition. We only make sense of the objects of our consciousness by locating them in a connected system which we have gradually developed by interpreting our experience. The world we understand and our understanding of it are not separable things but an interacting process. In the sphere of morals, Green took over from J. S. Mill the idea of self-realisation as the proper end of human conduct; it was the sense of an obligation to advance towards this idea which justified the title of 'idealist'. But the self could only be realised in society, by helping others to pursue the same end. The individual was called on as an urgent personal vocation to improve life for his neighbours even at the cost of his own pleasure. Morality consisted in the disinterested performance of self-imposed duties. Finally in the political sphere, rights were something which only acquired significance from taking part in society. They must therefore be closely linked with obligations. The individual could only plead that he needed them to perform his role in society if he was in fact prepared to perform that role.

> Freedom of contract and individual liberty are not ends in themselves but merely means to an end. That end is what I call freedom in the positive sense; in other words, the liberation of the powers of all men equally for contributions to the common good.[76]

Green inherited much of his approach from the Christian Socialists, but his Christianity was close to that of the Unitarians, seeing in Jesus an example rather than a saviour. Idealism provided an alternative for the moral earnestness of the Evangelicals in an age when men could no longer accept the Bible or the church as adequate foundations for faith. But it was essentially a creed for the advantaged, offering reasons (based ultimately on intuition) why someone who was relatively privileged had a duty to improve the position of someone else who was relatively less so.

But situations might occur in which, although an advantaged individual sought to improve the lot of the less advantaged, fulfilment of the duty called for the expenditure of more money or the exertion of more authority than he possessed. In such cases he would be justified in advocating intervention by the state. Just as the state had on occasion to intervene to prevent a majority oppressing a minority, so it should step in to prevent the iron laws of economics from resulting in living conditions which for many made all talk of their realising themselves meaningless.

Yet the admission of such a possibility carried with it dangers, of which Green was very conscious. In the first place the advantaged individual, in seeking to do his duty towards his less fortunate neighbours, might only too easily give them what he thought they ought to have rather than what they themselves wanted. When what they wanted was something obviously bad for them, such as too much drink, this paternalism was hard to avoid. It is an occupational weakness of meritocrats (see p. 30) and one to which some of Green's own pupils succumbed in their attitude to subject peoples. But since the real function of government was to maintain conditions in which morality was possible, and since morality consisted for Green in the disinterested performance of self-imposed duties, paternal government tended to make morality impossible by narrowing the room for the self-imposition of duties and for the play of disinterested motives. Moreover paternal government might easily end by sapping self-reliance.

If secondly the individual had an obligation to contribute to the common good even at the cost of his own apparent good, it might seem that his personal rights could not conflict with or even properly exist apart from that common good. From there it would be a short step to saying that the individual's true good coincided with the common good, even if he did not think so, and that the state was therefore justified in compelling him to conform. This was in fact the direction taken by German idealism and fear of such a development in Britain was one of the reasons why a group of younger Liberal theorists, Hobhouse, Hobson, Wallas and Ritchie, viewed Green's influence with mixed feelings. They for their part evolved a standpoint which, while it had many similarities with the idealists, retained more of the individualist tradition.[77]

Mill, while changing the proper object of individual life from happiness to self-realisation, had still considered the individual as distinct from society. The New Liberals took the next step by denying the possibility of such a distinct existence.[78] It was only through and in society that man could realise his potentialities; he could only hope to live the good life himself by seeking to enable others to do the same. Politics became inseparable from ethics, as they had been for Gladstone. The ideal society must be a just society, which the existing one was palpably not; the individual had not only an interest but also a duty to bring such a society into being.

For the New Liberals countered the authoritarian potentialities of Darwinism by seeing the extension of consciousness as an integral part of the evolutionary process. As that process advanced, the individual became increasingly aware both of himself and of his character as a social being. The recognition of mutual obligations between himself and his fellow-members emerged by a natural progress. Thus instead of evolution requiring all to compete against all, it was said to bring a growing sense of the need for all to cooperate with all. While this may have involved some wishful thinking, it did provide a rational explanation of how an intuitive moral imperative grew up. Moreover awareness of this situation involved awareness of ability to choose – an element lacking in the Darwinian hypothesis of natural selection – and thus of ability to steer society by mutual agreement towards conditions in which the possibility of individual self-realisation all round would be maximised by rational co-operation. This was the state of affairs towards which the New Liberals believed that progress was not merely desirable but actually occurring. They, more than Mill, deserved J. F. Stephen's charge of having formed too favourable a view of human nature (as they themselves began to realise after 1914).

If the political order had to conform to the ethical ideal of what was just, the individual had an obligation to work for this end. The state in turn had a collective responsibility for the well-being of its members, not necessarily by feeding, housing and clothing them but by taking care that economic conditions were such as to enable an able-bodied man to do so for himself by useful labour. It was therefore entitled to intervene where intervention was the only way of securing the external and material conditions needed to allow the highest possible average of individual self-realisation. Liberty thus ceased to be the over-riding objective; welfare acquired parity as an indispensable concomitant to it. The Welfare State rather than Marxist Socialism began to emerge as the answer to Britain's social problems.

A new concept of property replaced the Lockean view of it as the necessary adjunct to the maintenance of personality. Instead, the extent to which the community had contributed to its creation was taken as justifying a claim to a share in the advantages which it brought. 'Unearned increments' did not arise in relation to land alone but extended to all wealth of which the acquisition had been assisted by education, by the protection afforded through a legal system and by the opportunities of enlargement provided through the economic system. Those who had acquired an above average share (particularly if they had done so by inheritance or speculation) could be justly required to surrender some of it to the disadvantaged. Privilege and monopoly had always been targets for Liberalism. Now the desirability of reducing their economic impact was seen as justifying the financing of a welfare state by discriminatory taxation. The principles on which discrimination should be based were left indefinite.

Utilitarianism had thus been transformed into Social Democracy. If Socialism means treating man as a social being, with all which that principle entails, the New Liberals were socialists. But at the same time they were democrats. They were opposed to public ownership (although not to private co-operation) and to a centrally controlled economy, with all the inroads on liberty which such a concept must involve. They wanted to retain individual initiative as the mainspring of the economic system but make it socially responsible. This meant keeping competition and the profit motive in operation, although subject to regulation. They were a trifle evasive about the extent to which the state might coerce individuals who did not do their social duty. While favouring a more equitable distribution of wealth, they did not seek an equal one. They were gradualists who in the long run attached more importance to the regeneration of individuals than to the reshaping of machinery. The Marxist belief in the inevitability of class war was wholly alien to their thinking. Their overriding emphasis on the duty of individuals to co-operate in achieving a just society made them stress the need for everyone to have a chance of taking part in public life. As a corollary, they deprecated the formation of a party dedicated, like Labour, to advancing the interests of a single class, even if that class were the one most deserving public help. They condemned the stress laid by Liberal Imperialists and Fabians on 'national efficiency' as misplaced.[79] Not only was the term incapable of measurement and therefore practically useless but the notion of government in which it resulted was to them too mechanical. Too little attention was paid to ends and too much indifference shewn about means. The benefit which might accrue to society in making the individual more efficient was not the only thing to be considered; the effect on the human being was important as well. This overlooked the part played by efficiency in making ends meet in a competitive world.

These were the thinkers who told most of Britain's progressive governments after 1906 what to do, with the Fabians telling them how to do it. Yet the party for which the ideas were devised has been the one which has been least in power. Whatever else may have caused this anomaly, it was certainly not due to ideological bankruptcy on the Liberals' part.

Labour Goes It Alone

Men from the working classes had been sitting in Parliament since 1874, by agreement between the Liberals and the parliamentary committee which the Trades Union Congress set up in 1869 to look after workers' interests at Westminster. In 1885 their numbers had risen to twelve. One of them, Henry Broadhurst, held junior office in Gladstone's 1886 government; but they stood and in effect counted as rank and file Liberals. The first move to set up a party which would be independent both in organisation and policy was the Social Democratic Federation established in 1881. Under the influence of H. J. Hyndman, its predominantly bourgeois members became disciples of Marx and apostles of revolution. In 1884 there followed the Fabian Society, a 'think tank' with a title deliberately chosen to show that, although it too sought Socialism, it proposed to do so by the non-revolutionary strategy of 'permeating' existing bodies and primarily the Liberal Party; its membership, largely recruited in drawing-rooms, reached a peak of about 2,000 in the later 1890s. Both the SDF and the Fabians were mainly London-based. The SDF completely failed and the Fabians did not directly try to get candidates elected to anything.

In the aftermath of the 1884–7 recession, the trade unions, as has been said, gained strength and grew more militant. The view spread, particularly in the north, that labour's interests would never be adequately voiced in public until workers had a party of their own, led by men of working-class origin. The outcome was the foundation of the Independent Labour Party at Bradford in 1893. Although the party's objective was said to be the introduction of Socialist measures, that term was omitted from the title in the hope of winning support from trade unionists who were opposed to it. The moving spirits came from a variety of backgrounds: ex-radical (Keir Hardie), ex-SDF (Champion), Marxist (Aveling). Many had belonged to the Fabians but the society as such played little part in the new venture. Twenty-eight candidates were run in the 1895 election; none were successful. The TUC turned against the party and its efforts to build instead on a basis of individual membership were a failure.

The second recession from 1893 to 1896 was followed by a second wave of militant unionism, aggravated by an employers' counter-attack. The meagre record of the Liberals as regards social reform between 1892 and 1895 had angered the unions and Socialists who refused to appreciate why Home Rule had to be given priority. By 1900 the Liberals were in disarray over the Boer War and their chances of regaining power seemed slim. In 1899 the TUC voted in favour of combined action to get more workers into Parliament and in 1900 the Labour Representation Committee was formed. The LRC represented a compromise between the ILP on the left and the TUC on the right, with the half-hearted Fabians in the centre. The Committee was neither Marxist nor Socialist, although the Socialists were over-represented on it, and it was less under the thumb of the TUC than its predecessors, although the unions still remained its source of cash. Its sole function at the outset was to organise Labour candidates, who were to sit and vote in Parliament as a separate party with their own leaders and whips. Eight months after its formation, it ran fifteen candidates in the general election, two of whom were successful.

In 1903 the Committee decided that no organisation affiliated to it might support any other party, although they might work with one. In the same year the affiliated unions agreed to pay a penny for each of their members into an election fund; MPs who benefited had to vote as the majority of them wished. Before the 1906 election the LRC Secretary, Ramsay MacDonald, reached a secret agreement with the Liberal Chief Whip, Herbert Gladstone, by which Liberals refrained from putting up candidates in 30 constituencies, thus helping the LRC candidates to victory by leaving them as the only suitors for the progressive vote. The advantage of this bargain to the Liberals was that it saved them from having to spend money on contesting these seats and strengthened their appeal to working-class voters elsewhere. All thirty of the Committee's candidates were elected (as well as twenty-four of the usual 'Lib-Labs') and constituted themselves the Labour Party. The agreement with the Liberals left them free to cast their votes as they collectively chose.

Thus from 1903, if not from 1900, the possibility of progressive opinion being united in support of a single party disappeared (although the agreement with the Liberals held good for both the elections in 1910). This was to give Conservativism a distinct advantage after 1918, particularly when reinforced by the effect of the 'first past the post' system, and one is bound to ask whether the split could have been avoided. Clearly in a combined party working-class influence would have continued to grow and in time become dominant. But on the other hand the electoral appeal of Labour has been strongest when it has had a liberal flavour in its programme.[80]

The split was all the sadder because it need not have been the result of doctrinal difference. Nine out of the fourteen points in the programme which the Liberals adopted at Newcastle in 1891 were ones for which Labour bodies had been calling. Admittedly the slant was primarily political and it contained few of the economic items in the ILP programme of the same year. But the LRC programme of 1901 was to be considerably more moderate than the ILP one, to which on the other hand Chamberlain's 'Unauthorised Programme' of 1885 came distinctly closer. If that programme is taken in conjunction with later extensions and glosses, the gap between the two shrinks to a size which is hard to regard as beyond bridging. The causes which Chamberlain sponsored or with which he showed sympathy (see pp. 142–4, 146–50, 176, 204) included manhood suffrage; equal electoral districts; the payment of members; reform of the House of Lords; a shift to direct and progressive taxation; the purchase of land for housing by local authorities; loans to help workers buy houses; old-age pensions; health insurance; compensation for injured workmen; an eight-hour day; Labour Exchanges; Courts of Arbitration; the provision by local authorities of work for the unemployed; free and unsectarian primary education; measures to encourage the breaking-up of estates; the taxation of unearned increments in land value; wider public ownership of utilities. By the time such a programme had been executed, the decision on what to do next would have been for fresh leaders in a new world.

One issue which might have caused trouble was South Africa; judging by his previous record, Chamberlain would have advocated as a radical pretty much what he advocated as a Unionist. But, with Liberal colleagues to restrain him, he might have kept out of actual war, while the workers were by no means all pro-Boer.[81] Another possible area of disagreement was the spending of funds derived from taxes on schemes of social welfare; several condemnations of this can be quoted. But they all date from after 1892 – and what else had been meant by that notorious phrase 'pay ransom'? Ireland would *ex hypothesi* have been disposed of before he became leader.

The real cause of antagonism between Liberals and Labour were personal, social and organisational. The 'old guard' of Liberal leaders – Rosebery, Morley, Spencer and Harcourt – never saw the need to transform the party radically; even the most sympathetic would have regarded 40 to 50 working-class MPs as the maximum. This did not apply to Gladstone who said in 1891 that a substantial increase in labour representation was not only desirable but in the highest degree urgent.[82] His son thought that the Labour leaders were perfectly justified in creating an organisation of their own so as to compel the Liberals to transform official sympathy into positive action; as has been seen, he tried, when Chief Whip, to put this attitude into practice. But the departure of the Whigs and Liberal Unionists had deprived the central Liberal organisation of an important source of funds and constituencies were left more than ever dependent on local 'fat cats' who tended to be successful nonconformist employers. Such men were hostile to the ILP, did not see the need for attracting working-class votes and were unprepared to finance workers as candidates.[83]

Herbert Gladstone was told in 1892 that 'The long and the short of it is that the constituencies, for social, financial and trade reasons, are extremely slow to adopt Labour candidates'. All that the Liberal headquarters could do was 'to earnestly bespeak for a Labour candidate the generous support of the local Liberal Association'. Attempts at making the long march through the institutions as the Fabians wished came to grief on the tight control maintained by the Liberal establishment which kept off the agenda of council meetings subjects in which workers were interested, refused to accept amendments from the floor and considered that the job of the theoretically sovereign body was to ratify pre-arranged declarations. To this had the Caucus come! As soon as 'advanced' men began to get a majority in an association, the people with the money shut up their purses. 'It is only a waste of time for the workers to attend.' Ramsay MacDonald was hardly overstating things when he told Herbert Samuel in 1895 that 'we didn't leave the Liberals. They kicked us out and slammed the door in our faces'.[84]

Could Chamberlain have altered this if he had remained in the Liberal Party and in due course become its leader? An answer depends in part on whether it is supposed that his drift towards imperialism and protection was an inevitable accompaniment of growing old or whether separation from the Liberal Unionists and acceptance of Home Rule would have accentuated his radicalism. One must not judge what he might have become by what he did become. What can be said is that if he had moved in terms of both organisation and policy to make the Liberal Party acceptable to the working class he would have come into conflict with its middle-class leadership (to which of course he himself belonged). Had he been prepared to do so, would his authority (which by that time might have been formidable) have enabled him to prevail? Or would his headstrong and overbearing methods have aroused fatal antagonisms? If the price of victory had been the alienation of the right wing, could the party have won an election? Assuming that it did and that Chamberlain had held office at some stage of the 1890s to enact a programme of social reform, would not those in the Labour ranks who favoured working with the Liberals (and they were no negligible number) have won out against those who wanted independence? If so, it would be injudicious to dismiss too easily a hypothesis that Chamberlain's 'Pilgrimage' was bitter for Britain as well as for himself.

Notes to Chapter 7

1   P. Fraser, *Joseph Chamberlain: Radicalism and Empire* (1966), p. 104.
2   J. Cornford, 'The transformation of conservatism in nineteenth-century England', *Victorian Studies* (September 1963); G. L. Goodman, 'Liberal Unionism: the revolt of the Whigs', *Victorian Studies* (December 1959).
3   There is said to have been a convention preventing peers from taking part in elections. But in 1885 Granville, Spencer, Kimberley and Derby would all seem to have done so, and in 1886 Salisbury spoke several times at the start of the campaign.
4   Lady G. Cecil, *The Life of Lord Salisbury* (1921), Vol. 2, p. 302.
5   J. L. Garvin, *The Life of Joseph Chamberlain* (1933), Vol. 2, p. 264; Fraser, p. 111.
6   R. R. James, *Lord Randolph Churchill* (1959), p. 285.

7   M. Hurst, *Joseph Chamberlain and Liberal Reunion* (1967); A. G. Gardiner, *The Life of Sir William Harcourt* (1923), Vol. 3, pp. 23–37; Gavin, Vol. 2, pp. 277–94.

8   An incident at this time throws light on Chamberlain's relations with the press, not to mention his methods generally and the reasons why he was distrusted. On 3 January 1887 the *Birmingham Daily Post* published a report of an interview with him in which he denied that he had made 'fresh proposals towards the reunion of the Liberal Party' and expressed the belief that Gladstone's supporters were tiring of the existing situation and becoming convinced that Home Rule was impossible. Next day Chamberlain described the article to Dilke as 'inspired'. As has been appositely said, 'no enemy of Chamberlain's could inspire anything in that newspaper and a friend would not have acted without consulting him' (Hurst, p. 166). Yet he wrote to Harcourt, 'There is a stupid paragraph in the *BDP* this morning, professing to be by my authority. In case it is brought to your notice, I will say at once that it is quite inaccurate. I suppose one lie more or less does not matter but I should be sorry for you to think that I was in any way compromising the success of our joint efforts at reunion.' It will be noticed that he did not explicitly repudiate the paragraph or deny having been behind it; 'quite inaccurate' is delightfully ambiguous. What would be interesting is to know whether the piece was deliberately calculated or whether he had been talking off the top of his head, only to realise his unwisdom when he saw the result in print.

9   James, p. 257.

10 B. Webb (Potter) *Diary* (eds N. and J. Mackenzie, 1982), 15 March 1887.

11 Garvin (1934), Vol. 3, p. 303.

12 Recorded in a letter to G. Balfour from W. H. Hadow, who had been present at the meeting. I saw but destroyed it in 1930 without keeping a note of its date.

13 This section is primarily based on F. S. L. Lyons, *Charles Stewart Parnell* (1977). See also *The Fall of Parnell* (1960) by Lyons and his article 'Parnellism and crime', *Transactions of the Royal Historical Society*, Vol. 24 (1974).

14 Hurst, p. 125.

15 Lyons, *Charles Stewart Parnell*, p. 370 says that he had previously approached *The Times* without success; J. A. Cole, *Prince of Spies* (1984), p. 136 says that Buckle, the editor, insisted on seeing originals of the letters.

16 *The History of the Times 1884–1912* (1947), pp. 29–58; Lyons, 'Parnellism and crime,' p. 126.

17 H. Harrison, *Parnell Vindicated* (1931), p. 61.

18 Garvin, Vol. 2, p. 386.

19 E. Clarke, *The Story of My Life* (1918), p. 274; L. P. Curtis, *Coercion and Conciliation in Ireland* (1963), p. 281; Lord Alverstoke, *Recollections of Bar and Bench* (1914), pp. 142–53.

20 *The Times*, 31 July 1888.

21 Garvin, Vol. 2, p. 588.

22 Dilke papers, quoted by Harrison, p. 53.

23 Garvin, Vol. 2, p. 398.

24 A. Robbins, *Parnell, the Last Five Years* (1926), p. 132.

25 Garvin, Vol. 2, p. 400.

26 Letter of 1927 from Neville to Austen Chamberlain, quoted by D. Judd, *Radical Joe* (1976), p. 145. Judd also quotes a statement by Austen Chamberlain recording 'a vague recollection that O'Shea sought financial assistance from Father in his divorce proceedings and that . . . Father definitely refused any contribution for such a purpose'. But see note 29 below.

27 Garvin, Vol. 2, p. 401.

28 J. L. Hammond, *Gladstone and the Irish Nation* (1964), p. 611..

29 C. H. D. Howard, in *Irish Historical Studies* (1962) prints the letter, which is referred to by Garvin in a footnote (Vol. 2, p. 399), with all mention of a loan omitted.

30 H. Harrison, *Parnell, Chamberlain and Mr Garvin* (1938), pp. 201–4.

31 E. Hamilton, *The Diary of Sir Edward Hamilton*, ed. D. W. R. Bahlman (1972), 1 January 1890.

32 Lord Chilston, *Chief Whip* (1961), p. 203.

33 Hurst, p. 362.

34 Lady Randolph Churchill, *Reminiscences* (reprint; Bath, 1973), p. 154.
35 W. S. Churchill, *Lord Randolph Churchill* (1906), Vol. 2, p. 352.
36 M. Hurst, *Joseph Chamberlain and West Midland Politics* (*Dugdale Society*; Oxford, 1962).
37 Garvin (1932), Vol. 1, p. 334.
38 D. W. Laing, *Mistress of Herself* (Barre, Mass., 1965), p. 130.
39 Webb, 21 October 1891.
40 B. Dugdale, *Arthur James Balfour* (1936), Vol. 1, p. 211; Garvin, Vol. 2, pp. 623–32.
41 J. P. D. Dunbabin, 'The politics of the establishment of county councils', *HJ*, vol. 6 (1963).
42 Garvin, Vol. 2, p. 443.
43 T. H. Heyck, *The Dimensions of British Radicalism in the Case of Ireland* (Urbana, 1975), p. 217; P. Stansky, *Ambitions and Strategies* (Oxford, 1964), pp. 78–96.
44 Webb, *Diary* (1983), Vol. 2, 8 July 1895.
45 Diary of Lady D. Stanley, quoted by Cooke and Vincent, *The Governing Passion* (1974), p. 410.
46 Review by B. Pimlott in *The Times Literary Supplement*, 9 December 1983.
47 R. Floud and D. McCloskey, *The Economic History of Britain since 1700* (Cambridge, 1981), Vol. 2, pp. 8–9; P. Mathias, *The First Industrial Nation* (1978), p. 400.
48 J. H. Clapham, *An Economic History of Modern Britain* (Cambridge, 1963), Vol. 3, p. 122.
49 W. P. Kennedy, 'The institutional response to economic growth' in L. Hannah (ed.), *Management Strategy and Economic Development* (1975).
50 See M. Olson, *The Rise and Decline of Nations* (1982).
51 See especially P. Payne, 'Industrial Entrepreneurship and Management in Great Britain. The Critical Period 1870–1914', in *The Cambridge Economic History of Europe* (Cambridge, 1978), Vol. 7, part 1, pp. 201–11.
52 Kennedy; Mathias, p. 353.
53 R. A. Church, *The Kenricks in Hardware* (Newton Abbot, 1969), pp. 319–27.
54 B. Porter, *Critics of Empire* (1968), p. 45.
55 G. C. Allen, *The Industrial Development and the Black Country* (1929), p. 232.
56 Porter, pp. 207–29.
57 J. A. Hobson, *Imperialism* (3rd edn 1938), quoted by Porter, p. 213.
58 S. B. Saul, 'British trade 1870–1914', *EcHR*, Vol. 7 (1954); F. Crouzet, 'Trade and empire', in B. M. Ratcliffe (ed.), *Great Britain and Her World 1850–1914* (Manchester, 1975).
59 H. Feis, *Europe the World's Banker* (New Haven, 1930), p. 15; he gives the total of British overseas investments in 1913 as £4,000m. M. Edelstein, *Overseas Investment in the Age of High Imperialism* (New York, 1982), p. 27, gives the total as £3,932m. In 1913 British imports amounted to £769m. (c.i.f.) or £706m. (f.o.b.). See *British Economic Statistics 1900–64* (Cambridge, 1965), Table F.
60 House of Commons, 20 March 1893; W. Mock, *Imperiale Herrschaft und Nationales Interesse* (Stuttgart, 1982), pp. 178, 276; J. W. Mackail, *The Life and Letters of George Wyndham* (1924), Vol. 1, p. 621.
61 W. P. Kennedy, 'Foreign investment, trade and growth in the UK 1870–1939' in *Explorations in Economic History* (Cambridge, Mass., 1975), Vol. 11, pp. 425–6; A. K. Cairncross, *Home and Foreign Investment 1870–1913* (Cambridge, 1953); Edelstein, p. 157.
62 D. Aldcroft and H. Richardson, *The British Economy 1870–1939* (1969), pp. 14–16; L. G. Sandberg, 'The entrepreneur and technological change' in R. Floud and D. McCloskey, *The Economic History of Britain since 1700* (Cambridge, 1981), Vol. 2, p. 99–120.
63 A. P. Thornton, *The Imperial Idea and Its Enemies* (1959), p. 10.
64 In 1850 'colony' primarily meant an overseas land predominantly peopled by settlers of European origin. By 1950 it primarily meant one with an indigenous population which had always been coloured. So gradual was the change in usage as to make it often hard to be sure what the word is intended to denote.
65 C. A. Bodelsen, *Studies in Mid-Victorian Imperialism* (Copenhagen, 1924), pp. 205–14.
66 Speech of 9 April 1888.
67 Garvin, Vol. 1, p. 448.

68 Gladstone in the House of Commons, 26 April 1870, quoted by R. Koebner and H. D. Schmidt, *Imperialism* (Cambridge, 1964), p. 101.
69 See the letter of Queen Victoria to the Empress Frederick of 31 May 1898, quoted by E. Longford, *Victoria R.I.* (1964), p. 551.
70 Quoted, without detail of source, by R. Taylor, *Salisbury* (1975), p. 118.
71 R. Faber, *The Vision and the Need. Late-Victorian Imperial Aims* (1966), p. 129.
72 Speech at Glasgow, 5 December 1879.
73 *The Times*, 1 February 1897. This speech was not included in the Boyd selection.
74 B. Webb, *Our Partnership* (2nd edn 1979), p. 211; P. Thompson, *Socialists, Liberals and Labour: the Struggle for London 1885–1914* (1967), pp. 236–8.
75 M. Richter, *The Politics of Conscience* (1964); A. J. Milne, *The Social Philosophy of English Idealism* (1962).
76 T. H. Green, lecture on 'Liberal Legislation and the Freedom of Contract', 1880.
77 See L. T. Hobhouse in the *Manchester Guardian* for 31 July 1913, quoted by S. Collini, *Liberalism and Sociology* (Cambridge, 1979); also Hobhouse, *The Metaphysical Theory of the State* (1918).
78 See Collini; M. Freeden, *The New Liberalism* (Oxford, 1978); P. Clarke, *Liberals and Social Democrats* (Cambridge, 1978); C. Harvie, *The Lights of Liberalism* (1976); I. Bradley, *The Optimists* (1980); G. Watson, *The English Ideology* (1973).
79 H. G. C. Matthew, *The Liberal Imperialists* (Oxford, 1973); G. Searle, *The Quest for National Efficiency 1899–1914* (Oxford, 1971).
80 P. Thompson, pp. 232, 253; H. Pelling, *The Origins of the Labour Party* (Oxford, 1968).
81 R. Price, *An Imperial War and the British Working Class* (1972).
82 M. Barker, *Gladstone and Radicalism 1885–1894* (1975), p. 134.
83 A. Macbriar, *Fabian Socialism and English Politics* (1962), p. 240; Heyck, p. 166; P. Thompson, p. 107; G. Searle, 'The Edwardian Liberal Party and Business', *EHR*, Vol. 98 (1983).
84 Pelling, pp. 222–4; Barker, p. 152.

8 'Pushful Joe': 1895–1902

The Jameson Raid

On 1 July 1895 Chamberlain became Secretary of State for the Colonies, the post which he had coveted in 1886. His reasons for now making it his first choice are easier to see than those for having done so previously. Ireland had roused his interest in federalism. He was coming to believe that the empire offered Britain's best hope of salvation. The colonial post gave him a chance of making his name without stepping on Tory corns. But he told Salisbury that he would, if asked, go instead to the War Office, which was crying out for a vigorous reforming hand. Had he gone there, Britain might not have had to fight the Boers and, if she had, might have won more easily. But Salisbury judged it best to let his new ally do as he liked so that it was to sweep a department which had either been derided or forgotten that the new broom was applied. So much dust was stirred up that, even when the sweeper left, his minions had still not caught up with their arrears.[1]

Much of July was occupied by the election, so that the new 'Master' (as his staff promptly nicknamed him) had had little time to read himself in when on 1 August he was visited by his old friend Lord Grey (a former Whig back-bencher and a colleague on the missionary South Africa Committee) and Dr Rutherfoord Harris, a henchman of Cecil Rhodes who was to be the Captain O'Shea of the next episode. Chamberlain had met Rhodes at dinner six years earlier and had on his appointment received a congratulatory missive from one who was soon to boast that he never wrote letters. On both occasions willingness was shown on both sides to defer a judgment which inclined to be hostile. Rhodes had not endeared himself by giving Parnell £10,000 but had palliated the offence by making the gift conditional on the Irish MPs remaining at Westminster in the interests of imperial federation.[2] Grey and Harris were calling to tie up the handing-over of Bechuanaland Colony (see p. 131) to Cape Colony (of which Rhodes was Prime Minister) and to discuss the handing-over of the Bechuanaland Protectorate, further to the north, to the British South Africa Company (of which Rhodes was chairman and Grey a director).

Since Chamberlain had last dealt with South Africa as a minister, the scene had been transformed. Johannesburg, which did not appear on the map until gold was discovered on the Rand in 1886, had grown into a city of 50,000 'raw savages', less than an eighth of whom were Boers. It was easily the wealthiest place south of the Equator; the South African Gold Trust paid a dividend of 100 per cent in 1896.[3] As a result the Transvaal seemed set to dominate the rest of South Africa. The security of Britain's communications with India was thus tied up with the question of who ruled in Pretoria. To protect their hold on power in the face of so many immigrants, the Boers had raised the qualifications required for citizenship and only 2,087 'Uitlanders' were naturalised between 1890 and 1896.[4] Dutch was the language of all official business and of teaching in state schools (financed by taxes on English-speaking non-citizens). The governments of Gladstone, Rosebery and Salisbury had shewn sympathy with the Uitlander demand for equality of status. But the London Convention of 1884 (see p. 128) had left the British government with no explicit right of interference in the Republic's internal affairs. The Boers under their President Kruger showed every intention of resisting to the limit constitutional changes which would anglicise politics and society. In both South Africa and Ireland, Britain's Liberal Nationalism was being tested by collision with a rival national consciousness. But whereas in Ireland it was the other nation which was challenging the existing order, in South Africa the challenge came from the British side. To resolve the clash without resort to arms would call for straightforwardness, patience and tolerance – qualities for which Chamberlain was not conspicuous.

By 1895 the project of an Uitlander rising to seize power was being openly discussed. The chief uncertainty was whether the 'Randlords' would join in. The answer as regards the chief of them, Rhodes, was definite but concealed. He was engaged in providing encouragement, agents, money and arms with the immediate aim of escaping from Kruger's taxes (which hit him harder than most)[5] and the ultimate aim of bringing the Transvaal inside a British-led South Africa, including the territories which for eight decades were known by his name and which were for the time being administered under charter from the British government by his company. Rhodes described a rising as bound to take place; he covered up his intention of making sure that it did.

Distinct from but closely connected with the smoking volcano on the Rand was the project of strengthening communications between the chartered company's territories and the Cape. It was to prevent the Boers from blocking that route that Salisbury's 'Caretaker' government had in September 1885 annexed the south of Bechuanaland as a colony and proclaimed the rest to be a protectorate. A railway had been built into the colony as far as Mafeking. As a condition of his charter Rhodes had promised to continue it 500 miles northwards to Bulawayo and for this purpose wanted to get his hands on the protectorate. Chamberlain warmly approved of the railway but hesitated about abandoning the natives to the mercy of tycoons. He had in the 1880s belonged to the committee organised by the missionary John Mackenzie to humanise British policy and one of the three dominant elements in that policy was still 'the just and considerate treatment of the native population'.[6]

How the British government should react to a Johannesburg rising had been considered by the outgoing Liberal Cabinet. Their High Commissioner at the Cape had recommended that he should at once offer his services as a mediator between the rebels and the Pretoria government. To get a hearing he would need to have force behind him; he had already put some British troops into Mafeking and asked for 5,000 more. But any British government had to be circumspect. If it could be proved guilty of interfering in the home affairs of the Republic, the latter would have an excellent pretext for denouncing the London Convention. Britain would then find herself fighting a war 'not only without an ally but without a single sympathiser'.[7] Circumspection was all the more indicated because the German government was clearly itching to make mischief. The High Commissioner was therefore regarded in London as a dangerous activist and, instead of being given his extra troops, he was replaced in 1895 by the inappropriately christened Sir Hercules Robinson, who had held the post before and surprisingly managed to combine caution with the friendship of Rhodes. Chamberlain disapproved of the choice but reached office too late to stop it.[8]

The London government had always been anxious for Cape Colony to take over the Bechuanaland colony; how far the Liberals went towards promising the protectorate to Rhodes is obscure but he certainly thought his prospects of getting it to be good.[9] Naturally he wanted to control the land over which his railway would be built. He also wanted it as a jumping-off point for a force of his own brought from the north under his agent Dr Jameson, so that it could move over the Transvaal border immediately the rising began and thus ensure success. On the assumption that the rebels were 'rearing to go', the second objective was more urgent than the first. But when Grey and Harris arrived to negotiate the transfer, Chamberlain insisted on discussing it exclusively in the railway context. First Harris, and then Grey in a *tête-à-tête*, started referring to the rising in order to show why they wanted quick action. Chamberlain shut up Harris before he had made more than a 'guarded allusion' to the subject; he declined to receive Grey's information on the ground that, if it were pressed on him, he might have to use it 'officially'. He must have realised perfectly well why the company were in such a hurry to get troops into the protectorate, although he was afterwards to profess that he had no reason to doubt their attribution of this to the need to safeguard the railway and the border. As he admitted privately later, he did not want to know too much.[10]

Chamberlain did refuse to transfer the whole protectorate but offered to grant a strip in it instead. Harris, after a second interview with him on 13 August, sent a telegram to Rhodes saying that Chamberlain was ready to do anything to assist except hand over the administration of the protectorate 'provided he officially does not know anything of your plan'. After a further meeting on 21 August, Harris cabled 'You are aware Chamberlain states Dr Jameson's plan must not be mentioned to him'.[11] On 13 September the minister received three chiefs from the protectorate who had come to London to protest against the loss of their land and explained to them that the company must be allowed to take some of it for the railway; in return they and that section of British opinion which Rhodes contemptuously called 'negrophilist' were appeased by the promise that large native reserves would be established.

For the next seven weeks Chamberlain was on holiday in Spain. Kruger chose this juncture to interfere with traffic between Johannesburg and the south by requiring it to go by rail inside the Transvaal and thus pay the heavy rates charged for doing so. His object was to divert it to the newly-opened line to Delagoa Bay in Portuguese East Africa so as to benefit a route between the Republic and the outside world which was not under British control. Salisbury at once sounded a warning and Chamberlain, on getting home, fulminated against what he claimed to be a breach of the Convention. Kruger gave way, encouraging the belief that he would always yield to firmness.

On 6 November the chiefs were given larger reserves than originally contemplated while a strip along the east side of the Protectorate was handed over to the company, which promised to start building the railway at once. Harris reported that, as Grey was leaving, Chamberlain said to him 'You must allow a decent interval and delay the fireworks for a fortnight'.[12] Rhodes not surprisingly took the message to refer to the rising but its author later denied that any such meaning was intended, and he does seem unlikely to have realised that it lay with Rhodes to give the starting-signal – although power to apply the brake is another matter. The conspirators decided to wait until 28 December. Chamberlain independently arranged for two British regiments which were due to pass the Cape in mid-January in routine trooping movements to call at Table Bay.[13]

aid for Jameson Raiders

While in Spain Chamberlain had asked Robinson for his views on the prospects of a Johannesburg rising 'with or without assistance from outside'. The High Commissioner, who despite later denials also knew what was afoot, proposed that, if such an event occurred, he should call on the two sides to accept his arbitration, go to Pretoria and order the election of a constituent assembly by all adult males in the Transvaal. The London government should publicly endorse his action and announce that a large force would be sent to South Africa. Chamberlain cabled back his concurrence but added 'I take it that no movement will take place unless success is certain. A fiasco would be most disastrous'.[14]

At this point *The Times* took a hand in the game through its imperially-minded manager Moberly Bell and colonial correspondent Flora Shaw, an elegant operator familiar with the corridors of Chamberlain's office. She began with a simple inquiry to her Cape contact as to when 'plans' would commence and was told 'about the New Year'. She replied by cabling that delay would be dangerous since pressure from Europe, if allowed time to develop, might paralyse the government. On 17 December she wired again saying that Chamberlain (who had been down in Birmingham for the last eight days) was 'sound in case of interference European Powers but have special reason to believe wishes you must do it immediately'.[15]

The last statement probably referred to a distraction which had just supervened. Britain was disputing with Venezuela about the frontier of British Guiana and had refused to submit the matter to arbitration. On 17 December President Cleveland told Congress of his intention to appoint an arbitrator and enforce the award. The situation was less serious than it seemed since neither Britain nor the USA had any intention of fighting over such a triviality, although it defied Chamberlain's attempt to settle it by personal diplomacy in the following year. But for the moment a crisis in mid-1896 had to be reckoned with. Accordingly Chamberlain sent instructions to be conveyed to Maguire, Rhodes' agent in London:[16]

> Now as to Transvaal. Might it not come off just at the critical time if it is postponed now? The longer it is delayed the more chance there is of foreign intervention.
>
> It seems to me that either it should come *at once* or be postponed for a year or two at the least. Can we ensure this?
>
> If not, we had better not interfere, for we may bring about the very thing we want to avoid.
>
> If Fairfield [Under-Secretary at the C.O.] can make the situation clear to Maguire, I should like him to do so – then the responsibility must rest with Rhodes and we had better abstain even from giving advice. I again repeat, the *worst* time for trouble anywhere would be about six months hence. I cannot say that any time would be a good one but can the difficulty be indefinitely postponed?

Fairfield claimed later to have done his best to convince Maguire that postponement was possible and, on being satisfied that it was not, to have emphasised instead the need to move fast. This produced what became known as the 'Hurry up! For Pity!' telegram of 19 December. It has by now vanished without the text ever being revealed. But it led Rhodes to tell Johannesburg 'Our foreign suppliers urge immediate flotation'.[17]

In Johannesburg however things were going wrong. The potential rebels were developing cold feet, especially when they discovered that Rhodes proposed for them not independence but British rule with its unwelcome tenderness towards natives. Two delegations were sent to convince him that the flotation must be put off; their message was reluctantly accepted. But Jameson and his 470 men had been kicking their heels for nearly a month and were getting restive. On 23 December he was told that Johannesburg would rise on 28 December and that he should start a few hours earlier; on 26 December the order was cancelled and he was forbidden to move until told to do so by Cape Town. On 29 December however he took the bit between his teeth and, instead of invading the Transvaal after the rising had begun, did so to make it begin. He was sent several messages both from Johannesburg and Cape Town telling him to wait but his final warning to Rhodes that he was starting provoked no veto; it was delayed in transmission and by the time it arrived, the wires back had been cut. Two messages from the British authorities ordering him to halt did reach him *en route* but were disregarded. The story goes that a trooper who had been celebrating too well the imminence of action cut a fencing wire instead of the telegraph one, thus leaving a line of communication to the outside world which, by mischance, was the one to Kruger. The many misjudgments of the Raid's planners included an underestimation of the military effectiveness of the Boers who would have been more than a match for Jameson's force even if Johannesburg had risen to help it. After allowing it to reach the last village on the road, they forced it to surrender there on 2 January. Documents captured in the baggage, including the key to the code, enabled the Johannesburg ringleaders to be identified and arrested. Jameson and his associates were sent back to be tried in England.

Salisbury was wont to ride his Cabinets on a loose rein and gave to his Colonial Secretary more latitude than to most ministers. As a result the information which he had so far received about the Transvaal had been of the sketchiest. But on 26 December Chamberlain thought it expedient to warn him that a rising was imminent and that, if successful, 'it ought to turn to our advantage'.[18] On 27 December a cable from Robinson announced that it had collapsed and next day the news arrived via Rhodes' London solicitor that Jameson might be sent off on his own. Chamberlain promptly told Robinson to warn Rhodes that such a move would violate the company's charter. It would not have his support and Rhodes would do well to consider what would happen if the British government repudiated it. The message alarmed Rhodes but did not make him look for a way of halting Jameson.[19] On 30 December Flora Shaw brought round to the Colonial Office an indirect report that the doctor had set off; Chamberlain heard it at Highbury and wired Robinson to 'leave no stone unturned to prevent mischief'.[20] On reaching London after a night journey, he issued a proclamation condemning Jameson and forbidding British subjects to help him. He also wired to Kruger, saying that he regretted Jameson's action and wanted to co-operate in bringing about a peaceful settlement. He told Rhodes that, if the company proved to have been privy to the 'marauding action', Her Majesty's Government would at once face a demand for the charter to be revoked. This decided attitude met with some criticism, especially when *The Times* published a letter from Johannesburg (written in fact six weeks earlier but left undated) appealing for help on the plea that 'thousands of unarmed men, women and children' were at the mercy of well-armed Boers. Criticism moderated when the raid proved a failure and still more when the Kaiser, acting with some reluctance under pressure from his entourage,[21] sent his famous telegram of congratulations to Kruger.

During the eighteen months of *post mortems* which ensued, a game of poker was played behind the scenes. Rhodes, who was made by the Cape Boers to resign as Prime Minister, threatened to publish the telegrams between his London agents and himself, eight of which might have ended Chamberlain's political career by showing him to have known all along much more about what was going on than he in retrospect admitted. Rhodes hoped by this threat to prevent the government from agreeing to any formal inquiry. Chamberlain, while denying that the telegrams gave an accurate account of what he had said, and even hinting that they had been misleadingly phrased with the deliberate object of implicating him (which implied that Rhodes had been sent false information by his agents) forbade publication as being against the national interest.[22] He reinforced this veto by the threat that, if it were disregarded, he would have the charter rescinded. 'If they put me with my back to the wall, they will see some splinters.'[23] No formal agreement to refrain was ever signed; each side knew what the other could do and held back in consequence. Chamberlain correctly told Rhodes that, in view of public interest in Britain and Europe, some form of inquiry was inevitable. But when in July 1897 the report of that inquiry came to be debated, he defended Rhodes in terms which were, by general consent, unduly fulsome. Rumour had it that an MP sat through the debate with the unpublished telegrams in his pocket, prepared to read them out if the tribute was not lavish enough. This has been generally disbelieved. But the telegrams did not have to be in the House to exert an influence on Chamberlain.

The inquiry took the form of a Committee of fifteen MPs, including Harcourt, Hicks Beach, Labouchere, Campbell-Bannerman – and Chamberlain! The accused was allowed to join the judges. The verdict, although apparently an acquittal, was not wholly free from ambiguity. 'Neither the Secretary of State nor any of the officers of the Colonial

Office received any information which should have made them aware of the plot [which plot?] during its development.' Opinion abroad echoed the Liberal MP who spoke of the 'lying in State' at Westminster. There were several reasons apart from its composition which prevented the Committee from getting at the truth. One was lack of authority. Several witnesses, notably Rhodes and Flora Shaw, refused to answer questions which touched on the actions of third parties or on confidential conversations. One important witness had died and several potential ones, including Grey and Robinson, were not summoned at all, being ill or abroad, while Rhodes was allowed to go back to South Africa immediately after giving evidence so that he could not be recalled in the light of what later witnesses said. Chamberlain more than once reproved witnesses who volunteered evidence without being asked for it; he managed to visit Jameson secretly in prison to ensure that nothing awkward emerged from that source.[24] The British official who had done most of the negotiating in Cape Town was induced to ruin his career by pretending that he had not kept his superiors properly informed.

The Committee got hold of forty-six of the telegrams as well as ten to and from Flora Shaw. They established that an unspecified number [in fact 8] were held by Rhodes' solicitor, who refused to release them without his client's permission, which was not forthcoming. As this refusal was backed by Chamberlain (after he had himself got access to them and been forbidden by Salisbury to publish his comments) it is hardly surprising that a body which was essentially political did not report the recalcitrant persons to the House for contempt. Harcourt pulled his punches, perhaps out of patriotism, perhaps out of old friendships, perhaps for fear lest his own party's cupboard should prove to contain skeletons.[25]

A judicial inquiry which included or employed a first-class prosecuting counsel might have probed more relentlessly and brought more to light but the political repercussions would have been formidable. The Parnell, Marconi, Panama, Dreyfus and Eulenburg affairs all illustrate how elusive truth and justice can become once politics enter. Chamberlain said twice in the House that he would have preferred a judicial inquiry but, while the character of the body was still an open question, he advised his colleagues to accept a parliamentary one. 'I doubt whether they would be the most successful body for arriving at the truth but they would undoubtedly be most likely to satisfy the feeling in favour of enquiry which will probably dominate the House of Commons.' He went on to say that an investigation might be demanded not only into recent events but also into the whole history of the company. 'If I were a Director, I think I should prefer this as it will lengthen the enquiry and so widen the issue that their guilt – if they are guilty – in connection with the recent raid would be smothered up in comparatively irrelevant detail.'[26] No doubt he had the Parnell case in mind.

When Chamberlain heard of Jameson's start, he said 'If this succeeds, it will ruin me'.[27] It failed and he escaped ruin. Yet when all is said and done, the real case against him is not that he knew more than he let on and misled the public as to the extent of his knowledge. His professed stance was so implausible as to make many think him even more involved than the facts warranted. 'Pushful Joe is in it' was Robinson's reaction to the news that Jameson had launched forth,[28] and many other people inside and outside Britain thought the same. But Jameson's decision to start was his own and unprompted. Neither Chamberlain nor Rhodes knew of it in time or approved. And although Chamberlain realised that Rhodes was in league with the Johannesburg malcontents he did not appreciate how far they were being pushed and not pushing.

The charge which is hard to answer is not one of action but of inaction. It is that, knowing as much as he did and suspecting more as he must have done, he took pains not to know too much 'officially' and stood aside to let an attempt at overthrowing a foreign government go ahead. Indeed he took the positive step of facilitating it by handing over the railway strip to the company. He may have had defensible grounds for doing so but he thereby lost control over events.[29] Moreover he stood aside because he was in fundamental sympathy with the plotters. He thought he saw a way of getting what he wanted without involving the government in a charge of aggression. The lesson he drew from his experience as a minister between 1880 and 1885 was that the British Cabinet had been too generous in appeasing the Boers and had been ill-rewarded for their magnanimity. He judged the situation in the Transvaal to be intolerable; in his view an inferior race was trying to subdue a superior one.[30] An explosion was bound to come and he wanted to use it to bring the territory under British control as a step towards the unification of South Africa inside the empire. In this he and Rhodes saw eye to eye and one of the reasons why he gave Rhodes a 'certificate of honour' after the inquiry was his desire to preserve him and his company as a political force.

But the attempt to run with the hare and ride with the hounds was too clever by half. Admittedly Jameson upset the apple cart but an astute politician allows for Murphy's law that 'if things can go wrong, they will'. Not merely did Chamberlain emerge compromised in the eyes of all who were not convinced imperialists, but the British Cabinet and Parliament, by conniving in the hushing-up of his complicity, attracted to themselves a share of the suspicion which he had engendered. Britain's 'Bay of Pigs' immensely complicated the problem of handling the Boers. Plenty of people can be wise after the event; it is being wise before the event which marks the statesman.

The Prime Minister took it all with his usual calm, being chiefly concerned over the opportunities which might be given to Germany. 'It would be better if the revolution which transfers the Transvaal to British rulers were entirely the result of internal forces and not of Cecil Rhodes' intervention or ours.' 'Fortunately no great harm seems to have been done except to Rhodes' reputation. If filibustering fails, it is always disreputable.'[31] He refused Chamberlain's offer of resignation and there is no evidence that he bore any extra resentment against his Colonial Secretary for the scrape into which the government had been got. But if Chamberlain's colleagues allowed him a free hand abroad, his ability to extract concessions from them at home – and indeed his entire political position – can hardly have been strengthened.

West Africa and Egypt

'Experience teaches us', said Chamberlain in 1888, 'that trade follows the flag.'[32] In much British overseas development however the flag has followed trade. Merchants have led in establishing themselves wherever they saw a chance of venturing profitably. The armed forces of the home country and white government officials have only come on the scene when the need arose to establish the security without which trade cannot flourish. Money was something to be made by private enterprise, not wasted by public functionaries. Strategic areas like the Cape and East Africa were exceptions to this rule but West Africa did not come into that category. Lagos was annexed in 1861, to suppress the slave trade and encourage 'legitimate' commerce.[33] Consuls were established on the Nigerian coast in 1884 but their function was to get the local chiefs to accept British overlordship, not to supersede them. In 1885 a Protectorate was proclaimed along the coast in order to prevent it being appropriated by anybody else.

By the 1890s however this convenient state of affairs was passing away. There were two main causes. First the tide of modernisation was seeping up into the recesses of the rain forests and the sparser grasslands behind. The diversion to legitimate commerce of an economy built on slavery was having erosive effects. The primitive institutions of Ashanti and Yorubaland lost their nimbus of authority and with it their ability to keep order. Misgovernment in the former led to its occupation by British troops early in 1896. Chamberlain's justification was that[34]

the duty of this country in regard to all these savage countries over which we are called to exercise some sort of dominion is to establish at the earliest possible date *Pax Britannica* and to force these people to

235

keep the peace among themselves. Whatever may be the destruction of life in an expedition which brings about this result, it will be nothing if weighed in the balance against the annual loss of life which goes on as long as we keep away.

In general however the preferred remedy was not outright annexation but the consolidation of individual traders, on the model of the East India Company, into bodies capable of doing – and paying for – their own policing. In 1886 such a body, formed out of four firms, had been given a charter as the Royal Niger Company (thus antedating by three years Rhodes' British South Africa Company).

If the degenerating influence of civilisation had been the only novelty, the expedient might have sufficed. But Britain had also to pay in West Africa the bill for her break with France over Egypt (as well as for France's defeat at Sedan). Having lost out in Europe and in one part of Africa, the French salved their wounded self-esteem by stretching out in others, reviving an earlier dream of hoisting the tricolour all the way from Senegal to the Upper Nile – or even the Red Sea. The settlements which British merchants had created on the coast threatened, and were threatened from, the French enclaves of Guinea, the Ivory Coast and Dahomey on their flanks, as well as the Upper Niger in their rear. This was an expansion led by soldiers and diplomats as much as by traders and politicians; it sought glory as much as gain and snapped its fingers at Paris. On the Lower Niger where the threat was most acute, the company was ill-equipped to cope. For it was expected to be self-supporting; its troops and officials had to be paid out of profits. West Africa's chief product was palm-oil, for which world demand was depressed; before much money could be got out, even more would have to be put in. Railways had to be built, ports enlarged, policing extended and markets stabilised before the natives would go over to growing cash crops such as cocoa or ground-nuts for bulk export. In both strategy and economics, the capacity of private enterprise was reaching its limits.

Even before he took office Chamberlain had made clear his approach to this problem. 'It is not enough to occupy certain great spaces of the world's surface unless you can make the best of them.' 'I regard many of our colonies as being . . . estates which can never be developed without Imperial assistance!' 'If the people of this country are not willing to invest some of their superfluous wealth in the development of their great estate, than I see no future for these countries and it would have been better never to have gone there.' The self-made manufacturer argued that the capital expenditure which he proposed would in process of time bring in ample dividends to the economy as a whole. But he was preaching that the final verdict as to what should be done ought not to be left to market forces.

'Individual enterprise will till the fields and cut the timber and work the mines; but Government and Government alone can make the roads and the railways.'[35]

In the same August as he had his first interviews with Harris, he made encouraging noises to a deputation on West African railways. He also suggested to the Cabinet that the dividends on the government's Suez Canal shares should be used as a colonial development fund. This imaginative idea found no support from Hamilton at the Treasury. 'All new departures in financial arrangements are much to be deprecated'[36] – in other words, nothing should ever be done for the first time. An alternative scheme for using National Savings deposits to make colonial loans surmounted the Treasury hurdle only to encounter parliamentary insistence on sanctioning each loan before it was made. Chamberlain, who had rashly taken approval for granted, found himself committed to unauthorised expenditure of £3·5m. He managed to get what was in effect an Act of Indemnity passed. But Parliament's jealousy of its privileges, apathy on the part of his colleagues and Treasury doubts as to whether colonies could be made to pay were clearly going to set limits to the schemes which could be realised. Their disillusioned instigator reluctantly concluded that '*festina lente* is a just motto in the development of colonies in the possession of barbarous tribes'.[37]

The problem of keeping out the French remained. 1896 saw a number of their expeditions occupying a variety of posts on the Middle Niger. Hitherto the company had been content to demarcate its sphere of influence by making treaties with chiefs. But these were proving inadequate titles to suzerainty, especially when a chief signed up with both sides at once. Chamberlain pressed for occupation to be made more effective and early in 1897 Goldie, the company's man on the ground, overcame native resistance to take possession of two districts on the two sides of the river. But he refused to go further unless the government would promise both to meet his costs and to prolong his company's charter. This however Chamberlain would not do. He had decided that more was needed than the company could perform and that, in spite of his having a personal stake in it, it must be expropriated 'lock, stock and barrel'. Even before this was achieved, he persuaded the Cabinet to let him organise a West African Frontier Force and put it under the command of a Captain Lugard, whom he made Commissioner for the hinterland. The shape of Nigeria for the next eighty years was thereby largely if unwittingly determined. Chamberlain justified the cost of the Frontier Force in terms of the economic potential of the Middle Niger region, thus adopting the criteria of the French and Germans who made imperial rule a gamble on the chances of developing semi-deserts.[38] Before long Lugard's detachments were arriving at the same places as French ones. The focus of dispute shifted from Africa to Paris and Chamberlain found himself at odds with Salisbury.

For the Prime Minister's map of Africa was dominated by Egypt. The Franco-Russian Alliance of 1891 made the Admiralty uncomfortably aware of how weak the British fleet had in theory become. The naval estimates had risen sharply. If the 1894 increase proved too much for Gladstone, those for 1896–9 were higher still. Even so, the sailors were no longer willing to risk their 'porcelain' ships in the Bosporus as long as the French fleet remained intact behind them – and the Cabinet agreed. Instead, the route to India had to be defended at Suez, which meant that Britain must remain in Egypt until she had brought into being a native ruling class which could be relied on to run the country and stay on her side – two requirements which in an era of nationalism tended to conflict. Moreover Egypt was traditionally considered to be at the mercy of whoever controlled the Upper Nile. Admittedly the Dervishes who had done so since Gordon's death were incapable of interfering with the river. But they were taken to be merely keeping the bed warm until a European visitor arrived and the French clearly intended to despatch such a visitor via the Congo, the Niger or the Red Sea. Salisbury had long foreseen that, as he was to say in 1897, if the two countries met at Fashoda, the diplomatic crisis would be 'something to remember'.[39] Already in 1895 Edward Grey, as Liberal Under-Secretary for Foreign Affairs, had told Parliament without much premeditation that a French advance in that direction would be regarded as an 'unfriendly act'.

Ever since the disaster of 1885 the British public had fought shy of another push into the Sudan. This reluctance had been backed by Britain's agent in Egypt, not for nothing nicknamed 'over-Baring'; he saw that the cost would be charged to that country and wanted no interruption of the process by which he was gradually restoring its finances to solvency. Salisbury was thus left with two ways of preparing for the looming encounter. One was to push into the South Sudan from the south-east instead of the north; hence his activity in East Africa, notably the exchange of Heligoland for Zanzibar with Germany in 1890. But although his strategic railway up from Mombasa was the only one to get its finance without difficulty, physical obstacles slowed it down and in 1898 it still had a good way to go. The other expedient was to balance a blunt refusal of concessions in Egypt and the Sudan by offering some in other places, notably West Africa where only local trade might be at stake.

Already in 1889 and 1891 Salisbury had allowed the French to seal off the Gambia and Sierra Leone from their hinterlands and gave an impression of readiness to let the Gold Coast and Nigeria go the same way. In 1895 he revived the Anglo-French Commission which had been set up three years earlier to settle boundaries throughout the area; Chamberlain too at this stage favoured a comprehensive settlement of differences with France and Germany. But the Commission had scarcely started work than it was halted by the news that an Egyptian force was to move as far south as Dongola (with the unspoken expectation that it would thereafter go further still). For Italy's ambitions in Abyssinia had exceeded her capacities with painful results; her appeal for British help in extricating herself meant that Salisbury could get a majority in Cairo for expenditure on a move southwards, since Germany could not prudently vote against a project designed to rescue another member of the Triple Alliance. A stately advance was set going which was to bring Kitchener to Khartoum in September 1898, two months after Captain Marchand with seven other Frenchmen and 120 Africans had reached Fashoda from the Congo. This British advance southwards, coming as it did on top of the Jameson Raid, killed any French inclination to draw back on the Niger. Eighteen months however sufficed for dignity to be recovered and in the summer of 1897 Salisbury agreed to negotiations being resumed without insisting that, as a preliminary, the French must make their soldiers halt.

Salisbury has been described as 'cynical' and 'pessimistic' but neither adjective does justice to his shrewd and imperturbable outlook. He once, in discussing Russian advances in Central Asia, advised his critics to use large-scale maps; he equally favoured taking long-term views. As a devout high churchman he had a vivid awareness of human frailty and took the words out of Murphy's mouth when he said that 'Whatever happens will be for the worse and therefore it is in our interest that as little should happen as possible'.[40] This approach led him to view mankind's affairs with amused detachment; his descriptions of current events often qualified for the theatre of the absurd. It did not stop him from trying to improve the world but it prejudiced him against grandiose schemes and immunised him against disappointment. Both he and Gladstone were deeply religious men who had been born into a ruling class; otherwise a more complete contrast is hard to imagine – which makes it significant that Chamberlain should have managed to get as much across the one as across the other. Already in November 1895 Salisbury's niece was writing that 'I have never heard him talk of any colleague as he does of [Chamberlain], says that he wants to go to war with every Power in the world and has no thought but Imperialism'. A month later he himself wrote 'I read [Chamberlain's] letter with perfect dismay. Randolph at his wildest could not have made a madder suggestion'. In November 1897 he told the queen that 'Mr Chamberlain was a little too warlike and hardly sees the other side of the question'. In April 1898 he professed inability to decide whether it was Chamberlain's object to drive Britain into war with France, 'the indications differ from month to month'.[41]

Chamberlain was criticised by Salisbury for unwillingness to give things away. But in his eyes any possession was capable of development and thus a potential source of strength which Britain could not afford to lose if she was to maintain her world position in the twentieth century. 'My own idea', he wrote, 'was that the only hope of a peaceful arrangement was to convince the French from the first that they had tried our patience too far and must give way or take the consequences'.[42] On 1 December 1897 he told Salisbury that he could not agree to a Foreign Office proposal to concede the French a position on the west bank of the Niger. In January 1898 he could argue that 'if we have rights and interests in any part of the world and are unprepared to defend them, it is certain that other nations will know how to take advantage of our weakness'[43] – although on second thoughts he cut the sentence out of the paper he was circulating to the Cabinet. His views were shared by Goldie whom he sent to Paris to watch the negotiations and to whom he remarked that the British representatives had not 'enough stiffening in them to hold up a paper collar'.[44]

Salisbury knew that the country would not have its heart in a war over West Africa and the Cabinet appears to have told Chamberlain to pipe down. 'We cannot afford', said the Prime Minister, 'to have more than a limited area of the heather alight at any one time'.[45] On the other hand, he preferred not to drive the leader of his Liberal Unionist allies into resigning. By mid-June 1898 negotiations had narrowed down to ownership of Ilo, to which the French attached importance on the questionable ground that it was where one of their officers had been assassinated – by the enraged husband of his black inamorata. Salisbury was ready to give the place up. If refusal led to war, 'we cannot discern what difficulty it will open to us, but . . . its cost will certainly buy out the value of Ilo a hundred times over'.[46] When Chamberlain retorted that he could not defend any further surrender, the Prime Minister, like a true patriarch, seized on an alternative object for sacrifice:[47]

I am wholly unconvinced of the value of Ilo and I cannot discover on what our claim to it rests. But I should prefer giving up Bona because our title to Bona seems to me positively bad. It will be a pity if we break off negotiations, for it will add to our difficulties in the Nile valley. . . . If we are to send British or Indian troops in the hope of fighting another Plassey with Lugard as our Clive and Sokoto as our Bengal, the prospect becomes very much more serious. Our Clive will be in no danger of being astonished at his moderation. There is no loot to get except in Goldie's dreams. If you wish to come to terms it would be prudent to do so before we take Khartoum. We shall get nothing out of the French Assembly after that event.

Eleven days later an Anglo-French agreement settled the frontiers of Nigeria and the Gold Coast. Chamberlain had wanted to spin out the negotiations in the hope of using the time thus gained to acquire additional bargaining counters, but his colleagues overrode him. On the other hand he got more out of the French by standing up to them than might have resulted from an unrestrained desire to conciliate.

It was not as though he wanted West Africa to get priority over the Nile. He was whole-heartedly behind the refusal to evacuate Egypt, which he had visited in 1890. He spoke emphatically in favour of the expedition to Dongola, although privately nervous of it coming to grief. When the show-down arrived at Fashoda, he would appear to have told a German contact that Salisbury 'lacked the strength of mind to bring about the necessary crisis'![48] Yet Salisbury had consistently repeated that there could be no negotiations until Marchand had been withdrawn and that even then French possession of any part of the Nile was not a negotiable matter. If he showed himself more ready than Chamberlain and some other ministers to let France retain some shreds of dignity while climbing down, that is now recognised as an important part of crisis management. As things were, a new Cabinet in Paris found that its Russian ally would only give all aid short of help and that its fleet was consequently outnumbered.

Salisbury may have been wrong in accepting the conventional wisdom of the day about the need for Egypt's rulers to control the Upper Nile as well. But assuming that that part of the valley had to be held, he had acted like a skilful general who wins by massing superior force at the crucial place at the crucial moment. At a time when Europe seemed united in hostility to Britain, he had carried to completion the partition of Africa in such a way as to secure for her what he regarded as essential, and he had done so without having to fight a major war. This was hardly the occasion to criticise him for weakness yet that was what Chamberlain did. According to the German account he described how all his ministerial colleagues shared his view that Salisbury's policy of 'peace at any price' could not go on any longer and that England had to prove her capacity for action. 'As soon as we are ready, we shall present the bill to France . . . all over the globe and should she refuse to pay, then war.'[49] Yet within four years he was to reach the conclusion that Britain could not do without French support. France's willingness to sign the *Entente Cordiale* agreements of 1904 certainly owed much to her 'moment of truth' in November 1898. Once she realised the need to choose between Alsace and Africa, she had no doubt as to which came first. But to claim that this was why Chamberlain wanted to humiliate her would be far-fetched. His own change of view resulted from disillusionment over another miscalculation.

Amateur Negotiations[50]

Experience in Gladstone's Cabinet between 1880 and 1885 must already have disposed Chamberlain to borrow from Arnold the view of Britain as 'a weary Titan struggling under the too-vast orb of his fate'.[51] But things had grown worse while he was out of office, primarily because the signature of the Franco-Russian Alliance in 1891 made an apparently formidable combination out of two unimpressive components. Bismarck's first principle of foreign policy after 1870 had been to keep France isolated and he would never have given the Russians cause to establish a link which was ideologically so distasteful to them. In his eyes it was a direct threat to German security. But during its first decade Britain was the power to which it proved most threatening. France gave Russia moral support in the Balkans and Far East, Russia did the same to France in Africa and South-east Asia. The Kaiser, his Chancellor Bülow and the Foreign Office Counsellor Holstein, who were the chief orchestrators of German policy between 1897 and 1906, were lulled into the mistake of thinking that Britain needed them and not they Britain. According to the Kaiser, the Kruger telegram was intended to make Britain realise how important it was for her to secure the co-operation of the Triple Alliance.

Chamberlain at first disagreed. After filling Salisbury with dismay by the true but impracticable suggestion that Britain's best way out of her difficulties would be an alliance with the United States, he argued in January 1896 that 'we should occupy a stronger position in Europe as the friend of Russia rather than of the Triple Alliance' – an idea which Randolph Churchill had propounded in 1886. But although Salisbury exerted himself during the Tsar's visit to Balmoral in September 1896 to secure Russian co-operation over Turkey, and although he more than once thereafter expressed a wish for a closer friendship with Russia, the response was disappointing. Early in 1898, after the German acquisition of Kiao-Chou had started a scramble for toe-holds in China, he tried again. During the preceding years Britain and Russia had worked amicably on the basis of maintaining China's political integrity, while securing commercial predominance in the Yangtse valley and Manchuria respectively. But there were hawks as well as doves in St Petersburg and in 1897 the Russian Pacific fleet, after wintering in Port Arthur, showed no sign of leaving again. The British Cabinet had to choose between insisting on evacuation, if necessary to the point of war, or joining in the scramble by grabbing Wei-hai-Wei and obtaining compensation on the Yangtse. Chamberlain delivered a vigorous speech in favour of war and vehemently opposed any step which could be regarded as appeasement. But Salisbury remained obstinately cautious. 'Of course the Russians have behaved abominably and if it would be any satisfaction to my colleagues, I should have no objection to fighting them. But I don't think we carry enough guns to fight them and the French together. . . . In six months time we shall be on the verge of war with France. I can't afford to quarrel with the Russians now.'[52] In six months time, as a result, the Russians let the French down (see p. 241).

In the meantime Salisbury, who had been ill, went to France to recover, leaving foreign affairs in Arthur Balfour's charge. The latter was promptly asked to lunch by the banker Alfred Rothschild in pursuit of a scheme hatched in the German Embassy. Both the ambassador Paul von Hatzfeldt and the honorary counsellor Baron von Eckardstein ('that fat fellow who married Maple's daughter') wanted to improve their own reputations by improving Anglo–German relations and judged that they would get further through private chats than through official channels. They were well aware that their superiors in Berlin expected any approaches to come from the British side and as a result they concealed the extent to which they had themselves taken the initiative. Balfour gathered little from his talk with Hatzfeldt at Rothschild's 'except that the Germans did not at all like Joe's methods of procedure in Africa and felt aggrieved at our protest about Shantung'. Next Chamberlain himself, who had already seen Eckardstein (and possibly connived with him in starting off the whole process) was invited to meet Hatzfeldt at lunch. As Balfour told his uncle 'Joe is very impulsive and the Cabinet discussion of the preceding days [about China] had forced on his attention our isolated and therefore occasionally difficult position'.[53] [He told a friend 'the prospect is more gloomy than it has ever been in my recollection'.][54] 'He certainly went far in the expression of his own personal leaning towards a German alliance.'[55] His account of the conversation makes clear that outline terms for such an alliance were discussed and, as it omits to say which side propounded the idea, we can up to a point trust Hatzfeldt's statement to Berlin that the proposal came from the Englishman, who swept aside German complaints about colonial differences by saying that these could easily be settled once agreement had been reached on the great political interests. Admittedly the Colonial Secretary later told the Prime Minister that 'in every case the interviews were sought by the Germans and the initiative was taken by them'.[56] But with such an accomplished draughtsman the small print of statements is required reading and while 'interviews' are one thing, their content is another.

Chamberlain got Balfour's approval before going to the meal and reported to him afterwards. Moreover Balfour, in passing the report on to Salisbury, professed himself to favour an Anglo–German agreement. 'It must however if possible be made at the worst on equal terms. Of this loving couple, I should wish to be the one that lent the cheek, not that imprinted the kiss.'[57] The comment pinpoints the flaw in Chamberlain's procedure. For a minister not directly responsible for foreign affairs to propose, at a moment when the Prime Minister-cum-Foreign Secretary had gone away, a major departure from Britain's established policy of non-commitment was as remarkable as it had been for the President of the Board of Trade to try to settle the affairs of Ireland. What was even more unusual was to give the representative of the power with which alliance was being sought a clear hint that some members of the British Cabinet considered the country to need an ally, especially when no formal or even informal judgment to that effect had ever been reached collectively.[58] In combination with Hatzfeldt's misrepresentations these tactics gave the concoctors of German policy a distorted picture of the British outlook and hence an exaggerated idea of the strength from which they were playing. Balfour was well justified in describing the negotiations as 'amateur'.[59]

Holstein may have been suspicious by nature but, in deducing that Britain wanted an alliance in order to get German support against Russia, he was for once justified. The idea had no attraction for Bülow and Holstein because Germany had already snatched her own slice of China, did not want to see Britain increasing her slice, was only too glad to see Russian attention turning from the Balkans to the Far East and had no wish to revive tension along the Russo-German frontier. 'The good Chamberlain', wrote the Kaiser in one of his perspicacious moments, 'must not forget that in East Prussia I have three Russian armies and nine cavalry divisions standing opposite to one Prussian army corps, with no Chinese Wall to keep them apart and no British battleships to help in holding them off.'[60] He also doubted whether 'Brummagem Joe' could carry his colleagues with him. Hatzfeldt was told to parry with the argument that, as no British government could bind Parliament or its successors, Britain was ill-fitted for making long-term commitments. Chamberlain in a second interview denied this, presumably unaware that it was the argument which Salisbury had used in turning down offers of alliance in 1889, 1892 and 1896.[61] A good deal of talk followed about various conceivable contingencies without Chamberlain ever explaining or being asked to explain what benefit Germany was supposed to get out of an alliance. He did make clear his expectation that the obligation to go to one another's help would be reciprocal. But to conclude that this made an alliance worthwhile meant assuming that China was important enough to Germany for British help there to be worthwhile, even if it meant increasing Russian hostility in Europe where Britain could not help effectively, at any rate in a short war. Consequently Berlin's attitude remained unchanged.

A farcical interlude ensued in which Chamberlain told Balfour that Hatzfeldt wished to have another meeting with him which Hatzfeldt, on being so informed by Balfour, denied to be the case. Eckardstein then took a hand by making a direct personal approach to the Kaiser. He claimed to have found that impressionable character enthusiastically in favour of an alliance but by the time he had managed to get a rather unwilling Hatzfeldt to lunch with an equally unwilling Chamberlain by representing to each that the other wanted to meet him, prudence had reasserted itself and no progress was made. The Kaiser had laid down that negotiations were to be handled *freundlich aber dilatorisch*.[62] Hatzfeldt's line accordingly was that the best way to start would be to clear up differences over individual questions. Chamberlain replied that this was not good enough and that agreement with France and Russia would not be impossible for Britain if Germany would not play. The Englishman reminded the German that Frenchmen had a proverb about *le bonheur qui passe*.[63] Chamberlain may seem to have been dogged by unreliable intermediaries but that is apt to happen when people have to negotiate indirectly because they are not entitled to do so directly!

At this point Salisbury resumed control. Gladstone sent in a report of his 'curious' conversations and advocated a defensive treaty with Germany but left the decision to the man responsible for taking it. Salisbury told him that, if the Germans revived the idea, they could be informed that the government was prepared to regard it sympathetically. He agreed that a closer relationship with Germany was desirable 'but can we get it?'[64] His faith in Germany would seem to have been already as 'infinitesimal' as he later declared it. When Hatzfeldt told him that, if Britain wanted an alliance, she must be prepared to make some concessions outside Europe, he replied that 'you want too much for your friendship',[65] a phrase which was resented in Berlin because it showed that some influential people in Britain did not share the German view of the world balance of forces.

The Prime Minister went on to tell the Primrose League that 'we know that we shall have to maintain against all comers that which we possess, and we know that, in spite of the jargon about isolation, we are competent to do so'. Chamberlain was stung into saying, equally publicly, nine days later that, if Britain stuck to her policy of isolation, the fate of China would probably be decided in defiance of her interests there. But if she wished to continue trading on equal terms, 'we must not allow our Jingoes to drive us into quarrels with all the world at the same time [this less than three weeks after the speaker had threatened resignation if France were not quarrelled with over West Africa] and we must not reject the idea of alliance with those powers whose interests most nearly approximate to our own'.[66] Salisbury, when asked to reconcile the two speeches, took refuge in the time-honoured excuse that he had not yet read the full text. Chamberlain told the Commons that he had neither changed his mind nor been asked to resign. The Kaiser told the British ambassador that Chamberlain had been injudicious; the country whose alliance was being sought might demand a high price for it – just as Salisbury had said.

When the same ambassador came on leave in August, an unabashed Chamberlain invited four other ministers to meet him at lunch. The Prime Minister had once again gone off for a rest and the mice were quick to start playing. No record was kept of what was said over the cheese but the principal guest, on getting back to Germany, sought out the Kaiser and told him that the gathering had virtually amounted to a Cabinet Council at which all present had applauded Chamberlain's idea of a defensive alliance to come into effect only if either Germany or Britain were attacked by two (or more) powers simultaneously. William thought this an idea as bright as it was new but Bülow deflected him from following it up with the argument that it still involved alienating Russia and getting little in return.

Attention at this point switched to South Africa. Even before the Raid, the Germans had indicated that they would not tolerate the acquisition by Britain of either the Transvaal or Portuguese East Africa – although after the Raid they balanced the Kaiser's telegram by privately warning Kruger against being too provocative.[67] The reaction of Salisbury and his colleagues was to deny Germany any right to interfere in what was not her business. But the awkward fact remained that the railway to Delagoa Bay gave the Republic a door to the world which was not under British control, making the acquisition of such control an ace in the game to secure mastery in South Africa without fighting. Admittedly Germany was in no physical position to interfere; the Kaiser was fond of explaining that that was why he needed a navy. But she could make herself difficult in Egypt, China and elsewhere. The Kruger telegram however proved to be the high-water mark of German support for the Transvaal. The Kaiser was disappointed by the failure of other European governments to back him up; German bankers came to the conclusion that their interests would be best served if Britain took the Rand over.[68] Berlin became prepared to compromise provided the reward for doing so was big enough.

Since February 1897 desultory discussions had been going on in Lisbon about a deal by which Portugal would allow Britain virtual control of Delagoa Bay in the event of war with the Boers, receiving in return a loan to prop up her ailing finances. The Germans, hearing what was afoot, intimidated the Portuguese into dropping the idea. They proposed instead that Britain and Germany should agree on how Portugal's colonies should be shared out between them if the indigence of the present owners forced a sale. The British were slow to react; resentment at being, as they thought, blackmailed closed their eyes to the value of the prize which was coming within reach. Chamberlain however considered that blackmail was sometimes worth paying and in Salisbury's absence in August 1898 Balfour and he negotiated a Convention. This appeared to say merely that, if Portugal asked either party for a loan, the other would be informed and the possibility of a joint loan considered. As security for such a loan, Britain was to take the customs revenues of the southern part of Portuguese East Africa (including Delagoa Bay) and the central part of Portuguese West Africa, Germany the customs revenues of the rest (and of Timor). A secret annex provided that, if by any mischance the integrity of Portugal's possessions could not be preserved, they should be divided between the two countries on the lines laid down.

In practice the anticipated contingency never arose because Portugal eluded bankruptcy by getting a French loan on the security of her internal revenues. Then in 1899 Britain reaffirmed two seventeenth-century treaties by which she had promised to defend Portugal, colonies and all, while Portugal promised not to help Britain's enemies (as by letting arms go through to the Boers after war had broken out). The Portuguese were too timid to let this agreement be published but the Germans in due course learnt of it and felt they had been double-crossed. For they had read into Britain's willingness to sign the Convention a desire to bring it into effect which only they themselves in reality possessed. The people who had frustrated them were French and Portuguese rather than British but this did not alter the fact that they had played their best card without managing to take the trick. They could not well protest thereafter about British activity in an area which they had agreed as lying within Britain's zone of interest and they had to all intents and purposes abandoned the Boers. The disappointment disinclined them to make more separate agreements about individual areas.

This outcome was still maturing when in November 1899 the Kaiser came to Windsor. By then the Boer War had broken out. The German public was almost as keen as the Russian and French Foreign Offices to confront Britain with a continental coalition. A good deal depended on the attitude of the German government and in particular of its ruler and this in turn depended on what was settled not about South Africa and still less about Europe but about substituting partition for condominium in the three islands of the Samoan group. William had convinced himself that a base in one of them would be invaluable for his navy. But Salisbury's habitual reaction to pressure was to stonewall and in May 1899 he provoked the Kaiser into complaining petulantly to the queen that 'Lord Salisbury cares for us no more than for Portugal, Chile or the Patagonians'.[69] To the accusation of being 'my constant enemy throughout', the patrician replied 'I cannot make out what I have done to deserve that distinguished reputation. . . . So groundless is the charge that I cannot help feeling it indicates a consciousness on the part of His Majesty that he cherishes some design which is bound to make me his enemy and looks forward to the satisfaction of saying "I told you so". It is a great nuisance that one of the main factors in the European calculation should be so ultra-human.'[70] The Prime Minister's patent aversion to his critic was making him carry *insouciance* somewhat far.

Hatzfeldt and Eckardstein appealed to Chamberlain for help over a matter which was legitimately his business as minister responsible for relations with the Pacific colonies; the Australians and New Zealanders, on being told that the Germans in Samoa would not be very close and therefore not very dangerous neighbours, had replied that they preferred to have no neighbours at all. How anxious Chamberlain was to head off the Germans from supporting the Boers is shewn by his having been ready to offer them compensation in West Africa in return for an abandonment of the Samoan claim. But the Kaiser (misguidedly as it proved) was not to be diverted and had to be allowed his 'miserable island', regardless of the irritation which might be caused 'down under'. Only then did he agree to visit his grandmother and thus make clear to Europe that he was not going to enlist in any pro-Boer combination.

On the day that he and Bülow arrived, Salisbury's wife died; he had been more than usually dependent on her and felt unable to take part in political conversations. An unexpectedly large share therefore fell to Chamberlain, who was impressed by the Kaiser's 'versatile ability in ranging over matters large and small'[71] while Bülow thought the Colonial Secretary to be 'quite the modern businessman, determined, hard-headed, unscrupulous, quick-on-the-draw but withal realistic'.[72]

He repeated his desire for an understanding between Britain, Germany and the United States, in spite of having told Hatzfeldt a few weeks earlier that it was 'too late'. The visitors repeated the arguments against a formal commitment. Chamberlain said openly that Britain needed Germany, Bülow made clear that at the moment Germany felt she could do perfectly well without England. No mention was made of terms for a general alliance and there was agreement that the best way to proceed would be by repeating the Samoan case (although not, presumably, its frictions) and settling each issue separately. Chamberlain pointed to Asia Minor, where he encouraged the Germans to build a railway to Baghdad, and (taking up an old suggestion of Hatzfeldt's) Morocco. Bülow urged him to use his influence with the Americans in getting them to be nice to the Germans. Yet when he immediately afterwards made an injudicious speech at Leicester in which he applied too loosely the words 'alliance' and 'union' to the relations which he wanted to see between the three countries, he ran into not only a storm of criticism at home, in Europe and across the Atlantic but also a distinct douche of cold water from the German Foreign Secretary. The second German Navy Law of 1900 (which would start off the Anglo-German race in battleship building) was being prepared and Bülow needed to rouse anti-British feeling in order to get it through the *Reichstag*. Two months later he told the Budget Committee in private that

Britain had become Germany's most dangerous foe, the one power which could attack without risk to herself [in the middle of the Boer War!]. A conflict was described as being 'not outside the bounds of possibility'.[73]

This succession of rebuffs might have been expected to end, as it certainly cooled, Chamberlain's enthusiasm for a German connection. But, after an interval of fourteen months, during which those who had been speculating on a Boer victory were disillusioned, there was a further instalment. Although remaining Prime Minister, Lord Salisbury had handed over the Foreign Office to Lord Lansdowne who was more open-minded about accepting commitments to foreign countries. In January 1901 a house party was organised at Chatsworth to which Eckardstein was invited in common with Chamberlain. Although we have only a German account of their conversation, it seems clear that the latter still thought allies essential for Britain and preferred Germany to be one of them.[74] This time however he admitted that public animosities on both sides of the North Sea made a general agreement impossible and he therefore repeated the suggestion of beginning with an understanding about Morocco. Eckardstein was advised to wait until Salisbury was next out of the way and then raise the idea formally. Hardly had the party broken up than Queen Victoria died and the Kaiser, moved by an emotion which his subjects neither understood nor shared, hurried to England. On learning from Eckardstein of the Chatsworth conversation, he telegraphed in excitement to Bülow 'So they are coming, it seems, which is what we've been waiting for'.[75] But Bülow still read the world situation as putting time on Germany's side and William, although seeing the danger of falling between two stools, accepted the advice to play it long. He went home without seeing Chamberlain and it was to be with France rather than Germany that Britain made a Moroccan agreement. Instead Bülow denied that an agreement made in the previous year about maintaining an open door in China applied to Manchuria at all although the Germans knew that a desire to prevent the Russians from closing it in that province had been the chief motive of British ministers in negotiating and that they had only reluctantly accepted the weasel words 'so far as they can exercise influence' which the Germans had insisted on slipping in and now used as an excuse for slipping out.

Eckardstein was not however easily put off. Hatzfeldt's health was giving way and the honorary Counsellor thought that a diplomatic success would be the best qualification for getting appointed titular ambassador. He got little change out of Chamberlain who made clear his reluctance to burn his fingers again. 'We would gladly approach Germany with far-reaching proposals which would offer her at the least the same advantages as ourselves, if not greater. But, as we now know for certain that everything Berlin learns is at once passed on to St Petersburg [only a slight exaggeration], no one can be surprised if we impose on ourselves the greatest reserve towards Berlin in future.'[76] Eckardstein accordingly turned to Lansdowne, where he played his usual game of proposing an alliance and reporting to Berlin that the other side had begun it. As a result of this approach and of another by Hatzfeldt in May, the question of an alliance was considered seriously, although of course on a mistaken footing, by both governments for the rest of the summer, only for both to come to the conclusion that they would get better terms by waiting. The Germans doubted whether the British could mend their fences with the French and were convinced that, if this happened, it would lead to a break between the French and the Russians. The British thought that the Germans had many enemies and few reliable friends. Even the conclusion of the Anglo-Japanese Alliance in January 1902 (a project long favoured by Chamberlain) failed to shake Berlin's complacency because it was thought there that the looming Russo-Japanese war would be bound to precipitate a Franco–British one.

Chamberlain played no part in these final negotiations; he was said by Alfred Rothschild to have 'quite lost heart and will have nothing more to do with the people in Berlin'.[77] He may however be said to have brought on their obsequies. In October 1901, speaking in Edinburgh, he replied to those who criticised Britain for 'barbarity' in South Africa and mentioned other occasions when worse things had been done; these included the Franco–Prussian War. The German press was violent in its abuse and Hatzfeldt's successor (who was not Eckardstein) was instructed to demand an apology from the Foreign Office; he was told that, as no offence had been intended, no apology was needed. But this did not prevent Bülow from disregarding advice to leave well alone and saying that one had been given. Chamberlain hit back. 'I withdraw nothing. I qualify nothing. I defend nothing. I do not want to give lessons to a Foreign Minister and I will not accept any at his hands. . . . We have the feeling that we have to count on ourselves alone and I say it is the duty of the British people to count on themselves alone in a splendid isolation surrounded by our kinsfolk.'[78] But perhaps in vexation at having to eat so many of his words, he told Eckardstein at a reception, 'I have had enough of such treatment. There can be no question any longer of association between Britain and Germany'. The recipient of that rebuff claimed to have seen Chamberlain and the French ambassador a few minutes earlier in a deep conversation of which the only audible words were 'Egypt' and 'Morocco'.[79]

There has been much speculation about the possibility of a different outcome to the negotiations – if such a title can be bestowed on what was more like a dialogue of the deaf. 'If only the Germans had been as clever as the French, made an agreement about Morocco and waited to see what happened next!' But although they may have neglected Morocco, they did make agreements about the Portuguese colonies, China, Samoa and (way back in 1890) Heligoland and East Africa. What happened next in most cases was recrimination. British ministers regarded German attempts to take advantage of their embarrassments as blackmail; the Germans regarded British attempts to insist on a *quid* for every *quo* as a refusal to face facts. Holstein wrote to Eckardstein, 'Hardly any general treaty with England is conceivable for Germany that would not involve us in an almost certain danger of war. And Germany could only exact compensation comparable to the immense risks she was running if Britain had a more accurate, that is, a more modest opinion of her performances.'[80] But that was what Salisbury called asking too much for friendship. As long as there was such a discrepancy in the assessment of relative strengths, co-operation was bound to be difficult and agreements hard to reach. If the British estimate proved in the long run more realistic than the German, that is not what most non-British observers would have expected at the time. If Salisbury's attitude had been maintained and Britain continued to count on herself alone (even if surrounded by her kinsfolk), the German forecast might have proved right. Chamberlain was justified in saying that isolation must end. Where he miscalculated was in seeking agreement to preserve the *status quo* from the power whose main aim (outside Europe at any rate) was to change it.

Although the mirage of the Diamond Jubilee may have concealed the fact, the zenith of Britain's power was past; after 1870 her foreign policy was mainly on the defensive.[81] Chamberlain showed by his insistence on the need for an ally that he realised this. The zenith of Germany's power seemed to lie ahead and it was natural that she should seek to expand when Britain contracted. But as long as Britain refused to contract and claimed equal rights in those countries which Chamberlain called 'empty sacks'[82] because they could no longer stand upright on their own, she and Germany could not work easily together. Chamberlain's advocacy of the redistribution of property did not apply internationally! Britain's natural partners were the other countries threatened by German expansion, France, Russia and (on a long view) the United States. But the Germans, so far from realising that their challenge to the existing order was bound to draw the challenged together, complained of encirclement when this occurred. Neither side was as anxious to avoid war as they might have been if they had foreseen what industrialised war would be like and how much damage it would do to the world position of both. British nationalists took it for granted that 'what we have, we hold': German nationalists welcomed war as the natural way by which status is adjusted to power in international society. If the chief expanding power could have reached agreement with the chief contracting one, the waste of many human lives and much accumulated wealth could have been avoided. But an agreement to change peacefully is the most difficult of all international instruments to negotiate. As Chamberlain did not realise what he was attempting, he can hardly be blamed for failing in something infinitely harder than he realised.

South Africa – the Approach to War

For an astute politician, Chamberlain could be singularly obtuse. He was slow to realise how much the Raid had damaged Britain's position in South Africa. At Rhodes' prompting, he told Sir Hercules Robinson to go to Pretoria and mediate between Boers and Uitlanders. But with Jameson and his followers awaiting trial it was hardly the moment for 'the representative of the paramount Power' to demand definite promises of reform. The High Commissioner roused wrath in London by advising the Johannesburg ringleaders to surrender themselves unconditionally and retiring to the Cape without visiting them or their city. He then counter-manded orders from home for British troops to move to Mafeking, on the ground that they would irritate rather than intimidate, and told the Colonial Secretary that[83]

> to urge a claim for extended political privileges for the very men charged with treason would be ineffectual and impolitic. Any attempt to dictate in regard to the internal affairs of the Republic at this time would be resisted by all parties in South Africa and do great harm.

Three months later, when Chamberlain wanted to use a rebellion in Matabeleland as a pretext for reinforcing the British garrison, Robinson spoke out in words which were as prophetic as they were incisive:[84]

> Such a transparent excuse . . . would only confirm the burghers in their belief that we have designs on their independence. . . . The increase might precipitate action on their part which would involve us in war.

> To deal effectively with the Transvaal and Orange Free State, aided as they would be by the Boers of Cape Colony and Natal, would require a force of at least 30,000 men. Victory might require the whole strength of the Empire. It should also be considered that, when the operations have been brought to a successful issue, there will remain

the question of government of a people embittered by hatred and torn by internal dissensions which will for generations require the maintenance of a large permanent garrison.

Chamberlain fell back grumpily on the idea of inviting Kruger to London so that, as Salisbury put it, he could be 'drowned in turtle soup'.[85] But the President was too wily to overlook the risks of such softening up. He was further antagonised when a despatch demanding 'Home Rule for the Rand' was published in London before the top copy had reached Pretoria. It reasserted the British view that, while the South African Republic was a free and independent government as regards all the internal affairs not touched by the Convention [of 1884], 'as regards its external relations it is subject to the control of this country in accordance with the provisions of Article IV' (which bound the Republic not to conclude any treaty with any state other than the Orange Free State until it had been approved by the queen). Kruger replied that his government would not tolerate 'any interference or intermingling in its internal affairs' and demanded as a pre-condition of his journey that the British government agree to negotiate a new instrument superseding the Convention. Such a demand not only threw cold water on the project of reaching a new agreement in London but, by showing how widely the views of the two governments differed, threw it on the feasibility of reaching agreement at all. Since however there was no way of bringing the Boers to heel, it was hoped that leaving them to stew in their own insalubrious juice would prove as efficacious as immersion in any form of soup.

In the spring of 1897 various developments combined to produce a new crisis. First London detected Pretoria in the process of negotiating extradition treaties with the Netherlands and Portugal before they had been submitted to the government for approval. But Article IV proved to have been clumsily drafted and the Republic was thus enabled to take refuge in a distinction between 'conclusion' and 'completion' which it took the lawyers two years to straighten out. Two new republican laws were more serious. One authorised the government to expel without trial any alien considered 'a danger to the public peace and order', the other prohibited the entry into the country of any alien unable to prove that he could earn a living there. Both measures were held by the British government (although not by most of the international lawyers to whom the Boer government appealed) to infringe Article XIV of the Convention which assured to all persons, other than natives, 'full liberty to enter, travel and reside in the Republic.' For a time it looked as though arguments might lead to blows and the British forces in South Africa were raised by 60 per cent to 8,000. Then the Boers climbed down, reinforcing the dangerous but widespread impression among British ministers and officials that, if confronted firmly enough, they would always do so.

By this time Chamberlain had decided that Britain needed to be more forcefully represented in South Africa. To replace Robinson as Governor of Cape Colony and High Commissioner of the Protectorates he secured the services of Alfred Milner, a fine flower of Jowett's Balliol who had distinguished himself under Baring in Egypt and Goschen in the Treasury; he was destined to show how desirable it is for philosopher-kings to possess the milk of human kindness and for administrators to have a streak of laziness. The installation of a personality even more authoritarian than himself as second-in-command had a catalytic effect on Chamberlain; for the next two years he found himself in the unaccustomed stance of holding back rather than driving forward. That did not however lead him to modify his ultimate aim of combining South Africa under British rule and in proportion as it became clear that this was the ultimate question at stake so the chances of avoiding war by conciliatory tactics diminished. Yet it should not be forgotten that the underdog was illiberal, obstinate, corrupt and given to all sorts of subterfuges – not, in short, unlike his great-grandchildren.[86]

At first Chamberlain looked to 'municipal self-government' for Johannesburg as the solution to the Uitlanders grievances but could find nobody else to share this view; Birmingham, it seemed, did not export easily. He then sought by one means or another to keep grievances in perpetual prominence. But this was more productive of recrimination than results so that attention began to focus on the single big issue of enfranchisement in the hope that this, if settled, would provide the key to other reforms. As a rallying-cry however it had two drawbacks. It required those who were given votes to exchange British for Transvaal nationality and thus carried the danger that the ultimate result would still be a republic, composed in large part of persons who were of British origin but no longer subjects of the British crown. Secondly the process of settling what the new franchise was to be opened the door, particularly in 1899, to alternatives and arguments, making it hard to find a clear-cut breaking point.

The basic aim of the British was to make real their claim to 'suzerainty'. But as the word did not occur in the 1884 Convention, the legal basis for making the claim was flimsy; no lawyer with any title to impartiality was impressed by ingenious arguments about the Preamble to the 1881 Convention (which did contain it) never having been superseded. By repeating them, the British only maddened the Boers without achieving anything in return. On the other hand the Boer claim that the Republic was as much a sovereign international state as any other was hard to square with the limitations on both its external and internal freedom contained in Articles IV and XIV of the Convention. The strongest justification for

254

British intervention was not legal at all but lay, as Milner realised, in the inability of any government to remain aloof if any appreciable number of its nationals are being ill-treated in another state or if the actions of that other state are disturbing an adjacent territory which the first state controls.

The limits of manoeuvre on the British side were narrowed by the need to consider four separate publics. There were first of all the people of Dutch rather than British origin who made up rather more than half the population of Cape Colony, although being in a minority in Natal. In spite of owing a formal allegiance to Britain most of these were at heart Boers and, as such, sympathised with the rulers of the two Republics. When early in 1898 a group of them protested to Milner that aspersions on their loyalty were unjustified, he replied 'Of course you are loyal. It would be monstrous if you were not' and went on to tell them that, if they wanted peace, they must induce the Transvaal to reform. It was a group of such men, definitely not anti-British but firmly anti-war, who formed the government of Cape Colony from September 1898 onwards. If conciliated, they could bring considerable influence to bear in the Transvaal; if alienated, they would certainly not help Britain in a war and some might fight on the other side. Against them stood the English settlers. The great majority of these looked to the London government to assert its authority, establish clearly the English character of South Africa and remove the disabilities of the Uitlanders. Hints were frequent that, if these hopes should be disappointed, they would come to terms with the Boers and work for a South Africa which owed no allegiance to Britain.

At home their views were supported by a group of Tory nationalists, more vocal than numerous. But in the great mass of the public an aversion to war was combined in varying degrees with an attitude of 'what we have, we hold'. There was considerable animosity towards the 'money bags' of the Rand.[87] Conservatives remembered how the unsuccessful Zulu war of 1877 had helped to lose them the 1880 election. Even inside the Cabinet there were those, led by Hicks Beach the Chancellor, who doubted whether anything would be gained by fighting. The Liberals were split into the Liberal Imperialists such as Rosebery, Grey and Asquith (all friends of Milner) and the party faithful with Harcourt, Morley and Campbell-Bannerman, who sympathised with the Boers and mistrusted Chamberlain. No enthusiasm for a war could be expected in any circumstances from this last group and, if adequate backing was to be forthcoming elsewhere, matters had to be so handled as to suggest strongly that the Boers were in the wrong.

On the other hand a major aim of Chamberlain's strategy was to win the support and understanding of the enlarged post-1885 electorate for a

255

policy which combined social progress at home with imperial development overseas. He did not seek popular endorsement merely in order that, if and when war came, the government might have the country behind it, although that should be a duty of any minister who is steering on what may prove a collision course. Chamberlain wanted to use South Africa as an example to convince the public of the importance of the empire to Britain's continuance as a Great Power. Historians of Germany now consider that her leaders between 1890 and 1918 adopted an expansionary policy abroad largely because they wanted to distract attention from pressures at home (*Primat der Innenpolitik*). In somewhat the same way Chamberlain sought to make more of Britain's overseas possessions and to assert her claims where they were challenged or imprecise, as a way of preventing the polarisation of British politics on class lines. For that reason he went to unprecedented lengths in making publicly available in speeches and blue books a carefully selected presentation of background information and justifications of policy.

His long-range policy towards South Africa was part and parcel of this approach. He was not merely concerned to secure communications with India or bolster Britain's resources with the minerals of the high veldt (which could have been done without war). He aspired to see a Union of South Africa join the other three white dominions as a source of strength to a world-wide system based on London. That dream could not be fulfilled unless South Africa was united under British leadership. A republican United States of South Africa would not serve his purpose. For that reason Boer domination could not be tolerated indefinitely in the Transvaal and Orange Free State, since all the indications were that the wealth and population of the Rand would enable it to act as a magnet attracting the rest of the country round it. The Boers could be allowed a considerable amount of local autonomy, keeping their language and culture, but only on condition that they accepted British paramountcy as an unchallengeable fact. The male adult Uitlanders already approximately equalled the Boer ones in numbers and were expected to increase faster so that their enfranchisement meant sooner or later the transfer of power, with all its opportunities for influence, into their hands. Kruger was therefore in the long term justified when he said that 'it's our country you want' and Milner only justified in the short term when he denied that he and his masters wished to take away Boer independence.

By February 1898 Milner had come to the conclusion that 'there is no ultimate way out of the political troubles of South Africa except reform in the Transvaal or war. And at present the chances of reform are worse than ever.'[88] For Kruger was re-elected President with an increased majority and by dismissing his Chief Justice threw doubts on the impartiality which residents in the Transvaal might expect from its courts. But the spring of

1898, with trouble blowing up in the Sudan, West Africa and China, was no time for a show-down in South Africa. Chamberlain had to pass on the warning which he himself was receiving from his colleagues. 'For the present at any rate our greatest interest in South Africa is peace and all our policy must be directed to that object.'[89]

By the autumn however the other threats to Britain had begun to look less menacing and the Convention about the Portuguese colonies had made effective German help for the Boers unlikely. At this point the Cabinet's hand began to be forced by the British colonists who had formed themselves into a 'South Africa League' to agitate on behalf of the Uitlanders; behind the scenes the initiative had passed from Rhodes to the firm of Wernher-Beit who were hand-in-glove with Milner. In December the Johannesburg police, over-reacting to a quarrel between two Uitlanders, shot one of them dead. The League availed itself of the incident to draw up a petition to the queen, only to have it turned back by General Butler, the Irish Catholic commander-in-chief who was standing in as Governor while Milner was in England, on the ground that it had been published before presentation. In March 1899, with Milner back, a second attempt had more success; almost simultaneously the mine owners rebuffed a move by Kruger to buy them off and thus to split his opponents. Chamberlain summed up to his colleagues the dilemma which faced them:[90]

> If we ignore altogether the prayer of the petitioners, it is certain that British influence in South Africa will be severely shaken. If we send an ultimatum to Kruger, it is possible and in my opinion probable that we shall get an offensive reply and we shall then have to go to war or accept a humiliating check.

They were temporarily saved from this choice by the governments of the Cape and Orange Free State who, in their anxiety to avoid war, prevailed on Kruger to offer terms and brought him and Milner together at Bloemfontein on 31 May to negotiate an agreement. But Milner, thinking that the Boers were on the run, demanded more than was offered and, when more was refused, broke off the conference so hastily that a telegram from Chamberlain telling him to be patient arrived too late. Afterwards however the Boers made two separate offers of concessions, the intermediary in the second case being the young State Attorney Jan Christian Smuts. But the Governor had all along been more afraid of the risks involved in being conciliatory than of those involved in standing firm. 'The case for intervention is overwhelming. The spectacle of thousands of British subjects kept permanently in the position of helots . . . calling vainly to Her Majesty's Government for redress, steadily undermines the influence and reputation of Britain' (4 May, published 14 June). 'I don't want war but I think it may be the only way out' (17 May). 'Though I think the beginning of a war would be very unpleasant, I do not think the result doubtful' (14 June). 'Pretoria and its sympathisers are still bluffing and will yield further if pressure is kept up. The result depends on our staying power. They will collapse if we don't weaken or rather if we go on steadily turning the screw' (16 August). 'If the Transvaal were to disappear from the map as an independent state or if it were to become an Uitlander Republic, the "Afrikaner nation" idea would be for ever doomed' (6 September).[91]

The Colonial Office however laid down that the latest Boer proposals must be accepted for what they pretended to be. 'Public opinion insists on our using great patience and endeavouring to avoid war.'[92] The British government was prepared to rest content if it could get a reasonably large number of Uitlanders enfranchised reasonably quickly, hoping that this would in due course lead to a transfer of power. But such a transfer was exactly what the Boers were keen to avoid; while realising that they must make some concessions on enfranchisement, they hoped by some contrivance to keep them within limits. The British, suspecting as much, insisted on having the concessions spelt out in detail. The Boers, fearing that they would be pushed further than they liked, refused to commit themselves. Finally they made their offer dependent on Britain completely abandoning her claim to suzerainty. This enabled Chamberlain to assure his colleagues that 'what is now at stake is the position of Great Britain in the world and with it the estimate formed of our power and influence in our Colonies and throughout the world'.[93] Accordingly the Cabinet decided to raise the number of troops in South Africa from 12,000 to 22,000 and, as soon as the reinforcements had arrived, to demand the satisfaction of all their grievances. The Boers, like many belligerents who believe themselves to be in the long run the weaker side, had to choose between gaining the strategic and keeping the moral advantage. They decided to get their own ultimatum in first; when their demand for the withdrawal of British reinforcements was refused, they invaded Natal and Bechuanaland, thereby catching their opponents at a military disadvantage but weakening their case in the eyes of the world and, in particular, of the British public.

A compromise over the franchise which papered over the basic issues but opened a political door to the Uitlanders would not have been hard to reach if the will to do so had been present. One could have been achieved by General Butler, who had scant sympathy with the political policy of which the War Office had made him the military executant (and whose wife did so much by her pictures to make the pathos of war familiar to British homes). But he had made himself so unpopular, by saying that the

Boers would fight rather than sacrifice their independence, as to have resignation forced upon him. Milner by contrast had admitted before leaving England that Imperial Union was the one subject on which he did not have an open mind. He was not the man to make compromises liable to limit the spread of British power. For a peaceful settlement to have been reached, he would have to be superseded, either by being recalled or by being more closely controlled.

Chamberlain had however picked him specially for the job and acted on the generally sound principles of backing up his subordinate and giving discretion to the man on the spot. And although he often urged moderation on Milner, what made him cautious was the fear of getting into a war which the home public would not support or one which would have involved several enemies. Torn between long- and short-term aims, as well as between his hawklike countrymen overseas and his dovelike ones at home, he may seem to have been uncharacteristically undecided. But fundamentally he did not disagree with, and was for that reason not prepared to supersede, the thrusting proconsul. He cannot therefore be absolved of blame, perhaps the main blame, for the outcome. His Cabinet colleagues in turn often shook their heads over him. Salisbury in August 1899 wrote to Lansdowne:[94]

> The Boers will hate you for a generation, even if they submit. If they resist and are beaten, they will hate you still more. . . . [Milner's] view is too heated, if you consider the intrinsic significance and importance of the things which are in controversy. But it recks little to think of that now. What he has done cannot be effaced. We have to act upon a moral field prepared by him and his Jingo supporters. And therefore I see before us the necessity for considerable military effort – and all for a people whom we despise and for territory which will bring no profit and no power to England.

Balfour wrote that 'you are driving us over the edge of the cliff'.[95] Yet all the ministers had in varying degrees sympathy for the ultimate aims which, combined with the political difficulties involved in interfering, inhibited them from calling a halt until it was too late to do so with self-respect. In any case a compromise in 1899 would not have removed the fundamental conflict of will in Southern Africa. As long as the rulers of Britain were determined to dominate the whole of the area and as long as the Boers were not prepared to acquiesce, sooner or later force was almost bound to be invoked to settle the disagreement. Unfortunately force did not settle it either.

The Boer War

At the start of the war Britain had between 20,000 and 27,000 troops in South Africa. The two Boer Republics initially put 47,000 men into the field and these were helped by volunteers from Cape Colony who would not seem to have exceeded 10,000 at first, although estimates up to 40,000 occur later. They were well armed and had the advantages of the initiative, greater mobility and knowledge of the country. That they should have had a number of successes during the first three months is not therefore as surprising as many people in Britain found it. But their leadership was almost as timid (though not as incoherent) as the British. By the beginning of February 1900 the tide began to turn and with the capture of Pretoria in June major campaigning was at an end.

But it was at this point that the real difficulties began to emerge. For one thing, the British strategy of pressing ahead to the main centres of Bloemfontein, Johannesburg and Pretoria left pockets of resistance behind; the British refusal to be distracted from the main objectives meant that 'mopping up' had still to be carried out after those objectives had been secured. But even then a guerilla war went on. Obstinacy was an outstanding Boer characteristic. They enjoyed also the advantage which Mao has called as necessary to guerilla success as water to fish – a sympathetic population in a big country. They exploited proclamations of amnesty to make fighting into a spasmodic business, so that apparently peaceful farmers could turn into saboteurs and partisans the moment the coast was clear. They had no prospect of winning military victory and knew it but hoped to wear down the will of the British public and thus secure a peace which left their Republics independent.

A situation in which a beaten opponent refuses to accept defeat is as hard to deal with as any imaginable, especially before the days of air reconnaissance. By the time hostilities did end, Britain had deployed nearly 450,000 men against a foe who did not amount to more than a fifth of that number. Few of these troops were engaged in actual fighting; they were guarding stores and lines of communication and denying supplies to the enemy. For the only way of winning a struggle of this kind is to deprive the other side of the sinews of war. But prominent among these sinews are shelter and food, so that the British High Command was little by little led on to burning down farm-houses, destroying crops and 'concentrating' 'refugees' into camps.

The Boers, to organise sympathy, made the most of the sufferings which were being inflicted on non–combatants. It was of course the way in which they had chosen to prolong the war that drove the British leaders to use such methods and the plight of the refugees might have been no better if they had been left to starve in the ruins of their old homes. But the camps had to be hastily improvised and did not get high priority as regards supplies and staff. Although the torture which has now become associated with the name of 'concentration camp' was absent, 32,000 people died in them in thirteen months.[96] Campbell-Bannerman was not alone in talking of 'methods of barbarism'; eight months earlier Milner in a private letter to Chamberlain described farm-burning as '(1) barbarous and (2) ineffectual'.[97] He had hoped, by pressing ahead with reconstruction, to make the Boers see that it was in their own interest to surrender. The methods adopted by Kitchener, the commander-in-chief, frustrated this plan, but the civilian had no power to overrule the soldier. When, as a result of the outcry at home, he did get the camps under his control, conditions rapidly improved. But a lasting grievance had been left for repeated exploitation as a propaganda weapon. Passions rose high because principles were at stake which are as debatable as they are basic. How far should liberals allow their humane feelings to be exploited by illiberal opponents who use them merely as a tool for getting their own way? Is there a degree of suffering too great to be justified by any human end even if that end can only be reached by it?

The most remarkable feature of the war was that, except for Natal, Britain had no secure base. Chamberlain referred in September 1900 to 'the permanent fact of our situation which dominates the politics of the Colony [in the Cape], namely the existence of a Dutch majority largely consisting of persons disloyal to our rule'.[98] Milner three months earlier had estimated that nine-tenths of the Boers in the Colony sympathised with the Republics and that one-fifth (or rather over 10,000 men) had taken up arms on their behalf.[99] Merriman, a former British admirer of Chamberlain who had 'gone native', made the paradoxical claim that the people who should really be regarded as praiseworthy were the Boers who had not taken up arms since, if they had done so in the autumn of 1899, the whole country would have been lost to Britain for good.[100] When the false dawn appeared in 1900 and the Boer commandos withdrew from the Colony, leaving a spurious impression that it had been pacified, the question of how to treat the relapsed rebels produced a political crisis similar to that which had precipitated the war.

The Boers in the Colony deprecated any heavy punishment being inflicted on the ground that it would make the victims irreconcilable. The Cape British replied that, unless loyalty was rewarded, they would lose faith in the home government. As a compromise Chamberlain proposed a small fine and lasting disenfranchisement for the rank and file rebels, with heavier penalties for the leaders. But since neither courts-martial nor trial by jury were likely to impose appropriate sentences, he called on the Cape ministry to set up a special commission. This the ministry only agreed to do on the understanding that the victims would be few and the sentences light. When Chamberlain pressed for more, the ministry split and Schreiner, the Prime Minister, resigned. Although he was succeeded by the more loyal Sprigg, the latter depended for his majority on a certain number of Boer votes and there were accordingly limits to his readiness to fall in with the wishes of the British.

Milner, emphasising that 'no local Parliament elected by present constituencies including the rebels would support a loyal ministry',[101] pleaded more than once for the constitution to be suspended. Chamberlain, with his eye on public opinion at home, refused to consider this. Even though Britain's 'khaki election' of October 1900 had had the unusual result of increasing the government's majority, it only went up from 128 to 134 and the Tory-Unionists only secured 1·8m. votes as against 1·6m. Liberal ones. The Cape Parliament had however been prorogued in August 1900 and did not meet again for two years. The Boer MPs turned more openly than ever against the British and demanded a peace which would leave the Republics independent. When commandos again invaded the Colony at the turn of the year, many of the previous rebels, in flagrant disregard of the understanding on which they had been allowed to go home, took up their arms again. Almost the whole of the hinterland had to be put under martial law but when Kitchener wanted to extend this to the ports and Sprigg's Cabinet objected, Chamberlain sided with the civilians.

Milner and Kitchener were both high-handed men who wanted to have their own way. Each wished to combine firmness with conciliation but differed as to the time at which each would be appropriate. Kitchener's aim was to end the war as quickly as possible, partly to release him for his coveted post of commander-in-chief in India; he favoured being ruthless as long as resistance lasted but ready to compromise as soon as peace was sought. Milner wanted to avoid wartime acts which might leave lasting grievances but equally to avoid concessions which might complicate the task of reconstruction; he would have preferred to insist on the Boer surrender being unconditional. To draw a strict line between things military and things civilian was far from easy, so that each man was apt to accuse the other of trespassing. In November 1901 Milner sought to have Kitchener recalled but Chamberlain, although sympathetic, was not prepared for a show-down with the army and the Cabinet agreed with him.

By the spring of 1902 however there were still 20,000 Boers in the field and, although they were getting very short of food, horses and equipment, their strategy was paying off. The will of the British public was faltering and demands were growing for a compromise to end the war. The reputations of Chamberlain, of Unionism and 'Imperialism' stood increasingly in jeopardy. Chamberlain and Milner both decided that their weight would be better expended on influencing the terms to be offered than on preventing terms from being offered. They insisted on the Republics being annexed; on no date being set for the restoration of self-government; on primacy being given to English in public life and on Britain remaining free from responsibility for the debts which the Boers had incurred while fighting. The Boers, by arguing all the way, secured an amnesty for virtually all the rebels in the two Republics, an undertaking that self-government would be restored 'as soon as circumstances permit', a promise that Dutch could be taught in schools where the parents desired it and the offer of £3m. to be paid to loyalists and rebels alike, as compensation for war losses. A clause saying that the question of granting the franchise to natives would not be decided on until after the reintroduction of self-government was included on Milner's insistence. He was later to regret his firmness, since it worked to prevent the British government from doing anything for the natives while still in control of the Republics and, once self-government had been restored, a white majority in favour of any such concession was never to be had. But if the British negotiators had insisted on the door being kept open, they would have found not only the Boers but most of their own settlers against them. Typically, the document which was signed in Pretoria to end the war and which Milner entitled 'Terms of Surrender' has come to be known by the much less humiliating name of 'Treaty of Vereeniging' after the village at which the Boers finally agreed among themselves to accept it.

The war had been fought to make South Africa a British possession in which British ways of thought and life would predominate. But the fact that it had ended in a British victory did not necessarily mean that this would be the result. Britain clearly could not maintain indefinitely in the country the forces which she had had to deploy in order to win. This was to become all the more obvious as tension grew in Europe. To induce the Boers to surrender, she had virtually promised not to discriminate against them in peace time and further to allow them at some stage to join in self-government. Yet as they were expected at the end of the war to outnumber all the other white inhabitants put together, a liberal constitution which gave power to a majority might well mean handing over the government to people who were illiberal and anti-British. The likelihood of this happening was increased by the fact that, whereas the British South Africans were divided among themselves, the Boers were not merely well-disciplined but conscious of having only themselves to depend on, tough, shrewd and realistic, reminiscent in their political skill of the Magyar ruling class in Hungary.

Three policies offered a chance of preventing the war from having been fought in vain. One was to prolong the period of rule by British officials. Another was to bring in more Britons until they outnumbered the Boers. The third was to turn the Boers into people who would tolerate even if they did not embrace British ways of life; unconditional surrender might have contributed to this. Some people looked for a solution to federation but the only way in which this might make a difference would be if Rhodesia was brought into it.

Milner, who remained in South Africa as Governor of the Transvaal and High Commissioner until April 1905, placed his main hopes in the first two policies, while paying some lip-service to the third. Being himself a hard-working, honest and intelligent administrator with little use for politicians, he thought that what the country needed above all was efficient government to repair the damage done by the war (for which he obtained a £35m. reconstruction loan), to increase prosperity and thereby to attract both capital and manpower from abroad. He was frustrated by four things. One was weather; drought ruined the 1903 harvest and reduced a number of farmers to bankruptcy. The second was lack of labour for the mines which as a result took longer to get going again than had been expected. The mineowners sought to solve the difficulty by temporarily importing Chinese labour. For Milner to support them was economic sense but political folly; he aggravated the mistake by failing to secure the observation of a pledge about not flogging which he had encouraged his minister to give to Parliament. Thirdly his subordinates, in spite of the able 'kindergarten' imported from Britain, were too often arbitrary and inconsistent. Finally he could never bring himself to trust the Boers nor they him. As the net result, prosperity was slow to return and immigrants to settle; instead of the British making up 60 per cent of the white population in 1911, as Milner had hoped, they were only 54.[102] But the white residents of South Africa were not prepared to be ruled autocratically for long and Britain was not prepared to turn her rule into a military dictatorship. Had she done so, she would probably have lost the country in 1914 instead of 1948.

Chamberlain had greater hopes of finding a long-term solution by a mixture of firm adherence to the peace terms (in the face of Boer attempts to go back on them) and a generous policy of reconciliation thereafter – 'in victory, magnanimity; in peace, good will' (to use the words of the man who in December 1905 was to become the junior minister responsible for South Africa).[103] When the Cape British revived the proposal to suspend the Colony's constitution and Milner backed them, Chamberlain not merely took him to task for flying in face of the government's known wishes but refused to budge, partly on grounds of home politics but partly also on principle. Milner resigned but was persuaded to change his mind while the Secretary of State was in South Africa at the end of 1902. During a stay of two strenuous months, the visitor hardly put a foot wrong. Among other things, he made it clear that the import of Chinese labour would be anathema to the home public, but by the time this became an active issue, the responsibility was no longer his and, when Milner came under attack, his former superior defended him. When Chamberlain left South Africa, he professed an optimism which was probably genuine. Had he stayed longer, he might have come back more doubtful.

Chamberlain's last word on South Africa is to be found in a letter which he wrote in 1908 to Selborne, who had been his deputy at the Colonial Office and had become Milner's next-successor-but-one:[104]

> I do not believe that the Transvaal can ever be placed in the same position as it was before Kruger's time and this is something to look back on with satisfaction. At the same time I feel that the fear of a Transvaal which shall be like the Irish at home or the French in Canada is very real and I do not feel certain that some such result may not be the ultimate consequence of the presence of the two races on one continent.[105] . . . If the Dutch are in a majority over South Africa, and they appear to be in the Transvaal, the ORC and Cape Colony, are we sure that they will not make any effort to be supreme? Anyway . . . the only thing we can do is in the nature of good government and patience and not in the shape of force. Force alone will not keep the majority with us and the war shows that they are numerous enough and strong enough to hold their own.[106]

Does this amount to a recantation? If force alone could not keep the Boer majority from making a fresh attempt to run the country, what was the justification for adopting between 1895 and 1899 a policy which, by setting stiff terms for a peaceful settlement, made resort to force likely as an alternative? The success of British Imperialism in South Africa was short-lived. Its objectives – the predominance of the British South Africans, the safeguarding of the route to India and the strengthening of the empire's resources – were only temporarily secured. It failed because the amount of force needed to achieve those objectives was greater than the amount which the British were able and willing to supply. The chances of success were of course blighted by the two World Wars. But they were themselves a symptom of Britain's problem – how to maintain her position when the relative strengths of countries were changing to her disadvantage. Force had been resorted to in South Africa in the hope of redressing the shifting balance.

British Liberalism also failed in South Africa. It failed to open the way for a liberal society which offered all its members, black as well as white, an ultimate prospect of self-realisation. The Liberal government's act of faith in restoring self-government, in spite of its hopeful start, left a less durable impression than the traditions of Boer society. Would Liberalism have been more successful if it had been consistently applied and recourse

265

to force avoided (or kept in reserve until events had made clear that, without it, liberal ideas would not take root)? This seems unlikely. Liberalism assumes that the society in which it is applied is, or can be, integrated. Nearly all the white inhabitants of South Africa denied that their society could be. And where it is not possible and where power rests with a minority, that minority will probably regard the dangers involved in refusing to share it as preferable to those involved in applying the principle of 'one man, one vote'. The whites were not prepared to let liberal ideas induce them to run the risk of domination by, as they thought, an irremediably inferior race. Nobody has yet found a way of compelling them to do so. As we cannot tell what would have happened if they had, history may never disclose whether they made the right choice.

Notes to Chapter 8

1 J. L. Garvin, *The Life of Joseph Chamberlain* (1934), Vol. 3, p. 5; F. Graham, 1903, quoted by R. V. Kubicek, *The Administration of Imperialism* (Durham, N.C., 1969), p. 29.
2 J. G. Lockhart and C. M. Woodhouse, *Rhodes* (1963), pp. 161, 171, 216; Garvin, Vol. 3, p. 33.
3 F. M. L. Thompson, *English Landed Society in the Nineteenth Century* (1963), p. 306.
4 Firm figures for the population of South Africa are lacking until the first census in 1904. In 1891 there were thought to be 415,000 whites in Cape Colony, three-fifths being Boers; 280,000 in Transvaal, half being Uitlanders; 100,000 in the Orange Free State, predominantly Boers; 50,000 in Natal, predominantly British (R. H. Wilde, *Joseph Chamberlain and the South African Republic* (Cape Town, 1956). On that basis there would have been some 490,000 Boers to 321,000 other whites (all but about 75,000 British). Milner expected there to be at the end of the war 496,000 Boers to 368,000 British and 76,000 other whites (*The Milner Papers*, ed. C. Headlam (1933), Vol. 2, p. 280). The census showed a total population of 5·1m. of whom 1·1m. were white (no distinction being made between British and Boers, although N. Mansergh, *South African 1906–61* (1962) says that the proportion was 45:55. There was a steady tendency to underestimate Boer numbers. Thus Chamberlain at the beginning of the war said that there were 430,000 British and 410,000 Boers (R. Robinson and J. Gallagher, *Africa and the Victorians: The Official Mind of Imperialism* (1961), p. 454). Kruger at Bloemfontein in 1899 said that there were in the Transvaal 30,000 enfranchised burghers and 60,000–70,000 newcomers – but the Boers had an interest in playing their strength down. If the true balance had been known, British policy might have been different.
5 G. Blainey, 'Lost causes of the Jameson Raid', *EcHR*, Vol. 18 (1965).
6 From a proposed ultimatum to the Transvaal government (never delivered) 9 October 1899. E. Drus, 'Select documents from the Chamberlain papers concerning Anglo-Transvaal relations, 1896–1899', *Bulletin of the Institute of Historical Research*, Vol. 27 (1954).
7 J. Rose Innes, *Autobiography* (Cape Town, 1949), p. 157.
8 Garvin, Vol. 3, p. 58; J. van der Poel, *The Jameson Raid* (1951), p. 22.
9 J. Butler, *The Liberal Party and the Jameson Raid* (Oxford, 1968), pp. 43–7.
10 Garvin, Vol. 3, p. 83; E. Drus, 'The question of imperial complicity in the Jameson Raid', *EHR*, Vol. 68 (1953); Lockhart and Woodhouse, pp. 485–6.
11 E. Drus, 'A report on the papers of Joseph Chamberlain relating to the Jameson Raid and the Inquiry', *Bulletin of the Institute of Historical Research*, Vol. 25 (1952).
12 Garvin, Vol. 3, p. 112; Drus, 'Report on the Chamberlain papers', p. 49.
13 Garvin, Vol. 3, p. 78.

14 Garvin, Vol. 3, p. 63.
15 Van der Poel, p. 67.
16 Garvin, Vol. 3, p. 72.
17 Van der Poel, pp. 71–2.
18 Garvin, Vol. 3, p. 78.
19 Van der Poel, p. 82.
20 Garvin, Vol. 3, p. 89.
21 M. Balfour, *The Kaiser and His Times* (1964), p. 467.
22 The telegrams had been drafted in (abbreviated) English, then converted into code for transmission and decoded again on arrival. As a result the text as read by Rhodes was not identical with the London draft. In one telegram Harris said that he had spoken to Fairfield. There was no equivalent for the word 'spoken' in the code so it was transmitted *en clair*; the decoding clerk made a note of this with the result that the phrase became 'have spoken (open) to Fairfield', thereby provoking speculation as to what it was that had been said so openly (C. M. Woodhouse, 'The missing telegrams and the Jameson Raid', *History Today*, Vol. 12, 1962).
23 Garvin, Vol. 3, p. 116.
24 E. Longford, *Victoria R.I.* (1964), p. 544.
25 Butler, pp. 43–7; Drus, 'Report on the Chamberlain papers'.
26 Drus, 'Report on the Chamberlain papers'.
27 Garvin, Vol. 3, p. 89.
28 J. S. Marais, *The Fall of Kruger's Republic* (Oxford, 1961), p. 97.
29 Dr A. N. Porter has recently argued (*The Origins of the Boer War*, Manchester, 1980) that if Chamberlain had refused to help Rhodes and the revolt in Johannesburg had succeeded (as Chamberlain at first assumed it would do), imperial influence in South Africa would have been at an end (presumably because the Republic would have remained independent and Cape Colony would have joined it).

But this assumes that (a) either the rising could have taken place and succeeded without external assistance or (b) Rhodes could have given such assistance even if he had been denied freedom to post Jameson in the Protectorate. As regards (a), what chance was there of the rising taking place – and succeeding – in the absence of Jameson's force when it failed to occur with that force present? As to (b), why was Rhodes so insistent on getting control of the strip if he could have brought help to the rising without it? So far from retaining control over Rhodes and Jameson by ceding the strip, Chamberlain lost it and this is a main charge against his handling of the matter. He may well have reasoned as Dr Porter suggests but, if he did, it is a sign that he misjudged the situation.
30 House of Commons, 5 February 1900. The claim is never explicitly made but emerges from the general tenor of the speech.
31 Drus, 'Report on the Chamberlain papers'.
32 Speech of 9 April 1888. C. W. Boyd (ed.) *Mr Chamberlain's Speeches* (1914), Vol. 1, p. 322.
33 A. G. Hopkins, 'Economic Imperialism in West Africa', *EcHR*, Vol. 21 (1968).
34 R. Koebner and H. D. Schmidt, *Imperialism* (Cambridge, 1964), p. 210.
35 Garvin, Vol. 3, pp. 19–20; R. E. Dummett, 'Joseph Chamberlain, imperial finance and railway policy in British West Africa', *EHR*, Vol. 90 (1975).
36 Hamilton to Salisbury, 14 December 1895, quoted by Dummett.
37 Robinson and Gallagher, p. 402.
38 D. K. Fieldhouse, *Economics and Empire* (1973), p. 475.
39 Salisbury to Cromer, quoted by Lord Zetland, *Cromer* (1932), pp. 259–60.
40 R. Shannon, *The Crisis of Imperialism* (1974), p. 251.
41 Lady F. Balfour, *Ne Obliviscaris* (1930), Vol. 2, p. 270; K. Young, *Arthur James Balfour* (1963), p. 168; *Journals of Queen Victoria* (1968), 14 November 1897; B. Dugdale, *Arthur James Balfour* (1936), Vol. 1, p. 258.
42 Garvin, Vol. 3, p. 204.
43 Garvin, Vol. 3, p. 212.
44 J. C. Flint, *Sir George Goldie and the Making of Nigeria* (1960), p. 292.

45 J. A. S. Grenville, *Lord Salisbury and Foreign Policy* (1964), p. 122.
46 Garvin, Vol. 3, p. 122.
47 Garvin, Vol. 3, p. 220.
48 *Die grosse Politik der europäischen Kabinette* (Berlin, 1922–7), Vol. 14 (2), 3908; Grenville, p. 230.
49 *GP*, Vol. 14 (2), 3908. Of course Chamberlain may have been counting on the Germans leaking his remarks to the French, with a view to softening them up!
50 This section is primarily based on Grenville, chs 7, 8 and 14; W. L. Langer, *The Diplomacy of Imperialism* (2nd edn, New York, 1951), chs 15, 20 and 22; P. Kennedy, *The Rise of the Anglo-German Antagonism 1860–1914* (1980), ch. 13 and M. Balfour, ch. 8.
51 J. Amery, *The Life of Joseph Chamberlain* (1951), Vol. 4, p. 421.
52 A. L. Kennedy, *Salisbury 1830–1903. Portrait of a Statesman* (1953), p. 276.
53 Dugdale, Vol. 1, p. 259.
54 Chamberlain to Milner, 16 March 1898. *Milner Papers*, ed. C. Headlam (1931), Vol. 1, p. 229.
55 Dugdale, Vol. 1, p. 259.
56 Garvin, Vol. 3, p. 279.
57 Dugdale, Vol. 1, p. 260.
58 It may be objected that in those days ministerial responsibility was less circumscribed than now. But may it not have been the experience of laxity which led to tightening?
59 Dugdale, Vol. 1, p. 258.
60 *GP*, Vol. 14 (1), 3789.
61 Grenville, p. 155.
62 *GP*, Vol. 14 (1), 3790.
63 Garvin, Vol. 3, p. 274.
64 Garvin, Vol. 3, p. 279.
65 *GP*, Vol. 14 (1), 3796.
66 Garvin, Vol. 3, p. 283.
67 Robinson and Gallagher, p. 417.
68 W. Hallgarten, *Imperialismus vor 1914* (Munich, 1951), Vol. 1, p. 365.
69 *Letters of Queen Victoria 1886–1901*, ed. G. E. Buckle (1930), Vol. 3, pp. 376–7.
70 Salisbury to Lascelles, quoted by Grenville, p. 277.
71 Garvin, Vol. 3, p. 501.
72 *GP*, Vol. 15, 4398.
73 P. Kennedy, p. 240.
74 H. von Eckardstein, *Lebenserinnerungen und politische Denkwürdigkeiten* (Leipzig, 1919–21), Vol. 2, pp. 235–51; Amery, Vol. 4, p. 144.
75 *GP*, Vol. 17, 4982.
76 Eckardstein, Vol. 2, p. 278.
77 Amery, Vol. 4, p. 158.
78 Boyd, Vol. 2, p. 68.
79 Eckardstein, Vol. 2, p. 377.
80 Eckardstein, Vol. 2, p. 282.
81 D. C. M. Platt, *Finance, Trade and Politics in British Foreign Policy 1815–1914* (Oxford, 1968), p. 357.
82 *GP*, Vol. 15, 4398.
83 Marais, p. 107.
84 Marais, p. 116.
85 Garvin, Vol. 3, p. 127.
86 See Chamberlain's views on Kruger and Boers in Drus, 'Select documents'.
87 Chamberlain to Milner, 6 December 1899, Garvin, Vol. 3, p. 521.
88 *Milner Papers*, Vol. 1, p. 220.
89 16 March 1898, Garvin, Vol. 3, p. 368.
90 28 April 1899, Garvin, Vol. 3, p. 393.
91 *Milner Papers*, Vol. 1, dates as indicated.
92 Letter from Selborne to Milner, quoted by Marais, p. 305.

93   8 September 1899, Garvin, Vol. 3, p. 459.
94   Lord Newton, *Lord Lansdowne* (1929), p. 157.
95   Wilde, p. 148. See also memorandum of 1 June 1899 quoted by Drus, 'Select documents', which accepts the overestimate of British strength referred to in note 4 above.
96   T. Pakenham, *The Boer War* (1979), p. 518. The figure includes both whites and non-whites.
97   *Milner Papers* (1933), Vol. 2, p. 164.
98   Garvin, Vol. 3, p. 578.
99   *Milner Papers*, Vol. 2, p. 116.
100 G. H. L. Le May, *British Supremacy in South Africa* (Oxford, 1965), p. 68.
101 Le May, p. 57.
102 *Milner Papers*, Vol. 2, pp. 243, 280.
103 W. S. Churchill, *The Second World War. Moral of the Work* (1948).
104 Amery (1969), Vol. 6, p. 928.
105 Chamberlain, like Milner and others, habitually described as 'racial' the gap between British and Boers rather than that between white and black. Chamberlain also spoke of 'the Anglo-Saxon race' to describe what we would call the 'WASPish' inhabitants of the UK, the self-governing colonies and the USA. For his difficulty in distinguishing between 'race' and 'nation' in regard to Ireland, see Chapter 6, note 28.
106 'Force can be justified against a resistance which can be broken by a single blow but it can only be justified by necessity against a resistance which would have to be continually held down.' Bismarck, *Gesammelte Werke* (Berlin, 1924–31), Vol. 6, p. 319.

9 'Imperial Joe': 1902–14

Relations with the Tories

On 7 July 1902 a cab-horse which could not stand up and a cab-window which consequently fell down might be thought to have altered history. For the window fell on Chamberlain's forehead. Although nothing was broken, he lost blood, suffered from shock and was ordered to bed for a fortnight. He only stayed there ten days but during that time two events took place which, if he had been up and about, might conceivably have taken a different turning.

On 11 July Lord Salisbury offered his resignation as Prime Minister and advised the king to send for A. J. Balfour as his successor. Balfour had led the Conservatives in the Commons for eleven years and had been First Lord of the Treasury for eight of them, so that he was beyond question the obvious candidate. But there was an appreciable body of opinion which had been putting it around that Chamberlain would provide more initiative and direction. Balfour was careful to consult the invalid before accepting the king's commission; in such a context the only answer could be acquiescence. Chamberlain had indicated in public and private his readiness to serve under the younger man. He is said to have done this out of gratitude for the support which Balfour had given him during the black days of the war. But he may also have reflected on the difficulties which he might have in leading the Tories. His radical past had not been forgotten; he was suspect to the rank and file as an 'alien immigrant'.[1] The speed with which Salisbury's going followed on Chamberlain's accident naturally prompts a suspicion that the old and the young Premiers, uncle and nephew, were making assurance doubly sure by foreclosing on the job when it would have been hard for Chamberlain's fanciers to put a spoke in the wheel. But what in fact made the change imperative at that particular juncture seems to have been the shocking state of Salisbury's health.[2]

At his own wish, Chamberlain remained Colonial Secretary. He felt that nothing else was so important as the tasks which he saw ahead of him in South Africa and the empire at large. But there were those who regretted that he did not transfer to the Exchequer which 'Black Michael' Hicks Beach was quitting because he could not get his colleagues (and Chamberlain above all) to halt rising expenditure. Such disregard of the Treasury's power to control general policy would seem in retrospect unwise. What Chamberlain did as regards South Africa during the next fourteen months could have been done by someone else, especially by someone who was less handicapped by the need to live down past animosities. And it was in due course to prove of crucial importance that the Exchequer went to C. R. Ritchie, an abrasive and obstinate Scot who, in spite of having once proposed a motion for fair trade, became under the influence of his officials a convinced free trader. Among life's most difficult accomplishments is the art of leaving a good party five minutes before one has been there too long.

In the second place Balfour on 9 July allowed a free vote in the Commons over an amendment as to whether county and county borough councils should be left to decide for themselves about assuming responsibility for elementary education. The failure of both parties to take secondary education seriously was coming home to roost and a question of apparent detail being invested with acute political significance.

In 1870 the assumption had been that the job of the Board Schools was to instruct working-class children in the 3 Rs. But the Act, although including the word 'Elementary' in its title, failed to define what the term meant and as a result it was not long before enterprising Boards in some cities were setting up 'Higher Grade Schools' in which a considerably more advanced curriculum was being taught at the expense of ratepayers. Much the same happened over evening classes, to which adults were admitted. In 1889 however responsibility for 'technical' education was given to the newly created county and county borough councils. Whereas these councils and the voluntary schools were often Tory, the 2,500 School Boards, being mostly in urban areas, were often radical, so that Liberals were in the anomalous position of wanting to conserve them. Meanwhile, as the standards of education went up, its costs doubled.[3] The 10,000 voluntary schools, which were handling more than half the children, found it increasingly hard to make ends meet. The Established and Roman Catholic Churches were growing restive at the spread of secular influences. The public, bored by being called on to vote too often, were losing interest.[4]

Common sense suggested a compromise by which all public education in a locality would come under the control of a single authority and the voluntary schools, in return for losing their independence, would be paid for in part from the rates. The democratic solution was to make that authority an off-shoot of the new locally elected councils. Indeed, if the process of establishing a system of responsible government had been carried to completion after 1835, School Boards might never have been created; Chamberlain himself once said that he would have preferred to make councils responsible.[5] In 1896 a Bill was brought in which required councils to set up education committees responsible for all non-elementary education. It aroused so much opposition on so many grounds that, to

Chamberlain's undisguised relief, it was withdrawn and a series of minor measures substituted; one of these met the difficulties of the voluntary schools by increasing the central grant received by them since 1870.

In 1899 however the London District Auditor laid down that the go-ahead London School Board was exceeding its powers by providing to people who could not reasonably be regarded as children, education which could not reasonably be regarded as elementary.[6] In April 1901 the Court of Appeal upheld the decision and a Bill to regularise the situation became imperative. The Duke of Devonshire, who as Lord President was responsible for education, professed to have been so occupied over the subject as not really to understand it himself.[7] To Chamberlain's chagrin he decided that the best solution would be a bold one and Balfour, as the minister responsible in the Commons, agreed with him. The Bill introduced in March 1902 not only required county and county borough councils to take over (through education committees) secondary education but allowed them if they wished to take over all elementary education as well and pay for most of it out of the rates. In return they were to gain control over the secular teaching in voluntary schools and the right to appoint a third of the managers of such schools. It was this option which was turned into a requirement by the Commons amendment; School Boards were as a result to be abolished.

The nonconformists were at once up in arms. While they might have been expected to welcome voluntary schools being brought under public control, they disliked the fact that such schools would continue to be run by managers, two-thirds of whom would be appointed by the churches, while time had done nothing to blunt their objection to church schools getting help out of the rates. (A further cause of offence was a provision allowing denominational religious teaching to be given even in board schools and charged to the rates.) Chamberlain had long ceased to bother about the principle involved but the political repercussions worried him a good deal. He expected, rightly, that the Bill, if passed, would lead nonconformist Unionists to vote against the government.[8] Radical Unionists would be all the more inclined to revert to the Liberals now that Home Rule had ceased to be a live issue since the fall of Parnell and the loss by the Irish in the elections of 1895 and 1900 of their casting vote in Parliament. Such defections would weaken Chamberlain's own position *vis-à-vis* the Tories. Acquiescence over the schools would be tantamount to confession that he had overdone his opposition to the 1870 Act. He tried to get voluntary schools paid for out of grants rather than rates but such central money as might have been available had been swallowed by the war. He tried to persuade Balfour to give a majority on the management committees to governors appointed by the councils but Balfour refused, having decided that, as the nonconformists were going to oppose the Bill anyhow, he need not make concessions which his own supporters disliked. Chamberlain was left with the choice between knuckling under and resigning, which would have meant the end of his political influence as well as of his chances of clearing up South Africa and carrying out the grandiose schemes gathering in his mind. It was the logical consequence of his decision to break with Gladstone. He had to accept it but doing so must have been bitter.

In 1897 he persuaded the Conservatives, in spite of the apprehension of the mine owners and others about inroads on profitability, to pass a Workmen's Compensation Act which embodied the new principle that those injured at work should be compensated by their employers, regardless of whether negligence had been shown.[9] But this was his last success in social reform. In 1899 he returned to the subject of old-age pensions and pledged the government to do something about them, although both a Royal Commission (on which he sat) and a Treasury Committee had failed to find an acceptable scheme. Greater longevity, more lively compassion and growing labour strength were combining to make people uncomfortable about a society in which 40 per cent of those over 65 had to depend on parish relief, with all its stigmas, for the closing years of their lives.[10] But was a pension scheme to be voluntary or compulsory? Was it to be paid for, in whole or part, by contributions or financed out of public funds? The trade unions showed little enthusiasm for, and the friendly societies positive hostility towards, anything that was voluntary and/or contributory. The Treasury and industry held up their hands in horror at the thought of the £20m. which a universal scheme paid from taxes or rates was expected to cost. Others feared to discourage thrift; 'to remove the necessity of providing for old age would be to remove one of the most potent influences of civilisation'.[11] A Select Committee under a Conservative chairman hatched a proposal for a non-contributory scheme so safeguarded by means tests as to be little improvement on the Poor Law. Chamberlain, in recommending it to his colleagues, threw in a voluntary contributory scheme topped up by a modest government gratuity.[12] But the Cabinet were a good deal less than enthusiastic and in the autumn of 1899 there were other more urgent things on which he wanted their support. Moreover he had in 1895 told a colleague on the Royal Commission that the way to get the money was to tax imports of wheat.[13]

The Call for Preferences

The first bid for drawing the empire together which Chamberlain made as a minister came in March 1896 when he proposed that its members should learn by Germany's example and set up a *Zollverein* or customs union in which they let in one another's products free of duty but placed a common tariff on all imports from outside. Comment soon showed that this was a non-starter; most colonies were bent on protecting their own infant industries. But when eleven colonial Prime Ministers came to the Diamond Jubilee in 1897, the British Colonial Secretary, as chairman, invited them to consider a 'council of the empire', closer co-operation on defence and tariff preferences for the mother country on the model of the 12 per cent just offered by Canada.[14]

This Canadian preference, increased to 25 per cent in 1898 and to 33 per cent in 1900, involved trouble with Germany since it broke the terms of an 1875 trade agreement with Britain; Salisbury accordingly denounced the agreement and the duties on Canadian goods entering Germany were raised – in spite of which German-Canadian trade grew almost as fast as Anglo-Canadian. But the possibility of other colonies following Canada's example and the question of what, if anything, Britain might do in return had to await the outcome of the Boer War and the fusion of the six Australian states into a Commonwealth. By the time that the Prime Ministers gathered for the coronation in 1902, the moment for action was approaching. New Zealand was offering a preference of 10 per cent. The South Africans and Australians were making encouraging noises. But the Quebecois Prime Minister of Canada, Wilfrid Laurier, who had played a leading part in killing the proposals for general and defence co-operation, put the blunt question of what might be expected in return from the United Kingdom in the tariff field. The conference then passed a resolution urging Britain to introduce reciprocal preferences.[15] Chamberlain expressed sympathy but could merely promise to get the matter explored.

A few weeks before the conference met, Hicks Beach in his last budget had re-introduced, as a temporary measure to help meet the cost of the war, a small import duty on wheat which, having survived Peel's abolition of the other Corn Laws, had been abolished only in 1869 by Gladstone.[16] To make this duty permanent on foreign cereals but abolish it on wheat from the empire (chiefly Canada) stood out as an obvious first step towards meeting colonial desires. Before Chamberlain left for South Africa in November he put the matter to his colleagues, as he was in duty bound to do, and obtained from them a provisional decision, openly opposed only by the new Chancellor Ritchie, to maintain the duty and add a preference.

Ritchie however made the most of the opportunity offered by the absence of protection's protagonist, under the promptings of Mowatt, the Permanent Secretary to the Treasury, and Hamilton, Gladstone's former Private Secretary. Personal jealousy of Chamberlain increased his readiness to listen. Three weeks before the traveller got back the Chancellor circulated to his colleagues a proposal that some part of the anticipated surplus should, on grounds of justice and political expediency, go to the reduction of indirect taxation; at the same time he warned the Prime Minister of his intention to resign if the Cabinet stuck to the view it had taken in the previous autumn about the wheat duty. This was the situation with which Chamberlain was confronted three days after his triumphal return. His arguments in favour of retaining the tax and accompanying it by a preference were met by a repetition of Ritchie's threat. The rest of the Cabinet, including the Prime Minister, were not prepared to incur such a consequence. The departure of the budget's architect on the eve of its presentation involves obvious political difficulties (although they did not deter Macmillan in 1958) and they were not eased by the way Hicks Beach had refused to stay when Balfour took over. As Wilde almost said, to lose one Chancellor may be regarded as a misfortune; to lose two looks like recklessness. Moreover the decision to discontinue the duty did not necessarily imply a decision to maintain free trade; Chamberlain was given the right to reopen the whole question later.

All the same, there can be little doubt that he should, by a counter-threat of resignation, have forced Balfour to choose between Ritchie and himself. Even if his resignation had been accepted, his long-term position would have been no worse than it was to become. But the odds were against its acceptance. Inconvenient as Ritchie's departure would have been, it would have caused far less political damage than that of the returning hero at the pinnacle of his reputation, who could have gone to the Exchequer himself. The retention of the duty would have given the imperialists the initiative during the succeeding months; its abolition put the free traders in this position. But Chamberlain had come back tired and irritable; the crisis was upon him before he had had time to size up how politics lay at home. His friendship for the Prime Minister (returned, as has been well said, by nothing more than friendliness)[17] must have made him reluctant to cause embarrassment. He did not want to go down to history as the the man who had split not merely one party but two – although, as events were to prove, he would have done less serious damage to the Conservatives if he had pressed the issue at once. Paradox-ically the man who had so often threatened his resignation on wrong occasions held it back on the right one. What would have followed if he had forced a break and won is a fascinating but perhaps not very profitable speculation.

The reticence did not mean any drop in ardour for the cause. On the contrary, his experience in South Africa had made him all the more convinced. For one thing, he had given Canadian ministers to understand that he would do his best to get them a *quid pro quo*. He was very conscious of the danger that, if this opportunity of establishing a preferential system were missed, it might never recur and the colonies might establish tariff arrangements which gave Britain no advantage. Their coolness towards proposals for closer strategic and political collaboration suggested that trade afforded the only possible road to integration. Such integration in turn afforded in his view the best and perhaps the only way of preventing Britain from slipping steadily downhill. But vital though the empire was, it was still only one side of the picture. Hicks Beach had forced Britain's financial dilemma on Chamberlain's attention. The normal sources of revenue were running out at a time when demands for expenditure on defence and social services were rising. The South African War had brought home the dangers of economising on the armed forces; the situation in Europe, and particularly Germany's naval programme, did not suggest that strength could be run down with safety. A wave of imperial sentiment however might coax more help from the colonies. But rising social expenditure was also vital for Chamberlain's plans. His recipe for winning to the Unionist side the votes of the newly-enfranchised masses lay in combining pride in the empire with gratitude for rising standards of living. If the money for such benefits was obtained from direct taxation, it might, by raising industry's costs and reducing profits, aggravate the situation by hampering Britain's competitiveness; it would also alienate Tory voters. New sources of revenue had to be found.

A fresh assault on the Cabinet might simply result in a fresh failure. Pressure had to be brought on ministers from outside and on 15 May Chamberlain, on the pretext of telling his constituents about his trip, delivered a keynote speech on his home ground. The primary theme was the opportunity which the empire offered to Britain and the need for positive action to retain colonial good-will by meeting the offer of preferential tariffs. He suggested that the world had changed radically since Britain had adopted free trade and that the time had come to start discussing whether that policy was still appropriate. The economic case for protection was left unventilated. An observer said a few weeks later that Chamberlain gave the impression of a man who was seeking arguments to prop up conclusions which he had already reached on *a priori* grounds. His Permanent Secretary at the Board of Trade, Farrar, had described him as surprisingly ignorant on economic questions, although quick to learn. In a conversation at the end of June, he claimed to have always been an 'economic agnostic'. His decision to campaign for tariff reform owed much to the persuasiveness of W. A. S. Hewins, the director of the London School of Economics (an historian rather than a theorist in economics).[18] Certainly Chamberlain had arrived at his views by a political rather than an economic approach.

Nothing whatever was said at Birmingham about social policy or the way to finance it. But a week later, on 22 May, the House of Commons was debating old-age pensions. Lloyd George, towards whom Chamberlain had hitherto shown something of the jovial animosity maintained with Lord Randolph (even including a riot in Birmingham!), was in the middle of taunting ministers for having failed to fulfil their promises. When the Colonial Secretary, who was professedly at Westminster because he 'had some serious work to do', came 'accidentally' into the House, the Welsh barbs were directed more specifically at him. As a practitioner of the maxim that attack is the best defence, he immediately rose to reply and gave as good as he had received. He told Lloyd George that the universal provision of pensions at the expense of the state would not merely be an absolute impossibility on financial grounds but undesirable into the bargain because such a gift, 'without reference to previous character', would be the greatest blow ever struck at thrift in the country. His closing sentences were:

> Before any Government can consider a scheme of this kind, it must know where it is going to get the funds. I do not think Old Age Pensions is a dead question. I think it may be not impossible to find the funds; but that, no doubt, will involve a review of our fiscal system which I have indicated as necessary and desirable at an early date.

It was not much. But, coming on top of the Birmingham speech and a good deal of public discussion, it was enough to alert the corridors of power and induce Mowatt to spend a Saturday (less dedicated to leisure then than now) to composing an analysis calculated to keep the Chancellor from capitulating or resigning.

Now it so happened that an unholy alliance between two generations of fire-brands, Charles Dilke and Lloyd George, had put down a motion for 28 May aimed at exploiting a supposed discrepancy between Chamberlain's remarks at Birmingham and an answer which Balfour had given on the same afternoon to a deputation of disgruntled squires. It was inevitable that the Prime Minister should speak in reply; it was widely rumoured that Chamberlain would do so too. Ritchie told Balfour that, if Chamberlain repeated his remarks as to how pensions ought to be financed, the Chancellor would say openly that he had no Cabinet authority behind him. The Prime Minister reacted by extracting from the Colonial Secretary what he took to be a promise not to join in the debate but to keep away from the House. Why this plan foundered will probably never be known but not many speakers had followed Balfour when Chamberlain rose. Besides landing several broadsides on the opposition, he managed to air most of his ideas for the future, including an admission that they would include putting duties on imports of foreign foods. He pointed out in return the advantages which would accrue to home farmers, to home industry and even to Ireland. 'Animated and provocative as the speech was, it did not convince his hearers that he had thought the problem out.'[19] Then, before Ritchie managed to reply, the debate was over.[20]

As Margot Asquith said, the fat was in the fire. The Cabinet seemed to be so fundamentally divided as to put the continued existence of the government in question. But that was reckoning without the resource of the Prime Minister. He was unwilling to commit what he regarded as Peel's unforgivable sin of splitting his party. He was also concerned, like Chamberlain, to keep Britain a Great Power. But he chiefly looked to do so by diplomatic and military means. He had in mind various changes in the country's defence arrangements, including the establishment of the Committee of Imperial Defence. He wanted to strengthen the Japanese alliance and conclude the entente with France. He did not trust the Opposition to regard these as important and was therefore keen to stay in office until they were accomplished. When ministers met on 9 June, he allowed the discrepant views about tariff policy to be aired but then persuaded his colleagues to keep silent on the subject until Parliament rose in August and occupy the interval by establishing the facts. Ritchie was allowed to explain to the House that he personally remained a free trader, that Chamberlain spoke only for himself and that the rest of the government had merely decided on having the matter examined. Balfour conducted a skilful delaying action, professing some sympathy with the desire for change but emphasising the need for investigation to precede decision.

The vow of silence only applied to ministers as persons. It did not prevent friends and sympathisers from expressing opinions or peddling literature. Liberal Unionists, to whom free trade was important as the chief thing still uniting them, had already been provoked by the discovery that their central office was being used to distribute copies of the Birmingham speech. The instigator, when taxed by Devonshire, backed down but, in claiming liberty for his own Birmingham branch to act as it chose, hinted at the possibility of extending the operations of that branch outside the midlands. A deluge of pamphlets and articles spread into the press where the tariff reformers carried the heavier guns. By the end of July a Liberal Unionist Free Food League, a Liberal Free Trade League and a Tariff Reform League which professed to be non-party had all sprung up. In most of the discussions theoretical arguments won more prominence than detailed studies of the way trade was actually moving and the extent to which tariffs might be expected to divert or reduce it.

The Prime Minister however was showing the ability of the philosophic mind to turn itself to anything by quietly conducting a factual inquiry of very much this kind. Knowing the Treasury, his natural source, to be biased, he drew most of his material from the Board of Trade, of which his brother Gerald was conveniently President. He quickly convinced himself that free trade should no longer be regarded as beyond challenge. It made no sense for the British government to have no power of imposing tariffs when other countries were imposing them against it. Freedom to retaliate would be a justifiable precaution. But this should not mean automatic protection for all home industries against 'legitimate' competition. For one thing, Salisbury and Winston Churchill had forecast that, by such a policy, the Tories would turn themselves into a party dominated by businessmen and manufacturers (as of course they largely have done). Balfour expressed these conclusions in a paper, 'Economic Notes on Insular Free Trade', which he circulated to the Cabinet early in August.

But he circulated at the same time another memorandum which was intended as a draft declaration of government policy. This seemed to contemplate with equanimity the idea of imposing duties on some imports from foreign countries, so as to enable preferences to be given to the colonies. Now it was generally accepted that duties on imports of raw materials would put up the costs of British manufacturers and were therefore out of the question. But the colonies at the time sent few manufactured goods to Britain; the only permissible preferences which would be of use to them must therefore be on foodstuffs. Yet much of Britain's food, including three-quarters of her wheat imports, came from outside the empire. There was general agreement, which Chamberlain was reluctantly coming to share, that the public would not, for the time being at any rate, support anything in the nature of a 'stomach tax', making such a proposal tantamount to electoral suicide. Accordingly, after some vacillation, Balfour drew the line at putting it forward.

Thus his position was threefold:

(1) Free trade was no longer to be regarded as sacrosanct.
(2) Britain should take power to retaliate in suitable cases, although not to protect (which assumed that a workable distinction could be drawn between the two or that tariffs would amount to no more than anti-dumping duties).
(3) Colonial preferences, although not an available option for the moment, were not necessarily to be ruled out for ever.

He was taking up a central stance, opposed on grounds of principle to rigid free traders like Ritchie but opposed only on grounds of immediate expediency to protectionists like Chamberlain and not opposed at all to those who only objected to tariffs on food. With remarkable finesse he edged Ritchie and two other free trade ministers into resigning in mid-September under the impression that Chamberlain would stay, while retaining the Duke of Devonshire, influential not only as a person but also as the leader of the Liberal Unionists, by confidentially passing to him the information that Chamberlain had decided to go. The net result was that the government was split three ways instead of two and obtained twenty-seven more months of precarious existence.

For Chamberlain found himself in a dilemma of his own making. He was confronted by the fact that the idea of taxing food did not at the moment begin to command a majority in the country and accordingly did not stand a chance of being accepted by Parliament or the Cabinet. Yet such taxes were essential for his double scheme of imperial integration and social reform. His only chance of achieving his aim was to find some way of changing public opinion. This he could not hope to do as long as he remained in the Cabinet; the doctrine of collective responsibility would exercise a crippling restraint on his freedom of speech. On the other hand the considerations which had held him back from resigning in March retained force. But Balfour's position was so ingeniously chosen that he only differed from Chamberlain on grounds of practicability, not of principle. This opened for the latter the possibility of resigning, in order to get his tongue unfettered, without going into opposition. He therefore volunteered his resignation and acquiesced in its announcement being delayed until the exact tactical juncture which suited the Prime Minister's machinations. The arrangement was reinforced in two ways. First the manner in which Balfour elbowed out Ritchie and his colleagues was such as to make a reconciliation between him and the free traders impossible; it was the price paid to keep Chamberlain from outright opposition. Secondly Austen Chamberlain (who had been Postmaster-General since 1902) not only remained a minister but was given the key post of Chancellor of the Exchequer.

Only with the Duke of Devonshire did Balfour in the end fail. Although the shrewd but simple-minded septuagenarian did not appear to notice at the time the dexterity with which he was handled, it left him with an impression of sharp practice. This was heightened when he was accused of bad faith by Ritchie in a letter which his own Duchess was said to have inspired in the hope that, if her inert husband could be prodded into resigning and thereby bringing down Balfour, she might realise her ambition of becoming chatelaine of No. 10 Downing Street as well as of Chatsworth. But alas for her hopes! He did resign, did not bring the government down and during the remaining five years of his life lost steadily in political influence. He died at Cannes in 1908 only 500 yards from the hotel in which Chamberlain happened to be staying. In death as in life they were physically close but mentally distant.

The Last Years

Chamberlain's plan of action when he resigned was to stump the country in a second 'unauthorised' programme, with a view to demonstrating that a thoroughgoing tariff reform was practical politics, or in other words could win and not lose votes for the government. If he succeeded, Balfour would cease to regard the policy as merely a theoretical possibility and commit the party to its realisation. In a speech at Glasgow on 6 October, the evangelist put forward a combination of proposals which closely resembled the Minority Report of the 1886 Royal Commission on the Depression in Trade and Industry. A tariff was to be put on imports of wheat, meat, wine and fruit, with preferences which freed colonial produce from duty. In compensation, duties on tea, sugar, coffee and cocoa were to be reduced. Rates were to be fixed so as to involve no increase in the cost of living. A 10 per cent duty was to be put on imports of foreign manufactures and the revenue employed to reduce other taxes, while the possibility of concessions would be held out as a bait for tariff negotiations. But the idea of using the yield of tariffs to pay for new social services was played down because, if workers were to be won over, they had to be assured that the cost of living would not rise and most of the fresh cash would have to go to preventing that. Thus the programme had to be shorn of one of the features which originally inspired it.

Ten other speeches followed during the next four months, in a campaign of 'raging, tearing propaganda':[21] they were all staged in major cities in the belief that the person whose vote would be the most vital was the industrial worker. At first 'Joe's electric strength'[22] seemed to carry all before it; by the end of 1903 tariff reformers had won three by-elections. There was no lack of money. Hamilton, an unsympathetic observer, commented that[23]

> it is a marvellous testimony to the power of one man that he should have brought protection to life again and that he, a man with hair about his heels, should have carried with him all the bulk of the aristocracy and upper classes. No other public man has improved his position. Indeed the PM has done very much the reverse.

But then the tide began to turn. Chamberlain had committed himself to fighting single-handed. Although he quickly enlisted helpers and advisers, he no longer had the resources of a department behind him; ministers did little to assist. Moreover he was fighting in a field over which he could not claim expert knowledge; he was not the first – or the last – to find statistics tricky things. His weaknesses were exposed by Asquith who had a more highly trained mind and who, on Campbell-Bannerman's instructions, kept on his heels. The Trades Union Congress condemned tariff reform as a 'malignant disease'; the working man was not being won over. Economic trends did not suggest that a change of policy was urgent; between 1903 and 1906 exports rose by 33 per cent and imports by only 12 per cent. 1904 saw five by-election defeats in a row. The Prime Minister had every excuse for sticking to the non-committal position which he found so congenial; not for nothing was it said that his name would always be held in honour where hairs were to be split.[24] While Chamberlain could write of retaliation as 'a word – a device on paper – a philosopher's romance which could only be made into a practical commercial policy as a general tariff on manufactured imports',[25] Balfour could joke about 'attacks of fiscalitis'[26] while his acolytes talked of keeping the Tory Party 'free of the Protectionist taint'.[27] The endless arguments over theory and tactics concealed a clash of personal purposes. Chamberlain's ideas about the future involved applying to the Conservative Party caucus-like methods of democratisation, whereas one of its leaders said that 'the generals cannot be expected to take orders from the rank-and-file'.[28] If Chamberlain's tariff proposals had been accepted as official policy he would have become the virtual leader of the government and that was something to which the existing leader was naturally opposed, respecting as he must have done his own judgment more than that of the challenger. He had been complaining again about 'Joe's impulsiveness' (see p. 243). 'I could wish', wrote Joe now, 'that some of our leaders were a little more "impulsive".'[29]

If there was little joy in the present situation, the future did not look much brighter. As long as the government stayed in office, it would depend on the votes of some Unionist free traders, whose susceptibilities had accordingly to be spared. Chamberlain's itch for action made him eager for an election, especially if it could be fought on his positive programme. But Balfour's inner reasons for keeping power still operated and it was only with difficulty that he was nudged towards taking a more decided line; even when the Conservative Conference in October 1904 turned 'whole-hogger' as the best way of getting votes, he remained a 'little-pigger'. Chamberlain suggested calling another Colonial Conference; he hoped to demonstrate at it that a mutually satisfactory preference scheme could be devised and believed that, once the colonies had approved such a thing, the home government could not refuse to adopt it. Balfour countered by insisting that first one election should be held to approve the idea of a conference and then another to pass judgment on its results. Much breath, ink and patience were consumed before he could be dislodged from this position. Meanwhile the conviction was spreading on all sides that the Unionists were bound to lose the next election. Although supercilious assumptions about Liberal incompetence fostered the solacing thought that their spell in office would be as brief as it would be inglorious, even three years was a distasteful delay to a man on the verge of seventy. Chamberlain's fidelity to Balfour was sorely strained but his political sense held him from open revolt. The party discipline which meant that he would not be followed also meant that his aim could only be achieved through an established machine. The principle of systematic organisation which he had done so much to foster proved too strong for its advocate. Only in the autumn of 1905, by insisting on a programme which the free-fooders were bound to reject, did he force the Prime Minister to resign and thus precipitate an election.

The 'Liberal landslide' of January 1906 had a multitude of subsidiary causes, from Scottish church politics to Indian defence. As Chamberlain had foretold, the Education Act had alienated nonconformists; there were 180 of them in the Liberal majority. The Taff Vale judgment, Chinese slavery and the threat of a food tax had led working men to think that the government cared little for their interests. There had been fiascos over Irish reform and the redistribution of seats. The 'cold fit of peace', which according to Churchill always follows the 'hot fit of war', had become all the stronger by being denied practical effect for five years. But there is much in the view that the most damage had been done by the spectacle of a party steadily failing to make up its mind on a major issue, whereas the selfsame issue had reunited an opposition which was otherwise of very many minds, and even made it think what it could offer as a rival programme of social reform.[30]

In one respect defeat strengthened Chamberlain's position. Although there is argument as to exactly how many in the reduced Unionist ranks were his convinced supporters, they were certainly a majority and there was no longer the same need to conciliate the minority in order to stay in office.[31] The screw could therefore be turned upon the eel-like leader and, in letters exchanged on Valentine's Day 1906, an uncharacteristically firm commitment was extracted from him to accept fiscal reform as the first constructive task of the Unionist Party, with a view to obtaining more equal terms of competition for British trade and closer economic union with the colonies. While deferring decisions on how these aims were to be reached, Balfour recognised as 'not in principle objectionable' a small duty on foreign corn and a moderate duty on manufactured goods. At a party meeting which he was reluctantly induced to call, this stand-point was endorsed as official policy.

But the apparent victory proved barren. Balfour had no intention of doing as Chamberlain wanted and aggressively pressing a positive programme including both tariffs and social reform; he was convinced that any positive proposals made while in opposition were superfluous hostages to fortune. Although in due course this immobility was to turn his party against him, he was justified in so far that the change of government had passed to the Liberals the initiative in choosing the topics for political debate. Meanwhile there were ominous signs of Chamberlain's health giving way and not many more weeks of active life were left to him.

During them he defended Milner vigorously against a motion tantamount to censure; although he had himself disapproved of Chinese labour and warned of its political dangers, he skilfully transferred attention from the Governor's failure to keep his promises about flogging and from the inhumanitarian aspects of forced labour to an exordium on the duty which an empire has towards its public servants. He made one more attempt to solve the problem of religious education in state schools by reviving an old idea that each denomination should pay its own costs. This apparent glimpse of commonsense failed to deflect the government with the result that the Lords, by rejecting its Bill, took the first step to the constitutional conflict which lay ahead. On 7, 8 and 9 July an enthusiastic Birmingham joined him in celebrating the thirtieth anniversary of his election as its member and his seventieth birthday. Two days later a stroke paralysed his right arm and leg.

A kinder fate would have killed him outright. As it was he lingered on for another eight years, with his mental faculties largely unimpaired, able to take views about what was going on but unable to play any direct part. He was condemned to watch while many of the causes which he had backed were defeated. First of all a Colonial Conference, which in 1907 started to make suggestions about mutual preferences, was told by Churchill that the government would not look at them. Lloyd George's budget may have made all those who disliked higher taxes, Unionist free traders included, readier to consider tariffs as the only alternative way of paying for social reform. But the Lords' action in rejecting it, which Chamberlain fully endorsed, proved a miscalculation when the ensuing election left the government dependent for its majority on Labour and Irish votes. For their price for support was the Parliament Bill and Home Rule, compared with which protection and preference became secondary issues.

Chamberlain advised the peers to die hard by fighting the Parliament Bill to the last ditch and defying the threat that they would be swamped by new creations. One wonders what he would have said in his younger days about someone who tried to prevent the people's representatives from passing into law the promises on which they were elected, but aversion to Home Rule had become so deep-seated as to outweigh anything else. Balfour's counsels of surrender however carried the day, although the resentment against them was great enough to drive him into resigning afterwards. Thereupon the party which had considered Joseph Chamberlain too much of a cad to lead it decided that Austen Chamberlain was too much of a gentleman and chose as a compromise Bonar Law, a man who had never sat in a Cabinet. Law had been a firm believer in tariff reform but the need to win every possible vote on the bigger issues led him in January 1913 to drop the idea of taxing food imports as a likely vote-loser from the immediate programme. In so far as fiscal change remained a Unionist objective at all, it was in the shape of duties on manufactured imports designed to shelter home industrialists from competition. Both the idea of uniting the empire and of financing social reform had gone by the board. Conservatism was back in the position where its distinguishing mark was objection to change.

The old radical survived long enough to stop his wife talking to him about the Serajevo murder. He died on 2 July 1914, a month before Europe's lamps went out.

Post Mortem *on Tariff Reform*[32]

Judgment cannot be passed on the closing years of Chamberlain's active life unless some conclusion has been reached as to the validity of his arguments for tariff reform. How justified was his claim that it would draw the empire closer together, provide more employment at home, protect living standards and prevent the United Kingdom from declining into a fifth-rate nation?

Since the proposal for a customs union never won any serious support, there are only two schemes which need to be considered – mutual preferences and a UK tariff on imports of foreign manufactures. But the latter, taken by itself, was of relatively little interest to the rest of the empire, which sent few manufactures to the UK, and hardly therefore concerned imperial development at all.

Mutual Preferences   The proposal was that preferences for imports of UK manufactures into the self-governing colonies (which it will be convenient, if anachronistic, to describe as 'Dominions') should be balanced by preferences for imports of dominion products into the UK. The former would be primarily manufactured articles, the latter foodstuffs (since the Dominions had few manufactures to send and there was general agreement that duties on raw materials were out of the question as being liable to impair the ability of UK industry to sell at competitive prices in third markets).

Such duties would put up the price of food in the UK at a time when four-fifths of its food imports came from outside the empire (although duties might have stimulated a shift in this proportion, which was going to occur even without them). Except in so far as the higher prices were cancelled out by cuts in excise duties on goods like tea and sugar, or by foreign producers cutting their prices to hold their market (which would stultify the purpose of the duty) they would cause demands for higher wages and thus put up the costs of UK producers. Any diversion of supply from non-empire to empire countries would reduce the sterling earnings of the former and thus their ability to buy UK exports (although this might be offset by increased Dominion ability to do so). In so far as higher prices were cancelled out by reductions in other duties, the gain to the revenue by the duties on imported foreign foods would be balanced by the loss on the excise duties.

In the first decade of this century, the Dominions only took about 20 per cent of the UK's exports of manufactures. Another 20 per cent went to the colonies, where the UK power of control over imports was greater although not, for various reasons, unlimited.[33] The remaining 60 per cent went outside the empire and here competition might be expected to grow fiercer since those foreign producers who found themselves unable to sell any longer to the Dominions as a result of the preferences would look for alternative outlets. A preference is chiefly valuable to a producing country which can expect to sell most of its exportable output within the preferential area.[34] The advantage given to UK industry in the Dominions would do nothing to make it more competitive in foreign markets and might even encourage it to stick to old products instead of innovating.

Behind the proposal for mutual preferences stood the concept of turning the empire into a single-market trading area in which each part concentrated on doing what it was best at, i.e. the UK produced manufactures, the Dominions primary products. Although this outlook might be repudiated by leading protagonists of tariff reform, it kept on cropping up. How far it would have remained acceptable to the Dominions in the long term was questionable; while they wanted to raise their standards of life by developing their own industries, their resource endowments did largely consist of primary materials, so that the output of these was likely to play a large part in their economies for many years to come and they would need markets for that output.

Duties on manufactured imports into the UK   These were what substantial sections of UK industry (iron and steel, machinery, but not textiles, coal or shipbuilding) were demanding in the belief that it was similar tariffs in other industrialised countries which were depriving them of their markets in those countries. It is noteworthy that, although the Birmingham Chamber of Commerce had a number of members who were well acquainted with Germany, they went on believing that German (and American) ability to outsell them rested on some 'unfair' advantage rather than on lower prices, better quality and design, superior servicing, etc.[35]

The experience of the years 1932–9, when the UK, having imposed a tariff on imports, became the fastest growing economy in the world (with the possible exception of Nazi Germany), suggests that such a tariff, if imposed in 1903, would have given a once-for-all shot in the arm to UK industry.[36] The substitution of home-made products for imports would have meant a substantial increase in demand for such products, with multiplying repercussions, and given a corresponding stimulus to investment.[37] Some foreign firms would have set up factories in the UK, so as to produce inside the tariff wall, especially if they then also qualified for preferences in the Dominions: this investment would have been a further boost to home demand. There are those who consider that such a screen might have induced UK entrepreneurs to engage in the production of new products (notably electrical goods, chemicals and internal-combustion engines) – the field in which the UK's failure to keep abreast of the leaders was most apparent. On the other hand the existence of a secure and expanding home market might simply have enabled UK industry to go on turning out established products, while remaining uncompetitive in markets outside the empire where non-British producers would have been fiercely trying to recoup the sales which they had lost in the UK.[38]

Experience after 1932 certainly confirms Balfour's view that a tariff on manufactures would be valuable as a counter in bargaining. Before 1939 trade treaties were secured with Scandinavia, the Argentine, the United States and the European Steel Cartel. After 1945 the UK, if it had not had tariffs, would have been in a distinctly weaker negotiating position in the various bargaining rounds under the General Agreement on Tariffs and Trade.

On the other hand, the industries which were still competitive in 1903 would have gained little by a tariff, unless it had enabled them to keep a home market which they would otherwise have proceeded to lose. Multilateral trade (see p. 207), which was of growing importance, would have been seriously disrupted, some customers of the UK being deprived of the means with which to buy its products. UK earnings from merchandising, finance and services would undoubtedly have been impaired by the creation of barriers to the free movement of goods – which explains the almost unanimous hostility of the City to Chamberlain's proposals.[39] It is a fallacy to suppose that the UK owes its prosperity predominantly to its role as a manufacturer of industrial products.

The closing of the world's major free market, even if only partial, would have been bound to intensify competition elsewhere. This would have been likely to induce some Governments to take diplomatic and administrative action in support of their businessmen and so to heighten international animosities. Some countries would undoubtedly have retaliated with measures of various kinds (perhaps including devaluations) against UK goods. In particular, relations with the United States would have deteriorated and, as Chamberlain was one of the first to maintain, American friendship was going to be of growing importance to the UK in the coming years.

But increased material prosperity was only one aspect of what Chamberlain hoped to gain by tariff reform. He also hoped to ease the problem of financing social reform at home and to integrate the empire.

Tariffs and social reform   Here two difficulties arose. On the one hand there was the need, as a matter of political tactics, to prevent tariffs from putting up prices, especially of food. Countering this by reducing other duties meant that the net gain in revenue would be small. Duties on foreign manufactures would have brought in more than duties on foreign food. But here the second problem came in. If tariffs are effective in keeping out competitive goods, they bring in little revenue; if they bring in revenue, it means that they are not keeping out competitive goods. How much social reform could have been paid for out of tariffs is therefore hard to conjecture.

A particular area in which there may have been a social case for protection is agriculture. If it is considered that a flourishing (or at any rate non-decaying) countryside is important to the social well-being of any community, then farmers in an industrialised economy with a high standard of living require protection against imports from low-cost producers elsewhere, including those inside the empire. But in a country which must in any case import a large proportion of its food, this is best given by a system of guaranteed prices and bounties, putting the cost of protection on the taxpayer rather than the consumer.

Imperial integration   No doubt the vision of an integrated empire was what really excited the advocates of tariff reform and especially those who thought in political rather than economic terms. But when one comes to ask exactly what extra non-economic advantages might have flowed from it, a convincing answer is not easy to find.

Defence is one obvious area. Thanks to the exceptional combination of circumstances described in the first chapter of this book, Britain had acquired a world position which was in the long run disproportionate to her relative resources and which was therefore bound to be challenged sooner or later. She could have saved herself much expense of wealth and blood if she had been able to establish an international system of peaceful change. That however is something which still evades mankind even when the need for it has become far more obvious than was the case a century ago. But, if in its absence Britain had to reckon with an armed challenge, she was going to need allies who could provide not only men but also materials and money to reinforce her inadequate reserves. But the white population of the Dominions was only 11m. (of whom 1·5m. were Boers and French Canadian) while for arms and loans they were as likely to need help as to give it. The only potential ally large and stable enough to provide the necessary support was the United States and they were more likely to come to the aid of a liberal free-trade Britain than of an exclusive imperialist one. And if after 1914 the sympathies of many neutrals inclined towards her, it was because she appeared to be fighting in the cause of all freedoms including their own, whereas Germany did not.

In any case the UK obtained valuable help from the Dominions in 1899, 1914 and 1939. It is hard to see that the absence of a preferential system did any more to diminish the amount of that help in the first two wars than its presence did to augment the help given in the third. Much the same arguments apply to intellectual and cultural co-operation. This has occurred on a gratifying scale. But it surely depends on tradition and the common use of the English language, to which the existence of preferences would have added little.

The upshot of the foregoing paragraphs would seem to be that the question whether the game would have been worth the candle is hard to judge but that for this very reason the gains, if any, would have been unlikely to have been as great as the tariff reformers prophesied. As far as economics were concerned, the main handicaps of Britain were technical backwardness, slow growth and unduly high costs. Duties-cum-preferences on foodstuffs would have been unlikely to have had any effect on the first two but (unless compensated for) would have had an adverse one on the third. Duties on manufactures might have done something to remedy the first two but would almost certainly have aggravated the third. Both types would have made the UK economy less flexible instead of encouraging it to adapt to change.

Notes to Chapter 9

1 W. A. S. Hewins, *The Apologia of an Imperialist* (1929), Vol. 1, pp. 154–5.
2 P. Marsh, *The Discipline of Popular Government: Lord Salisbury's Domestic Statecraft 1881–1902* (Brighton, 1978), pp. 319–20.
3 J. E. B. Munson, 'The Unionist Coalition and Education 1895–1902', *HJ*, Vol. 20 (1977). Cost for each child in average attendance at voluntary schools in 1870 was £1 5s 5d; cost in 1900 at Board Schools £2 17s 7d, and at voluntary schools £2 6s 4d.
4 E. Eaglesham, *From School Board to Local Authority* (1956).
5 House of Commons, 13 March 1877.
6 A. MacBriar, *Fabian Socialism and English Politics* (1962), p. 212.
7 Quoted by Munson, p. 629.
8 B. Holland, *The Life of Spencer Compton, Eighth Duke of Devonshire* (1911), Vol. 2, p. 284; J. Amery, *The Life of Joseph Chamberlain* (1951), Vol. 4, ch. 96.
9 D. C. Hanes, *The First British Workmen's Compensation Act of 1897* (New Haven, 1968).
10 C. Booth at Birmingham, 25 March 1899, quoted by B. B. Gilbert, *The Evolution of National Insurance in Great Britain* (1966), p. 192.
11 C. L. Mowat, *The Charity Organisation Society* (1961), p. 142.
12 Gilbert, pp. 181–211; P. Fraser, *Joseph Chamberlain: Radicalism and Empire* (1966), pp. 232–3.
13 H. Maxwell, *Evening Memories* (1932), pp. 245–6.

14 J. F. Kendle, *The Colonial and Imperial Conferences 1887–1911* (1967), pp. 26–30.
15 Kendle, pp. 26–30.
16 For the rest of this section, see especially Amery, Vol. 5; A. Gollin, *Balfour's Burden* (1965); R. Rempel, *Unionists Divided* (Newton Abbot, 1972): A. Sykes, *Tariff Reform in British Politics 1903–13* (Oxford, 1979), chs 2 and 3.
17 Amery (1969), Vol. 5, p. 70.
18 A. West, *Contemporary Portraits* (1920), p. 68; E. Hamilton, *Diary*, ed. D. W. R. Bahlman (1972), 30 June 1903; Hewins, Vol. 1, p. 68; B. Semmel, *Imperialism and Social Reform* (1960), p. 82.
19 A. Fitzroy, *Memoirs* (1923), 29 May 1903.
20 Chamberlain spoke in the House about pensions on both 22 May and 28 May (B. Dugdale (*Arthur James Balfour*, Vol. 1, p. 348) says the first occasion was on 19 May and Rempel (p. 32) says 21 May). In both debates he spoke after Lloyd George. Balfour, in a letter to Devonshire of 27 August 1903 (Amery, Vol. 5, p. 227), claimed that the speech of 22 May was a violation of an arrangement to which they had come. Amery says there is nothing in the Chamberlain papers to indicate what this arrangement may have been.

Ritchie, in a memorandum written after his resignation in September 1903 (Rempel, pp. 33, 205), said that Balfour told him of Chamberlain's intention of speaking on old-age pensions. Ritchie had then threatened that if this happened, he would rise and repudiate such a statement on behalf of the Cabinet. As a result Balfour saw Chamberlain, which led to a message being sent to Ritchie through Gerald Balfour that Chamberlain had abandoned his intention and would absent himself from the House. Notwithstanding this apparent undertaking, Chamberlain attended the debate and delivered his speech. Ritchie attached this story to the speech on 22 May.

But Margot Asquith, in her *Autobiography* (1920, Vol. 2, p. 33), recorded having gone to the House on 28 May to hear whether the Prime Minister would take the opportunity to make clear that he did not agree with Chamberlain. Meeting Sandars, Balfour's secretary, she said, 'Tell Arthur that this is a *most* important occasion and do not let him think that he can slip out of it'. Sandars replied, 'Joe is not going to speak today and all will be well'. 'Mr Chamberlain did however speak; Mr Balfour did not repudiate him.'

It is tempting to disbelieve the notoriously inaccurate Margot. But she can hardly have invented the episode and her story is keyed to an occasion when Balfour spoke, which he did not do on the 22nd. Moreover there is no evidence that Chamberlain intended to speak on the 22nd or that such an intention was known in advance. He professed only to have come into the House 'accidentally', although it would have been strange for him to have kept away from a debate on a subject which so interested him.

If all the evidence is accepted at its face value, there was trouble *twice* about Chamberlain's speech, he gave two undertakings and broke both of them. This seems improbable, especially as nobody accused him of breaking faith twice. All becomes clear if Balfour and Ritchie are assumed to have confused the later debate in retrospect with the earlier. Confusion would have been easy, since both debates involved pensions and in both Lloyd George provoked Chamberlain. The speech on the 28th was much more calculated to annoy Balfour than that on the 22nd, but the latter went far enough to make it intelligible why Mowatt should have written his memorandum next day.
21 The phrase was coined by Chamberlain's now hostile brother Arthur; D. Dilkes, *Neville Chamberlain* (Cambridge, 1984), Vol. 1, p. 92.
22 Churchill to Rosebery, 9 October 1903; R. Churchill, *Winston S. Churchill* (1969), Companion Vol. 2, p. 227.
23 E. Hamilton, *Diary*, quoted by M. Egremont, *Balfour* (1980), p. 187.
24 G. W. E. Russell, *Prime Ministers and Some Others* (1918), p. 67.
25 Amery (1969), Vol. 6, p. 644.
26 Dugdale, Vol. 1, p. 363.
27 Amery, Vol. 6, p. 688.
28 Lansdowne, quoted by P. Fraser, p. 275.
29 Amery, Vol. 5, p. 377 and Vol. 6, p. 650.
30 J. Harris, *Unemployment and Politics 1886–1914* (Oxford, 1972), p. 214.

31 N. Blewett, 'Free Fooders, Balfourites, Whole Hoggers: factionalism within the Unionist Party 1906–1910', *HJ*, Vol. 11 (1968).

32 In addition to the sources mentioned at various points, and general books on British economic history, the following have been used in this section:

F. Crouzet, 'Trade and empire, the British experience from the establishment of free trade until the First World War', in B. M. Ratcliffe (ed.), *Great Britain and Her World 1850–1914* (Manchester, 1975).

W. P. Kennedy, 'Foreign investment, trade and growth in the UK 1870–1913', in *Explorations in Economic History*, Vol. 2 (Cambridge, Mass., 1974).

M. W. Kirby, *The Decline of British Power since 1870* (1981), pp. 21–3.

D. MacDougall, 'British and American Exports', *The Economic Journal* (September 1952).

33 This statement is based on W. Schlote, *British Overseas Trade from the 1700s to the 1930s* (tr. Oxford, 1952). Schlote only gives figures for overall exports and allowance should be made for the possibility that the proportion of manufactures was higher for empire than for non-empire markets.

34 S. B. Saul, 'The economic significance of constructive imperialism', *The Journal of Economic History* (June 1957).

35 J. R. Hay, 'The British business community: social insurance and the German example', in W. Mommsen and W. Mock, *The Emergence of the Welfare State in Britain and Germany* (1981), pp. 117–19.

36 Letter from Lord Kaldor in *The Times*, 27 March 1983.

37 F. C. Benham, *Great Britain Under Protection* (New York, 1941), pp. 193–5.

38 M. Edelstein, *Overseas Investment in the Age of High Imperialism: The United Kingdom 1850–1914* (New York, 1982), p. 213.

39 W. Mock, *Imperiale Herrschaft und Nationales Interesse* (Stuttgart, 1982), pp. 286–305.

10 Conclusion: 'Joe and his World'

'Joe'

Chamberlain once applied to himself a phrase of Gambetta's, saying that he was *'un radical autoritaire'*,[1] and there is abundant evidence that the self-made man from Birmingham possessed what is now known as 'an authoritarian personality'.[2] His upbringing and surroundings had a strong enough influence to direct his energies initially into liberal channels and, even after he developed a national radicalism, to keep this from assuming the intolerant totalitarianism which characterised it elsewhere.

He was no original thinker and indeed such a faculty can be a handicap for an active politician. 'His mind was open to ideas, to new subjects, new interests and purposes but sceptical about generalised systems for unravelling the tangles of the world.'[3] It was not his way to deduce his opinions by the aid of well-thought-out principles from carefully observed facts.[4] Instead, by his own admission, he decided first and found reasons and methods afterwards.[5] He had a keen, calculating intellect, admirable in manipulating practical detail and in adapting means to ends.[6] He owed his success in politics, as in business, to being a man of action, quick to see how any ideas which he came across could be used as arguments in favour of what he wanted to do or see done; he was less good at foreseeing the long-term problems to which short-term policies might lead. Milner said that he was swayed by big permanent ideas; 'wherever he gets them from, they have deep roots inside him'.[7] An observer in 1880 compared him to 'a sparrow-hawk among a flock of decorous finches'.[8]

He was driven by strong emotions. 'His convictions are passionately held, his whole energy is thrown into the attempt to realise them.'[9] Enthusiasm and self-will were the governing forces in his mind. Milner's friend Gell found the keystone of his character in pugnacity, antagonism and self-will.[10] From this derived what Ramsay MacDonald called his 'tribal instincts'[11] – the conviction that any group with which he was associated was preferable to the groups with which other people were associated.

Two characteristics followed from this fundamental vigour. One was a desire to dominate. Mundella in 1877 called him 'a born wire-puller and intriguer. He wants to have as many puppets as possible so that he can

292

manipulate them.'[12] He once said that on every committee of thirteen, there are twelve who go to a meeting having given no thought to the subject and prepared to accept someone else's lead. One goes having made up his mind what he means shall be done. 'I always make it my business to be that one.'[13] (Characteristically he did not allow for the possibility of there being not one but two, with minds made up in different ways!) He had considerable ability as a negotiator and could charm when he considered that charm was called for.[14] As a speaker he could be very persuasive; Asquith and he were the only people whom Balfour thought it 'worth crossing the street' to hear, while Speaker Peel said that he was the best speaker in the House bar Gladstone and the best debater bar none.[15] But he did not hesitate to bully when up against an opponent whom he disliked or considered weak.

Secondly he was impatient. This may have been partly due to the gout from which he was a chronic sufferer (unless the gout itself derived from some element in his make-up which generated the energy and the emotion). Being quick to grasp what might be done, he was unduly inclined to take over the direction of events himself, if he thought that others were being timid or blind. His friend Milner (of whom he could never so think) said that 'he was very bold and loved the forward game';[16] his enemy Sandars said that in the long run his masterfulness and lack of restraint were bound to prejudice, if not ruin, any cause in which he was engaged.[17] Beatrice Potter said that his enthusiasm for a cause was accompanied by a passionate desire to *crush* opposition to *his will*, a longing to put his foot on the necks of others, although he would persuade himself that he represented the right and his enemies the wrong.[18] His impulse towards achievement made him disinclined to leave well alone and helps to explain his inability to get on with either Gladstone, who believed in the tendency of things, when left to themselves, to work out for good, or Salisbury, who believed that whatever happened would be for the worse.

His impatience led to quick changes of plan. If he could not get his way by one means, he would not hesitate before trying another. This provoked charges of impressionability, of opportunism, of being uninhibited over switching from one side to another.[19] Certainly he was inherently uncomfortable in a moderate position.[20] Such charges of insincerity and lack of principle are often brought against public figures and are hard to assess. Beatrice Potter probably came closest to the answer when she questioned whether his convictions were in fact honestly based on experience but, having originated as the tools of ambition, had become so inextricably woven into his love of power that even in his own mind their origin was no longer recognisable.[21]

Another of his characteristics was extreme sensitivity. His ally Dilke wrote of 'the unforgiving ferocity which he displays when people don't do as he and I want'.[22] Mundella said he was 'implacable in his hatreds and unceasing in his intrigues'.[23] Balfour called him 'the most vindictive of men',[24] Selborne said in 1897 that 'he takes being sold much amiss and is apt to let off steam in resentment'.[25] A major victim of such resentment was God (see p. 58). But intense sensitiveness to his own wrongs was not tempered by any corresponding sensitiveness to the feelings and rights of others.[26] His impetuosity and preoccupation with himself made him pay too little attention to dissentient voices. Even his hagiographer Garvin admitted that he never understood the strength of Irish nationalism, while Morley said he was slow to realise 'the scale, the proportions, the prodigious magnitude and complexity of the Irish problem'.[27]

According to Margot Asquith, Salisbury, after saying that Gladstone was much hated but also much loved, went on to ask whether anyone ever loved Joe.[28] The answer is that, in spite of his admission that he did not allow divergent opinions to be expressed in his household, there are no tales of feuds or rancours in it.[29] And the people of Birmingham kept him as their member for thirty-eight years even though for the last eight he was incapable of speaking in Parliament. Morley, despite their quarrels, said he had 'a genius for friendship'.[30] Certainly he was devoted to those who devoted themselves body and soul to him. In the two Churchills he recognised kindred spirits and, in spite of sparring matches, there was no lasting animosity between them. Winston wrote that, when he began to take an interest in politics, Chamberlain was the most live, sparkling and insurgent figure;[31] he it was who drove the younger man to describe a lie as a 'terminological inexactitude'.

All the same there can be no disputing the hate which he could arouse. The Tories hated him for the invective of his radical days, the Liberals hated him for abandoning Home Rule, the Liberal Unionists hated him for advocating tariffs. The Hamilton Diary is full of the theme in the 1880s. 'Joe is by far the best hated man in public life now.' 'Everything he says is discounted owing to his being so unfairly hated and distrusted.' 'The dislike and fear of Joe among the moderate section of the Party are strong.'[32] Queen Victoria described him in 1882 as 'Gladstone's evil genius'[33] – although she had come to regard him very differently by the time he had the last audience in January 1901. Gladstone, after the defeat of Home Rule in 1886, said that, while Hartington behaved like and was a thorough gentleman, 'of Chamberlain it is better not to speak'.[34] At the other end of the social scale, a radical Daventry poacher hated Chamberlain above all men, as a renegade.[35] The animosity lasted. Campbell-Bannerman, having described him in the late 1880s as 'the Opposition's evil genius, for he is always guided by spite and therefore a poor tactician', said in 1900 that 'the thing we have to keep going for is Chamberlain – the vulgarity, recklessness, caddishness, snobbery of it'.[36] Asquith said in 1900 that he had 'the manners of a cad and the tongue of a bargee'.[37] Goldwin-Smith wrote to Bryce in 1903 that 'England had been ruled by bad men before now but never by a cad'.[38] In 1904 Balfour said that some Unionist free traders had been as much animated by distrust and even hatred of Joe as by a scientific ardour for the truth.[39]

Yet in spite of all the moral and social disapproval, few specific charges of crooked conduct have been brought against him and none proven. The Dilke, Parnell and Raid cases have already been discussed (see pp. 159, 194–200, 226–34). The only one on which a charge can be established is the Raid, but it is not the one which was widely made at the time; if the rising had succeeded, Harris's telegrams might have gone down to history as the British counterpart of that sent from Ems! Grave suspicion is justified in the Parnell case but his conduct would even there only have been dishonest if he knew the Piggott documents to be forged or paid O'Shea to bring the divorce case. With Dilke there is insufficient evidence to say whether it was all or nothing. Perhaps the most sinister thing is that there were three such cases; they give the impression of a man who, through over-eagerness to achieve his ends, habitually sailed close to the wind.[40] The charges of inability to keep secrets are partly the sign of a generation gap, partly a genuine difference of view (which still persists) as to how far questions of high policy ought only to be discussed behind a screen which is not removed until the moment for action arrives. Three charges of sharp practice in the business field – that he was ruthless to competitors (see p. 57), that his family made money out of Corporation Street (see p. 79) and out of the Boer War ('the more the Empire expands, the more the Chamberlains contract') – are not sufficiently documented to afford a basis for judgment.

Chamberlain and Gladstone were both by temperament excessively vigorous men with strong emotions. Both could be extremely vindictive. But Gladstone was acutely aware of the resulting dangers. He made superhuman efforts at restraint, prostrating himself continually before his maker. He had his loved and adoring 'Pussy' to act as a calming influence. Chamberlain was for most of his life denied both advantages by fate. Had either of his first two wives lived, had he met his third earlier and had he retained his faith, he might have been a different and more effective man. Gladstone's religion filled him in his more equable moments with respect for human personality and a belief in the superiority of persuasion to force, the two hall marks of genuine liberalism. Chamberlain by contrast took pride in impetuosity – the business man's love of getting things done. He sought to improve by reforming society rather than by changing men's hearts. His anxiety to make people happy lost force when they wanted to be happy in their own way rather than his. He instinctively shunned the loss of power involved in setting men free. He was thus a hard rather than a soft progressive, radical rather than liberal. When he changed sides he became a hard rather than a soft conservative, anxious to act rather than to leave well alone.[41]

Tragedy has been described as the story of how men are undone by the excesses of their qualities. Chamberlain's tragedy was that the man who was so anxious to achieve left few lasting achievements behind him other than one or two institutions which someone else would have established anyway. His passion and impatience led him into advocating policies without due consideration, only to find, when he was already committed, that the obstacles and opponents were far stronger than he had realised. Consequently his career was 'strewn with the debris of abandoned hypotheses'.[42] Education, Egypt, Ireland, West Africa, merchant shipping, foreign policy, tariff reform, sisal – all alike illustrate this and it is a formidable list. His chief legacy lay in two linked ideas: social reform and imperial development. But by breaking up the Liberal Party so that it was out of power for twenty vital years, he set back the first more than he advanced it while in the second he had the tide against him. Instead of countering the movement of the middle classes into the conservative camp, he exemplified and accentuated it. Had he stood out against it, his historical reputation would have been higher and he would have left behind him a happier and more successful pair of islands, as well as a commonwealth which was no less – although possibly also no more – united.

But even if one supposes that the individual could have behaved differently, how much would this have done to halt or slow down the decline in Britain's world position?

His World

The first chapter of this book ended by suggesting that the Industrial Revolution presented Britain with four problems, which can be conveniently identified by the labels revolution, alienation, self-indulgence and decline. The time has come to consider how far she succeeded in meeting them.

The likelihood of revolution had passed by 1850 (see p. 48). This was chiefly because after that date the benefits of industrialisation began to spread more widely. But that spreading itself owed a good deal to the continuity of the Roundhead–Whig–Liberal–Radical tradition and its success – belated perhaps but all the same effective – in widening the franchise. This widening, by occurring in stages, satisfied the claims of the most articulate outsiders and allowed time for them to be integrated into the community before the next admission became due. The logical conclusion to this trend was the introduction of universal adult suffrage, which is the essence of the radical doctrine (see pp. 22, 24).

Chamberlain stood in this tradition and did his share in bringing about the third widening. His 'Unauthorised Programme' advocated manhood suffrage, although it was not achieved until after his death. There are those who consider (see p. 39) that the absence of revolution was a disadvantage which, by consolidating Britain's inherited social system, made it inflexible and prejudiced her chances of adapting to change. But if there was a time when a revolution might have done good, it was at the end of the century when Britain was losing impetus, and by then it had become unlikely.

If anyone had asked in July 1914 whether the second problem of alienation had been overcome, the answer could only have been hesitant.[43] Whether class antagonisms were stronger than they had been a century earlier is impossible to measure but they were certainly powerful and the division between parties was increasingly based upon them. Ireland was on the brink of civil war, with His Majesty's Opposition egging Ulster on to defy Parliament. The workers were growing truculent, hit by the fall in real wages since 1906. A general strike in the autumn was well on the cards. The suffragettes were as active as ever. Fear of the future was helping to raise the export of capital to record levels.

A month later the answer would of course have been different. The spectacle of Germany invading Belgium produced a sudden burst of solidarity, just as the spectacle of Russia invading East Prussia resolved a similarly tense situation inside Germany. The strength of national feeling had, as so often, been underestimated. But Bismarck's social legislation is thought to have played a part in causing the Social Democrats to vote for the war credits and, although British social legislation can be criticised as inadequate and tardy, it cannot have been altogether without effect. The first measures had been regulative rather than redistributive. But the Chartists had demanded that the doctrine of the right of the individual to a say in society must apply to how he lived as well as to whether he voted. Chamberlain repeated the claim. 'Men are born with natural rights, with the right to existence and the right to a fair and reasonable opportunity of enjoying it.'[44] To a younger follower, he alone among the leading men 'seemed to apprehend the truth that political reform is related to social reform as the means to the end, that politics, in its widest sense, is the science of human happiness'.[45] His proposals, other than for education, did not involve the spending of much public money. But by the end of his career the possibilities of what could be done within this limit were almost exhausted, as the argument over pensions showed. And once the decisive voice in elections passed into the hands of those who paid no income tax and who thus, in defiance of Ireton's principle (see p. 22), acquired a power which was out of proportion to their stake in the country, *laissez-faire* and all that went with it were doomed.[46] The 1906 Education (Provision of Meals) Act has been identified as the first step towards creating a welfare state.[47] One of Chamberlain's last acts in Parliament was to vote against its principle. But in doing so he turned his back on his earlier insistence that 'property' [the haves] must be prepared to pay an 'insurance' for the security it enjoyed. If he had stuck to that view, the situation in 1914 might have been less tense, since it was in part the hang-over from twenty years of Conservative rule between 1886 and 1905.

But the cost of mitigating alienation is notorious. Taxation began to be used (in the eyes of the left) as an engine of social justice and (in the eyes of the right) as an instrument of plunder.[48] The public sector's share of the Gross National Product rose from 8·9 per cent in 1890 through 12·4 per cent in 1913 and 30 per cent in 1938 to over 50 per cent in the 1970s.[49] At this point the thesis lies ready to hand that the solution of the alienation problem by the palliative of self-indulgence made decline inevitable. Economic resources were taken away from people likely to save and given to people likely to spend. Industry was starved of the capital which it needed to keep abreast of its challengers. The future was sacrificed to the present. The result has been unduly slow growth and unduly high costs. Resources increased less fast than did demand, with inflation as the inevitable result. We spent too much on being kind and comfortable and cultivated, forgetting that such things can only be afforded if the productive machine is creating a sufficient surplus over necessities. Society has thus ceased to fulfil the crucial requirement of giving top priority to productive investment (see p. 8). People who are short of the necessities of life find it hard to understand the need to hold resources back. Powerful sanctions of a religious, moral or intellectual character are required if the temptation to consume rather than save is to be held in check. These tend to be undermined by success; they certainly lost efficacy in Britain as the nineteenth century passed into the twentieth and they were assailed from various sides by plausible criticisms.

But this thesis, while containing elements of truth, is not the whole story. The Edwardian upper classes were notorious for 'conspicuous consumption'; they are said to have spent more on sport than on the Navy![50] The lower classes can hardly be blamed for taking their ideas about the way to live from the example set by their superiors. Moreover the extra demand which higher consumption implied should have encouraged producers to extend their capacity and thus have led to investment, some parts of which should have helped exports (although too much demand at home may reduce the incentive to export yet increase the bill for imports). What is significant is the paucity of evidence, before 1914 at any rate, of industry having been unable to obtain the capital it sought.[51] If more had been saved, it would probably only have gone to swell the flood pouring overseas.

One of the main arguments of this book is that too little investment occurred at home (see pp. 208–10). A low level of investment, and particularly home investment, went together with a slow growth rate, in marked contrast to the situation in the two economies which were taking over the industrial lead, Germany and the United States (see Table 10.1). In this perspective private enterprise failed the country (which is not to imply that public enterprise would have done any better). The causal relationship between investment and growth can, of course, be two-way; if the former produces the latter, the latter also makes the former look more attractive. But the two trends taken together are undeniably signs of a defect. There may often have been good microeconomic reasons why investment did not take place but this only complicates the problem. It looks as though there had been a divergence between the long-term interests of the British economy and the short-term interests of individual enterprises, putting in question the conventional assumption that adding together individual best interests is the most effective way of approximating to the best interest of the country as a whole.

But this assumption was one of those tenets which become so taken for granted that the possibility of them being capable of and even requiring revision goes unrealised. Leaving decisions to the free judgment of the individual was and in many quarters still is regarded as one of the secrets of British success. If the individual chooses to invest overseas rather than at home, then investment overseas is accepted as the right thing to do. A similar assumption was that the cultural and ethical values which had been developed in a largely agrarian society – all that was associated with the word 'gentleman' – needed no modification in what had become not merely an industrial society but one in which Britain could no longer count on keeping the lead. This was particularly evident in the field of education. A similar unchallenged assumption held that the methods of handling labour in a deferential society with wide class differences would suffice for one where the differences were smaller and the education of the workforce higher. Those who had been keen for the individual to have a say in the state were much less keen to give him a say in his place of work.

Many people saw that Britain must adapt herself to changing conditions. It was much harder to identify the things which needed to be discarded and those which should be retained. It is not perhaps surprising that attention should first have fastened on the rather obvious issue of free trade. The failure of other countries to follow Britain in opening their markets was palpable and naturally prompted the question whether she ought not to have second thoughts. The rejection of the proposal was probably wise (see p. 288); in any case it did not go to the heart of the matter. But what those responsible for its rejection failed to see – or at any rate to act on – was that if Britain was going to keep to classical principles and behave as though the world market was open, she would need to observe the fundamental requirement of that market by remaining competitive within it. This she failed to do, growing too slowly and investing too little. The higher productivity which would have been involved called for changes in attitude and behaviour which neither management nor labour were prepared to make, partly because they did not see the need, partly because they shrank from the risks and sacrifices involved.

Where beliefs and procedures had become so firmly set, there is little that a single statesman can do, especially when state intervention is decried. Even if Chamberlain had not been a self-made man from Birmingham, with many of the views and prejudices of the species, even if he had remained a radical and become Prime Minister, he would have been unlikely to restore dynamism to the British economy.

Some may think that this was just as well, that the price of remaining competitive might have been to give prosperity and money-making undue priority over freedom, amenity and humanity. Others, watching how failure to grow seems to be increasing social tensions, may deplore Britain's loss of drive, which it is tempting to connect with the migration of the middle classes from the progressive to the conservative camp. It almost seems as though a society which had successfully managed to respond to one challenge was exhausted by the creative effort involved and lacked the inspiration to repeat the process.

Table 10.1   Investment and Growth in the Leading Industrial Countries[52]

	UK	France	Germany	USA
Population (1891)	38·1m	38·2m	49·4m	63m
Gross National Product per head (1899)	$830	$360	$525	$790
Total investment as % of GNP Annual average (1851–1913)	12·8	20·2	21·2	22·1
Investment abroad as % of Total Investment Annual average (1870–1913)	32·2	12?	9	6 (max.)
Investment abroad as % of GNP Annual average (1870–1913)	5·2	2 to 3	2–	1·5
Growth Rate average % increase per year (1873–1913)	0·4[a]	n.a.	0·9[b]	1·2

(a) The British rate fell from 1·0 in 1882–90 to 0·1 in 1900–07
(b) The German rate was pulled down by a figure of −0·3 in 1873–82

Some of these figures are rough approximations. The discrepancies are big enough to justify this being disregarded.

Notes to Chapter 10

1 J. Austen Chamberlain, *Politics from the Inside* (1936), p. 81. W. L. Strauss, *Joseph Chamberlain and the Theory of Imperialism* (Washington, 1942), p. 123 says that Gladstone called Chamberlain '*un homme autoritaire*' but this must be the result of some confusion.
2 N. Sandford, T. Adorno *et al.*, *The Authoritarian Personality* (New York, 1950).
3 J. Morley, *Recollections* (1917), Vol. 1, pp. 147–62.
4 B. Webb (Potter), *Diary* (eds N. and J. Mackenzie, 1982), 12 January 1884.
5 W. S. Hewins, *The Apologia of an Imperialist* (1929), Vol. 1, p. 225.
6 Webb, 12 January 1884.
7 J. Amery, *The Life of Joseph Chamberlain* (1951), Vol. 4, p. 342.
8 Lady F. Balfour, *Ne Obliviscaris* (1930), Vol. 1, p. 278.
9 Webb, 26 September 1883.
10 Gell to Milner, 19 September 1903, quoted by R. V. Kubicek, *The Administration of Imperialism* (Durham, N.C., 1969), p. 172.
11 R. MacDonald in A. Milner, J. A. Spender, H. Lucy and R. MacDonald, *The Life of Joseph Chamberlain* (1912), p. 148.
12 W. H. G. Armytage, *A. J. Mundella 1825–1897* (1951), p. 178.
13 A. G. Gardiner, *Pillars of Society* (1914), p. 19.
14 E. Hamilton, *Diary*, ed. D. W. R. Bahlman (1972), 30 June 1903; Webb, 12 January 1884.
15 B. Dugdale, *Arthur James Balfour* (1936), Vol. 1, p. 219; J. Austen Chamberlain, *Down the Years* (1935), p. 78.
16 *Milner Papers*, ed. C. Headlam (1931), Vol. 1, p. 153.
17 A. Fitzroy, *Memoirs* (1923), 18 March 1905.
18 Webb, 12 January 1884.
19 Armytage, p. 179; J. Cambon in Amery, Vol. 4, p. 205; Granville to Gladstone in A. Ramm (ed.), *Political Correspondence* (1952), Vol. 2, p. 42; Granville to Spencer, 24 December 1886, quoted in M. Hurst, *Joseph Chamberlain and Liberal Reunion* (1967), p. 126.
20 Webb, 12 January 1884; R. Jenkins, *Asquith* (1964), p. 129.
21 Webb, 26 September 1883.
22 Letter to Mrs Pattison, October 1881, quoted by R. Jenkins, *Sir Charles Dilke, a Victorian Tragedy* (2nd edn 1965), p. 134.
23 W. H. G. Armytage, 'The railway rates question and the fall of the third Gladstone ministry', *EHR*, vol. 65 (1950).
24 Dugdale, Vol. 1, p. 95.
25 Selborne to Milner, 24 May 1897, *Milner Papers*, Vol. 1, p. 69.
26 Webb, 18 November 1888.
27 J. L. Garvin, *The Life of Joseph Chamberlain* (1932), Vol. 1, p. 584; Morley, Vol. 1, p. 162.
28 M. Asquith, *Autobiography* (1920), Vol. 1, p. 156.
29 Webb, 12 January 1884.
30 Gardiner, p. 15.
31 W. S. Churchill, *Great Contemporaries* (1937).
32 Hamilton, *Diary*, 11 July 1882, 24 February 1883, 2 March 1884.
33 Queen Victoria to Granville, quoted by Ramm, Vol. 1, p. xxxv.
34 Ramm, Vol. 2, p. 458.
35 G. Christian (ed.), *James Hawker's Journal* (1961), p. 74.
36 J. Wilson, *C-B: A Life of Henry Campbell-Bannerman* (1973), p. 148; C-B to Bryce, 29 October 1900, Bryce Papers (Bodleian Library UB21).
37 Asquith to H. Gladstone, quoted by G. Searle, *The Quest for National Efficiency* (Oxford, 1976), p. 144.
38 Goldwin-Smith to Bryce, 17 May 1903, quoted by C. Harvie, *The Lights of Liberalism* (1976), p. 237.
39 Balfour to Hugh Cecil, 6 December 1904, quoted by R. Rempel, *Unionists Divided* (Newton Abbot, 1972), p. 143.

40 Webb, 9 June 1887.
41 H. Eysenck, *The Psychology of Politics* (1954).
42 Fitzroy, 22 June 1903.
43 G. Dangerfield, *The Strange Death of Liberal England* (2nd edn 1966).
44 Speech of 15 September 1885.
45 G. W. E. Russell in *The Contemporary Review* September 1889. Chamberlain in fact used the last eleven words in the speech referred to in note 44.
46 H. Pelling, *The Origins of the Labour Party* (Oxford, 1968), p. 69.
47 B. B. Gilbert, *The Evolution of National Insurance in Great Britain* (1966), p. 100.
48 'Instrument of Plunder'; Lord Salisbury (then Lord Robert Cecil) in *The Quarterly Review* (April 1860), pp. 523–4:

> The taxation of the State is an engine which may be used almost without limit for the transfer of property from one class to another ... Wherever democracy has prevailed, the power of the state has been used to plunder the well-to-do for the benefit of the poor.

> See also remarks by Salisbury quoted by D. Southgate, *The Conservative Leadership* (1974), p. 104.

49 A. T. Peacock and F. Wiseman, *The Growth of Public Expenditure in the UK* (2nd edn 1967), p. 41.
50 C. Aslet, *The Last Country Houses* (1982).
51 See Chapter 7, note 62.
52 GNP: A. Maizels, *Industrial Growth and World Trade* (Cambridge, 1963). Total Investment: M. Floud and D. McCloskey, *The Economic History of Britain since 1700* (Cambridge, 1981), Vol. 2, p. 14.

Foreign Investment: M. Edelstein, *Overseas Investment in the Age of High Imperialism: The United Kingdom 1850–1914* (New York, 1982), pp. 3, 21, 25, 233.

Index